Puranas. Bhāgavatapurāna.

Śrīmad-Bhāgavatam

Fourth Canto
"The Creation of the Fourth Order"

(Part Two–Chapters 9-19)

With the Original Sanskrit Text,
Its Roman Transliteration, Synonyms,
Translation and Elaborate Purports by

His Divine Grace
A.C. Bhaktivedanta Swami Prabhupāda
Founder-Ācārya of the International Society for Krishna Consciousness

THE BHAKTIVEDANTA BOOK TRUST
New York · Los Angeles · London · Bombay

Readers interested in the subject matter of this book
are invited by the International Society for Krishna Consciousness
to correspond with its Secretary.

International Society for Krishna Consciousness
3959 Landmark Street
Culver City, California 90230

Library of Congress Catalogue Card Number: 75-189067
International Standard Book Number: 0-912776-47-1

Printed by Dai Nippon Printing Co., Ltd., Tokyo, Japan

TABLE OF CONTENTS

CHAPTER NINETEEN

King Pṛthu's One Hundred Horse Sacrifices

CHAPTER NINE

Dhruva Mahārāja Returns Home

TEXT 1

मैत्रेय उवाच
त एवमुत्सन्नभया उरुक्रमे
कृतावनामाः प्रययुस्त्रिविष्टपम् ।
सहस्रशीर्षापि ततो गरुत्मता
मधोर्वनं भृत्यदिदृक्षया गतः ॥ १ ॥

maitreya uvāca
ta evam utsanna-bhayā urukrame
kṛtāvanāmāḥ prayayus tri-viṣṭapam
sahasraśīrṣāpi tato garutmatā
madhor vanaṁ bhṛtya-didṛkṣayā gataḥ

maitreyaḥ uvāca—the great sage Maitreya continued; *te*—the demigods; *evam*—thus; *utsanna-bhayāḥ*—being freed from all fears; *urukrame*—unto the Supreme Personality of Godhead, whose actions are uncommon; *kṛta-avanāmāḥ*—they offered their obeisances; *prayayuḥ*—they returned; *tri-viṣṭapam*—to their respective heavenly planets; *sahasra-śīrṣā api*—also the Personality of Godhead known as Sahasraśīrṣa; *tataḥ*—from there; *garutmatā*—getting up on the back of Garuḍa; *madhoḥ vanam*—the forest known as Madhuvana; *bhṛtya*—servant; *didṛkṣayā*—wishing to see him; *gataḥ*—went.

TRANSLATION

The great sage Maitreya told Vidura: When the demigods were reassured by the Personality of Godhead, they were freed from all fears, and after offering their obeisances, they returned to their heavenly planets. Then the Lord, who is nondifferent from the Sahasraśīrṣa incarnation, got on the back of Garuda, who carried Him to the Madhuvana Forest to see His servant Dhruva.

PURPORT

The word *sahasraśīrṣa* refers to the Personality of Godhead known as Garbhodakaśāyī Viṣṇu. Although the Lord appeared as Kṣīrodakaśāyī Viṣṇu, He has been described here as Sahasraśīrṣa Viṣṇu because He is non-different from Garbhodakaśāyī Viṣṇu. According to Śrīla Sanātana Gosvāmī in his *Bhāgavatāmṛta,* the Sahasraśīrṣa Personality of Godhead who appeared at that time was the incarnation known as Pṛśnigarbha. He created the planet known as Dhruvaloka for the habitation of Dhruva Mahārāja.

TEXT 2

स वै धिया योगविपाकतीव्रया
हृत्पद्मकोशे स्फुरितं तडित्प्रभम् ।
तिरोहितं सहसैवोपलक्ष्य
बहिःस्थितं तदवस्थं ददर्श ॥ २ ॥

sa vai dhiyā yoga-vipāka-tīvrayā
hṛt-padma-kośe sphuritaṁ taḍit-prabham
tirohitaṁ sahasaivopalakṣya
bahiḥ sthitaṁ tad-avasthaṁ dadarśa

saḥ—Dhruva Mahārāja; *vai*—also; *dhiyā*—by meditation; *yoga-vipāka-tīvrayā*—on account of mature realization of the yogic process; *hṛt*—the heart; *padma-kośe*—on the lotus of; *sphuritam*—manifested; *taḍit-prabham*—brilliant like lightning; *tirohitam*—having disappeared; *sahasā*—all of a sudden; *eva*—also; *upalakṣya*—by observing; *bahiḥ sthitam*—externally situated; *tat-avastham*—in the same posture; *dadarśa*—was able to see.

TRANSLATION

The form of the Lord, which was brilliant like lightning and in which Dhruva Mahārāja, in his mature yogic process, was fully absorbed in meditation, all of a sudden disappeared. Thus Dhruva was perturbed, and his meditation broke. As soon as he opened his eyes he saw the Supreme Personality of Godhead personally present, just as he had been seeing Him in his heart.

PURPORT

Because of his mature position in yogic meditation, Dhruva Mahārāja was constantly observing the form of the Personality of Godhead within his heart, but all of a sudden, when the Supreme Personality disappeared from his heart, he thought that he had lost Him. He was perturbed, but upon opening his eyes and breaking his meditation he saw the same form of the Lord before him. In the *Brahma-saṁhitā* (5.38) it is said, *premāñjana-cchurita-bhakti-vilocanena:* a saintly person who has developed love of Godhead by devotional service always sees the Lord's transcendental form of Śyāmasundara. This Śyāmasundara form of the Lord within the heart of a devotee is not imagination. When a devotee becomes mature in his prosecution of devotional service, he sees eye to eye the same Śyāmasundara he has thought of during the entire course of his devotional service. Since the Supreme Lord is absolute, the form within the heart of a devotee, the form in the temple and the original form in Vaikuṇṭha, Vṛndāvana-dhāma, are all the same; they are nondifferent from one another.

TEXT 3

तद्दर्शनेनागतसाध्वसः क्षिता-
ववन्दताङ्गं विनमय्य दण्डवत् ।
दृग्भ्यां प्रपश्यन् प्रपिबन्निवार्भक-
श्चुम्बन्निवास्येन भुजैरिवाश्लिषन् ॥ ३ ॥

tad-darśanenāgata-sādhvasaḥ kṣitāv
avandatāṅgaṁ vinamayya daṇḍavat
dṛgbhyāṁ prapaśyan prapibann ivārbhakaś
cumbann ivāsyena bhujair ivāśliṣan

tat-darśanena—after seeing the Lord; *āgata-sādhvasaḥ*—Dhruva Mahārāja, being greatly confused; *kṣitau*—on the ground; *avandata*—offered obeisances; *aṅgam*—his body; *vinamayya*—prostrating; *daṇḍa-vat*—just like a rod; *dṛgbhyām*—with his eyes; *prapaśyan*—looking upon; *prapiban*—drinking; *iva*—like; *arbhakaḥ*—the boy; *cumban*—kissing; *iva*—like; *āsyena*—with his mouth; *bhujaiḥ*—with his arms; *iva*—like; *āśliṣan*—embracing.

TRANSLATION

When Dhruva Mahārāja saw his Lord just in front of him, he was greatly agitated and offered Him obeisances and respect. He fell flat before Him like a rod and became absorbed in love of God. Dhruva Mahārāja, in ecstasy, looked upon the Lord as if he were drinking the Lord with his eyes, kissing the lotus feet of the Lord with his mouth, and embracing the Lord with his arms.

PURPORT

Naturally, when Dhruva Mahārāja personally saw the Supreme Personality of Godhead face to face, he was very much agitated in awe and respect, and it appeared as if he were drinking the entire body of the Lord with his eyes. The devotee's love for the Supreme Personality of Godhead is so intense that he wants to kiss the lotus feet of the Lord constantly, and he wants to touch the tips of the toes of the Lord and constantly embrace His lotus feet. All these features of Dhruva Mahārāja's bodily expression indicate that upon seeing the Lord eye to eye he developed the eight kinds of transcendental ecstasy in his body.

TEXT 4

स तं विवक्षन्तमतद्विदं हरि-
ज्ञार्त्वास्य सर्वस्य च हृद्यवस्थितः ।
कृताञ्जलिं ब्रह्ममयेन कम्बुना
पस्पर्श बालं कृपया कपोले ॥ ४ ॥

sa taṁ vivakṣantam atadvidaṁ harir
jñātvāsya sarvasya ca hṛdy avasthitaḥ
kṛtāñjaliṁ brahmamayena kambunā
pasparśa bālaṁ kṛpayā kapole

saḥ—the Supreme Personality of Godhead; *tam*—Dhruva Mahārāja; *vivakṣantam*—wanting to offer prayers describing his qualities; *a-tat-vidam*—not experienced at that; *hariḥ*—the Personality of Godhead; *jñātvā*—having understood; *asya*—of Dhruva Mahārāja; *sarvasya*—of everyone; *ca*—and; *hṛdi*—in the heart; *avasthitaḥ*—being situated; *kṛta-añjalim*—situated with folded hands; *brahma-mayena*—just up to the words of the Vedic hymns; *kambunā*—with His conchshell; *pasparśa*—touched; *bālam*—the boy; *kṛpayā*—out of causeless mercy; *kapole*—on the forehead.

TRANSLATION

Although Dhruva Mahārāja was a small boy, still he wanted to offer prayers to the Supreme Personality of Godhead in suitable language. But because he was inexperienced, he could not adjust himself immediately. The Supreme Personality of Godhead, being situated in everyone's heart, could understand Dhruva Mahārāja's awkward position. Out of His causeless mercy He touched His conchshell to the forehead of Dhruva Mahārāja, who stood before Him with folded hands.

PURPORT

Every devotee wants to chant the transcendental qualities of the Lord. Devotees are always interested in hearing about the transcendental qualities of the Lord, and they are always eager to glorify these qualities, but sometimes they feel inconvenienced by humbleness. The Personality of Godhead, being situated in everyone's heart, specifically gives a devotee intelligence to describe Him. It is therefore understood that when a devotee writes or speaks about the Supreme Personality of Godhead, it is dictated by the Lord from within. This is confirmed in *Bhagavad-gītā,* Tenth Chapter: to those who constantly engage in the transcendental loving service of the Lord, the Lord, from within, dictates what to do next in order to serve Him. When Dhruva Mahārāja felt hesitant, not knowing how to describe the Lord for want of sufficient experience, the Lord, out of His causeless mercy, touched His conchshell to Dhruva's forehead, and he was transcendentally inspired. This transcendental inspiration is called *brahmamaya* because when one is thus inspired, the sound he produces exactly corresponds to the sound vibration of the *Vedas*. This is not the ordinary sound vibration of this material world. Therefore the sound vibration of the Hare Kṛṣṇa *mantra*, although presented in the ordinary alphabet, should not be taken as mundane or material.

TEXT 5

स वै तदैव प्रतिपादितां गिरं
दैवीं परिज्ञातपरात्मनिर्णयः ।
तं भक्तिभावोऽभ्यगृणादसत्वरं
परिश्रुतोरुश्रवसं ध्रुवक्षितिः ॥ ५ ॥

sa vai tadaiva pratipāditāṁ giraṁ
daivīṁ parijñāta-parātma-nirṇayaḥ
taṁ bhakti-bhāvo 'bhyagṛṇād asatvaraṁ
pariśrutoru-śravasaṁ dhruva-kṣitiḥ

saḥ—Dhruva Mahārāja; *vai*—certainly; *tadā*—at that time; *eva*—just; *pratipāditām*—having attained; *giram*—speech; *daivīm*—transcendental; *parijñāta*—understood; *para-ātma*—of the Supreme Soul; *nirṇayaḥ*—the conclusion; *tam*—to the Lord; *bhakti-bhāvaḥ*—situated in devotional service; *abhyagṛṇāt*—offered prayers; *asatvaram*—without any hasty conclusion; *pariśruta*—widely known; *uru-śravasam*—whose fame; *dhruva-kṣitiḥ*—Dhruva, whose planet would not be annihilated.

TRANSLATION

At that time Dhruva Mahārāja became perfectly aware of the Vedic conclusion and understood the Absolute Truth and His relationship with all living entities. In accordance with the line of devotional service to the Supreme Lord, whose fame is widespread, Dhruva, who in the future would receive a planet which would never be annihilated, even during the time of dissolution, offered his deliberate and conclusive prayers.

PURPORT

There are many important items to be considered in this verse. First of all, the relationship between the Absolute Truth and the relative material and spiritual energies is here understood by a student who has complete knowledge of the Vedic literature. Dhruva Mahārāja never went to any school or academic teacher to learn the Vedic conclusion, but because of his devotional service to the Lord, as soon as the Lord appeared and touched his forehead with His conchshell, automatically the entire Vedic conclusion was revealed to him. That is the process of understanding Vedic literature. One cannot understand it simply by academic learning. The *Vedas* indicate that only to one who has unflinching faith in the Supreme Lord as well as in the spiritual master is the Vedic conclusion revealed.

The example of Dhruva Mahārāja is that he engaged himself in devotional service to the Lord according to the order of his spiritual master, Nārada Muni. As a result of his rendering such devotional service with great determination and austerity, the Personality of Godhead personally manifested Himself before him. Dhruva was only a child. He wanted to offer nice prayers to the Lord, but because he lacked sufficient knowledge, he hesitated; but by the mercy of the Lord, as soon as the Lord's conchshell touched his forehead, he became completely aware of the Vedic conclusion. That conclusion is based on proper understanding of the difference between *jīva* and Paramātmā, the individual soul and the Supersoul. The individual soul is forever a servant of the Supersoul, and therefore his relationship with the Supersoul is to offer service. That is called *bhakti-yoga* or *bhakti-bhāva*. Dhruva Mahārāja offered his prayers to the Lord not in the way of the impersonalist philosophers, but as a devotee. Therefore, it is clearly said here, *bhakti-bhāva*. The only prayers worth offering are those offered to the Supreme Personality of Godhead, whose reputation is spread far and wide. Dhruva Mahārāja wanted to have the kingdom of his father, but his father refused to even allow him to get on his lap. In order to fulfill his desire, the Lord had already created a planet known as the Pole Star, Dhruvaloka, which was never to be annihilated even at the time of the dissolution of the universe. Dhruva Mahārāja did not attain this perfection by acting hastily, but by patiently executing the order of his spiritual master, and therefore he became so successful that he saw the Lord face to face. Now he was further enabled, by the causeless mercy of the Lord, to offer fitting prayers to the Lord. To glorify or offer prayers unto the Supreme, one needs the Lord's mercy. One cannot write to glorify the Lord unless one is endowed with His causeless mercy.

TEXT 6

ध्रुव उवाच
योऽन्तः प्रविश्य मम वाचमिमां प्रसुप्तां
संजीवयत्यखिलशक्तिधरः स्वधाम्ना ।
अन्यांश्च हस्तचरणश्रवणत्वगादीन्
प्राणान्नमो भगवते पुरुषाय तुभ्यम् ॥ ६ ॥

dhruva uvāca
yo 'ntaḥ praviśya mama vācam imāṁ prasuptāṁ
sañjīvayaty akhila-śakti-dharaḥ sva-dhāmnā
anyāṁś ca hasta-caraṇa-śravaṇa-tvag-ādīn
prāṇān namo bhagavate puruṣāya tubhyam

dhruvaḥ uvāca—Dhruva Mahārāja said; *yaḥ*—the Supreme Lord who; *antaḥ*—within; *praviśya*—entering; *mama*—my; *vācam*—words; *imām*—all these; *prasuptām*—which are all inactive or dead; *sañjīvayati*—rejuvenates; *akhila*—universal; *śakti*—energy; *dharaḥ*—possessing; *sva-dhāmnā*—by His internal potency; *anyān ca*—other limbs also; *hasta*—like hands; *caraṇa*—legs; *śravaṇa*—ears; *tvak*—skin; *ādīn*—and so on; *prāṇān*—life force; *namaḥ*—let me offer my obeisances; *bhagavate*—unto the Supreme Personality of Godhead; *puruṣāya*—the Supreme Person; *tubhyam*—unto You.

TRANSLATION

Dhruva Mahārāja said: My dear Lord, You are all-powerful. After entering within me, You have enlivened all my sleeping senses—my hands, legs, ears, touch sensation, life force and especially my power of speech. Let me offer my respectful obeisances unto You.

PURPORT

Dhruva Mahārāja could understand very easily the difference between his condition before and after attaining spiritual realization and seeing the Supreme Personality of Godhead face to face. He could understand that his life force and activities had been sleeping. Unless one comes to the spiritual platform, his bodily limbs, mind and other facilities within the body are understood to be sleeping. Unless one is spiritually situated, all his activities are taken as a dead man's activities or ghostly activities. Śrīla Bhaktivinoda Ṭhākura has composed a song in which he addresses himself: "O living entity, get up! How long shall you sleep on the lap of *māyā*? Now you have the opportunity of possessing a human form of body; now try to get up and realize yourself." The *Vedas* also declare, "Get up! Get up! You have the opportunity, the boon of the human form of life—now realize yourself." These are the Vedic injunctions.

Dhruva Mahārāja actually experienced that upon enlightenment of his senses on the spiritual platform he could understand the essence of Vedic instruction—that the Supreme Godhead is the Supreme Person; He is not impersonal. Dhruva Mahārāja could immediately understand this fact. He was aware that for a very long time he was practically sleeping, and he felt the impetus to glorify the Lord according to the Vedic conclusion. A mundane person cannot offer any prayer or glorify the Supreme Personality of Godhead because he has no realization of the Vedic conclusion.

When Dhruva Mahārāja, therefore, found this difference within himself, he could immediately understand that it was because of the causeless mercy of the Lord. He offered obeisances to the Lord with great respect and reverence, completely understanding that the Lord's favor was upon him. This spiritual enlivenment of Dhruva Mahārāja's senses, mind, etc., was due to the action of the internal potency of the Lord. In this verse, therefore, the word *sva-dhāmnā* means by spiritual energy. Spiritual enlightenment is possible by the mercy of the spiritual energy of the Lord. The chanting of the Hare Kṛṣṇa *mantra* is first addressed to the spiritual energy of the Lord, Hare. This spiritual energy acts when a living entity fully surrenders and accepts his position as an eternal servitor. When a person places himself at the disposal or order of the Supreme Lord, that is called *sevonmukha;* at that time the spiritual energy gradually reveals the Lord to him.

Without revelation by the spiritual energy, one is unable to offer prayers glorifying the Lord. Any amount of philosophical speculation or poetic expression by mundane persons is still considered to be the action and reaction of the material energy. When one is actually enlivened by the spiritual energy, all his senses become purified, and he engages only in the service of the Lord. At that time his hands, legs, ear, tongue, mind, genitals—everything—engage in the service of the Lord. Such an enlightened devotee no longer has any material activities, nor has he any interest in being materially engaged. This process of purifying the senses and engaging them in the service of the Lord is known as *bhakti,* or devotional service. In the beginning, the senses are engaged by the direction of the spiritual master and *śāstra*, and after realization, when the same senses are purified, the engagement continues. The difference is that in the beginning the senses are engaged in a mechanical way, but after realization they are engaged in spiritual understanding.

TEXT 7

एकस्त्वमेव भगवन्निदमात्मशक्त्या
मायाख्ययोरुगुणया महदाद्यशेषम् ।
सृष्ट्वानुविश्य पुरुषस्तदसद्गुणेषु
नानेव दारुषु विभावसुवद्विभासि ॥ ७ ॥

ekas tvam eva bhagavann idam ātma-śaktyā
māyākhyayoru-guṇayā mahadādy-aśeṣam
sṛṣṭvānuviśya puruṣas tad-asad-guṇeṣu
nāneva dāruṣu vibhāvasu-vad vibhāsi

ekaḥ—one; *tvam*—you; *eva*—certainly; *bhagavan*—O my Lord; *idam*—this material world; *ātma-śaktyā*—by Your own potency; *māyā-ākhyayā*—of the name *māyā; uru*—greatly powerful; *guṇayā*—consisting of the modes of nature; *mahat-ādi*—the *mahat-tattva,* etc.; *aśeṣam*—unlimited; *sṛṣṭvā*—after creating; *anuviśya*—then after entering; *puruṣaḥ*—the Supersoul; *tat*—of *māyā; asat-guṇeṣu*—into the temporarily manifested qualities; *nānā*—variously; *iva*—as if; *dāruṣu*—into pieces of wood; *vibhāvasu-vat*—just like fire; *vibhāsi*—you appear.

TRANSLATION

My Lord, You are the Supreme One, but by Your different energies You appear differently in the spiritual and material worlds. You create the total energy of the material world by Your external potency, and after creation You enter within the material world as the Supersoul. You are the Supreme Person, and through the temporary modes of material nature You create varieties of manifestation, just as fire, entering into wood of different shapes, burns brilliantly in different varieties.

PURPORT

Dhruva Mahārāja realized that the Supreme Absolute Truth, the Personality of Godhead, acts through His different energies, not that He becomes void or impersonal and thus becomes all-pervading. The Māyāvādī philosopher thinks that the Absolute Truth, being spread throughout the cosmic manifestation, has no personal form. But here Dhruva Mahārāja, upon realization of the Vedic conclusion, says, "You are spread all over the cosmic manifestation by Your energy." This energy is basically spiritual, but because it acts in the material world temporarily, it is called *māyā,* or illusory energy. In other words, for everyone but the devotees the Lord's energy acts as external energy. Dhruva Mahārāja could understand this fact very nicely, and he could understand also that the energy and the energetic are one and the same. The energy cannot be separated from the energetic.

The identity of the Supreme Personality of Godhead in the feature of Paramātmā or Supersoul is admitted herein. His original spiritual energy enlivens the material energy, and thus the dead body appears to have life force. Voidist philosophers think that under certain material conditions symptoms of life occur in the material body, but the fact is that the material body cannot act on its own. Even a machine needs separate energy (electricity, steam, etc.). It is stated in this verse that the material energy acts in varieties of material bodies, just as fire burns differently in different wood according to the size and quality of the wood. In the case of devotees the same energy is transformed into spiritual energy; this is possible because the energy is originally spiritual, not material. As it is said, *viṣṇu-śaktiḥ parā proktā*. The original energy inspires a devotee, and thus he engages all his bodily limbs in the service of the Lord. The same energy, as external potency, engages the ordinary nondevotees in material activities for sense enjoyment. We should mark the difference between *māyā* and *sva-dhāma*—for devotees the *sva-dhāma* acts, whereas in the case of nondevotees the *māyā* energy acts.

TEXT 8

त्वद्दत्तया वयुनयेदमचष्ट विश्वं
सुप्तप्रबुद्ध इव नाथ भवत्प्रपन्नः ।
तस्यापवर्ग्यशरणं तव पादमूलं
विस्मर्यते कृतविदा कथमार्तबन्धो ॥ ८ ॥

tvad-dattayā vayunayedam acaṣṭa viśvaṁ
supta-prabuddha iva nātha bhavat-prapannaḥ
tasyāpavargya-śaraṇaṁ tava pāda-mūlaṁ
vismaryate kṛtavidā katham ārtabandho

tvat-dattayā—given by You; *vayunayā*—by knowledge; *idam*—this; *acaṣṭa*—could see; *viśvam*—whole universe; *supta-prabuddhaḥ*—a man rising from sleep; *iva*—like; *nātha*—O my Lord; *bhavat-prapannaḥ*—Lord Brahmā, who is surrendered unto You; *tasya*—his; *āpavargya*—of persons desiring liberation; *śaraṇam*—the shelter; *tava*—Your; *pāda-mūlam*—lotus feet; *vismaryate*—can be forgotten; *kṛta-vidā*—by a learned person; *katham*—how; *ārta-bandho*—O friend of the distressed.

TRANSLATION

O my master, Lord Brahmā is fully surrendered unto You. In the beginning You gave him knowledge, and thus he could see and understand the entire universe, just as a person awakens from sleep and visualizes his immediate duties. You are the only shelter of all persons who desire liberation, and You are the friend of all who are distressed. How, therefore, can a learned person who has perfect knowledge ever forget You?

PURPORT

The Supreme Personality of Godhead cannot be forgotten even for a moment by His surrendered devotees. The devotee understands that the Lord's causeless mercy is beyond his estimation; he cannot know how much he is benefited by the grace of the Lord. The more a devotee engages himself in the devotional service of the Lord, the more encouragement is supplied by the energy of the Lord. In the *Bhagavad-gītā* the Lord says that to those who are constantly engaged in devotional service with love and affection, the Supreme Personality of Godhead gives intelligence from within, and thus they may make further progress. Being so encouraged, the devotee can never forget, at any moment, the Personality of Godhead. He always feels obliged to Him for having achieved increased power in devotional service by His grace. Saintly persons like Sanaka, Sanātana and Lord Brahmā were able to see the entire universe, by the mercy of the Lord, through knowledge of the Lord. The example is given that a person may apparently abstain from sleep all day, but as long as he is not spiritually enlightened he is actually sleeping. He may sleep at night and perform his duties in the daytime, but as long as he does not come to the platform of working in spiritual enlightenment he is considered to be always sleeping. A devotee, therefore, never forgets the benefit derived from the Lord.

The Lord is addressed here as *ārtabandhu*, which means friend of the distressed. As stated in the *Bhagavad-gītā*, after many, many births of executing severe austerities in search of knowledge, one comes to the point of real knowledge and becomes wise when he surrenders unto the Supreme Personality of Godhead. The Māyāvādī philosopher who does not surrender unto the Supreme Person is understood to be lacking in real knowledge. The devotee in perfect knowledge cannot forget his obligation to the Lord at any moment.

TEXT 9

नूनं विमुष्टमतयस्तव मायया ते
ये त्वां भवाप्ययविमोक्षणमन्यहेतोः ।
अर्चन्ति कल्पकतरुं कुणपोपभोग्य-
मिच्छन्ति यत्स्पर्शजं निरयेऽपि नृणाम् ॥९॥

nūnaṁ vimuṣṭa-matayas tava māyayā te
ye tvāṁ bhavāpyaya-vimokṣaṇam anya-hetoḥ
arcanti kalpaka-taruṁ kuṇapopabhogyam
icchanti yat sparśa-jaṁ niraye 'pi nṛṇām

nūnam—certainly; *vimuṣṭa-matayaḥ*—those who have lost their right intelligence; *tava*—Your; *māyayā*—by influence of the illusory energy; *te*—they; *ye*—who; *tvām*—You; *bhava*—from birth; *apyaya*—and death; *vimokṣaṇam*—the cause of liberation; *anya-hetoḥ*—for other purposes; *arcanti*—worship; *kalpaka-tarum*—who are like the desire tree; *kuṇapa*—of this dead body; *upabhogyam*—sense gratification; *icchanti*—they desire; *yat*—that which; *sparśa-jam*—derived by touch sensation; *niraye*—in hell; *api*—even; *nṛṇām*—for persons.

TRANSLATION

Persons who worship You simply for the sense gratification of this bag of skin are certainly influenced by Your illusory energy. In spite of having You, who are like a desire tree and are the cause of liberation from birth and death, foolish persons, such as me, desire benediction from You for sense gratification, which is available even for those who live in hellish conditions.

PURPORT

Dhruva Mahārāja repented because he came to the Lord to render devotional service for material profit. He here condemns his attitude. Only due to gross lack of knowledge does one worship the Lord for material profit or for sense gratification. The Lord is like a desire tree. Anyone can have whatever he desires from the Lord, but people in general do not know what kind of benediction they should ask from Him. Happiness derived from the touch of skin, or sensuous happiness, is present in the life of hogs and dogs. Such happiness is very insignificant. If a devotee worships the Lord for such insignificant happiness, he must be considered devoid of all knowledge.

TEXT 10

या निर्वृतिस्तनुभृतां तव पादपद्म-
ध्यानाद्भवज्जनकथाश्रवणेन वा स्यात् ।
सा ब्रह्मणि स्वमहिमन्यपि नाथ मा भूत्
किं त्वन्तकासिलुलितात्पततां विमानात् ॥१०॥

yā nirvṛtis tanu-bhṛtāṁ tava pāda-padma-
dhyānād bhavaj-jana-kathā-śravaṇena vā syāt
sā brahmaṇi sva-mahimany api nātha mā bhūt
kiṁ tv antakāsi-lulitāt patatāṁ vimānāt

yā—that which; *nirvṛtiḥ*—blissfulness; *tanu-bhṛtām*—of the embodied; *tava*—your; *pāda-padma*—lotus feet; *dhyānāt*—from meditating upon; *bhavat-jana*—from Your intimate devotees; *kathā*—topics; *śravaṇena*—by hearing; *vā*—or; *syāt*—comes into being; *sā*—that bliss; *brahmaṇi*—in the impersonal Brahman; *sva-mahimani*—Your own magnificence; *api*—even; *nātha*—O Lord; *mā*—never; *bhūt*—exists; *kim*—what to speak of; *tu*—then; *antaka-asi*—by the sword of death; *lulitāt*—being destroyed; *patatām*—of those who fall down; *vimānāt*—from their airplanes.

TRANSLATION

My Lord, the transcendental bliss derived from meditating upon Your lotus feet or hearing about Your glories from pure devotees is so unlimited that it is far beyond the stage of brahmānanda, wherein one thinks himself merged in the impersonal Brahman as one with the Supreme. Since brahmānanda is also defeated by the transcendental bliss derived

from devotional service, what to speak of the temporary blissfulness of elevating oneself to the heavenly planets, which is ended by the separating sword of time? Although one may be elevated to the heavenly planets, he falls down in due course of time.

PURPORT

The transcendental bliss derived from devotional service, primarily from *śravaṇaṁ kīrtanam*, hearing and chanting, cannot be compared with the happiness derived by *karmīs* by elevating themselves to the heavenly planets or by *jñānīs* or *yogīs* who enjoy oneness with the supreme impersonal Brahman. *Yogīs* generally meditate upon the transcendental form of Viṣṇu, but devotees not only meditate upon Him but actually engage in the direct service of the Lord. In the previous verse we find the phrase *bhavāpyaya,* which means birth and death. The Lord can give relief from the chain of birth and death. It is a misunderstanding to think, as do the monists, that when one gets relief from the process of birth and death he merges into the Supreme Brahman. Here it is clearly said that the transcendental bliss derived from *śravaṇaṁ kīrtanam* by pure devotees cannot be compared with *brahmānanda,* or the impersonal conception of transcendental bliss derived by merging into the Absolute.

The position of *karmīs* is still more degraded. Their aim is to elevate themselves to the higher planetary systems. It is said, *yānti deva-vratā devān:* persons who worship the demigods are elevated to the heavenly planets (Bg. 9.25). But elsewhere in *Bhagavad-gītā* (Bg. 9.21) we find, *kṣīṇe puṇye martya-lokaṁ viśanti:* those who are elevated to the higher planetary systems must come down again as soon as the results of their pious activities are exhausted. They are like the modern astronauts who go to the moon; as soon as their fuel is used up, they are obliged to come back down to this earth. As the modern astronauts who go to the moon or other heavenly planets by force of jet propulsion have to come down again after exhausting their fuel, so also do those who are elevated to the heavenly planets by force of *yajñas* and pious activities. *Antakāsi-lulitāt:* by the sword of time one is cut from his exalted position within this material world, and he comes down again. Dhruva Mahārāja appreciated that the results of devotional service are far more valuable than merging into the Absolute or being elevated to the heavenly planets. The words *patatāṁ vimānāt* are very significant. *Vimāna* means airplane: those who are elevated to the heavenly planets are like airplanes, which drop when they run out of fuel.

TEXT 11

भक्तिं मुहुः प्रवहतां त्वयि मे प्रसङ्गो
भूयादनन्त महताममलाशयानाम् ।
येनाञ्जसोल्बणमुरुव्यसनं भवाब्धिं
नेष्ये भवद्गुणकथामृतपानमत्तः ॥११॥

bhaktiṁ muhuḥ pravahatāṁ tvayi me prasaṅgo
bhūyād ananta mahatām amalāśayānām
yenāñjasolbaṇam uru-vyasanaṁ bhavābdhiṁ
neṣye bhavad-guṇa-kathāmṛta-pāna-mattaḥ

bhaktim—devotional service; *muhuḥ*—constantly; *pravahatām*—of those who perform; *tvayi*—unto You; *me*—my; *prasaṅgaḥ*—intimate association; *bhūyāt*—may it become; *ananta*—O unlimited; *mahatām*—of the great devotees; *amala-āśayānām*—whose hearts are freed from material contamination; *yena*—by which; *añjasā*—easily; *ulbaṇam*—terrible; *uru*—great; *vyasanam*—full of dangers; *bhava-abdhim*—the ocean of material existence; *neṣye*—I shall cross; *bhavat*—Your; *guṇa*—transcendental qualities; *kathā*—pastimes; *amṛta*—nectar, eternal; *pāna*—by drinking; *mattaḥ*—mad.

TRANSLATION

Dhruva Mahārāja continued: O unlimited Lord, kindly bless me so that I can be associated with great devotees who engage in Your transcendental loving service constantly, as the waves of a river constantly flow. Such transcendental devotees are completely situated in an uncontaminated state of life. By the process of devotional service I shall surely be able to cross the nescient ocean of material existence, which is filled with the waves of blazing, firelike dangers. It will be very easy for me, for I am becoming mad to hear about Your transcendental qualities and pastimes, which are eternally existent.

PURPORT

The significant point in Dhruva Mahārāja's statement is that he wanted the association of pure devotees. Transcendental devotional service cannot be complete and cannot be relishable without the association of devotees. We have, therefore, established the International Society for Krishna Consciousness. Anyone who is trying to be aloof from this Krishna Consciousness Society and yet engage in Kṛṣṇa consciousness is living in a great hallucination, for this is not possible. From this statement of Dhruva Mahārāja it is clear that unless one is associated with devotees, his devotional service does not mature; it does not become distinct from material activities. The Lord says, *satāṁ prasaṅgān mama vīrya-saṁvido bhavanti hṛt-karṇa-rasāyanāḥ kathāḥ.* Only in the association of pure devotees can the words of Lord Kṛṣṇa be fully potent and relishable to the heart and ear. (*Bhāg.* 3.25.25) Dhruva Mahārāja explicitly wanted the association of devotees. That association in devotional activities is just like the waves of an incessantly flowing river. In our Krishna Consciousness Society we have full engagement twenty-four hours a day. Every moment of our time is always busily engaged in the service of the Lord. This is called the incessant flow of devotional service.

A Māyāvādī philosopher may question us, "You may be very happy in the association of devotees, but what is your plan for crossing the ocean of material existence?" Dhruva Mahārāja's answer is that it is not very difficult. He clearly says that this ocean can be crossed very easily if one simply becomes mad to hear the glories of the Lord. *Bhavad-guṇa-kathā:* for anyone who persistently engages in hearing the topics of the Lord from *Śrīmad Bhagavad-gītā, Śrīmad-Bhāgavatam* and *Caitanya-caritāmṛta* and who is actually addicted to this process, just as one becomes addicted to intoxicants, it is very easy to cross the nescience of material existence. The ocean of material nescience is compared with a blazing fire, but to a devotee this blazing fire is insignificant because he is completely absorbed in devotional service. Although the material world is blazing fire, to a devotee it appears full of pleasure (*viśvaṁ pūrṇaṁ sukhāyate*).

The purport of this statement by Dhruva Mahārāja is that devotional service in the association of devotees is the cause of the development of further devotional service. By devotional service only is one elevated to the transcendental planet Goloka Vṛndāvana, and there also there is only devotional service, for the activities of devotional service both in this world and in the spiritual world are one and the same. Devotional service does not change. The example of a mango can be given here. If one gets an unripe mango, it is still a mango, and when it is ripe it remains the same mango, but it becomes more tasteful and relishable. Similarly, there is devotional service performed according to the direction of the spiritual master and the injunctions and regulative principles of *śāstra,* and there is devotional service in the spiritual world rendered directly in association with the Supreme Personality of Godhead. But they are both the same. There is no change. The difference is that one stage is unripe and the other is ripe and more relishable. It is possible to mature in devotional service only in the association of devotees.

TEXT 12

ते न स्मरन्त्यतितरां प्रियमीश मर्त्यं
ये चान्वदः सुतसुहृद्गृहवित्तदाराः ।
ये त्वब्जनाभ भवदीयपदारविन्द-
सौगन्ध्यलुब्धहृदयेषु कृतप्रसङ्गाः ॥१२॥

te na smaranty atitarāṁ priyam īśa martyaṁ
ye cānv adaḥ suta-suhṛd-gṛha-vitta-dārāḥ
ye tv abja-nābha bhavadīya-padāravinda-
saugandhya-lubdha-hṛdayeṣu kṛta-prasaṅgāḥ

te—they; *na*—never; *smaranti*—remember; *atitarām*—highly; *priyam*—dear; *īśa*—O Lord; *martyam*—material body; *ye*—they who; *ca*—also; *anu*—in relationship with; *adaḥ*—that; *suta*—sons; *suhṛt*—friends; *gṛha*—home; *vitta*—wealth; *dārāḥ*—and wife; *ye*—those who; *tu*—then; *abja-nābha*—O Lord who has a lotus navel; *bhavadīya*—of Your; *pada-aravinda*—lotus feet; *saugandhya*—the fragrance; *lubdha*—have achieved; *hṛdayeṣu*—with devotees whose hearts; *kṛta-prasaṅgāḥ*—have association.

TRANSLATION

O Lord who has a lotus navel, if a person happens to associate with a devotee whose heart always hankers after Your lotus feet, seeking always their fragrance, he is never attached to the material body or, in relationship with it, offspring, friends, home, wealth, and wife, which are very, very dear to materialistic persons. He does not care for them.

PURPORT

A special advantage in devotional service is that devotees not only enjoy the transcendental pastimes of the Lord by hearing and chanting and glorifying them, but also they are not very much attached to their bodies, unlike the *yogīs,* who are too attached to the body and who think that by performing bodily gymnastic exercises they will advance in spiritual consciousness. *Yogīs* are generally not very much interested in devotional service; they want to regulate the breathing process. This is simply a bodily concern. Here Dhruva Mahārāja plainly says that a devotee has no more bodily interest. He knows that he is not the body. From the very beginning, therefore, without wasting time in bodily exercises, a devotee searches out a pure devotee, and simply by his association becomes more advanced in spiritual consciousness than any *yogī.* Because a devotee knows that he is not the body, he is never affected by bodily happiness or distress. He is not interested in bodily relationships with wife, children, home, bank balance, etc., or in the distress or happiness which comes from these things. This is the special advantage of being a devotee. This status of life is possible only when a person is interested in associating with a pure devotee who always enjoys the fragrance of the lotus feet of the Lord.

TEXT 13

तिर्यङ्नगद्विजसरीसृपदेवदैत्य-
मर्त्यादिभिः परिचितं सदसद्विशेषम् ।
रूपं स्थविष्ठमज ते महदाद्यनेकं
नातः परं परम वेद्मि न यत्र वादः ॥१३॥

tiryaṅ-naga-dvija-sarīsṛpa-deva-daitya-
martyādibhiḥ paricitaṁ sad-asad-viśeṣam
rūpaṁ sthaviṣṭham aja te mahad-ādy-anekaṁ
nātaḥ paraṁ parama vedmi na yatra vādaḥ

tiryak—by animals; *naga*—trees; *dvija*—birds; *sarīsṛpa*—reptiles; *deva*—demigods; *daitya*—demons; *martya-ādibhiḥ*—by men, etc.; *paricitam*—pervaded; *sat-asat-viśeṣam*—with varieties manifest and nonmanifest; *rūpam*—form; *sthaviṣṭham*—gross universal; *aja*—O unborn; *te*—Your; *mahat-ādi*—caused by the total material energy, etc.; *anekam*—various causes; *na*—not; *ataḥ*—from this; *param*—transcendental; *parama*—O Supreme; *vedmi*—I know; *na*—not; *yatra*—where; *vādaḥ*—various arguments.

TRANSLATION

My dear Lord, O Supreme Unborn, I know that the different varieties of living entities, such as animals, trees, birds, reptiles, demigods and human beings, are spread throughout the universe, which is caused by the total material energy, and I know that they are sometimes manifest and sometimes unmanifest; but I have never experienced the supreme form I behold as I see You now. Now all kinds of theorizing processes are finished.

PURPORT

In the *Bhagavad-gītā* the Lord says that He has spread Himself throughout the universe, but although everything is resting upon Him, He is aloof.

The same concept is expressed here by Dhruva Mahārāja. He states that before seeing the transcendental form of the Lord, he had experienced only the varieties of material forms, which are counted at 8,400,000 species of aquatics, birds, beasts, etc. The fact is that unless one engages in the devotional service of the Lord, it is impossible for him to understand the ultimate form of the Lord. This is also confirmed in the *Bhagavad-gītā* (Bg. 18.55). *Bhaktyā mām abhijānāti:* factual understanding of the Absolute Truth, who is the Supreme Person, cannot be obtained by any process other than devotional service.

Dhruva Mahārāja here compares his previous state of understanding with the perfection of understanding in the presence of the Supreme Lord. The position of a living entity is to render service; unless he comes to the stage of appreciating the Supreme Personality of Godhead, he engages in the service of the various forms of trees, reptiles, animals, men, demigods, etc. One can experience that one man engages in the service of a dog, another serves plants and creepers, another the demigods, and another humanity or his boss in the office—but no one is engaged in the service of Kṛṣṇa. Aside from common men, even men who are elevated in terms of spiritual understanding are at the utmost engaged in the service of the *virāṭa-rūpa,* or, unable to understand the ultimate form of the Lord, they worship voidism by meditation. Dhruva Mahārāja, however, had been blessed by the Supreme Lord. When the Lord touched His conchshell to Dhruva's forehead, real knowledge was revealed from within, and Dhruva could understand the Lord's transcendental form. Dhruva Mahārāja here admits that not only was he ignorant, but by years he was only a child. It would not have been possible for an ignorant child to appreciate the supreme form of the Lord had he not been blessed by the Lord, who touched His conchshell to Dhruva's forehead.

TEXT 14

कल्पान्त एतदखिलं जठरेण गृह्णन्
शेते पुमान् स्वदृगनन्तसखस्तदङ्के ।
यन्नाभिसिन्धुरुहकाञ्चनलोकपद्म-
गर्भे द्युमान् भगवते प्रणतोऽस्मि तस्मै ॥ १४ ॥

kalpānta etad akhilaṁ jaṭhareṇa gṛhṇan
śete pumān sva-dṛg ananta-sakhas tad-aṅke
yan-nābhi-sindhu-ruha-kāñcana-loka-padma-
garbhe dyumān bhagavate praṇato 'smi tasmai

kalpa-ante—at the end of the millennium; *etat*—this universe; *akhilam*—all; *jaṭhareṇa*—within the belly; *gṛhṇan*—withdrawing; *śete*—lies down; *pumān*—the Supreme Person; *sva-dṛk*—looking upon Himself; *ananta*—the unlimited being Śeṣa; *sakhaḥ*--accompanied by; *tat-aṅke*—on His lap; *yat*—from whose; *nābhi*—navel; *sindhu*—ocean; *ruha*—sprouted; *kāñcana*—golden; *loka*—planet; *padma*—of the lotus; *garbhe*—on the whorl; *dyumān*—Lord Brahmā; *bhagavate*—unto the Supreme Personality of Godhead; *praṇataḥ*—offering obeisances; *asmi*—I am; *tasmai*—unto Him.

TRANSLATION

My dear Lord, at the end of each millennium the Supreme Personality of Godhead Garbhodakaśāyī Viṣṇu dissolves everything manifested within the universe in His belly. He lies down on the lap of Śeṣanāga, from His navel sprouts a golden lotus flower on a stem, and on that lotus Lord Brahmā is created. I can understand that You are the same Supreme Godhead. I therefore offer my respectful obeisances unto You.

PURPORT

Dhruva Mahārāja's understanding of the Supreme Personality of Godhead is complete. In the *Vedas* it is said, *yasmin vijñāte sarvam evaṁ vijñātaṁ bhavanti:* knowledge received through the transcendental causeless mercy of the Lord is so perfect that by that knowledge the devotee becomes acquainted with all the different manifestations of the Lord. Lord Kṣīrodakaśāyī Viṣṇu was present before Dhruva Mahārāja, who could also understand the Lord's two other forms, namely Garbhodakaśāyī Viṣṇu and Kāraṇodakaśāyī (Mahā) Viṣṇu. Regarding Mahā-Viṣṇu, it is stated in the *Brahma-saṁhitā:*

yasyaika-niśvasita-kālam athāvalambya
jīvanti loma-vilajā jagadaṇḍa-nāthāḥ
viṣṇur mahān sa iha yasya kalā-viśeṣo
govindam ādi-puruṣaṁ tam ahaṁ bhajāmi (Bs. 5.48)

At the end of each and every millennium, when all the material worlds are dissolved, everything enters the body of Garbhodakaśāyī Viṣṇu, who is lying on the lap of Śeṣanāga, another form of the Lord.

Those who are not devotees cannot understand the different forms of Viṣṇu and their positions in regard to the creation. Sometimes the atheists argue, "How can a flower stem sprout from the navel of

Garbhodakaśāyī Viṣṇu?" They consider all the statements of the *śāstras* to be stories. As a result of their inexperience in the Absolute Truth and their reluctance to accept authority, they become more and more atheistic; they cannot understand the Supreme Personality of Godhead. But a devotee like Dhruva Mahārāja, by the grace of the Lord, knows all the manifestations of the Lord and their different positions. It is said that anyone who has even a little of the Lord's grace can understand His glories; others may go on speculating on the Absolute Truth, but they will always be unable to understand the Lord. In other words, unless one comes in contact with a devotee it is not possible to understand the transcendental form or the spiritual world and its transcendental activities.

TEXT 15

त्वं नित्यमुक्तपरिशुद्धविबुद्ध आत्मा
कूटस्थ आदिपुरुषो भगवांस्त्र्यधीशः ।
यद्बुद्ध्यवस्थितिमखण्डितया स्वदृष्ट्या
द्रष्टा स्थितावधिमखो व्यतिरिक्त आस्से ॥१५॥

tvaṁ nitya-mukta-pariśuddha-vibuddha ātmā
kūṭa-stha ādi-puruṣo bhagavāṁs try-adhīśaḥ
yad buddhy-avasthitim akhaṇḍitayā sva-dṛṣṭyā
draṣṭā sthitāv adhimakho vyatirikta āsse

tvam—You; *nitya*—eternally; *mukta*—liberated; *pariśuddha*—uncontaminated; *vibuddha*—full of knowledge; *ātmā*—the Supreme Soul; *kūṭa-sthaḥ*—changeless; *ādi*—original; *puruṣaḥ*—person; *bhagavān*—the Lord full with six opulences; *tri-adhīśaḥ*—master of the three modes; *yat*—whence; *buddhi*—of intellectual activities; *avasthitim*—all stages; *akhaṇḍitayā*—unbroken; *sva-dṛṣṭyā*—by transcendental vision; *draṣṭā*—You witness; *sthitau*—for maintaining (the universe); *adhimakhaḥ*—enjoyer of the results of all sacrifices; *vyatiriktaḥ*—differently; *āsse*—You are situated.

TRANSLATION

My Lord, by Your unbroken transcendental glance You are the supreme witness of all stages of intellectual activities. You are eternally liberated, Your existence is situated in pure goodness, You are existent in the Supersoul without change, You are the original Personality of Godhead, full with six opulences, and You are eternally the master of the three modes of material nature. Thus, You are always different from the

ordinary living entities. As Lord Viṣṇu, You maintain all the affairs of the entire universe, and yet You stand aloof and are the enjoyer of the results of all sacrifices.

PURPORT

An atheistic argument against the supremacy of the Supreme Personality of Godhead states that if God, the Supreme Person, appears and disappears and sleeps and awakens, then what is the difference between God and the living entity? Dhruva Mahārāja is carefully distinguishing the existence of the Supreme Personality of Godhead from that of the living entities. He points out the following differences. The Lord is eternally liberated. Whenever He appears, even within this material world, He is never entangled by the three modes of material nature. He is known, therefore, as *try-adhīśa,* the master of the three modes of material nature. In *Bhagavad-gītā* (7.14) it is said, *daivī hy eṣā guṇamayī mama māyā duratyayā:* the living entities are all entangled in the three modes of material nature. The external energy of the Lord is very strong, but the Lord, as the master of the three modes of nature, is ever liberated from the action and reaction of those modes. He is, therefore, uncontaminated, as it is stated in the *Īśopaniṣad.* The contamination of the material world does not affect the Supreme Godhead. Kṛṣṇa therefore says in the *Bhagavad-gītā* that those who are rascals and fools think of Him as an ordinary human being, not knowing His *paraṁ bhāvam. Paraṁ bhāvam* refers to His being always transcendentally situated. Material contamination cannot affect Him.

Another difference between the Lord and the living entity is that a living entity is always in darkness. Even though he may be situated in the mode of goodness, there are still so many things which are unknown to him. But it is not the same for the Supreme Personality of Godhead. He knows past, present and future and everything that is happening in everyone's heart. *Bhagavad-gītā* confirms this *(vedāhaṁ samatītāni).* The Lord is not part of the soul—He is the unchangeable Supreme Soul, and the living entities are His parts and parcels. The living entity is forced to appear in this material world under the direction of *daiva-māyā,* but when the Lord appears, He comes by His own internal potency, *ātma-māyā.* Besides that, a living entity is within the time of past, present and future. His life has a beginning, a birth, and in the conditioned state his life ends with death. But the Lord is *ādi-puruṣa,* the original person. In the *Brahma-saṁhitā* Lord Brahmā offers his respect to the *ādi-puruṣa,* Govinda, the original person, who has no beginning, whereas the creation of this material world has a beginning. The *Vedānta* says, *janmādy asya yataḥ:* everything is born from the Supreme, but the Supreme has no birth. He has all the six opulences in full and beyond comparison, He is the master of material nature, His intelligence is not broken under any circumstances, and He stands aloof, although He is the maintainer of the whole creation. As stated in the *Vedas* (*Kaṭha Up.* 2.2.13), *nityo nityānāṁ cetanaś cetanānām.* The Lord is the supreme maintainer. Living entities are meant to serve Him by offering sacrifices, for He is the rightful enjoyer of the results of all sacrifices. Everyone, therefore, should engage himself in the devotional service of the Lord with his life, his riches, his intelligence and his words. This is the original, constitutional position of the living entities. One should never compare the sleeping of an ordinary living entity with the sleeping of the Supreme Personality of Godhead in the Causal Ocean. There is no stage at which the living entity can compare to the Supreme Person. The Māyāvādī philosophers, being unable to adjust to all this, come to the conclusion of impersonalism or voidism.

TEXT 16

यस्मिन् विरुद्धगतयो ह्यनिशं पतन्ति
विद्यादयो विविधशक्तय आनुपूर्व्यात् ।
तद्ब्रह्म विश्वभवमेकमनन्तमाद्य-
मानन्दमात्रमविकारमहं प्रपद्ये ॥१६॥

yasmin viruddha-gatayo hy aniśaṁ patanti
vidyādayo vividha-śaktaya ānupūrvyāt
tad brahma viśva-bhavam ekam anantam ādyam
ānanda-mātram avikāram ahaṁ prapadye

yasmin—in whom; *viruddha-gatayaḥ*—of opposite character; *hi*—certainly; *aniśam*—always; *patanti*—are manifest; *vidyā-ādayaḥ*—knowledge and ignorance, etc.; *vividha*—various; *śaktayaḥ*—energies; *ānupūrvyāt*—continually; *tat*—that; *brahma*—Brahman; *viśva-bhavam*—the cause of material creation; *ekam*—one; *anantam*—unlimited; *ādyam*—original; *ānanda-mātram*—simply blissful; *avikāram*—changeless; *aham*—I; *prapadye*—offer my obeisances.

TRANSLATION

My dear Lord, in Your impersonal manifestation of Brahman there are always two opposing elements, knowledge and ignorance. Your multi-

energies are continually manifest, but the impersonal Brahman, which is undivided, original, changeless, unlimited and blissful, is the cause of the material manifestation. Because You are the same impersonal Brahman, I offer my respectful obeisances unto You.

PURPORT

In the *Brahma-saṁhitā* it is said that the unlimited impersonal Brahman is the effulgence of the transcendental body of Govinda. In that unlimited effulgent aura of the Supreme Personality of Godhead there are innumerable universes with innumerable planets of different categories. Although the Supreme Person is the original cause of all causes, still His impersonal effulgence, known as Brahman, is the immediate cause of the material manifestation. Dhruva Mahārāja, therefore, offered his respectful obeisances unto the impersonal feature of the Lord. One who realizes this impersonal feature can enjoy the unchangeable *brahmānanda* described here as spiritual bliss.

Śrīla Viśvanātha Cakravartī Ṭhākura describes that this impersonal feature or Brahman manifestation of the Supreme Lord is meant for persons who are essentially very advanced but still not able to understand the personal features or variegatedness of the spiritual world. Such devotees are known as *jñāna-miśra-bhaktas,* or devotees whose devotional service is mixed with empiric knowledge. Because the impersonal Brahman realization is a partial understanding of the Absolute Truth, Dhruva Mahārāja offers his respectful obeisances.

It is said that this impersonal Brahman is the distant realization of the Absolute Truth. Although apparently Brahman seems to be devoid of energy, factually it has different energies working under the headings of knowledge and ignorance. On account of these different energies, there is continually a manifestation of *vidyā* and *avidyā. Vidyā* and *avidyā* are very nicely described in *Īśopaniṣad.* It is said there that sometimes, due to *avidyā*, or a poor fund of knowledge, one accepts the Absolute Truth as ultimately impersonal. But in fact the impersonal and personal realizations develop in proportion to the development of devotional service. The more we develop our devotional service, the more closely we approach the Absolute Truth, which, in the beginning, when we realize the Absolute Truth from a distant place, is manifest as impersonal.

People in general, who are under the influence of *avidyā-śakti,* or *māyā,* have neither knowledge nor devotion. But when a person who is a little advanced and is therefore called a *jñānī* advances even more, he is in the category of a *jñāna-miśra-bhakta,* or a devotee whose love is mixed with material knowledge. When he is still further advanced, he can realize that the Absolute Truth is a person with multi-energies. An advanced devotee can understand the Lord and His creative energy. As soon as one accepts the creative energy of the Absolute Truth, the six opulences of the Supreme Personality of Godhead are also understood. Devotees who are still further advanced, in full knowledge, can understand the transcendental pastimes of the Lord. Only on that platform can one fully enjoy transcendental bliss. An example is given in this connection by Viśvanātha Cakravartī Ṭhākura of a person proceeding towards a destination. As he approaches, he sees the destination from a distant place, just as we see a city from a distance. At that time he simply understands that the city is situated at a distance. When, however, he comes still nearer, he sees the domes and flags. But as soon as he enters the city, he sees various paths, gardens, lakes, and marketplaces with shops and persons buying. He sees varieties of cinema houses, and he sees dancing and jubilation. When a person actually enters the city and personally sees the activities of the city, he becomes satisfied.

TEXT 17

सत्याशिषो हि भगवंस्तव पादपद्म-
माशीस्तथानुभजतः पुरुषार्थमूर्तेः ।
अप्येवमर्य भगवान् परिपाति दीनान्
वाश्रेव वत्सकमनुग्रहकातरोऽस्मान् ॥१७॥

satyāśiṣo hi bhagavaṁs tava pāda-padmam
āśīs tathānubhajataḥ puruṣārtha-mūrteḥ
apy evam arya bhagavān paripāti dīnān
vāśreva vatsakam anugraha-kātaro 'smān

satyā—real; *āśiṣaḥ*—compared with other benedictions; *hi*—certainly; *bhagavan*—my Lord; *tava*—Your; *pāda-padmam*—lotus feet; *āśīḥ*—benediction; *tathā*—in that way; *anubhajataḥ*—for the devotees; *puruṣa-artha*—of the real goal of life; *mūrteḥ*—the personification; *api*—although; *evam*—thus; *arya*—O Lord; *bhagavān*—the Personality of Godhead; *paripāti*—maintains; *dīnān*—the poor in heart; *vāśrā*-a cow; *iva*-like; *vatsakam*—unto the calf; *anugraha*-to bestow mercy; *kātaraḥ*—eager; *asmān*—upon me.

TRANSLATION

My Lord, O Supreme Lord, You are the supreme personified form of all benediction. Therefore, for one who abides in Your devotional service

with no other desire, worshiping Your lotus feet is better than becoming king and lording it over a kingdom. That is the benediction of worshiping Your lotus feet. To ignorant devotees like me, You are the causelessly merciful maintainer, just like a cow, who takes care of the newly born calf by supplying milk and giving it protection from attack.

PURPORT

Dhruva Mahārāja was cognizant of the defective nature of his own devotional service. Pure devotional service is without material form and is not covered by mental speculation or fruitive activities. Pure devotional service is therefore called *ahaitukī,* unmotivated. Dhruva Mahārāja knew that he came to worship the Lord in devotional service with a motive—to get the kingdom of his father. Such an adulterated devotee can never see the Supreme Personality of Godhead face to face. He therefore felt very grateful for the causeless mercy of the Lord. The Lord is so merciful that He not only fulfills the desires of a devotee who is driven by ignorance and desires for material benefit, but He also gives him all protection, just as a cow gives milk to a newly born calf. In the *Bhagavad-gītā* it is said that the Lord gives intelligence to the constantly engaged devotee so that he may gradually approach the Lord without difficulty. A devotee must be very sincere in his devotional service; then, although there may be many things wrong on the devotee's part, Kṛṣṇa will guide him and gradually elevate him to the highest position of devotional service.

The Lord is addressed herein by Dhruva Mahārāja as *puruṣārtha-mūrti,* the ultimate goal of life. Generally *puruṣārtha* is taken to mean execution of a type of religious principle or worship of God in order to get material benediction. Prayers for material benediction are intended for satisfying the senses. And when one is frustrated and cannot fully satisfy the senses in spite of all endeavor, he desires liberation, or freedom from material existence. These activities are generally called *puruṣārtha.* But actually the ultimate goal is to understand the Supreme Personality of Godhead. This is called *pañca-puruṣārtha,* the ultimate goal of life. Lord Caitanya therefore taught us not to ask from the Supreme Personality any benediction such as material wealth, popularity or a good wife. One should simply pray to the Lord to be constantly engaged in His transcendental loving service. Dhruva Mahārāja, being cognizant of his desire for material benefit, wanted protection from the Lord so that he might not be misled or deviated from the path of devotional service by material desires.

TEXT 18

मैत्रेय उवाच
अथाभिष्टुत एवं वै सत्संकल्पेन धीमता ।
भृत्यानुरक्तो भगवान् प्रतिनन्द्येदमब्रवीत् ॥१८॥

maitreya uvāca
athābhiṣṭuta evaṁ vai
sat-saṅkalpena dhīmatā
bhṛtyānurakto bhagavān
pratinandyedam abravīt

maitreyaḥ uvāca—Maitreya said; *atha*—then; *abhiṣṭutaḥ*—being worshiped; *evam*—thus; *vai*—certainly; *sat-saṅkalpena*—by Dhruva Mahārāja, who had only good desires in his heart; *dhīmatā*—because he was very intelligent; *bhṛtya-anuraktaḥ*—very favorably disposed to devotees; *bhagavān*—the Supreme Personality of Godhead; *pratinandya*—having congratulated him; *idam*—this; *abravīt*—said.

TRANSLATION

The great sage Maitreya continued: My dear Vidura, when Dhruva Mahārāja, who had good intentions in his heart, finished his prayer, the Supreme Lord, the Personality of Godhead, who is very kind to His devotees and servants, congratulated him, speaking as follows.

TEXT 19

श्रीभगवानुवाच
वेदाहं ते व्यवसितं हृदि राजन्यबालक ।
तत्प्रयच्छामि भद्रं ते दुरापमपि सुव्रत ॥१९॥

śrī bhagavān uvāca
vedāhaṁ te vyavasitaṁ
hṛdi rājanya-bālaka
tat prayacchāmi bhadraṁ te
durāpam api suvrata

śrī bhagavān uvāca—the Personality of Godhead said; *veda*—know; *aham*—I; *te*—your; *vyavasitam*—determination; *hṛdi*—within the heart; *rājanya-bālaka*—O son of the King; *tat*—that; *prayacchāmi*—I shall give you; *bhadram*—all good fortune; *te*—unto you; *durāpam*—although it is very difficult to obtain; *api*—in spite of; *su-vrata*—one who has taken a pious vow.

TRANSLATION

The Personality of Godhead said: My dear Dhruva, son of the King, you have executed pious vows, and I also know the desire within your heart. Although your desire is very ambitious and very difficult to fulfill, still I shall favor you with its fulfillment. All good fortune unto you.

PURPORT

The Lord is so merciful to His devotee that He immediately said to Dhruva Mahārāja, "Let there be all good fortune for you." The fact is that Dhruva Mahārāja was very much afraid in his mind, for he had aspired after material benefit in discharging his devotional service and this was hampering him from reaching the stage of love of God. In the *Bhagavad-gītā* (2.44) it is said, *bhogaiśvarya-prasaktānām:* those who are addicted to material pleasure cannot be attracted to devotional service. It was true that at heart Dhruva Mahārāja wanted a kingdom that would be far better than Brahmaloka. This was a natural desire for a *kṣatriya.* He was also only five years old, and in his childish way he desired to have a kingdom far greater than his father's, grandfather's or great-grandfather's. His father, Uttānapāda, was the son of Manu, and Manu was the son of Lord Brahmā. Dhruva wanted to excel all these great family members. The Lord, however, knew Dhruva Mahārāja's childish ambition, but at the same time how was it possible to offer him a position more exalted than Lord Brahmā's?

The Lord assured Dhruva Mahārāja that he would not be bereft of His love. He encouraged Dhruva not to be worried that he childishly had material desires and at the same time had the pure aspiration to be a great devotee. Generally, the Lord does not award a pure devotee material opulence, even though he may desire it. But Dhruva Mahārāja's case was different. The Lord knew that he was such a great devotee that in spite of having material opulence he would never be deviated from love of God. This example illustrates that a highly qualified devotee can have the facility of material enjoyment and at the same time execute love of God. This, however, is a special case for Dhruva Mahārāja.

TEXTS 20-21

नान्यैरधिष्ठितं भद्र यद्भ्राजिष्णु ध्रुवक्षिति ।
यत्र ग्रहर्क्षताराणां ज्योतिषां चक्रमाहितम् ॥२०॥
मेढ्यां गोचक्रवत्स्थास्नु परस्तात्कल्पवासिनाम् ।
धर्मोऽग्निः कश्यपः शुक्रो मुनयो ये वनौकसः ।
चरन्ति दक्षिणीकृत्य भ्रमन्तो यत्सतारकाः ॥२१॥

nānyair adhiṣṭhitaṁ bhadra
yad bhrājiṣṇu dhruva-kṣiti
yatra grahar̥kṣa-tārāṇāṁ
jyotiṣāṁ cakram āhitam
meḍhyāṁ go-cakravat sthāsnu
parastāt kalpa-vāsinām
dharmo 'gniḥ kaśyapaḥ śukro
munayo ye vanaukasaḥ
caranti dakṣiṇī-kṛtya
bhramanto yat satārakāḥ

na—never; *anyaiḥ*—by others; *adhiṣṭhitam*—was ruled over; *bhadra*—my good boy; *yat*—which; *bhrājiṣṇu*—brightly glowing; *dhruva-kṣiti*—the land known as Dhruvaloka; *yatra*—where; *graha*—planets; *ṛkṣa*—constellations; *tārāṇām*—and stars; *jyotiṣām*—by luminaries; *cakram*—encirclement; *āhitam*—is done; *meḍhyām*—around a central pole; *go*—of bulls; *cakra*—a multitude; *vat*—like; *sthāsnu*—stationary; *parastāt*—beyond; *kalpa*—a day of Brahmā (millennium); *vāsinām*—those who live; *dharmaḥ*—Dharma; *agniḥ*—Agni; *kaśyapaḥ*—Kaśyapa; *śukraḥ*—Śukra; *munayaḥ*—great sages; *ye*—all of them who; *vana-okasaḥ*—living in the forest; *caranti*—move; *dakṣiṇī-kṛtya*—keeping it to their right; *bhramantaḥ*—circumambulating; *yat*—which planet; *sa-tārakāḥ*—with all the stars.

TRANSLATION

The Supreme Personality of Godhead continued: My dear Dhruva, I shall award you the glowing planet known as the Pole Star, which will continue to stay even after the dissolution at the end of the millennium. No one has ever ruled over this planet, which is surrounded by all the solar systems, planets and stars. All the luminaries in the sky circumambulate this planet, just as bulls go around a central pole for the purpose of crushing grains. Keeping it to their right, all the stars inhabited by the great sages like Dharma, Agni, Kaśyapa and Śukra

circumambulate this planet, which continues to exist even after the dissolution of all others.

PURPORT

Although the Pole Star existed before its occupation by Dhruva Mahārāja, there was no predominating deity. Dhruvaloka, our Pole Star, is the center for all other stars and solar systems, for all of them circle around Dhruvaloka just as a bull crushes grains by walking around and around a central pole. Dhruva wanted the best of all planets, and although it was a childish prayer, the Lord satisfied his demand. A small child may demand something from his father which his father has never given to anyone else, yet out of affection the father offers it to the child; similarly, this unique planet, Dhruvaloka, was offered to Mahārāja Dhruva. The specific significance of this planet is that until the entire universe is annihilated, this planet will remain, even during the devastation which takes place during the night of Lord Brahmā. There are two kinds of dissolutions, one during the night of Lord Brahmā and one at the end of Lord Brahmā's life. At the end of Brahmā's life, selected personalities go back home, back to Godhead. Dhruva Mahārāja is one of them. The Lord assured Dhruva that he would exist beyond the partial dissolution of this universe. Thus at the end of the complete dissolution, Dhruva Mahārāja would go directly to Vaikuṇṭhaloka, to a spiritual planet in the spiritual sky. Śrīla Viśvanātha Cakravartī Ṭhākura comments in this connection that Dhruvaloka is one of the *lokas* like Śvetadvīpa, Mathurā and Dvārakā. They are all eternal places in the kingdom of Godhead, which is described in the *Bhagavad-gītā* (*tad dhāma paramam*) and in the *Vedas* (*oṁ tad viṣṇoḥ paramaṁ padaṁ sadā paśyanti sūrayaḥ).* The words *parastāt kalpa-vāsinām,* transcendental to the planets inhabited after the dissolution, refer to the Vaikuṇṭha planets. In other words, Dhruva Mahārāja's promotion to the Vaikuṇṭhalokas was guaranteed by the Supreme Personality of Godhead.

TEXT 22

प्रस्थिते तु वनं पित्रा दत्त्वा गां धर्मसंश्रयः ।
षट्त्रिंशद्वर्षसाहस्रं रक्षिताव्याहतेन्द्रियः ॥२२॥

prasthite tu vanaṁ pitrā
dattvā gāṁ dharma-saṁśrayaḥ
ṣaṭ-triṁśad-varṣa-sāhasraṁ
rakṣitāvyāhatendriyaḥ

prasthite—after departure; *tu*—but; *vanam*—to the forest; *pitrā*—by your father; *dattvā*-awarding; *gām*—the whole world; *dharma-saṁśrayaḥ*—under the protection of piety; *ṣaṭ-triṁśat*—thirty-six; *varṣa*—years; *sāhasram*—one thousand; *rakṣitā*—you will rule; *avyāhata*—without decay; *indriyaḥ*—the power of the senses.

TRANSLATION

After your father goes to the forest and awards you the rule of his kingdom, you will rule the entire world continually for 36,000 years, and all your senses will continue to be as strong as they are now. You will never become old.

PURPORT

In the Satya-yuga people generally lived for 100,000 years. Dhruva Mahārāja's ruling the world for 36,000 years was quite possible in those days.

TEXT 23

त्वद्भ्रातर्युत्तमे नष्टे मृगयायां तु तन्मनाः ।
अन्वेषन्ती वनं माता दावाग्निं सा प्रवेक्ष्यति ॥२३॥

tvad-bhrātary uttame naṣṭe
mṛgayāyāṁ tu tan-manāḥ
anveṣantī vanaṁ mātā
dāvāgniṁ sā pravekṣyati

tvat—your; *bhrātari*—brother; *uttame*—Uttama; *naṣṭe*—being killed; *mṛgayāyām*—in hunting; *tu*—then; *tat-manāḥ*—being too afflicted; *anveṣantī*—while searching out; *vanam*—in the forest; *mātā*—the mother; *dāva-agnim*—in the forest fire; *sā*—she; *pravekṣyati*—will enter.

TRANSLATION

The Lord continued: Sometime in the future your brother Uttama will go hunting in the forest, and while absorbed in hunting, he will be killed. Your stepmother Suruci, being maddened upon the death of her son, will go to search him out in the forest, but she will be devoured by a forest fire.

PURPORT

Dhruva Mahārāja came to the forest to search out the Supreme Personality of Godhead with a revenging spirit against his stepmother. His stepmother insulted Dhruva, who was not an ordinary person, but a great Vaiṣṇava. An offense at the lotus feet of a Vaiṣṇava is the greatest offense in this world. Because of her insulting Dhruva Mahārāja, Suruci would become mad upon the death of her son and would enter a forest fire, and thus her life would be ended. This was specifically mentioned by the Lord to Dhruva because he was determined for revenge against her. From this we should take the lesson that we should never try to insult a Vaiṣṇava. Not only should we not insult a Vaiṣṇava, but we should not insult anyone unnecessarily. When Suruci insulted Dhruva Mahārāja, he was just a child. She of course did not know that Dhruva was a great recognized Vaiṣṇava, and so her offense was committed unknowingly. Similarly, if one serves a Vaiṣṇava unknowingly, there is a good result. When one serves a Vaiṣṇava without knowledge, he still gets the good result, and if he unknowingly insults a Vaiṣṇava, one suffers the bad result. A Vaiṣṇava is especially favored by the Supreme Personality of Godhead. Pleasing him or displeasing him directly affects the pleasure and displeasure of the Supreme Lord. Śrīla Viśvanātha Cakravartī Ṭhākura, in his eight stanzas of prayer to the spiritual master, has sung, *yasya prasādād bhagavat-prasādaḥ:* by pleasing the spiritual master, who is a pure Vaiṣṇava, one pleases the Personality of Godhead, but if one displeases the spiritual master he does not know where he is going.

TEXT 24

इष्ट्वा मां यज्ञहृदयं यज्ञैः पुष्कलदक्षिणैः ।
भुक्त्वा चेहाशिषः सत्या अन्ते मां संस्मरिष्यसि ।२४।

iṣṭvā māṁ yajña-hṛdayaṁ
yajñaiḥ puṣkala-dakṣiṇaiḥ
bhuktvā cehāśiṣaḥ satyā
ante māṁ saṁsmariṣyasi

iṣṭvā—after worshiping; *mām*—Me; *yajña-hṛdayam*—the heart of all sacrifices; *yajñaiḥ*—by great sacrifices; *puṣkala-dakṣiṇaiḥ*—comprehending distribution of great charities; *bhuktvā*--after enjoying; *ca*—also; *iha*—within this world; *āśiṣaḥ*—blessings; *satyāḥ*—true; *ante*—at the end; *mām*—Me; *saṁsmariṣyasi*—you will be able to remember.

TRANSLATION

The Lord continued: I am the heart of all sacrifices. You will be able to perform many great sacrifices and also give great charities. In this way

you will be able to enjoy the blessings of material happiness in this life, and at the time of your death you will be able to remember Me.

PURPORT

The most important factor in this verse is the Lord's instructions regarding how to remember the Supreme Personality of Godhead at the end of life. *Ante nārāyaṇa-smṛtiḥ:* the result of whatever we do in executing spiritual activities is successful if we can remember Nārāyaṇa, the Supreme Personality of Godhead. This program of constant remembrance can be disturbed by many things, but Dhruva Mahārāja's life would be so pure, as assured by the Lord Himself, that he would never forget Him. Thus at the time of his death he would remember the Supreme Lord, and before his death he would enjoy this material world, not by sense gratification, but by performing great sacrifices. As stated in the *Vedas,* when one performs great sacrifices he must give in charity, not only to the *brāhmaṇas,* but also to the *kṣatriyas, vaiśyas* and *śūdras.* It is assured here that Dhruva Mahārāja would be able to perform such activities. In this age of Kali, however, the great sacrifice is the performance of *saṅkīrtana-yajña.* Our Kṛṣṇa consciousness movement is designed to teach people (and to learn ourselves) the exact instruction of the Personality of Godhead. In this way we shall continue to perform the *saṅkīrtana-yajña* continually and continually chant the Hare Kṛṣṇa *mantra.* Then certainly at the end of our lives we shall be able to remember Kṛṣṇa, and our program of life will be successful. In this age, distribution of *prasāda* has replaced distribution of money. No one has sufficient money to distribute, but if we distribute *kṛṣṇa-prasāda* as far as possible, it is more valuable than the distribution of money.

TEXT 25

ततो गन्तासि मत्स्थानं सर्वलोकनमस्कृतम् ।
उपरिष्टादृषिभ्यस्त्वं यतो नावर्तते गतः ॥२५॥

tato gantāsi mat-sthānaṁ
sarva-loka-namas-kṛtam
upariṣṭād ṛṣibhyas tvaṁ
yato nāvartate gataḥ

tataḥ—thereafter; *gantāsi*—you will go; *mat-sthānam*—to My abode; *sarva-loka*—by all planetary systems; *namaḥ-kṛtam*—offered obeisances to; *upariṣṭāt*—situated higher; *ṛṣibhyaḥ*—than the planetary systems of the *ṛṣis;*

tvam—you; *yataḥ*—wherefrom; *na*—never; *āvartate*—will come back; *gataḥ*—having gone there.

TRANSLATION

The Personality of Godhead continued: My dear Dhruva, after your material life in this body, you will go to My planet, which is always offered obeisances by the residents of all other planetary systems. It is situated above the planets of the seven ṛṣis, and when you go there you never have to come back again to this material world.

PURPORT

In this verse the word *nāvartate* is very significant. The Lord says, "You will not come back to this material world because you will reach *mat-sthānam,* My abode." Therefore Dhruvaloka, or the Pole Star, is the abode of Lord Viṣṇu within this material world. Upon it there is an ocean of milk, and within that ocean there is an island known as Śvetadvīpa. It is clearly indicated that this planet is situated above the seven planetary systems of the *ṛṣis,* and because this planet is Viṣṇuloka, it is worshiped by all other planetary systems. It may be questioned here what will happen to the planet known as Dhruvaloka at the time of the dissolution of this universe. The answer is simple: Dhruvaloka remains, like other Vaikuṇṭhalokas, beyond this universe. Śrīla Viśvanātha Cakravartī Ṭhākura has commented in this connection that the very word *nāvartate* indicates that this planet is eternal.

TEXT 26

मैत्रेय उवाच

इत्यर्चितः स भगवानतिदिश्यात्मनः पदम् ।
बालस्य पश्यतो धाम स्वमगाद्गरुडध्वजः ॥२६॥

maitreya uvāca
ity arcitaḥ sa bhagavān
atidiśyātmanaḥ padam
bālasya paśyato dhāma svam
agād garuḍa-dhvajaḥ

maitreyaḥ uvāca—the great sage Maitreya continued to speak; *iti*—thus; *arcitaḥ*—being honored and worshiped; *saḥ*—the Supreme Lord; *bhagavān*—Personality of Godhead; *atidiśya*—after offering; *ātmanaḥ*—His personal; *padam*—residence; *bālasya*—while the boy; *paśyataḥ*—was looking on;

dhāma—to His abode; *svam*—own; *agāt*—He returned; *garuḍa-dhvajaḥ*—Lord Viṣṇu, whose flag bears the emblem of Garuḍa.

TRANSLATION

The great sage Maitreya said: After being worshiped and honored by the boy, Dhruva Mahārāja, and offering him His abode, Lord Viṣṇu returned to His abode on the back of Garuḍa as Dhruva Mahārāja looked on.

PURPORT

From this verse it appears that Lord Viṣṇu awarded Dhruva Mahārāja the same abode in which He resides. His abode is described in the *Bhagavad-gītā* (15.6): *yad gatvā na nivartante tad dhāma paramaṁ mama.*

TEXT 27

सोऽपि संकल्पजं विष्णोः पादसेवोपसादितम् ।
प्राप्य संकल्पनिर्वाणं नातिप्रीतोऽभ्यगात्पुरम् ॥२७॥

so 'pi saṅkalpajaṁ viṣṇoḥ
pāda-sevopasāditam
prāpya saṅkalpa-nirvāṇaṁ
nātiprīto 'bhyagāt puram

saḥ—he (Dhruva Mahārāja); *api*—although; *saṅkalpa-jam*—the desired result; *viṣṇoḥ*—of Lord Viṣṇu; *pāda-sevā*—by serving the lotus feet; *upasāditam*—obtained; *prāpya*—having achieved; *saṅkalpa*—of his determination; *nirvāṇam*—the satisfaction; *na*—not; *atiprītaḥ*—very much pleased; *abhyagāt*—he returned; *puram*—to his home.

TRANSLATION

Despite having achieved the desired result of his determination by worshiping the lotus feet of the Lord, Dhruva Mahārāja was not very pleased. Thus he returned to his home.

PURPORT

By worshiping the lotus feet of the Lord in devotional service as instructed by Nārada Muni, Dhruva Mahārāja achieved the desired result. His desire was to get a very exalted position, excelling those of his father, grandfather and great-grandfather, and although it was a somewhat childish determination because Dhruva Mahārāja was nothing but a small child, still Lord Viṣṇu, the Supreme Personality of Godhead, is so kind and merciful that He fulfilled his desire. Dhruva Mahārāja wanted a residence more exalted than any ever occupied by anyone else in his family. Therefore he was offered the planet in which the Lord personally resides, and his determination was completely satisfied. Still, when Dhruva Mahārāja returned home he was not very much pleased because although in pure devotional service there is no demand from the Lord, because of his childish nature he had demanded something, and although the Lord also fulfilled his desire, he was not very pleased. Rather, he was ashamed that he had demanded something from the Lord, for he should not have done this.

TEXT 28

विदुर उवाच
सुदुर्लभं यत्परमं पदं हरे-
र्मायाविनस्तच्चरणार्चनार्जितम् ।
लब्ध्वाप्यसिद्धार्थमिवैकजन्मना
कथं स्वमात्मानममन्यतार्थवित् ॥२८॥

vidura uvāca
sudurlabhaṁ yat paramaṁ padaṁ harer
māyāvinas tac-caraṇārcanārjitam
labdhvāpy asiddhārtham ivaika-janmanā
kathaṁ svam ātmānam amanyatārtha-vit

viduraḥ uvāca—Vidura continued to inquire; *sudurlabham*—very rare; *yat*—that which; *paramam*—is the supreme; *padam*—situation; *hareḥ*—of the Supreme Personality of Godhead; *māyāvinaḥ*—very affectionate; *tat*—His; *caraṇa*—lotus feet; *arcana*—by worshiping; *arjitam*—achieved; *labdhvā*—having attained; *api*—although; *asiddha-artham*—not fulfilled; *iva*—as if; *eka-janmanā*—in the duration of one life; *katham*—why; *svam*—own; *ātmānam*—heart; *amanyata*—he felt; *artha-vit*—being very wise.

TRANSLATION

Śrī Vidura inquired: My dear brāhmaṇa, the abode of the Lord is very difficult to attain. It can be attained only by pure devotional service, which alone pleases the most affectionate, merciful Lord. Dhruva Mahārāja achieved this position even in one life, and he was very wise and conscientious. Why, then, was he not very pleased?

PURPORT

Saint Vidura's inquiry is very relevant. The word *artha-vit,* which refers to one who knows how to discriminate between reality and unreality, is very significant in this connection. An *artha-vit* is also called *paramahaṁsa.* A *paramahaṁsa* accepts only the active principle of everything; just as a swan accepts only the milk from a mixture of water and milk, a *paramahaṁsa* accepts only the Supreme Personality of Godhead as his life and soul, neglecting all external material things. Dhruva Mahārāja was in this category, and due to his determination he achieved the result he desired, but still when he returned home he was not very pleased.

TEXT 29

मैत्रेय उवाच
मातुः सपत्न्या वाग्बाणैर्हृदि विद्धस्तु तान् स्मरन् ।
नैच्छन्मुक्तिपतेर्मुक्तिं तस्मात्तापमुपेयिवान् ॥२९॥

maitreya uvāca
mātuḥ sapatnyā vāgbāṇair
hṛdi viddhas tu tān smaran
naicchan mukti-pater muktiṁ
tasmāt tāpam upeyivān

maitreyaḥ uvāca—the great sage Maitreya replied; *mātuḥ*—of his mother; *sa-patnyāḥ*—of the co-wife; *vāk-bāṇaiḥ*—by the arrows of harsh words; *hṛdi*—in the heart; *viddhaḥ*—pierced; *tu*—then; *tān*—all of them; *smaran*—remembering; *na*—not; *aicchat*—desired; *mukti-pateḥ*—from the Lord, whose lotus feet give liberation; *muktim*—salvation; *tasmāt*—therefore; *tāpam*—grief; *upeyivān*—he suffered.

TRANSLATION

Maitreya answered: Dhruva Mahārāja's heart, which was pierced by the arrow of the harsh words of his stepmother, was greatly aggrieved, and thus when he fixed upon his goal of life he did not forget her misbehavior. He did not demand actual liberation from this material world, but at the end of his devotional service, when the Supreme Personality of Godhead appeared before him, he was simply ashamed of the material demands he had in his mind.

PURPORT

This important verse has been discussed by many stalwart commentators. Why was Dhruva Mahārāja not very pleased, even after achieving the goal of life he desired? A pure devotee is always free from any kind of material desires. In the material world, one's material desires are all most demonic; one thinks of others as one's enemies, one thinks of revenge against one's enemies, one aspires to become the topmost leader or topmost person in this material world, and thus one competes with all others, etc. This has been described in the *Bhagavad-gītā*, Sixteenth Chapter, as asuric. A pure devotee has no demand from the Lord. His only concern is to serve the Lord sincerely and seriously, and he is not at all concerned about what will happen in the future. In the *Mukunda-mālā-stotra,* King Kulaśekhara, author of the book, states in his prayer: "My dear Lord, I don't want any position of sense gratification within this material world. I simply want to engage in Your service perpetually." Similarly, Lord Caitanya, in His *Śikṣāṣṭaka,* also prayed, "My Lord, I do not want any amount of material wealth, I do not want any number of materialistic followers, nor do I want any attractive wife to enjoy. The only thing I want is that I may engage life after life in Your service." Lord Caitanya did not pray even for *mukti,* or liberation.

In this verse Maitreya replied to Vidura that Dhruva Mahārāja, influenced by a revengeful attitude towards his insulting stepmother, did not think of *mukti,* nor did he know what *mukti* is. Therefore he failed to aim for *mukti* as his goal in life. But a pure devotee also does not want liberation. He is a soul completely surrendered to the Supreme Lord, and he does not demand anything from the Lord. This position was realized by Dhruva Mahārāja when he saw the Supreme Personality of Godhead present personally before him because he was elevated to the *vāsudeva* platform. The *vāsudeva* platform refers to the stage at which material contamination is conspicuous by absence only, or in other words where there is no question of the material modes of nature—goodness, passion and ignorance—and one can therefore see the Supreme Personality of Godhead. Because on the *vāsudeva* platform one can see God face to face, the Lord is also called Vāsudeva.

Dhruva Mahārāja's demand was for a position so exalted that it was never enjoyed even by Lord Brahmā, his great-grandfather. Kṛṣṇa, the Supreme Personality of Godhead, is so affectionate and kind towards His devotee, especially to a devotee like Dhruva Mahārāja, who went to render devotional service in the forest alone at the age of only five years, that although the motive might be impure, the Lord does not consider the motive; He is concerned with the service. But if a devotee has a particular motive, the Lord directly or indirectly knows it, and therefore He does not leave the devotee's material desires unfulfilled. These are some of the special favors by the Lord to a devotee.

Dhruva Mahārāja was offered Dhruvaloka, a planet that was never resided upon by any conditioned soul. Even Brahmā, although the topmost living creature within this universe, was also not allowed to enter the Dhruvaloka. Whenever there is a crisis within this universe, the demigods go to see the Supreme Personality of Godhead Kṣīrodakaśāyī Viṣṇu, and they stand on the beach of the Milk Ocean. So the fulfillment of Dhruva Mahārāja's demand—a position more exalted than that of even his great-grandfather Brahmā—was offered to him.

Here in this verse the Lord is described as *mukti-pati*, which means one under whose lotus feet there are all kinds of *mukti.* There are five kinds of *mukti—sāyujya, sārūpya, sālokya, sāmīpya,* and *sārṣṭi.* Out of these five *muktis,* which can be achieved by any person engaged in devotional service to the Lord, the one which is known as *sāyujya* is generally demanded by Māyāvādī philosophers; they demand to become one with the impersonal Brahman effulgence of the Lord. In the opinion of many scholars, this *sāyujya-mukti,* although counted among the five kinds of *mukti,* is not actually *mukti* because from *sāyujya-mukti* one may again fall down to this material world. This information we have from *Śrīmad-Bhāgavatam,* wherein it is said *patanty adaḥ,* which means "they again fall down." The monist philosopher, after executing severe austerity, merges into the impersonal effulgence of the Lord, but the living entity always wants reciprocation in loving affairs. Therefore, although the monist philosopher is elevated to the status of being one with the effulgence of the Lord, because there is no facility for associating with the Lord and rendering service unto Him, he again falls down into this material world, and his service propensity is satisfied by material welfare activities like humanitarianism, altruism and philanthropy. There are many instances of such falldowns, even for great *sannyāsīs* in the Māyāvāda school.

Therefore Vaiṣṇava philosophers do not accept *sāyujya-mukti* to be within the category of *mukti.* According to them, *mukti* means transferral to the loving service of the Lord from one's position of serving *māyā.* Lord Caitanya also says in this connection that the constitutional position of a living entity is to render service to the Lord. That is real *mukti.* When one is situated in his original position, giving up artificial positions, he is called *mukta*, or liberated. In the *Bhagavad-gītā* this is confirmed: anyone who engages in rendering transcendental loving service to the Lord is considered to be *mukta* or *brahma-bhūta*. It is said in *Bhagavad-gītā* that a devotee is considered to be on the *brahma-bhūta* platform when he has no material contamination. In the *Padma Purāṇa* this is also confirmed: *mukti* means engagement in the service of the Lord.

The great sage Maitreya explained that Dhruva Mahārāja did not desire in the beginning to engage in the service of the Lord, but he wanted an exalted position better than his great-grandfather's. This is more or less not service to the Lord but service to the senses. Even if one gets the position of Brahmā, the most exalted position in this material world, he is a conditioned soul. Śrīla Prabodhānanda Sarasvatī says that if one is elevated to real, pure devotional service, he considers even great demigods like Brahmā and Indra to be on an equal level with an insignificant insect. The reason is that an insignificant insect has a desire for sense gratification, and even a great personality like Lord Brahmā also wants to dominate this material nature.

Sense gratification means domination over material nature. The whole competition between conditioned souls is based upon domination of this material nature. Modern scientists are proud of their knowledge because they are discovering new methods to dominate the laws of material nature. They think that this is the advancement of human civilization—the more they can dominate the material laws, the more advanced they think they are. Dhruva Mahārāja's propensity in the beginning was like that. He wanted to dominate this material world in a greater position than Lord Brahmā. Therefore elsewhere it is described that after the appearance of the Lord, when Dhruva Mahārāja thought and compared his determination to his final reward, he realized that he had wanted a few particles of broken glass but instead had received many diamonds. As soon as he saw the Supreme Personality of Godhead face to face, he immediately became conscious of the unimportance of his demand from the Lord to have an exalted position better than Lord Brahmā's.

When Dhruva Mahārāja became situated on the *vāsudeva* platform due to seeing the Lord face to face, all his material contamination was cleared. Thus he became ashamed of what his demands were and what he had achieved. He was very much ashamed to think that although he had gone to Madhuvana, giving up the kingdom of his father, and he had gotten a spiritual master like Nārada Muni, still he was thinking of revenge against his stepmother and wanted to occupy an exalted post within this material world. These were the causes for his moroseness even after he received all the desired benedictions from the Lord.

When Dhruva Mahārāja factually saw the Supreme Personality of Godhead, there was no question of a revengeful attitude towards his stepmother nor any aspiration to lord it over the material world, but the Supreme Personality is so kind that He knew that Dhruva Mahārāja wanted these. Speaking before Dhruva Mahārāja, He used the word *vedāham* because when Dhruva Mahārāja demanded material benefits, the Lord was present within his heart and so knew everything. The Lord always knows everything that a man is thinking. This is confirmed in *Bhagavad-gītā* also: *vedāhaṁ samatītāni.*

The Lord fulfilled all Dhruva Mahārāja's desires. His revengeful attitude towards his stepmother and stepbrother was satisfied. He wanted a more exalted position than his great-grandfather. That was also fulfilled. And at the same time, his eternal position in Dhruvaloka was fixed. Although Dhruva Mahārāja's achievement of an eternal planet was not conceived by him, Kṛṣṇa thought, "What will Dhruva do with an exalted position within this material world?" Therefore He gave him the opportunity to rule this material world for 36,000 years with unchangeable senses and the chance to perform many great sacrifices and thus become the most reputed king within this material world. And, after finishing with all this material enjoyment, he would be promoted to the spiritual world, which includes the Dhruvaloka.

TEXT 30

ध्रुव उवाच
समाधिना नैकभवेन यत्पदं
विदुः सनन्दादय ऊर्ध्वरेतसः ।
मासैरहं षड्भिरमुष्य पादयो-
श्छायामुपेत्यापगतः पृथङ्मतिः ॥३०॥

dhruva uvāca
samādhinā naika-bhavena yat padaṁ
viduḥ sanandādaya ūrdhva-retasaḥ
māsair ahaṁ ṣaḍbhir amuṣya pādayoś
chāyām upetyāpagataḥ pṛthaṅ-matiḥ

dhruvaḥ uvāca—Dhruva Mahārāja said; *samādhinā*—by practicing *yoga* in trance; *na*—never; *eka-bhavena*—by one birth; *yat*—which; *padam*—position; *viduḥ*—understood; *sananda-ādayaḥ*—the four *brahmacārīs* headed by Sanandana; *ūrdhva-retasaḥ*—infallible celibates; *māsaiḥ*—within months; *aham*—I; *ṣaḍbhiḥ*—six; *amuṣya*—of Him; *pādayoḥ*—of the lotus feet; *chāyām*—shelter; *upetya*—achieving; *apagataḥ*—fell down; *pṛthak-matiḥ*—my mind fixed on things other than the Lord.

TRANSLATION

Dhruva Mahārāja thought to himself: To endeavor to be situated in the shade of the lotus feet of the Lord is not an ordinary task because even the great brahmacārīs headed by Sanandana, who practiced the aṣṭāṅga-yoga in trance, attained the shelter of the lotus feet of the Lord only after many, many births. Although within six months I achieved the same result, nevertheless, due to my thinking differently from the Lord, I fell down from my position.

PURPORT

In this verse Dhruva Mahārāja himself explains the cause of his moroseness. First he laments that to see the Supreme Personality of Godhead directly is not easy. Even great saintly persons like the four celebrated *brahmacārīs* headed by Sanandana—Sanaka, Sanātana, Sanatkumāra and Sanandana—practiced the *yoga* system for many, many births and remained in trance before getting the opportunity to see the Supreme Lord face to face. As far as Dhruva Mahārāja was concerned, he saw the Supreme Lord personally after only six months of practice in devotional service. He expected, therefore, that as soon as he met the Supreme Lord, the Lord would take him to His abode immediately, without waiting. Dhruva Mahārāja could understand very clearly that the Lord had offered him the rule of the world for 36,000 years because in the beginning he was under the spell of material energy and wanted to take revenge against his stepmother and rule over his father's kingdom. Dhruva Mahārāja greatly lamented his propensity for ruling the material world and his revengeful attitude toward other living entities.

TEXT 31

अहो बत ममानात्म्यं मन्दभाग्यस्य पश्यत ।
भवच्छिदः पादमूलं गत्वायाचे यदन्तवत् ॥३१॥

aho bata mamānātmyaṁ
manda-bhāgyasya paśyata
bhava-cchidaḥ pāda-mūlaṁ
gatvā yāce yad antavat

aho—oh; *bata*—alas; *mama*—my; *anātmyam*—bodily consciousness; *manda-bhāgyasya*—of the unfortunate; *paśyata*—just see; *bhava*—material existence; *chidaḥ*—of the Lord who can cut off; *pāda-mūlam*—the lotus feet; *gatvā*—having approached; *yāce*—I prayed for; *yat*—that which; *antavat*—perishable.

TRANSLATION

Alas, just look at me! I am so unfortunate. I approached the lotus feet of the Supreme Personality of Godhead, who can immediately cut the chain of the repetition of birth and death, but still, out of my foolishness, I prayed for things which are perishable.

PURPORT

The word *anātmyam* is very significant in this verse. *Ātmā* means the soul, and *anātmya* means without any conception of the soul. Śrīla Ṛṣabhadeva instructed his sons that unless a human being comes to the point of understanding the *ātmā*, or spiritual position, whatever he does is ignorance, and this brings only defeat in his life. Dhruva Mahārāja regrets his unfortunate position, for although he approached the Supreme Personality of Godhead, who is always able to give His devotee the highest benediction of cessation of the repetition of birth and death, which is impossible for any demigod to offer, he foolishly wanted something perishable. When Hiraṇyakaśipu asked immortality from Lord Brahmā, Lord Brahmā expressed his inability to offer such a benediction because he himself is not immortal; therefore immortality or complete cessation of the chain of repeated birth and death can be offered by the Supreme Lord, the Personality of Godhead Himself, not by others. *Hariṁ vinā na sṛtiṁ taranti.* It is said that without the blessings of Hari, the Supreme Personality of Godhead, no one can stop the continuous chain of birth and death within this material world. Therefore the Supreme Lord is also called *bhava-cchida.* The Vaiṣṇava philosophy in the process of Kṛṣṇa consciousness prohibits the devotee from all kinds of material aspirations. A Vaiṣṇava devotee should always be *anyābhilāṣitā-śūnya,* free from all material aspirations for the results of fruitive activities or empiric philosophical speculation. Dhruva Mahārāja was actually initiated by Nārada Muni, the greatest Vaiṣṇava, in the chanting of *oṁ namo bhagavate vāsudevāya*. This *mantra* is a *viṣṇu-mantra,* for by practicing the chanting of this *mantra* one is elevated to the Viṣṇuloka. Dhruva Mahārāja regrets that although he was initiated in the *viṣṇu-mantra* by a Vaiṣṇava, he still aspired for material benefits. That was another cause for lamentation. Although he got the result of the *viṣṇu-mantra* by the causeless mercy of the Lord, he lamented how foolish he was to strive for material benefits while practicing devotional service. In other words, every one of us who is engaged in devotional service in Kṛṣṇa consciousness should be completely free from all material aspirations. Otherwise we will have to lament like Dhruva Mahārāja.

TEXT 32

मतिर्विदूषिता देवैः पतद्भिरसहिष्णुभिः ।
यो नारदवचस्तथ्यं नाग्राहिषमसत्तमः ॥३२॥

matir vidūṣitā devaiḥ
patadbhir asahiṣṇubhiḥ
yo nārada-vacas tathyaṁ
nāgrāhiṣam asattamaḥ

matiḥ—intelligence; *vidūṣitā*—contaminated; *devaiḥ*—by the demigods; *patadbhiḥ*—who will fall down; *asahiṣṇubhiḥ*—intolerant; *yaḥ*—I who; *nārada*—of the great sage Nārada; *vacaḥ*—of the instructions; *tathyam*—the truth; *na*—not; *agrāhiṣam*—could accept; *asat-tamaḥ*—the most wretched.

TRANSLATION

Since all the demigods who are situated in the higher planetary system will have to come down again, they are all envious of my being elevated to Vaikuṇṭhaloka by devotional service. These intolerant demigods have dissipated my intelligence, and only for this reason could I not accept the genuine benediction of the instructions of Sage Nārada.

PURPORT

As shown by many instances in the Vedic literature, when a person undergoes severe austerities, the demigods become very much perturbed because they are always afraid of losing their posts as the predominating deities of the heavenly planets. It is known to them that their position in the higher planetary system is not permanent, as it is stated in the *Bhagavad-gītā*, Ninth Chapter. It is said in the *Gītā* that after exhausting the results of their pious activities, all the demigods who are inhabitants of the higher planetary system have to come back again to this earth.

It is a fact that the demigods control the different activities of the limbs of our bodies. Factually we are not free even in moving our eyelids. Everything is controlled by them. Dhruva Mahārāja's conclusion is that these demigods, being envious of his superior position in devotional service, conspired against him to pollute his intelligence, and thus although he was the disciple of a great Vaiṣṇava, Nārada Muni, he could not accept his valid instructions. Now Dhruva Mahārāja regretted very much that he had neglected these instructions. Nārada Muni had asked him, "Why should you bother about insult or adoration from your stepmother?" He of course informed Dhruva Mahārāja that since he was only a child, what did he have to do with such insult or adoration? But Dhruva Mahārāja was determined to achieve the benediction of the Supreme Personality of Godhead, and therefore Nārada advised him to go back home for the time being, and in mature time he could try to practice devotional service. Dhruva Mahārāja regretted that he had rejected the advice of Nārada Muni and was adamant in asking him for something perishable, namely revenge against his stepmother for her insult and possession of the kingdom of his father.

Dhruva Mahārāja regretted very much that he could not take seriously the instruction of his spiritual master and that his consciousness was therefore contaminated. Still, the Lord is so merciful that due to Dhruva's execution of devotional service He offered him the ultimate Vaiṣṇava goal.

TEXT 33

दैवीं मायामुपाश्रित्य प्रसुप्त इव भिन्नदृक् ।
तप्ये द्वितीयेऽप्यसति भ्रातृभ्रातृव्यहृद्रुजा ॥३३॥

daivīṁ māyām upāśritya
prasupta iva bhinna-dṛk
tapye dvitīye 'py asati
bhrātṛ-bhrātṛvya-hṛd-rujā

daivīm—of the Personality of Godhead; *māyām*—the illusory energy; *upāśritya*—taking shelter of; *prasuptaḥ*—dreaming while asleep; *iva*—like; *bhinna-dṛk*—having separated vision; *tapye*—I lamented; *dvitīye*—in the illusory energy; *api*—although; *asati*—temporary; *bhrātṛ*—brother; *bhrātṛvya*—enemy; *hṛt*—within the heart; *rujā*—by lamentation.

TRANSLATION

Dhruva Mahārāja lamented: I was under the influence of the illusory energy; being ignorant of the actual facts, I was sleeping on her lap. Under a vision of duality, I saw my brother as my enemy, and falsely I lamented within my heart, thinking, "They are my enemies."

PURPORT

Real knowledge is revealed to a devotee only when he comes to the right conclusion about life by the grace of the Lord. Our creation of friends and enemies within this material world is something like dreaming at night. In dreams we create so many things out of various impressions in the subconscious mind, but all such creations are simply temporary and unreal. In the same way, although apparently we are awake in material life, because we have no information of the soul and the Supersoul, we create many friends and enemies simply out of imagination. Śrīla Kṛṣṇadāsa Kavirāja Gosvāmī says that within this material world or material consciousness, good and bad are the same. The distinction between good and bad is simply a mental concoction. The actual fact is that all living entities are sons of God, or by-products of His marginal energy. Because of our being contaminated by the modes of material nature, we distinguish one spiritual spark from another. That is also another kind of dreaming. It is stated in the *Bhagavad-gītā* that those who are actually learned do not make any distinction between a learned scholar, a *brāhmaṇa*, an elephant, a dog and a *caṇḍāla;* they do not see in terms of the external body, but they see the person as spirit soul. By higher understanding one can know that the material body is nothing but a combination of the five material elements. In that sense also the bodily construction of a human being and that of a demigod are one and the same. From the spiritual point of view we are all spiritual sparks, parts and parcels of the Supreme Spirit, God. Either materially or spiritually we are basically one, but we make friends and enemies as dictated by the illusory energy. Dhruva Mahārāja therefore said, *daivīṁ māyām upāśritya:* the cause of his bewilderment was his association with the illusory material energy.

TEXT 34

मयैतत्प्रार्थितं व्यर्थं चिकित्सेव गतायुषि ।
प्रसाद्य जगदात्मानं तपसा दुष्प्रसादनम् ।
भवच्छिदमयाचेऽहं भवं भाग्यविवर्जितः ॥३४॥

mayaitat prārthitaṁ vyarthaṁ
cikitseva gatāyuṣi
prasādya jagad-ātmānaṁ
tapasā duṣprasādanam
bhava-cchidam ayāce 'haṁ
bhavaṁ bhāgya-vivarjitaḥ

mayā—by me; *etat*—this; *prārthitam*—prayed for; *vyartham*—uselessly; *cikitsā*—treatment; *iva*—like; *gata*—has ended; *āyuṣi*—for one whose life;

prasādya—after satisfying; *jagat-ātmānam*—the soul of the universe; *tapasā*—by austerity; *duṣprasādanam*—who is very difficult to satisfy; *bhava-chidam*—the Personality of Godhead, who can cut the chain of birth and death; *ayāce*—prayed for; *aham*—I; *bhavam*—again repetition of birth and death; *bhāgya*—fortune; *vivarjitaḥ*—being without.

TRANSLATION

It is very difficult to satisfy the Supreme Personality of Godhead, but in my case, although I have satisfied the Supersoul of the whole universe, I have prayed only for useless things. My activities were exactly like treatment given to a person who is already dead. Just see how unfortunate I am, for in spite of meeting the Supreme Lord, who can cut one's link with birth and death, I have prayed for the same conditions again.

PURPORT

Sometimes it so happens that a devotee engaged in the loving service of the Lord desires some material benefit in exchange for this service. This is not the proper way to discharge devotional service. Out of ignorance, of course, sometimes a devotee does so, but Dhruva Mahārāja regrets his personal behavior in this connection.

TEXT 35

स्वाराज्यं यच्छतो मौढ्यान्मानो मे भिक्षितो बत ।
ईश्वरात्क्षीणपुण्येन फलीकारानिवाधनः ॥३५॥

svārājyaṁ yacchato mauḍhyān
māno me bhikṣito bata
īśvarāt kṣīṇa-puṇyena
phalī-kārān ivādhanaḥ

svārājyam—His devotional service; *yacchataḥ*—from the Lord, who was willing to offer; *mauḍhyāt*—by foolishness; *mānaḥ*—material prosperity; *me*—by me; *bhikṣitaḥ*—was asked for; *bata*—alas; *īśvarāt*—from a great emperor; *kṣīṇa*—reduced; *puṇyena*—whose pious activities; *phalī-kārān*—broken particles of husked rice; *iva*—like; *adhanaḥ*—a poor man.

TRANSLATION

Because of my state of complete foolishness and paucity of pious activities, although the Lord offered me His personal service, still I wanted material name, fame and prosperity. My case is just like that of the poor man

who, when he satisfied a great emperor who wanted to give him anything he might ask, out of ignorance asked only a few broken grains of husked rice.

PURPORT

In this verse the word *svārājyam*, which means complete independence, is very significant. A conditioned soul does not know what complete independence is. Complete independence means situation in one's own constitutional position. The real independence of a living entity, who is part and parcel of the Supreme Personality of Godhead, is to remain always dependent on the Supreme Lord, just like a child who plays in complete independence, guided by his parents, who watch over him. The independence of the conditioned soul does not mean to fight with the obstacles offered by *māyā*, but to surrender to Kṛṣṇa. In the material world, everyone is trying to become completely independent simply by fighting against the obstacles offered by *māyā.* This is called the struggle for existence. Real independence is to be reinstated in the service of the Lord. Anyone who goes to the Vaikuṇṭha planets or Goloka Vṛndāvana planet is freely offering his service to the Lord. That is complete independence. Just contrary to this is material overlordship, which we wrongly take to be independence. Many great political leaders have tried to establish independence, but due to such so-called independence the people's dependence has only increased. The living entity cannot be happy trying to be independent in the material world. One has to surrender, therefore, unto the lotus feet of the Lord and engage in His original eternal service.

Dhruva Mahārāja regrets that he wanted material opulence and greater prosperity than that of his great-grandfather, Lord Brahmā. His begging from the Lord was like a poor man's asking a great emperor for a few grains of broken rice. The conclusion is that anyone who is engaged in the loving service of the Lord should never ask for material prosperity from the Lord. The awarding of material prosperity simply depends on the stringent rules and regulations of the external energy. Pure devotees ask the Lord only for the privilege of serving Him. This is our real independence. If we want anything else, it is a sign of our misfortune.

TEXT 36

मैत्रेय उवाच

न वै मुकुन्दस्य पदारविन्दयो

रजोजुषस्तात भवादृशा जनाः ।

वाञ्छन्ति तद्दास्यमृतेऽर्थमात्मनो
यदृच्छया लब्धमनःसमृद्धयः ॥३६॥

maitreya uvāca
na vai mukundasya padāravindayo
rajo-juṣas tāta bhavādṛśā janāḥ
vāñchanti tad-dāsyam ṛte 'rtham ātmano
yadṛcchayā labdha-manaḥ-samṛddhayaḥ

maitreyaḥ uvāca—the great sage Maitreya continued; *na*—never; *vai*—certainly; *mukundasya*—of the Lord, who can give liberation; *pada-aravindayoḥ*—of the lotus feet; *rajaḥ-juṣaḥ*—persons who are eager to taste the dust; *tāta*—my dear Vidura; *bhavādṛśāḥ*—like yourself; *janāḥ*—persons; *vāñchanti*—desire; *tat*—His; *dāsyam*—servitorship; *ṛte*—without; *artham*—interest; *ātmanaḥ*—for themselves; *yadṛcchayā*—automatically; *labdha*—by what is achieved; *manaḥ-samṛddhayaḥ*—considering themselves to be very rich.

TRANSLATION

The great sage Maitreya continued: My dear Vidura, persons who, like you, are pure devotees of the lotus feet of Mukunda [the Supreme Personality of Godhead, who can offer liberation] and who are always attached to the honey of His lotus feet, are always satisfied in serving at the lotus feet of the Lord. In any condition of life, such persons remain satisfied, and thus they never ask the Lord for material prosperity.

PURPORT

In the *Bhagavad-gītā* the Lord says that He is the supreme enjoyer, the supreme proprietor of everything and anything within this creation, and the supreme friend of everyone. When one knows these things perfectly, he is always satisfied. The pure devotee never hankers after any kind of material prosperity. The *karmīs*, however, or *jñānīs* or *yogīs*, endeavor always for their own personal happiness. *Karmīs* work day and night to improve their economic condition, *jñānīs* undergo severe austerities in order to get liberation, and *yogīs* also undergo severe austerities by practicing the *yoga* system for attainment of wonderful mystic powers. A devotee, however, is not interested in such activities; he does not want mystic powers or liberation or material prosperity. He is satisfied in any condition of life, as long as he is constantly engaged in the service of the Lord. The Lord's feet are compared with the lotus, wherein there is saffron dust. A devotee is always engaged in drinking the honey from the lotus feet of the Lord. Unless one is freed from all material desires, he cannot actually taste the honey from the Lord's lotus feet. One has to discharge his devotional duties without being disturbed by the coming and going of material circumstances. This desirelessness for material prosperity is called *niṣkāma.* One should not mistakenly think that *niṣkāma* means giving up all desires. That is impossible. A living entity is eternally existent, and he cannot give up desires. A living entity must have desires; that is the symptom of life. When there is a recommendation to become desireless, it is to be understood that this means that we should not desire anything for our sense gratification. For a devotee this state of mind, *niḥspṛha,* is the right position. Actually every one of us already has an arrangement for our standard of material comforts. A devotee should always remain satisfied with the standard of comforts offered by the Lord, as stated in the *Īśopaniṣad* (*tena tyaktena bhuñjīthā*). This saves time for executing Kṛṣṇa consciousness.

TEXT 37

आकर्ण्यात्मजमायान्तं सम्परेत्य यथाऽऽगतम् ।
राजा न श्रद्दधे भद्रमभद्रस्य कुतो मम ॥३७॥

ākarṇyātma-jam āyāntaṁ
samparetya yathāgatam
rājā na śraddadhe bhadram
abhadrasya kuto mama

ākarṇya—having heard; *ātma-jam*—his son; *āyāntam*—coming back; *samparetya*—after dying; *yathā*—as if; *āgatam*—coming back; *rājā*—King Uttānapāda; *na*—did not; *śraddadhe*—have any confidence; *bhadram*—good fortune; *abhadrasya*—of the impious; *kutaḥ*—whence; *mama*—my.

TRANSLATION

When King Uttānapāda heard that his son Dhruva was coming back home, as if coming back to life after death, he could not put his faith in this message, for he was doubtful how it could happen. He considered himself the most wretched, and therefore he thought that it was not possible for him to attain such good fortune.

PURPORT

Dhruva Mahārāja, a five-year-old boy, went to the forest for penance and austerity, and the King could not at all believe that a small boy of such a tender age could live in the forest. He was certain that he was dead.

He therefore could not fix his faith in the message that Dhruva Mahārāja was coming back home again. For him this message said that a dead man was coming back home, and so he could not believe it. After Dhruva Mahārāja's departure from home, King Uttānapāda thought that he was the cause of his leaving, and thus he considered himself the most wretched. Therefore, even though it was possible that his lost son was coming back from the kingdom of death, he thought that since he was most sinful it was not possible for him to be so fortunate as to get back his lost son.

TEXT 38

श्रद्धाय वाक्यं देवर्षेर्हर्षवेगेन धर्षितः ।
वार्ताहर्तुरतिप्रीतो हारं प्रादान्महाधनम् ॥३८॥

śraddhāya vākyaṁ devarṣer
harṣa-vegena dharṣitaḥ
vārtā-hartur atiprīto
hāraṁ prādān mahā-dhanam

śraddhāya—keeping faith; *vākyam*—in the words; *devarṣeḥ*—of the great sage Nārada; *harṣa-vegena*—by great satisfaction; *dharṣitaḥ*—overwhelmed; *vārtā-hartuḥ*—with the messenger who brought the news; *atiprītaḥ*—being very satisfied; *hāram*—a pearl necklace; *prādāt*—offered; *mahā-dhanam*—very valuable.

TRANSLATION

Although he could not believe the words of the messenger, he had full faith in the word of the great sage, Nārada. Thus he was greatly overwhelmed by the news, and immediately he offered the messenger a highly valuable garland in great satisfaction.

TEXTS 39-40

सदश्वं रथमारुह्य कार्तस्वरपरिष्कृतम् ।
ब्राह्मणैः कुलवृद्धैश्च पर्यस्तोऽमात्यबन्धुभिः ॥३९॥
शङ्खदुन्दुभिनादेन ब्रह्मघोषेण वेणुभिः ।
निश्चक्राम पुरात्तूर्णमात्मजाभीक्षणोत्सुकः ॥४०॥

sad-aśvaṁ ratham āruhya
kārtasvara-pariṣkṛtam
brāhmaṇaiḥ kula-vṛddhaiś ca
paryasto 'mātya-bandhubhiḥ

śaṅkha-dundubhi-nādena
brahma-ghoṣeṇa veṇubhiḥ
niścakrāma purāt tūrṇam
ātma-jābhīkṣaṇotsukaḥ

sat-aśvam—drawn by very fine horses; *ratham*—chariot; *āruhya*—getting on; *kārtasvara-pariṣkṛtam*—bedecked with golden filigree; *brāhmaṇaiḥ*—with *brāhmaṇas; kula-vṛddhaiḥ*—along with elderly personalities of the family; *ca*—also; *paryastaḥ*—being surrounded; *amātya*—by officers and ministers; *bandhubhiḥ*—and friends; *śaṅkha*—of conchshells; *dundubhi*—and kettledrums; *nādena*—with the sound; *brahma-ghoṣeṇa*—by the chanting of Vedic *mantras; veṇubhiḥ*—by flutes; *niścakrāma*—he came out; *purāt*—from the city; *tūrṇam*—with great haste; *ātma-ja*—son; *abhīkṣaṇa*—to see; *utsukaḥ*—very eager.

TRANSLATION

Then King Uttānapāda, being very eager to see the face of his lost son, mounted a chariot drawn by excellent horses and bedecked with golden filigree. Taking with him many learned brāhmaṇas, all the elderly personalities of his family, his officers, his ministers, and his immediate friends, he immediately left the city. As he proceeded in this parade, there were auspicious sounds of conchshells, kettledrums, flutes, and the chanting of Vedic mantras to indicate all good fortune.

TEXT 41

सुनीतिः सुरुचिश्चास्य महिष्यौ रुक्मभूषिते ।
आरुह्य शिबिकां सार्धमुत्तमेनाभिजग्मतुः ॥४१॥

sunītiḥ suruciś cāsya
mahiṣyau rukma-bhūṣite
āruhya śibikāṁ sārdham
uttamenābhijagmatuḥ

sunītiḥ—Queen Sunīti; *suruciḥ*—Queen Suruci; *ca*—also; *asya*—of the King; *mahiṣyau*—queens; *rukma-bhūṣite*—being decorated with golden ornaments; *āruhya*—getting on; *śibikām*—a palanquin; *sārdham*—along with; *uttamena*—the King's other son, Uttama; *abhijagmatuḥ*-all proceeded along.

TRANSLATION

Both the queens of King Uttānapāda, namely Sunīti and Suruci, along with his other son, Uttama, appeared in the procession. The queens were seated on a palanquin.

PURPORT

After the departure of Dhruva Mahārāja from the palace, the King was very afflicted, but by the kind words of Saint Nārada he was partially satisfied. He could understand the great fortune of his wife Sunīti and the great misfortune of Queen Suruci, for these facts were certainly very open in the palace. But still when the news reached the palace that Dhruva Mahārāja was returning, his mother, Sunīti, out of her great compassion and due to being the mother of a great Vaiṣṇava, did not hesitate to take the other wife, Suruci, and her son Uttama, on the same palanquin. That is the greatness of Queen Sunīti, the mother of the great Vaiṣṇava Dhruva Mahārāja.

TEXTS 42-43

तं दृष्ट्वोपवनाभ्याश आयान्तं तरसा रथात् ।
अवरुह्य नृपस्तूर्णमासाद्य प्रेमविह्वलः ॥४२॥
परिरेभेऽङ्गजं दोर्भ्यां दीर्घोत्कण्ठमनाः श्वसन् ।
विष्वक्सेनाङ्घ्रिसंस्पर्शहताशेषाघबन्धनम् ॥४३॥

taṁ dṛṣṭvopavanābhyāśa
āyāntaṁ tarasā rathāt
avaruhya nṛpas tūrṇam
āsādya prema-vihvalaḥ

parirebhe 'ṅgajaṁ dorbhyāṁ
dīrghotkaṇṭha-manāḥ śvasan
viṣvaksenāṅghri-saṁsparśa-
hatāśeṣāgha-bandhanam

tam—him (Dhruva Mahārāja); *dṛṣṭvā*—having seen; *upavana*—the small forest; *abhyāśe*—near; *āyāntam*—returning; *tarasā*—with great haste; *rathāt*—from the chariot; *avaruhya*—got down; *nṛpaḥ*—the King; *tūrṇam*—immediately; *āsādya*—coming near; *prema*—with love; *vihvalaḥ*—overwhelmed; *parirebhe*—he embraced; *aṅga-jam*—his son; *dorbhyām*—with his arms; *dīrgha*—for a long time; *utkaṇṭha*—anxious; *manāḥ*—the King, whose mind; *śvasan*—breathing heavily; *viṣvaksena*—of the Lord; *aṅghri*—by the lotus feet; *saṁsparśa*—being touched; *hata*—were destroyed; *aśeṣa*—unlimited; *agha*—material contamination; *bandhanam*—whose bondage.

TRANSLATION

Upon seeing Dhruva Mahārāja approaching the neighboring small forest, King Uttānapāda with great haste got down from his chariot. He had been

very anxious for a long time to see his son Dhruva, and therefore with great love and affection he went forward to embrace his long lost boy. Breathing very heavily, he embraced him with both arms. But Dhruva Mahārāja was not the same as before; he was completely sanctified by spiritual advancement due to being touched by the lotus feet of the Supreme Personality of Godhead.

TEXT 44

अथाजिघ्रन्मुहुर्मूर्ध्नि शीतैर्नयनवारिभिः ।
स्नापयामास तनयं जातोद्दाममनोरथः ॥४४॥

athājighran muhur mūrdhni
śītair nayana-vāribhiḥ
snāpayām āsa tanayaṁ
jātoddāma-mano-rathaḥ

atha—thereupon; *ājighran*—smelling; *muhuḥ*—again and again; *mūrdhni*—on the head; *śītaiḥ*—cold; *nayana*—of his eyes; *vāribhiḥ*—with the water; *snāpayām āsa*—he bathed; *tanayam*—son; *jāta*—fulfilled; *uddāma*—great; *manaḥ-rathaḥ*—his desire.

TRANSLATION

Reunion with Dhruva Mahārāja fulfilled King Uttānapāda's long cherished desire, and for this reason he smelled Dhruva's head again and again and bathed him with torrents of very cold tears.

PURPORT

By nature's way, when a man cries, there may be two causes. When one cries in great happiness upon the fulfillment of some desire, the tears coming forth from the eyes are very cold and pleasing, whereas tears in times of distress are very hot.

TEXT 45

अभिवन्द्य पितुः पादावाशीर्भिश्चाभिमन्त्रितः ।
ननाम मातरौ शीर्ष्णा सत्कृतः सज्जनाग्रणीः ॥४५॥

abhivandya pituḥ pādāv
āśīrbhiś cābhimantritaḥ
nanāma mātarau śīrṣṇā
sat-kṛtaḥ saj-janāgraṇīḥ

abhivandya—worshiping; *pituḥ*—of his father; *pādau*—the feet; *āśīrbhiḥ*—with benedictions; *ca*—and; *abhimantritaḥ*—was addressed; *nanāma*—he bowed; *mātarau*—to his two mothers; *śīrṣṇā*—with his head; *sat-kṛtaḥ*—was honored; *sat-jana*—of the nobles; *agraṇīḥ*—the foremost.

TRANSLATION

Then Dhruva Mahārāja, the foremost of all nobles, first of all offered his obeisances at the feet of his father and was honored by his father with various questions. He then bowed his head at the feet of his two mothers.

PURPORT

It may be questioned why Dhruva Mahārāja offered his respect not only to his mother but also to his stepmother, due to whose insults he had to leave home. The answer is that after achieving perfection by self-realization and seeing the Supreme Personality of Godhead face to face, Dhruva Mahārāja was completely freed from all contamination of material desire. Feelings of insult or honor in this material world are never perceived by a devotee. Lord Caitanya therefore says that one has to be humbler than the grass, and, He recommends, more tolerant than the tree, to execute devotional service. Dhruva Mahārāja, therefore, has in this verse been described as *saj-janāgraṇīḥ,* the foremost of noble men. The pure devotee is the noblest of all, and he has no feelings of animosity towards anyone. Duality due to animosity is a creation of this material world. There is no such thing in the spiritual world, which is the absolute reality.

TEXT 46

सुरुचिस्तं समुत्थाप्य पादावनतमर्भकम् ।
परिष्वज्याह जीवेति बाष्पगद्गदया गिरा ॥४६॥

surucis taṁ samutthāpya
pādāvanatam arbhakam
pariṣvajyāha jīveti
bāṣpa-gadgadayā girā

suruciḥ—Queen Suruci; *tam*—him; *samutthāpya*—having picked up; *pāda-avanatam*—fallen at her feet; *arbhakam*—the innocent boy; *pariṣvajya*—embracing; *āha*—she said; *jīva*—may you live long; *iti*—thus; *bāṣpa*—with tears; *gadgadayā*—choked up; *girā*—with words.

TRANSLATION

Suruci, the younger mother of Dhruva Mahārāja, seeing that the innocent boy had fallen at her feet, immediately picked him up, embracing

him with her hands, and with tears of feeling she blessed him with the words, "My dear boy, long may you live!"

TEXT 47

यस्य प्रसन्नो भगवान् गुणैर्मैत्र्यादिभिर्हरिः ।
तस्मै नमन्ति भूतानि निम्नमाप इव स्वयम् ॥४७॥

yasya prasanno bhagavān
guṇair maitryādibhir hariḥ
tasmai namanti bhūtāni
nimnam āpa iva svayam

yasya—anyone with whom; *prasannaḥ*—is pleased; *bhagavān*—the Personality of Godhead; *guṇaiḥ*—by qualities; *maitrī-ādibhiḥ*—by friendship, etc.; *hariḥ*—Lord Hari; *tasmai*—unto him; *namanti*—offer respect; *bhūtāni*—all living entities; *nimnam*—to low ground; *āpaḥ*—water; *iva*—just as; *svayam*—automatically.

TRANSLATION

Anyone who has transcendental qualities due to friendly behavior with the Supreme Personality of Godhead receives honor from all living entities, just as water automatically flows down by nature.

PURPORT

The question may be raised in this connection why Suruci, who was not at all favorably disposed towards Dhruva, blessed him, "Long may you live," which means that she also desired good fortune for him. The answer is given in this verse. Since Dhruva Mahārāja was blessed by the Lord, due to his transcendental qualities everyone was bound to offer him all respects and benediction, just as water, by its nature, flows downward. A devotee of the Lord does not demand respect from anyone, but wherever he goes he is honored by everyone throughout the whole world with all respect. Śrīnivāsa Ācārya said that the six Gosvāmīs of Vṛndāvana are respected throughout the entire universe because a devotee, having pleased the Supreme Personality of Godhead, the source of all emanations, automatically pleases everyone, and thus everyone offers him respect.

TEXT 48

उत्तमश्च ध्रुवश्चोभावन्योन्यं प्रेमविह्वलौ ।
अङ्गसङ्गादुत्पुलकावस्रौघं मुहुरूहतुः ॥४८॥

uttamaś ca dhruvaś cobhāv
anyonyaṁ prema-vihvalau
aṅga-saṅgād utpulakāv
asraughaṁ muhur ūhatuḥ

uttamaḥ ca—also Uttama; *dhruvaḥ ca*—Dhruva also; *ubhau*—both; *anyonyam*—one another; *prema-vihvalau*—being overwhelmed with affection; *aṅga-saṅgāt*—by embracing; *utpulakau*—their hair stood up; *asru*—of tears; *ogham*—torrents; *muhuḥ*—again and again; *ūhatuḥ*—they exchanged.

TRANSLATION

The two brothers Uttama and Dhruva Mahārāja also exchanged their tears. They were overwhelmed by the ecstasy of love and affection, and when they embraced one another, the hair on both their bodies stood up.

TEXT 49

सुनीतिरस्य जननी प्राणेभ्योऽपि प्रियं सुतम् ।
उपगुह्य जहावाधिं तदङ्गस्पर्शनिर्वृता ॥४९॥

sunītir asya jananī
prāṇebhyo 'pi priyaṁ sutam
upaguhya jahāv ādhiṁ
tad-aṅga-sparśa-nirvṛtā

sunītiḥ—Sunīti, the real mother of Dhruva Mahārāja; *asya*—his; *jananī*—mother; *prāṇebhyaḥ*—more than life air; *api*—even; *priyam*—dear; *sutam*—son; *upaguhya*—embracing; *jahau*—gave up; *ādhim*—all grief; *tat-aṅga*—his body; *sparśa*—touching; *nirvṛtā*—being satisfied.

TRANSLATION

Sunīti, the real mother of Dhruva Mahārāja, embraced the tender body of her son, who was dearer to her than her own life, and thus forgot all material grief, for she was very pleased.

TEXT 50

पयः स्तनाभ्यां सुस्राव नेत्रजैः सलिलैः शिवैः ।
तदाभिषिच्यमानाभ्यां वीर वीरसुवो मुहुः ॥५०॥

payaḥ stanābhyāṁ susrāva
netra-jaiḥ salilaiḥ śivaiḥ
tadābhiṣicyamānābhyāṁ
vīra vīra-suvo muhuḥ

payaḥ—milk; *stanābhyām*—from both breasts; *susrāva*—began to flow down; *netra-jaiḥ*—from the eyes; *salilaiḥ*—by tears; *śivaiḥ*—auspicious; *tadā*—at that time; *abhiṣicyamānābhyām*—being wetted; *vīra*—my dear Vidura; *vīra-suvaḥ*—of the mother who gave birth to a hero; *muhuḥ*—constantly.

TRANSLATION

My dear Vidura, Sunīti was the mother of a great hero. Her tears, together with the milk flowing from her breasts, wet the whole body of Dhruva Mahārāja. This was a great auspicious sign.

PURPORT

When Deities are installed, They are washed with milk, yogurt and water, and this ceremony is called *abhiṣeka*. In this verse it has been especially mentioned that the tears which flowed down from the eyes of Sunīti were all-auspicious. This auspiciousness of the *abhiṣeka* ceremony performed by his beloved mother is the indication that in the very near future Dhruva Mahārāja would be installed on the throne of his father. The history of Dhruva Mahārāja's leaving home was that his father refused to give him a place on his lap, and Dhruva Mahārāja determined that unless he got the throne of his father he would not come back. Now this *abhiṣeka* ceremony performed by his beloved mother was an indication that he would occupy the throne of Mahārāja Uttānapāda.

It is also significant in this verse that Sunīti, mother of Dhruva Mahārāja, is described as *vīra-sū*, a mother who produced a great hero. There are many heroes in the world, but there is no comparison with Dhruva Mahārāja, who was not only a heroic emperor of this planet, but also a great devotee. A devotee is also a great hero because he conquers the influence of *māyā*. When Lord Caitanya inquired from Rāmānanda Rāya about the most famous man in this world, the latter replied that anyone who is known as a great devotee of the Lord is to be accepted as the most famous.

TEXT 51

तां शशंसुर्जना राज्ञीं दिष्ट्या ते पुत्र आर्तिहा ।
प्रतिलब्धश्चिरं नष्टो रक्षिता मण्डलं भुवः ॥५१॥

tāṁ śaśaṁsur janā rājñīṁ
diṣṭyā te putra ārti-hā
pratilabdhaś ciraṁ naṣṭo
rakṣitā maṇḍalaṁ bhuvaḥ

tām—unto Queen Sunīti; *śaśaṁsuḥ*—offered praise; *janāḥ*—the people in general; *rājñīm*—unto the Queen; *diṣṭyā*—by fortune; *te*—your; *putraḥ*—son; *ārti-hā*—will vanquish all your pains; *pratilabdhaḥ*—now returned; *ciram*—since a long time; *naṣṭaḥ*—lost; *rakṣitā*—will protect; *maṇḍalam*—the globe; *bhuvaḥ*—earthly.

TRANSLATION

The residents of the palace praised the Queen: Dear Queen, your beloved son was lost a long time ago, and it is your great fortune that he now has come back. It appears, therefore, that your son will be able to protect you for a very long time and will put an end to all your material pangs.

TEXT 52

अभ्यर्चितस्त्वया नूनं भगवान् प्रणतार्तिहा ।
यदनुध्यायिनो धीरा मृत्युं जिग्युः सुदुर्जयम् ।।५२।।

abhyarcitas tvayā nūnaṁ
bhagavān praṇatārti-hā
yad-anudhyāyino dhīrā
mṛtyuṁ jigyuḥ sudurjayam

abhyarcitaḥ—worshiped; *tvayā*—by you; *nūnam*—however; *bhagavān*—the Supreme Personality of Godhead; *praṇata-ārti-hā*—who can deliver His devotees from the greatest danger; *yat*—whom; *anudhyāyinaḥ*—constantly meditating upon; *dhīrāḥ*—great saintly persons; *mṛtyum*—death; *jigyuḥ*—conquered; *sudurjayam*—which is very, very difficult to overcome.

TRANSLATION

Dear Queen, you must have worshiped the Supreme Personality of Godhead, who delivers His devotees from the greatest danger. Persons who constantly meditate upon Him surpass the course of birth and death. This perfection is very difficult to achieve.

PURPORT

Dhruva Mahārāja was the lost child of Queen Sunīti, but during his absence she always meditated upon the Supreme Personality of Godhead, who is able to rescue His devotee from all dangers. While Dhruva Mahārāja was absent from his home, not only did he undergo severe austerities in the forest of Madhuvana, but at home also his mother prayed to the Supreme Lord for his safety and good fortune. In other words, the Lord was worshiped by both the mother and the son, and both were able to achieve the supreme benediction from the Supreme Lord. The word *sudurjayam*, an adjective which indicates that no one can conquer death, is very significant. When Dhruva Mahārāja was away from his home, his father thought that he was dead. Ordinarily a king's son only five years old and away from home in the forest would certainly be supposed dead, but by the mercy of the Supreme Personality of Godhead, not only was he saved, but he was blessed with the highest perfection.

TEXT 53

लाल्यमानं जनैरेवं ध्रुवं सभ्रातरं नृपः ।
आरोप्य करिणीं हृष्टः स्तूयमानोऽविशत्पुरम् ॥५३॥

lālyamānaṁ janair evaṁ
dhruvaṁ sabhrātaraṁ nṛpaḥ
āropya kariṇīṁ hṛṣṭaḥ
stūyamāno 'viśat puram

lālyamānam—being thus praised; *janaiḥ*—by the people in general; *evam*—thus; *dhruvam*—Mahārāja Dhruva; *sa-bhrātaram*—with his brother; *nṛpaḥ*—the King; *āropya*—placing; *kariṇīm*—on the back of a she-elephant; *hṛṣṭaḥ*—being so pleased; *stūyamānaḥ*—and being so praised; *aviśat*—returned; *puram*—to his capital.

TRANSLATION

The sage Maitreya continued: My dear Vidura, when everyone was thus praising Dhruva Mahārāja, the King was very happy, and he had Dhruva and his brother seated on the back of a she-elephant. Thus he returned to his capital, where he was praised by all classes of men.

TEXT 54

तत्र तत्रोपसंक्लृप्तैर्लसन्मकरतोरणैः ।
सवृन्दैः कदलीस्तम्भैः पूगपोतैश्च तद्विधैः ॥५४॥

tatra tatropasaṅkḷptair
lasan-makara-toraṇaiḥ
savṛndaiḥ kadalī-stambhaiḥ
pūga-potaiś ca tad-vidhaiḥ

tatra tatra—here and there; *upasaṅkḷptaiḥ*—set up; *lasat*—brilliant; *makara*—shark-shaped; *toraṇaiḥ*—with arched gateways; *sa-vṛndaiḥ*—with bunches of fruits and flowers; *kadalī*—of banana trees; *stambhaiḥ*—with columns; *pūga-potaiḥ*—with young betel nut trees; *ca*—also; *tat-vidhaiḥ*—of that kind.

TRANSLATION

The whole city was decorated with columns of banana trees containing bunches of fruits and flowers, and betel nut trees with leaves and branches were seen here and there. There were also many gates set up which were structured to give the appearance of sharks.

PURPORT

Auspicious ceremonies with decorations of the green leaves of palms, coconut trees, betel nut trees and banana trees and with fruits, flowers and leaves are an age-old custom in India. To receive his great son Dhruva Mahārāja, King Uttānapāda arranged a good reception, and all the citizens very enthusiastically took part with great jubilation.

TEXT 55

चूतपल्लववासःस्रङ्मुक्तादामविलम्बिभिः ।
उपस्कृतं प्रतिद्वारमपां कुम्भैः सदीपकैः ॥५५॥

cūta-pallava-vāsaḥ-sraṅ-
muktā-dāma-vilambibhiḥ
upaskṛtaṁ pratidvāram
apāṁ kumbhaiḥ sadīpakaiḥ

cūta-pallava—with mango leaves; *vāsaḥ*—cloth; *srak*—flower garlands; *muktā-dāma*—strings of pearls; *vilambibhiḥ*—hanging; *upaskṛtam*—decorated; *pratidvāram*—at every gate; *apām*—full of water; *kumbhaiḥ*—with water pots; *sa-dīpakaiḥ*—with burning lamps.

TRANSLATION

At each and every gate there were burning lamps and big water pots decorated with differently colored cloth, strings of pearls, flower garlands, and hanging mango leaves.

TEXT 56

प्राकारैर्गोपुरागारैः शातकुम्भपरिच्छदैः ।
सर्वतोऽलंकृतं श्रीमद्विमानशिखरद्युभिः ॥५६॥

prākārair gopurāgāraiḥ
śāta-kumbha-paricchadaiḥ
sarvato 'laṅkṛtaṁ śrīmad-
vimāna-śikhara-dyubhiḥ

prākāraiḥ—with surrounding walls; *gopura*—city gates; *āgāraiḥ*—with houses; *śāta-kumbha*—golden; *paricchadaiḥ*—with ornamental work; *sarvataḥ*—on all sides; *alaṅkṛtam*—decorated; *śrīmat*—valuable, beautiful; *vimāna*—airplanes; *śikhara*—domes; *dyubhiḥ*—glittering.

TRANSLATION

In the capital city there were many palaces, city gates and surrounding walls, which were already very, very beautiful, and on this occasion all of them were decorated with golden ornaments. The domes of the city palaces glittered, as did the domes of the beautiful airplanes which hovered over the city.

PURPORT

Regarding the mention of airplanes here, it is suggested by Śrīmad Vijayadhvaja Tīrtha that on this occasion the demigods from higher planetary systems also came in their airplanes to bestow their blessings on Dhruva Mahārāja on his arrival at the capital of his father. It also appears that all the domes of the city palaces as well as the pinnacles of the airplanes were decorated with ornamental work in gold, and, being reflected by the sunshine, they were all glittering. We can observe a specific distinction between Dhruva Mahārāja's time and modern days, for the airplanes in those days were made of gold, whereas at the present moment airplanes are made of base aluminum. This just gives a hint of the opulence of Dhruva Mahārāja's days and the poverty of modern times.

TEXT 57

मृष्टचत्वररथ्याट्टमार्गं चन्दनचर्चितम् ।
लाजाक्षतैः पुष्पफलैस्तण्डुलैर्बलिभिर्युतम् ॥५७॥

mṛṣṭa-catvara-rathyāṭṭa-
mārgaṁ candana-carcitam
lājākṣataiḥ puṣpa-phalais
taṇḍulair balibhir yutam

mṛṣṭa—fully cleansed; *catvara*—quadrangles; *rathya*—highways; *aṭṭa*—raised sitting places; *mārgam*—lanes; *candana*—with sandalwood; *carcitam*—sprinkled; *lāja*—with fried rice; *akṣataiḥ*—and barley; *puṣpa*—with flowers; *phalaiḥ*—and fruits; *taṇḍulaiḥ*—with rice; *balibhiḥ*—auspicious presentations; *yutam*—provided with.

TRANSLATION

All the quadrangles, lanes and streets in the city, and the raised sitting places at the crossings, were thoroughly cleansed and sprinkled with sandalwood water; and all over the city auspicious grains such as rice and barley and flowers, fruits and many other auspicious presentations were scattered.

TEXTS 58-59

ध्रुवाय पथि दृष्टाय तत्र तत्र पुरस्त्रियः ।
सिद्धार्थाक्षतदध्यम्बुदूर्वापुष्पफलानि च ॥५८॥
उपजह्रुः प्रयुञ्जाना वात्सल्यादाशिषः सतीः ।
शृण्वंस्तद्वल्गुगीतानि प्राविशद्भवनं पितुः ॥५९॥

dhruvāya pathi dṛṣṭāya
tatra tatra pura-striyaḥ
siddhārthākṣata-dadhy-ambu-
dūrvā-puṣpa-phalāni ca

upajahruḥ prayuñjānā
vātsalyād āśiṣaḥ satīḥ
śṛṇvaṁs tad-valgu-gītāni
prāviśad bhavanaṁ pituḥ

dhruvāya—on Dhruva; *pathi*—on the road; *dṛṣṭāya*—seen; *tatra tatra*—here and there; *pura-striyaḥ*—household ladies; *siddhārtha*—white mustard seed; *akṣata*—barley; *dadhi*—curd; *ambu*—water; *dūrvā*—newly grown grass; *puṣpa*—flowers; *phalāni*—fruits; *ca*—also; *upajahruḥ*—they showered; *prayuñjānāḥ*—uttering; *vātsalyāt*—out of affection; *āśiṣaḥ*—blessings; *satīḥ*—gentle ladies; *śṛṇvan*—hearing; *tat*—their; *valgu*—very pleasing; *gītāni*—songs; *prāviśat*—he entered; *bhavanam*—the palace; *pituḥ*—of his father.

TRANSLATION

Thus, as Dhruva Mahārāja passed on the road, from every place in the neighborhood all the gentle household ladies assembled to see him, and out of maternal affection they offered their blessings, showering him with white mustard seed, barley, curd, water, newly grown grass, fruits and flowers. In this way Dhruva Mahārāja, while hearing the pleasing songs sung by the ladies, entered the palace of his father.

TEXT 60

महामणिव्रातमये स तस्मिन् भवनोत्तमे ।
लालितो नितरां पित्रा न्यवसद्दिवि देववत् ॥६०॥

mahāmaṇi-vrāta-maye
sa tasmin bhavanottame
lālito nitarāṁ pitrā
nyavasad divi devavat

mahāmaṇi—greatly valuable jewels; *vrāta*—groups of; *maye*—bedecked with; *saḥ*—he (Dhruva Mahārāja); *tasmin*—in that; *bhavana-uttame*—brilliant house; *lālitaḥ*—being raised; *nitarām*—always; *pitrā*—by the father; *nyavasat*—lived there; *divi*—in the higher planetary systems; *deva-vat*—like the demigods.

TRANSLATION

Dhruva Mahārāja thereafter lived in his father's palace, which had walls bedecked with highly valuable jewels. His affectionate father took particular care of him, and he dwelled in that house just as the demigods live in their palaces in the higher planetary systems.

TEXT 61

पयःफेननिभाः शय्या दान्ता रुक्मपरिच्छदाः।
आसनानि महार्हाणि यत्र रौक्मा उपस्कराः ॥६१॥

payaḥ-phena-nibhāḥ śayyā
dāntā rukma-paricchadāḥ
āsanāni mahārhāṇi
yatra raukmā upaskarāḥ

payaḥ—milk; *phena*—foam; *nibhāḥ*—like; *śayyāḥ*—bedding; *dāntāḥ*—made of ivory; *rukma*—golden; *paricchadāḥ*—with embellishments; *āsanāni*—sitting places; *mahā-arhāṇi*—very valuable; *yatra*—where; *raukmāḥ*—golden; *upaskarāḥ*—furniture.

TRANSLATION

The bedding in the palace was as white as the foam of milk and was very soft. The bedsteads were made of ivory with embellishments of gold, and the chairs, benches and other sitting places and furniture were made of gold.

TEXT 62

यत्र स्फटिककुड्येषु महामारकतेषु च ।
मणिप्रदीपा आभान्ति ललनारत्नसंयुताः ॥६२॥

yatra sphaṭika-kuḍyeṣu
mahā-mārakateṣu ca
maṇi-pradīpā ābhānti
lalanā-ratna-saṁyutāḥ

yatra—where; *sphaṭika*—made of marble; *kuḍyeṣu*—on walls; *mahā-mārakateṣu*—bedecked with valuable jewels like sapphires; *ca*—also; *maṇi-pradīpāḥ*—lamps made of jewels; *ābhānti*—shined; *lalanā*—female figures; *ratna*—made of jewels; *saṁyutāḥ*—held by.

TRANSLATION

The palace of the King was surrounded by walls made of marble with many engravings made of valuable jewels like sapphires, which depicted beautiful women with shining jewel lamps in their hands.

PURPORT

The description of King Uttānapāda's palace depicts the state of affairs many hundreds and thousands of years ago, long before *Śrīmad-Bhāgavatam* was compiled. Since it is described that Mahārāja Dhruva ruled for 36,000 years, he must have lived in the Satya-yuga, when people lived for 100,000 years. The life durations in the four *yugas* are also mentioned in the Vedic literature. In the Satya-yuga people used to live for 100,000 years, in the Tretā-yuga people lived for 10,000 years, in Dvāpara-yuga they lived for 1,000 years, and in this age, Kali-yuga, people may live up to 100 years.

With the progressive advance of each new *yuga,* the duration of human life is reduced by ninety percent—from 100,000 to 10,000, from 10,000 to 1,000, and from 1,000 to 100.

It is said that Dhruva Mahārāja is the great-grandson of Lord Brahmā. This indicates that Dhruva Mahārāja's time was in the Satya-yuga in the beginning of creation. During one day of Lord Brahmā, as stated in the *Bhagavad-gītā,* there are many Satya-yugas. According to the Vedic calculation, at the present moment the twenty-eighth millennium is current. It can be calculated that Dhruva Mahārāja lived many millions of years ago, but the description of the palace of Dhruva's father is so glorious that we cannot accept that advanced human civilization did not exist even 40,000 or 50,000 years ago. There were walls like those in the palace of Mahārāja Uttānapāda even very recently, during the Mogul period. Anyone who has seen the Red Fort in Delhi must have marked that the walls were made of marble and were once decorated with jewels. During the British Period all these jewels were taken away and dispatched to the British Museum.

The conception of worldly opulence was formerly based mainly on natural resources such as jewels, marble, silk, ivory, gold and silver. The advancement of economic development was not based on big motor cars. Advancement of human civilization does not depend on industrial enterprises, but on possession of natural wealth and natural food, which is all supplied by the Supreme Personality of Godhead so that we may save time for self-realization and success in the human form of body.

Another aspect of this verse is that Dhruva Mahārāja's father, Uttānapāda, would very soon give up attachment for his palaces and would go to the forest for self-realization. From the description of *Śrīmad-Bhāgavatam,* therefore, we can make a very thorough comparative study of modern civilization and the civilization of mankind in the other millenniums, Satya-yuga, Tretā-yuga and Dvāpara-yuga.

TEXT 63

उद्यानानि च रम्याणि विचित्रैरमरद्रुमैः ।
कूजद्विहङ्गमिथुनैर्गायन्मत्तमधुव्रतैः ॥६३॥

udyānāni ca ramyāṇi
vicitrair amara-drumaiḥ
kūja-dvihaṅga-mithunair
gāyan-matta-madhuvrataiḥ

udyānāni—gardens; *ca*—also; *ramyāṇi*—very beautiful; *vicitraiḥ*—various; *amara-drumaiḥ*—with trees brought from the heavenly planets; *kūja*—singing; *dvihaṅga*—of birds; *mithunaiḥ*—with pairs; *gāyat*—humming; *matta*—mad; *madhu-vrataiḥ*—with bumblebees.

TRANSLATION

The King's residence was surrounded by gardens wherein there were varieties of trees brought from the heavenly planets, and in those trees there were pairs of sweetly singing birds and almost mad bumblebees who made a very relishable buzzing sound.

PURPORT

In this verse the word *amara-drumaiḥ,* "with trees brought from the heavenly planets," is very significant. The heavenly planets are known as *amaraloka,* the planets where death is very much delayed, because the people there live for 10,000 years according to the calculations of the demigods, in which our six months are equal to one day. The demigods live in the heavenly planets for months, years and ten thousands of years according to demigod time, and then again, after the results of their pious activities are exhausted, they fall down again to this earth. These are the statements that can be collected from Vedic literature. As the people there live for 10,000 years, so also do the trees. Of course, here on this earth there are many trees which live for 10,000 years, so what to speak of the trees on the heavenly planets? They must live for more than many ten thousands of years, and sometimes, as practiced even now, some valuable trees are taken from one place to another.

It is elsewhere stated that when Lord Kṛṣṇa went to the heavenly planets with His wife Satyabhāmā He took a *pārijāta* flower tree from heaven and brought it to the earth. There was a fight between Kṛṣṇa and the demigods due to the *pārijāta* tree's being taken from heaven to this planet. The *pārijāta* was planted in the palace of Lord Kṛṣṇa which was occupied by Queen Satyabhāmā. The flower and fruit trees in the heavenly planets are superior, for they are very pleasant and tasteful, and it appears that in the palace of Mahārāja Uttānapāda there were many varieties of such trees.

TEXT 64

वाप्यो वैदूर्यसोपानाः पद्मोत्पलकुमुद्वतीः ।
हंसकारण्डवकुलैर्जुष्टाश्चक्राह्वसारसैः ॥६४॥

vāpyo vaidūrya-sopānāḥ
padmotpala-kumudvatīḥ
haṁsa-kāraṇḍava-kulair
juṣṭāś cakrāhva-sārasaiḥ

vāpyaḥ—lakes; *vaidūrya*—emerald; *sopānāḥ*—with staircases; *padma*—lotuses; *utpala*—blue lotuses; *kumud-vatīḥ*—full of lilies; *haṁsa*—swans; *kāraṇḍava*—and ducks; *kulaiḥ*—by flocks of; *juṣṭāḥ*—inhabited; *cakrāhva*—by *cakravākas* (geese); *sārasaiḥ*—and by cranes.

TRANSLATION

There were emerald staircases which led to lakes full of variously colored lotus flowers and lilies, and swans, kāraṇḍavas, cakravākas, cranes and similar other valuable birds were visible in those lakes.

PURPORT

It appears that the palace was not only surrounded by compounds and gardens with varieties of trees, but there were small man-made lakes also where the water was full of many colorful lotus flowers and lilies, and to get down to the lakes there were staircases made of valuable jewels such as emeralds. By the beautifully positioned garden houses there were many luxuriant birds, such as swans, *cakravākas, kāraṇḍavas* and cranes. These birds generally do not live in filthy places like crows. The atmosphere of the city was very healthy and beautiful; it can simply be imagined from its description.

TEXT 65

उत्तानपादो राजर्षिः प्रभावं तनयस्य तम् ।
श्रुत्वा दृष्ट्वाद्भुततमं प्रपेदे विस्मयं परम् ॥६५॥

uttānapādo rājarṣiḥ
prabhāvaṁ tanayasya tam
śrutvā dṛṣṭvādbhuta-tamaṁ
prapede vismayaṁ param

uttānapādaḥ—King Uttānapāda; *rājarṣiḥ*—great saintly king; *prabhāvam*—influence; *tanayasya*—of his son; *tam*—that; *śrutvā*—hearing; *dṛṣṭvā*—seeing; *adbhuta*—wonderful; *tamam*—in the superlative degree; *prapede*—happily felt; *vismayam*—wonder; *param*—supreme.

TRANSLATION

The saintly King Uttānapāda, hearing of the glorious deeds of Dhruva Mahārāja and personally seeing also how influential and great he was, felt very satisfied, for Dhruva's activities were wonderful to the supreme degree.

PURPORT

When Dhruva Mahārāja was in the forest executing his austerities, his father, Uttānapāda, heard everything about his very wonderful activities. Although Dhruva Mahārāja was not only the son of a king but was only five years old, he went to the forest and executed devotional service under strict austerity. Therefore his acts were all wonderful, and when he came back home, naturally, because of his spiritual qualifications, he became very popular amongst the citizens. He must have performed many wonderful activities by the grace of the Lord. No one is more satisfied than the father of a person who is credited with glorious activities. Mahārāja Uttānapāda was not an ordinary king; he was a *rājarṣi,* a saintly king. Formerly this earth was ruled by one saintly king only. Kings were trained to become saintly; therefore they had no other concern than the welfare of the citizens. These saintly kings were properly trained, and as mentioned in *Bhagavad-gītā* also, the science of God, or the *yoga* system of devotional service known as *Bhagavad-gītā,* was spoken to the saintly king of the sun planet, and gradually it descended through the *kṣatriya* kings who were generated from the sun and the moon. If the head of the government is saintly, certainly the citizens not only become saintly, but they are very happy because both their spiritual and physical needs and hankerings are satisfied.

TEXT 66

वीक्ष्योढवयसं तं च प्रकृतीनां च सम्मतम् ।
अनुरक्तप्रजं राजा ध्रुवं चक्रे भुवः पतिम् ॥६६॥

vīkṣyoḍha-vayasaṁ taṁ ca
prakṛtīnāṁ ca sammatam
anurakta-prajaṁ rājā
dhruvaṁ cakre bhuvaḥ patim

vīkṣya—after seeing; *ūḍha-vayasam*—mature in age; *tam*—Dhruva; *ca*—and; *prakṛtīnām*—by the ministers; *ca*—also; *sammatam*—approved of; *anurakta*—

beloved; *prajam*—by his subjects; *rājā*—the King; *dhruvam*—Dhruva Mahārāja; *cakre*—made; *bhuvaḥ*—of the earth; *patim*—master.

TRANSLATION

When, after concentration, King Uttānapāda saw that Dhruva Mahārāja was suitably mature to take charge of the kingdom and that his ministers were agreeable and the citizens were also very fond of him, he enthroned him as Emperor of this planet.

PURPORT

Although it is misconceived that formerly the monarchial government was autocratic, from the description of this verse it appears that not only was King Uttānapāda a *rājarṣi,* but before installing his beloved son Dhruva on the throne of the empire of the world, he consulted his ministerial officers, considered the opinion of the public, and also personally examined Dhruva's character. Then he installed him on the throne to take charge of the affairs of the world.

When a Vaiṣṇava king like Dhruva Mahārāja is the head of the government of the entire world, the world is so happy that it is not possible to imagine or describe. Even now, if people would all become Kṛṣṇa conscious, the democratic government of the present day would be exactly like the kingdom of heaven. If all people became Kṛṣṇa conscious they would vote for persons who are of the category of Dhruva Mahārāja. If the post of chief executive were occupied by such a Vaiṣṇava, all the problems of satanic government would be solved. The youthful generation of the present day is very enthusiastic in trying to overthrow the government in different parts of the world. Unless people are Kṛṣṇa conscious like Dhruva Mahārāja, there will be no appreciable changes in government because people who hanker to attain political position by hook or by crook cannot think of the welfare of the people. They are only busy to keep their position of prestige and monetary gain. They have very little time to think of the welfare of the citizens.

TEXT 67

आत्मानं च प्रवयसमाकलय्य विशाम्पतिः ।
वनं विरक्तः प्रातिष्ठद्विमृशन्नात्मनो गतिम् ॥६७॥

ātmānaṁ ca pravayasam
ākalayya viśām patiḥ
vanaṁ viraktaḥ prātiṣṭhad
vimṛśann ātmano gatim

ātmānam—himself; *ca*—also; *pravayasam*—advanced in age; *ākalayya*—considering; *viśām patiḥ*—King Uttānapāda; *vanam*—to the forest; *viraktaḥ*—detached; *prātiṣṭhat*—departed; *vimṛśan*—deliberating on; *ātmanaḥ*—of the self; *gatim*—salvation.

TRANSLATION

After considering his advanced age and deliberating on the welfare of his spiritual self, King Uttānapāda detached himself from worldly affairs and entered the forest.

PURPORT

This is the sign of a *rājarṣi.* King Uttānapāda was very opulent and was Emperor of the world, and these attachments were certainly very great. Modern politicians are not as great as kings like Mahārāja Uttānapāda, but because they get some political power for some days, they become so much attached to their positions that they never retire unless they are removed from their posts by cruel death or killed by some opposing political party. It is within our experience that the politicians in India do not quit their positions until death. This was not the practice in olden days, as it is evident from the behavior of King Uttānapāda. Immediately after installing his worthy son Dhruva Mahārāja on the throne, he left his home and palace. There are hundreds and thousands of instances like this in which kings, in their mature age, would give up their kingdoms and go to the forest to practice austerity. Practice of austerity is the main business of human life. As Mahārāja Dhruva practiced austerity in his early age, similarly his father, Mahārāja Uttānapāda, in his old age, also practiced austerity in the forest. It is, however, not possible in modern days to give up one's home and go to the forest to practice austerity, but if people of all ages would take shelter of the Kṛṣṇa consciousness movement and practice the simple austerities of no illicit sex, no intoxication, no gambling and no meat eating, and chant the Hare Kṛṣṇa *mantra* regularly (sixteen rounds), by this practical method it would be a very easy task to get salvation from this material world.

Thus end the Bhaktivedanta purports of the Fourth Canto, Ninth Chapter, of the Śrīmad-Bhāgavatam, *entitled "Dhruva Mahārāja Returns Home."*

CHAPTER TEN

Dhruva Mahārāja's Fight with the Yakṣas

TEXT 1

मैत्रेय उवाच
प्रजापतेर्दुहितरं शिशुमारस्य वै ध्रुवः ।
उपयेमे भ्रमिं नाम तत्सुतौ कल्पवत्सरौ ॥ १ ॥

maitreya uvāca
prajāpater duhitaraṁ
śiśumārasya vai dhruvaḥ
upayeme bhramiṁ nāma
tat-sutau kalpa-vatsarau

maitreyaḥ uvāca—the great sage Maitreya continued; *prajā-pateḥ*—of the *prajāpati; duhitaram*—daughter; *śiśumārasya*—of Śiśumāra; *vai*—certainly; *dhruvaḥ*—Dhruva Mahārāja; *upayeme*—married; *bhramim*—Bhrami; *nāma*—named; *tat-sutau*—her sons; *kalpa*—Kalpa; *vatsarau*—Vatsara.

TRANSLATION

The great sage Maitreya said: My dear Vidura, thereafter Dhruva Mahārāja married the daughter of Prajāpati Śiśumāra, whose name was Bhrami, and two sons named Kalpa and Vatsara were born of her.

PURPORT

It appears that Dhruva Mahārāja married after being installed on the throne of his father and after the departure of his father for the forest for self-realization. It is very important to note in this connection that since Mahārāja Uttānapāda was greatly affectionate towards his son, and since it is the duty of a father to get his sons and daughters married as quickly as possible, why did he not get his son married before he left home? The answer is that Mahārāja Uttānapāda was a *rājarṣi*, saintly king. Although he was busy in his political affairs and duties of government management, still he was very anxious for self-realization. Therefore as soon as his son, Dhruva Mahārāja, was quite worthy to take charge of the government, he took this opportunity to leave home, just like his son, who, without fear, left home for self-realization, even at the age of five years. These are rare instances from which we can see that the importance of spiritual realization is above all other important work. Mahārāja Uttānapāda knew very well that to get his son, Dhruva Mahārāja, married was not so important that it should take preference to his going away to the forest for self-realization.

TEXT 2

इलायामपि भार्यायां वायोः पुत्र्यां महाबलः ।
पुत्रमुत्कलनामानं योषिद्रत्नमजीजनत् ॥ २ ॥

ilāyām api bhāryāyāṁ
vāyoḥ putryāṁ mahā-balaḥ
putram utkala-nāmānaṁ
yoṣid-ratnam ajījanat

ilāyām—unto his wife named Ilā; *api*—also; *bhāryāyām*—unto his wife; *vāyoḥ*—of the demigod Vāyu (controller of air); *putryām*—unto the daughter; *mahā-balaḥ*—the greatly powerful Dhruva Mahārāja; *putram*—son; *utkala*—Utkala; *nāmānam*—of the name; *yoṣit*—female; *ratnam*—jewel; *ajījanat*—he begot.

TRANSLATION

The greatly powerful Dhruva Mahārāja had another wife named Ilā, who was the daughter of the demigod Vāyu. In her he begot a son named Utkala and a very beautiful daughter.

TEXT 3

उत्तमस्त्वकृतोद्वाहो मृगयायां बलीयसा ।
हतः पुण्यजनेनाद्रौ तन्मातास्य गतिं गता ॥ ३ ॥

uttamas tv akṛtodvāho
mṛgayāyāṁ balīyasā
hataḥ puṇya-janenādrau
tan-mātāsya gatiṁ gatā

uttamaḥ—Uttama; *tu*—but; *akṛta*—without; *udvāhaḥ*—marriage; *mṛgayāyām*—on a hunting excursion; *balīyasā*—very powerful; *hataḥ*—was killed; *puṇya-janena*—by a Yakṣa; *adrau*—on the Himalayan Mountains; *tat*—his; *mātā*—mother (Suruci); *asya*—of her son; *gatim*—way; *gatā*—followed.

TRANSLATION

Dhruva Mahārāja's younger brother Uttama, who was still unmarried, once went on a hunting excursion and was killed by a powerful Yakṣa in the Himalayan Mountains. Along with him, his mother, Suruci, also followed the path of her son [died].

TEXT 4

ध्रुवो भ्रातृवधं श्रुत्वा कोपामर्षशुचार्पितः ।
जैत्रं स्यन्दनमास्थाय गतः पुण्यजनालयम् ॥ ४ ॥

dhruvo bhrātṛ-vadhaṁ śrutvā
kopāmarṣa-śucārpitaḥ
jaitraṁ syandanam āsthāya
gataḥ puṇya-janālayam

dhruvaḥ—Dhruva Mahārāja; *bhrātṛ-vadham*—killing of his brother; *śrutvā*—hearing this news; *kopa*—anger; *amarṣa*—vengeance; *śucā*—lamentation; *arpitaḥ*—being filled with; *jaitram*—victorious; *syandanam*—chariot; *āsthāya*—getting on; *gataḥ*—went; *puṇya-jana-ālayam*—to the city of the Yakṣas.

TRANSLATION

When Dhruva Mahārāja heard of the killing of his brother Uttama by the Yakṣas in the Himalayan Mountains, being overwhelmed with lamentation and anger, he got on his chariot and went for victory over the city of the Yakṣas, Alakāpurī.

PURPORT

Dhruva Mahārāja's becoming angry, overwhelmed with grief, and envious of the enemies was not incompatible with his position as a great devotee. It is a misunderstanding that a devotee should not be angry, envious or overwhelmed by lamentation. Dhruva Mahārāja was the King, and when his brother was unceremoniously killed, it was his duty to take revenge against the Yakṣas from the Himalayas.

TEXT 5

गत्वोदीचीं दिशं राजा रुद्रानुचरसेविताम् ।
ददर्श हिमवद्द्रोण्यां पुरीं गुह्यकसंकुलाम् ॥ ५ ॥

gatvodīcīṁ diśaṁ rājā
rudrānucara-sevitām

dadarśa himavad-droṇyāṁ
purīṁ guhyaka-saṅkulām

gatvā—going; *udīcīm*—northern; *diśam*—direction; *rājā*—King Dhruva; *rudra-anucara*—by followers of Rudra, Lord Śiva; *sevitām*—inhabited; *dadarśa*—saw; *himavat*—Himalayan; *droṇyām*—in a valley; *purīm*—a city; *guhyaka*—ghostly persons; *saṅkulām*—full of.

TRANSLATION

Dhruva Mahārāja went to the northern direction of the Himalayan range. In a valley he saw a city that was full of ghostly persons who were followers of Lord Śiva.

PURPORT

In this verse it is stated that the Yakṣas are more or less devotees of Lord Śiva. By this indication the Yakṣas may be taken to be the Himalayan tribes like the Tibetans.

TEXT 6

दध्मौ शङ्खं बृहद्बाहुः खं दिशश्चानुनादयन् ।
येनोद्विग्नदृशः क्षत्तरुपदेव्योऽत्रसन्भृशम् ॥ ६ ॥

dadhmau śaṅkhaṁ bṛhad-bāhuḥ
khaṁ diśaś cānunādayan
yenodvigna-dṛśaḥ kṣattar
upadevyo 'trasan bhṛśam

dadhmau—blew; *śaṅkham*—conchshell; *bṛhat-bāhuḥ*—the mighty-armed; *kham*—the sky; *diśaḥ ca*—and all directions; *anunādayan*—causing to resound; *yena*—by which; *udvigna-dṛśaḥ*—appeared to be very anxious; *kṣattaḥ*—my dear Vidura; *upadevyaḥ*—the wives of the Yakṣas; *atrasan*—became frightened; *bhṛśam*—greatly.

TRANSLATION

Maitreya continued: My dear Vidura, as soon as Dhruva Mahārāja reached Alakāpurī, he immediately blew his conchshell, and the sound reverberated throughout the entire sky and in every direction. The wives of the Yakṣas became very much frightened. From their eyes it was apparent that they were full of anxiety.

TEXT 7

ततो निष्क्रम्य बलिन उपदेवमहाभटाः ।
असहन्तस्तन्निनादमभिपेतुरुदायुधाः ॥ ७ ॥

tato niṣkramya balina
upadeva-mahā-bhaṭāḥ
asahantas tan-ninādam
abhipetur udāyudhāḥ

tataḥ—thereafter; *niṣkramya*—coming out; *balinaḥ*—very powerful; *upadeva*—of Kuvera; *mahā-bhaṭāḥ*—great soldiers; *asahantaḥ*—unable to tolerate; *tat*—of the conchshell; *ninādam*—sound; *abhipetuḥ*—attacked; *udāyudhāḥ*—equipped with various weapons.

TRANSLATION

O hero Vidura, the greatly powerful heroes of the Yakṣas, unable to tolerate the resounding vibration of the conchshell of Dhruva Mahārāja, came forth from their city with weapons and attacked Dhruva.

TEXT 8

स तानापततो वीर उग्रधन्वा महारथः ।
एकैकं युगपत्सर्वानहन् बाणैस्त्रिभिस्त्रिभिः ॥ ८ ॥

sa tān āpatato vīra
ugra-dhanvā mahā-rathaḥ
ekaikaṁ yugapat sarvān
ahan bāṇais tribhis tribhiḥ

saḥ—Dhruva Mahārāja; *tān*—all of them; *āpatataḥ*—falling upon him; *vīraḥ*—hero; *ugra-dhanvā*—powerful bowman; *mahā-rathaḥ*—who could fight with many chariots; *eka-ekam*—one after another; *yugapat*—simultaneously; *sarvān*—all of them; *ahan*—killed; *bāṇaiḥ*—by arrows; *tribhiḥ tribhiḥ*—by threes.

TRANSLATION

Dhruva Mahārāja, who was a great charioteer and certainly a great bowman also, immediately began to kill them by simultaneously discharging arrows at the rate of three at a time.

TEXT 9

ते वै ललाटलग्नैस्तैरिषुभिः सर्व एव हि ।
मत्वा निरस्तमात्मानमाशंसन् कर्म तस्य तत् ॥ ९ ॥

te vai lalāṭa-lagnais tair
iṣubhiḥ sarva eva hi
matvā nirastam ātmānam
āśaṁsan karma tasya tat

te—they; *vai*—certainly; *lalāṭa-lagnaiḥ*—intent upon their heads; *taiḥ*—by those; *iṣubhiḥ*—arrows; *sarve*—all of them; *eva*—certainly; *hi*—without fail; *matvā*—thinking; *nirastam*—defeated; *ātmānam*—themselves; *āśaṁsan*—praised; *karma*—action; *tasya*—of him; *tat*—that.

TRANSLATION

When the heroes of the Yakṣas saw that all their heads were being thus threatened by Dhruva Mahārāja, they could very easily understand their awkward position, and they concluded that they would certainly be defeated. But, as heroes, they lauded the action of Dhruva.

PURPORT

This spirit of fighting in a sporting attitude is very significant in this verse. The Yakṣas were severely attacked. Dhruva Mahārāja was their enemy, but still upon witnessing the wonderful heroic action of Mahārāja Dhruva, they were very pleased with him. This straightforward appreciation of an enemy's prowess is a characteristic of real *kṣatriya* spirit.

TEXT 10

तेऽपि चामुममृष्यन्तः पादस्पर्शमिवोरगाः ।
शरैरविध्यन् युगपद् द्विगुणं प्रचिकीर्षवः ॥१०॥

te 'pi cāmum amṛṣyantaḥ
pāda-sparśam ivoragāḥ
śarair avidhyan yugapad
dvi-guṇaṁ pracikīrṣavaḥ

te—the Yakṣas; *api*—also; *ca*—and; *amum*—at Dhruva; *amṛṣyantaḥ*—being intolerant of; *pāda-sparśam*—being touched by the feet; *iva*—like; *uragāḥ*—serpents; *śaraiḥ*—with arrows; *avidhyan*—struck; *yugapat*—simultaneously; *dvi-guṇam*—twice as much; *pracikīrṣavaḥ*—trying to retaliate.

TRANSLATION

Just like serpents, who cannot tolerate being trampled upon by anyone's feet, the Yakṣas, being intolerant of the wonderful prowess of Dhruva

Mahārāja, threw twice as many arrows—six from each of the soldiers—and thus they very valiantly exhibited their prowess.

TEXTS 11-12

ततः परिघनिस्त्रिंशैः प्रासशूलपरश्वधैः ।
शक्त्यृष्टिभिर्भुशुण्डीभिश्चित्रवाजैः शरैरपि ॥११॥
अभ्यवर्षन् प्रकुपिताः सरथं सहसारथिम् ।
इच्छन्तस्तत्प्रतीकर्तुमयुतानां त्रयोदश ॥१२॥

tataḥ parigha-nistriṁśaiḥ
prāsaśūla-paraśvadhaiḥ
śakty-ṛṣṭibhir bhuśuṇḍībhiś
citra-vājaiḥ śarair api

abhyavarṣan prakupitāḥ
sarathaṁ saha sārathim
icchantas tat pratīkartum
ayutānāṁ trayodaśa

tataḥ—thereupon; *parigha*—with iron bludgeons; *nistriṁśaiḥ*—and swords; *prāsaśūla*—with tridents; *paraśvadhaiḥ*—and lances; *śakti*—with pikes; *ṛṣṭibhiḥ*—and spears; *bhuśuṇḍībhiḥ*—with *bhuśuṇḍī* weapons; *citra-vājaiḥ*—having various feathers; *śaraiḥ*—with arrows; *api*—also; *abhyavarṣan*—they showered Dhruva; *prakupitāḥ*—being angry; *sa-ratham*—along with his chariot; *saha sārathim*—along with his charioteer; *icchantaḥ*—desiring; *tat*—Dhruva's activities; *pratīkartum*—to counteract; *ayutānām*—of ten-thousands; *trayodaśa*—thirteen.

TRANSLATION

The Yakṣa soldiers were 130,000 strong, all greatly angry and all desiring to defeat the wonderful activities of Dhruva Mahārāja. With full strength they showered various types of feathered arrows, parighas [iron bludgeons], nistriṁśas [swords], prāsaśūlas [tridents], paraśvadhas [lances], śaktis [pikes], ṛṣṭis [spears], and bhuśuṇḍī weapons upon Mahārāja Dhruva along with his chariot and charioteer.

TEXT 13

औत्तानपादिः स तदा शस्त्रवर्षेण भूरिणा ।
न एवादृश्यताच्छन्न आसारेण यथा गिरिः ॥१३॥

auttānapādiḥ sa tadā
śastra-varṣeṇa bhūriṇā
na evādṛśyatācchanna
āsāreṇa yathā giriḥ

auttānapādiḥ—Dhruva Mahārāja; *saḥ*—he; *tadā*—at that time; *śastra-varṣeṇa*—by a shower of weapons; *bhūriṇā*—incessant; *na*—not; *eva*—certainly; *adṛśyata*—was visible; *ācchannaḥ*—being covered; *āsāreṇa*—by constant rainfall; *yathā*—as; *giriḥ*—a mountain.

TRANSLATION

Dhruva Mahārāja was completely covered by an incessant shower of weapons, just as a mountain becomes covered by incessant rainfall.

PURPORT

Śrīla Viśvanātha Cakravartī Ṭhākura points out in this connection that although Dhruva Mahārāja was covered by the incessant arrows of the enemy, this does not mean that he succumbed in the battle. The example of a mountain peak's being covered by incessant rain is just suitable, for when a mountain is covered by incessant rain, all dirty things are washed from the body of the mountain. Similarly, the incessant shower of arrows from the enemy gave Dhruva Mahārāja new vigor to defeat them. In other words, whatever incompetency he might have had was washed away.

TEXT 14

हाहाकारस्तदैवासीत्सिद्धानां दिवि पश्यताम् ।
हतोऽयं मानवः सूर्यो मग्नः पुण्यजनार्णवे ॥१४॥

hāhā-kāras tadaivāsīt
siddhānāṁ divi paśyatām
hato 'yaṁ mānavaḥ sūryo
magnaḥ puṇya-janārṇave

hāhā-kāraḥ—tumult of disappointment; *tadā*—at that time; *eva*—certainly; *āsīt*—became manifest; *siddhānām*—of all the residents of Siddhaloka; *divi*—in the sky; *paśyatām*—who were observing the fight; *hataḥ*—killed; *ayam*—this; *mānavaḥ*—grandson of Manu; *sūryaḥ*—sun; *magnaḥ*—set; *puṇya-jana*—of the Yakṣas; *arṇave*—in the ocean.

TRANSLATION

All the Siddhas from the higher planetary systems were observing the fight from the sky, and when they saw that Dhruva Mahārāja had been covered by the incessant arrows of the enemy, they roared tumultuously, "The grandson of Manu, Dhruva, is now lost!" They cried that Dhruva Mahārāja was just like the sun and that now he had set within the ocean of the Yakṣas.

PURPORT

In this verse *mānava* is very significant. Generally this word is used to mean "human being." Dhruva Mahārāja is also described here as *mānava.* Not only is Dhruva Mahārāja a descendant of Manu, but all human society descends from Manu. According to Vedic civilization, Manu is the lawgiver. Even today Hindus in India follow the laws given by Manu. Everyone, therefore, in human society is a *mānava*, or descendant from Manu, but Dhruva Mahārāja is a distinguished *mānava* because he is a great devotee.

The denizens of the planet Siddhaloka, where the residents can fly in the sky without airplanes, were anxious over Dhruva Mahārāja's welfare in the battlefield. Śrīla Rūpa Gosvāmī says, therefore, that a devotee is not only well protected by the Supreme Lord, but all the demigods, and even ordinary men, are anxious for his security and safety. The comparison given here that Dhruva Mahārāja appeared to merge in the ocean of the Yakṣas is also significant. When the sun sets on the horizon, it appears that the sun drowns in the ocean, but factually the sun has no difficulty. Similarly, although Dhruva appeared to drown in the ocean of the Yakṣas, he had no difficulty. As the sun rises again in due course at the end of night, so Dhruva Mahārāja, although he might have been in difficulty (because, after all, it was a fight, and in any fighting activities there are reverses), that did not mean that he was defeated.

TEXT 15

नदत्सु यातुधानेषु जयकाशिष्वथो मृधे ।
उदतिष्ठद्रथस्तस्य नीहारादिव भास्करः ॥१५॥

nadatsu yātudhāneṣu
jayakāśiṣv atho mṛdhe
udatiṣṭhad rathas tasya
nīhārād iva bhāskaraḥ

nadatsu—while exclaiming; *yātudhāneṣu*—the ghostly Yakṣas; *jaya-kāśiṣu*—proclaiming victory; *atho*—then; *mṛdhe*—in the fighting; *udatiṣṭhat*—appeared; *rathaḥ*—the chariot; *tasya*—of Dhruva Mahārāja; *nīhārāt*—from the mist; *iva*—like; *bhāskaraḥ*—the sun.

TRANSLATION

The Yakṣas, being temporarily victorious, exclaimed that they had conquered Dhruva Mahārāja. But in the meantime Dhruva's chariot suddenly appeared, just as the sun suddenly appears from within foggy mist.

PURPORT

Here Dhruva Mahārāja is compared to the sun and the great assembly of the Yakṣas to foggy mist. Fog is insignificant in comparison with the sun. Although the sun is sometimes seen to be covered by fog, in fact the sun cannot be covered by anything. Our eyes may be covered by a cloud, but the sun is never covered. By this comparison with the sun, the greatness of Dhruva Mahārāja in all circumstances is affirmed.

TEXT 16

धनुर्विस्फूर्जयन्दिव्यं द्विषतां खेदमुद्वहन् ।
अस्त्रौघं व्यधमद्बाणैर्घनानीकमिवानिलः ॥१६॥

dhanur visphūrjayan divyaṁ
dviṣatāṁ khedam udvahan
astraughaṁ vyadhamad bāṇair
ghanānīkam ivānilaḥ

dhanuḥ—his bow; *visphūrjayan*—twanging; *divyam*—wonderful; *dviṣatām*—of the enemies; *khedam*—lamentation; *udvahan*—creating; *astra-ogham*—different types of weapons; *vyadhamat*—he scattered; *bāṇaiḥ*—with his arrows; *ghana*—of clouds; *anīkam*—an army; *iva*—like; *anilaḥ*—the wind.

TRANSLATION

Dhruva Mahārāja's bow and arrows twanged and hissed, causing lamentation in the hearts of his enemies. He began to shoot incessant arrows shattering all their different weapons, just as the blasting wind scatters the assembled clouds in the sky.

TEXT 17

तस्य ते चापनिर्मुक्ता भित्त्वा वर्माणि रक्षसाम् ।
कायानाविविशुस्तिग्मा गिरीनशनयो यथा ॥१७॥

tasya te cāpa-nirmuktā
bhittvā varmāṇi rakṣasām
kāyān āviviśus tigmā
girīn aśanayo yathā

tasya—of Dhruva; *te*—those arrows; *cāpa*—from the bow; *nirmuktāḥ*—released; *bhittvā*—having pierced; *varmāṇi*—shields; *rakṣasām*—of the demons; *kāyān*—bodies; *āviviśuḥ*—entered; *tigmāḥ*—sharp; *girīn*—mountains; *aśanayaḥ*—thunderbolts; *yathā*—just like.

TRANSLATION

The sharp arrows released from the bow of Dhruva Mahārāja pierced the shields and bodies of the enemy, like the thunderbolts released by the King of heaven, which dismantle the bodies of the mountains.

TEXTS 18-19

भल्लैः संछिद्यमानानां शिरोभिश्चारुकुण्डलैः ।
ऊरुभिर्हेमतालाभैर्दोर्भिर्वलयवल्गुभिः ॥१८॥
हारकेयूरमुकुटैरुष्णीषैश्च महाधनैः ।
आस्तृतास्ता रणभुवो रेजुर्वीरमनोहराः ॥१९॥

bhallaiḥ sañchidyamānānāṁ
śirobhiś cāru-kuṇḍalaiḥ
ūrubhir hema-tālābhair
dorbhir valaya-valgubhiḥ

hāra-keyūra-mukuṭair
uṣṇīṣaiś ca mahā-dhanaiḥ
āstṛtās tā raṇa-bhuvo
rejur vīra-mano-harāḥ

bhallaiḥ—by his arrows; *sañchidyamānānām*—of the Yakṣas who were cut to pieces; *śirobhiḥ*—with heads; *cāru*—beautiful; *kuṇḍalaiḥ*—with earrings; *ūrubhiḥ*—with thighs; *hema-tālābhaiḥ*—like golden palm trees; *dorbhiḥ*—with arms; *valaya-valgubhiḥ*—with beautiful bracelets; *hāra*—with garlands; *keyūra*—armlets; *mukuṭaiḥ*—and helmets; *uṣṇīṣaiḥ*—with turbans; *ca*—also; *mahā-dhanaiḥ*—very valuable; *āstṛtāḥ*—covered; *tāḥ*—those; *raṇa-bhuvaḥ*—battlefields; *rejuḥ*—began to glimmer; *vīra*—of the heroes; *manaḥ-harāḥ*—bewildering the minds.

TRANSLATION

The great sage Maitreya continued: My dear Vidura, the heads of those who were cut to pieces by the arrows of Dhruva Mahārāja were decorated very beautifully with earrings and turbans. The legs of their bodies were as beautiful as golden palm trees, their arms were decorated with golden bracelets and armlets, and on their heads there were very valuable helmets bedecked with gold. All these ornaments lying on that battlefield were very attractive and could bewilder the mind of a hero.

PURPORT

It appears that in those days soldiers used to go to the battlefield highly decorated with golden ornaments and with helmets and turbans, and when they were dead the booty was taken by the enemy party. Their falling dead in battle with their many golden ornamental dresses was certainly a lucrative opportunity to the heroes on the battlefield.

TEXT 20

हतावशिष्टा इतरे रणाजिराद्
रक्षोगणाः क्षत्रियवर्यसायकैः ।
प्रायो विवृक्णावयवा विदुद्रुवु-
र्मृगेन्द्रविक्रीडितयूथपा इव ॥२०॥

hatāvaśiṣṭā itare raṇājirād
rakṣo-gaṇāḥ kṣatriya-varya-sāyakaiḥ
prāyo vivṛkṇāvayavā vidudruvur
mṛgendra-vikrīḍita-yūthapā iva

hata-avaśiṣṭāḥ—the remaining soldiers who were not killed; *itare*—others; *raṇa-ajirāt*—from the battlefield; *rakṣaḥ-gaṇāḥ*—the Yakṣas; *kṣatriya-varya*—of the greatest of the *kṣatriyas* or warriors; *sāyakaiḥ*—by the arrows; *prāyaḥ*—mostly; *vivṛkṇa*—cut to pieces; *avayavāḥ*—their bodily limbs; *vidudruvuḥ*—fled; *mṛgendra*—by a lion; *vikrīḍita*—being defeated; *yūthapāḥ*—elephants; *iva*—like.

TRANSLATION

The remaining Yakṣas who somehow or other were not killed had their limbs cut to pieces by the arrows of the great warrior Dhruva Mahārāja. Thus they began to flee, just as elephants flee when defeated by a lion.

TEXT 21

अपश्यमानः स तदाऽऽततायिनं
महामृधे कंचन मानवोत्तमः ।
पुरीं दिदृक्षन्नपि नाविशद्द्विषां
न मायिनां वेद चिकीर्षितं जनः ॥२१॥

apaśyamānaḥ sa tadātatāyinaṁ
mahā-mṛdhe kañcana mānavottamaḥ
purīṁ didṛkṣann api nāviśad dviṣāṁ
na māyināṁ veda cikīrṣitaṁ janaḥ

apaśyamānaḥ—while not observing; *saḥ*—Dhruva; *tadā*—at that time; *ātatāyinam*—armed opposing soldier; *mahā-mṛdhe*—in that great battlefield; *kañcana*—any; *mānava-uttamaḥ*—the best of the human beings; *purīm*—the city; *didṛkṣan*—wishing to see; *api*—although; *na āviśat*—did not enter; *dviṣām*—of the enemies; *na*—not; *māyinām*—of the mystics; *veda*—knows; *cikīrṣitam*—the plans; *janaḥ*—anyone.

TRANSLATION

Dhruva Mahārāja, the best of human beings, observed that in that great battlefield not one of the opposing soldiers was left standing with proper weapons. He then desired to see the city of Alakāpurī, but he thought to himself, "No one knows the plans of the mystic Yakṣas."

TEXT 22

इति ब्रुवंश्चित्ररथः स्वसारथिं
यत्तः परेषां प्रतियोगशङ्कितः ।
शुश्राव शब्दं जलधेरिवेरितं
नभस्वतो दिक्षु रजोऽन्वदृश्यत ॥२२॥

iti bruvaṁś citra-rathaḥ sva-sārathiṁ
yattaḥ pareṣāṁ pratiyoga-śaṅkitaḥ
śuśrāva śabdaṁ jaladher iveritaṁ
nabhasvato dikṣu rajo 'nv adṛśyata

iti—thus; *bruvan*—talking; *citra-rathaḥ*—Dhruva Mahārāja, whose chariot was very beautiful; *sva-sārathim*—to his charioteer; *yattaḥ*—being on guard;

pareṣām—from his enemies; *pratiyoga*—counterattack; *śaṅkitaḥ*—being apprehensive; *śuśrāva*—heard; *śabdam*—sound; *jaladheḥ*—from the ocean; *iva*—as if; *īritam*—resounded; *nabhasvataḥ*—because of wind; *dikṣu*—in all directions; *rajaḥ*—dust; *anu*—then; *adṛśyata*—was perceived.

TRANSLATION

In the meantime, while Dhruva Mahārāja, doubtful of his mystic enemies, was talking with his charioteer, they heard a tremendous sound, as if the whole ocean were there, and they found that from the sky a great dust storm was coming over them from all directions.

TEXT 23

क्षणेनाच्छादितं व्योम घनानीकेन सर्वतः ।
विस्फुरत्तडिता दिक्षु त्रासयत्स्तनयित्नुना ॥२३॥

kṣaṇenācchāditaṁ vyoma
ghanānīkena sarvataḥ
visphurat-taḍitā dikṣu
trāsayat-stanayitnunā

kṣaṇena—within a moment; *ācchāditam*—was covered; *vyoma*—the sky; *ghana*—of dense clouds; *anīkena*—with a mass; *sarvataḥ*—everywhere; *visphurat*—dazzling; *taḍitā*—with lightning; *dikṣu*—in all directions; *trāsayat*—threatening; *stanayitnunā*—with thundering.

TRANSLATION

Within a moment the whole sky was overcast with dense clouds, and severe thundering was heard. There was glittering electric lightning and severe rainfall.

TEXT 24

ववृषू रुधिरौघासृक्पूयविण्मूत्रमेदसः ।
निपेतुर्गगनादस्य कबन्धान्यग्रतोऽनघ ॥२४॥

vavṛṣū rudhiraughāsṛk-
pūya-viṇ-mūtra-medasaḥ
nipetur gaganād asya
kabandhāny agrato 'nagha

vavṛṣuḥ—showered; *rudhira*—of blood; *ogha*—an inundation; *asṛk*—mucus; *pūya*—pus; *viṭ*—stool; *mūtra*—urine; *medasaḥ*—and marrow; *nipetuḥ*—began to fall; *gaganāt*—from the sky; *asya*—of Dhruva; *kabandhāni*—trunks of bodies; *agrataḥ*—in front; *anagha*—O faultless Vidura.

TRANSLATION

My dear faultless Vidura, in that rainfall there was blood, mucus, pus, stool, urine and marrow falling heavily before Dhruva Mahārāja, and there were trunks of bodies falling from the sky.

TEXT 25

ततः खेऽदृश्यत गिरिर्निपेतुः सर्वतोदिशम् ।
गदापरिघनिस्त्रिंशमुसलाः साश्मवर्षिणः ॥२५॥

tataḥ khe 'dṛśyata girir
nipetuḥ sarvato-diśam
gadā-parigha-nistriṁśa-
musalāḥ sāśma-varṣiṇaḥ

tataḥ—thereafter; *khe*—in the sky; *adṛśyata*—was visible; *giriḥ*—a mountain; *nipetuḥ*—fell down; *sarvataḥ-diśam*—from all directions; *gadā*—clubs; *parigha*—iron bludgeons; *nistriṁśa*—swords; *musalāḥ*—maces; *sāśma*—great pieces of stone; *varṣiṇaḥ*—with a shower of.

TRANSLATION

Next, a great mountain was visible in the sky, and from all directions hailstones fell, along with lances, clubs, swords, iron bludgeons and great pieces of stone.

TEXT 26

अहयोऽशनिनिःश्वासा वमन्तोऽग्निं रुषाक्षिभिः ।
अभ्यधावन् गजा मत्ताः सिंहव्याघ्राश्च यूथशः ॥२६॥

ahayo 'śani-niḥśvāsā
vamanto 'gniṁ ruṣākṣibhiḥ
abhyadhāvan gajā mattāḥ
siṁha-vyāghrāś ca yūthaśaḥ

ahayaḥ—serpents; *aśani*—thunderbolts; *niḥśvāsāḥ*—breathing; *vamantaḥ*—vomiting; *agnim*—fire; *ruṣā akṣibhiḥ*—with angry eyes; *abhyadhāvan*—came forward; *gajāḥ*—elephants; *mattāḥ*—mad; *siṁha*—lions; *vyāghrāḥ*—tigers; *ca*—also; *yūthaśaḥ*—in groups.

TRANSLATION

Dhruva Mahārāja also saw many big serpents with angry eyes, vomiting forth fire and coming to devour him, along with groups of mad elephants, lions and tigers.

TEXT 27

समुद्र ऊर्मिभिर्भीमः प्लावयन् सर्वतो भुवम् ।
आससाद महाह्रादः कल्पान्त इव भीषणः ॥२७॥

samudra ūrmibhir bhīmaḥ
plāvayan sarvato bhuvam
āsasāda mahā-hrādaḥ
kalpānta iva bhīṣaṇaḥ

samudraḥ—the sea; *ūrmibhiḥ*—with waves; *bhīmaḥ*—fierce; *plāvayan*—inundating; *sarvataḥ*—in all directions; *bhuvam*—the earth; *āsasāda*—came forward; *mahā-hrādaḥ*—making great sounds; *kalpa-ante*—(the dissolution) at the end of a *kalpa; iva*—like; *bhīṣaṇaḥ*—fearful.

TRANSLATION

Then, as if it were the time of the dissolution of the whole world, the fierce sea with foaming waves and great roaring sounds came forward before him.

TEXT 28

एवंविधान्यनेकानि त्रासनान्यमनस्विनाम् ।
ससृजुस्तिग्मगतय आसुर्या माययासुराः ॥२८॥

evaṁ vidhāny anekāni
trāsanāny amanasvinām
sasṛjus tigma-gataya
āsuryā māyayāsurāḥ

evam vidhāni—(phenomena) like this; *anekāni*—many varieties of; *trāsanāni*—fearful; *amanasvinām*—to the less intelligent men; *sasṛjuḥ*—they created; *tigma-gatayaḥ*—of heinous nature; *āsuryā*—demoniac; *māyayā*—by illusion; *asurāḥ*—the demons.

TRANSLATION

The demon Yakṣas are by nature very heinous, and by their demoniac power of illusion they can create many strange phenomena to frighten one who is less intelligent.

TEXT 29

ध्रुवे प्रयुक्तामसुरैस्तां मायामतिदुस्तराम् ।
निशम्य तस्य मुनयः शमाशंसन् समागताः ॥२९॥

dhruve prayuktām asurais
tāṁ māyām atidustarām
niśamya tasya munayaḥ
śam āśaṁsan samāgatāḥ

dhruve—against Dhruva; *prayuktām*—inflicted; *asuraiḥ*—by the demons; *tām*—that; *māyām*—mystic power; *atidustarām*—very dangerous; *niśamya*—after hearing; *tasya*—his; *munayaḥ*—the great sages; *śam*—good fortune; *āśaṁsan*—giving encouragement for; *samāgatāḥ*—assembled.

TRANSLATION

When the great sages heard that Dhruva Mahārāja was overpowered by the illusory mystic tricks of the demons, they immediately assembled to offer him auspicious encouragement.

TEXT 30

मुनय ऊचुः
औत्तानपाद भगवांस्तव शार्ङ्गधन्वा
देवः क्षिणोत्ववनतार्तिहरो विपक्षान् ।
यन्नामधेयमभिधाय निशम्य चाद्धा
लोकोऽञ्जसा तरति दुस्तरमङ्ग मृत्युम् ॥३०॥

munaya ūcuḥ
auttānapāda bhagavāṁs tava śārṅgadhanvā
devaḥ kṣiṇotv avanatārti-haro vipakṣān
yan-nāmadheyam abhidhāya niśamya cāddhā
loko 'ñjasā tarati dustaram aṅga mṛtyum

munayaḥ ūcuḥ—the sages said; *auttānapāda*—O son of King Uttānapāda; *bhagavān*—the Supreme Personality of Godhead; *tava*—your; *śārṅga-*

dhanvā—one who bears the bow called Śārṅga; *devaḥ*—the Lord; *kṣiṇotu*—may He kill; *avanata*—of the surrendered soul; *ārti*—the distresses; *haraḥ*—who removes; *vipakṣān*—enemies; *yat*—whose; *nāmadheyam*—holy name; *abhidhāya*—uttering; *niśamya*—hearing; *ca*—also; *addhā*—immediately; *lokaḥ*—persons; *añjasā*—fully; *tarati*—overcome; *dustaram*—insurmountable; *aṅga*—O Dhruva; *mṛtyum*—death.

TRANSLATION

All the sages said: Dear Dhruva, O son of King Uttānapāda, may the Supreme Personality of Godhead known as Śārṅgadhanus, who relieves the distresses of His devotees, kill all your threatening enemies. The holy name of the Lord is as powerful as the Lord Himself. Therefore, simply by chanting and hearing the holy name of the Lord, many men can be fully protected from fierce death without difficulty. Thus a devotee is saved.

PURPORT

The great *ṛṣis* approached Dhruva Mahārāja at a time when his mind was very perplexed due to the magical feats exhibited by the Yakṣas. A devotee is always protected by the Supreme Personality of Godhead. By His inspiration only the sages came to encourage Dhruva Mahārāja and assure him that there was no danger because he was a soul fully surrendered to the Supreme Lord. By the grace of the Lord, if a devotee can simply chant His holy name—Hare Kṛṣṇa, Hare Kṛṣṇa, Kṛṣṇa Kṛṣṇa, Hare Hare/ Hare Rāma, Hare Rāma, Rāma Rāma, Hare Hare—at the time of death, then he immediately surpasses the great ocean of the material sky and enters the spiritual sky. He never has to come back for repetition of birth and death. Simply by chanting the holy name of the Lord, one can surpass the ocean of death, so Dhruva Mahārāja was certainly able to surpass the illusory magical feats of the Yakṣas which for the time being disturbed his mind.

Thus end the Bhaktivedanta purports of the Fourth Canto, Tenth Chapter, of the Śrīmad-Bhāgavatam, *entitled "Dhruva Mahārāja's Fight with the Yakṣas."*

CHAPTER ELEVEN

Svāyambhuva Manu Advises Dhruva Mahārāja to Stop Fighting

TEXT 1

मैत्रेय उवाच
निशम्य गदतामेवमृषीणां धनुषि ध्रुवः ।
संदधेऽस्त्रमुपस्पृश्य यन्नारायणनिर्मितम् ॥ १ ॥

maitreya uvāca
niśamya gadatām evam
ṛṣīṇāṁ dhanuṣi dhruvaḥ
sandadhe 'stram upaspṛśya
yan nārāyaṇa-nirmitam

maitreyaḥ uvāca—the sage Maitreya continued to speak; *niśamya*—having heard; *gadatām*—the words; *evam*—thus; *ṛṣīṇām*—of the sages; *dhanuṣi*—upon his bow; *dhruvaḥ*—Dhruva Mahārāja; *sandadhe*—fixed; *astram*—an arrow; *upaspṛśya*—after touching water; *yat*—that which; *nārāyaṇa*—by Nārāyaṇa; *nirmitam*—was made.

TRANSLATION

Śrī Maitreya said: My dear Vidura, when Dhruva Mahārāja heard the encouraging words of the great sages, he performed the ācamana by touching water and then took up his arrow, which was made by Lord Nārāyaṇa, and fixed it upon his bow.

PURPORT

Dhruva Mahārāja was given a specific arrow made by Lord Nārāyaṇa Himself, and he now fixed it upon his bow to finish the illusory atmosphere created by the Yakṣas. As it is stated in the *Bhagavad-gītā, mām eva ye prapadyante māyām etāṁ taranti te.* (Bg. 7.14) Without Nārāyaṇa, the Supreme Personality of Godhead, no one is able to overcome the action of the illusory energy. Śrī Caitanya Mahāprabhu has also given us a nice weapon for this age, as stated in the *Bhāgavatam: sāṅgopāṅgāstra*—in this age, the Nārāyaṇāstra, or weapon to drive away *māyā*, is the chanting of the Hare Kṛṣṇa *mantra* in pursuance of the associates of Lord Caitanya, such as Advaita Prabhu, Nityānanda, Gadādhara and Śrīvāsa.

TEXT 2

संधीयमान एतस्मिन्माया गुह्यकनिर्मिताः ।
क्षिप्रं विनेशुर्विदुर क्लेशा ज्ञानोदये यथा ॥ २ ॥

sandhīyamāna etasmin
māyā guhyaka-nirmitāḥ
kṣipraṁ vineśur vidura
kleśā jñānodaye yathā

sandhīyamāne—while joining to his bow; *etasmin*—this Nārāyaṇāstra; *māyāḥ*—the illusions; *guhyaka-nirmitāḥ*—created by the Yakṣas; *kṣipram*—very soon; *vineśuḥ*—were destroyed; *vidura*—O Vidura; *kleśāḥ*—illusory pains and pleasures; *jñāna-udaye*—upon the arising of knowledge; *yathā*—just as.

TRANSLATION

As soon as Dhruva Mahārāja joined the Nārāyaṇāstra arrow to his bow, the illusion created by the Yakṣas was immediately vanquished, just as all material pains and pleasures are vanquished when one becomes fully cognizant of the self.

PURPORT

Kṛṣṇa is like the sun, and *māyā*, or the illusory energy of Kṛṣṇa, is like darkness. Darkness means absence of light; similarly, *māyā* means absence of Kṛṣṇa consciousness. Kṛṣṇa consciousness and *māyā* are always there, side by side. As soon as there is awakening of Kṛṣṇa consciousness, all the illusory pains and pleasures of material existence are vanquished. *Māyām etāṁ taranti te:* constant chanting of the *mahā-mantra* will keep us always aloof from the illusory energy of *māyā*.

TEXT 3

तस्यार्षास्त्रं धनुषि प्रयुञ्जतः
सुवर्णपुङ्खाः कलहंसवाससः ।

विनिःसृता आविविशुर्द्विषद्बलं
यथा वनं भीमरवाः शिखण्डिनः ॥ ३ ॥

tasyārṣāstraṁ dhanuṣi prayuñjataḥ
suvarṇa-puṅkhāḥ kalahaṁsa-vāsasaḥ
viniḥsṛtā āviviśur dviṣad-balaṁ
yathā vanaṁ bhīma-ravāḥ śikhaṇḍinaḥ

tasya—while Dhruva; *ārṣa-astram*—the weapon given by Nārāyaṇa Ṛṣi; *dhanuṣi*—on his bow; *prayuñjataḥ*—fixed; *suvarṇa-puṅkhāḥ*—(arrows) with golden shafts; *kalahaṁsa-vāsasaḥ*—with feathers like the wings of a swan; *viniḥsṛtāḥ*—sprang out; *āviviśuḥ*—entered; *dviṣat-balam*—the soldiers of the enemy; *yathā*—just as; *vanam*—into a forest; *bhīma-ravāḥ*—making a tumultuous sound; *śikhaṇḍinaḥ*—peacocks.

TRANSLATION

Even as Dhruva Mahārāja fixed the weapon made by Nārāyaṇa Ṛṣi onto his bow, arrows with golden shafts and feathers like the wings of a swan flew out from it. They entered the enemy soldiers with a great hissing sound, just as peacocks enter a forest with tumultuous crowing.

TEXT 4

तैस्तिग्मधारैः प्रधने शिलीमुखै-
रितस्ततः पुण्यजना उपद्रुताः ।
तमभ्यधावन् कुपिता उदायुधाः
सुपर्णमुन्नद्धफणा इवाहयः ॥ ४ ॥

tais tigma-dhāraiḥ pradhane śilī-mukhair
itas tataḥ puṇya-janā upadrutāḥ
tam abhyadhāvan kupitā udāyudhāḥ
suparṇam unnaddha-phaṇā ivāhayaḥ

taiḥ—by those; *tigma-dhāraiḥ*—which had a sharp point; *pradhane*—on the battlefield; *śilī-mukhaiḥ*—arrows; *itas tataḥ*—here and there; *puṇya-janāḥ*—the Yakṣas; *upadrutāḥ*—being greatly agitated; *tam*—toward Dhruva Mahārāja; *abhyadhāvan*—rushed; *kupitāḥ*—being angry; *udāyudhāḥ*—with upraised weapons; *suparṇam*—toward Garuḍa; *unnaddha-phaṇāḥ*—with upraised hoods; *iva*—like; *ahayaḥ*—serpents.

TRANSLATION

Those sharp arrows dismayed the enemy soldiers, who became almost unconscious, but various Yakṣas on the battlefield, in a rage against Dhruva Mahārāja, somehow or other collected their weapons and attacked. Just as serpents agitated by Garuḍa rush toward him with upraised hoods, so all the Yakṣa soldiers prepared to overcome Dhruva Mahārāja with their upraised weapons.

TEXT 5

स तान् पृषत्कैरभिधावतो मृधे
निकृत्तबाहूरुशिरोधरोदरान् ।
निनाय लोकं परमर्कमण्डलं
व्रजन्ति निर्भिद्य यमूर्ध्वरेतसः ॥ ५ ॥

sa tān pṛṣatkair abhidhāvato mṛdhe
nikṛtta-bāhūru-śirodharodarān
ināya lokaṁ param arka-maṇḍalaṁ
vrajanti nirbhidya yam ūrdhva-retasaḥ

saḥ—he (Dhruva Mahārāja); *tān*—all the Yakṣas; *pṛṣatkaiḥ*—by his arrows; *abhidhāvataḥ*—coming forward; *mṛdhe*—in the battlefield; *nikṛtta*—being separated; *bāhu*—arms; *ūru*—thighs; *śiraḥ-dhara*—necks; *udarān*—and bellies; *nināya*—delivered; *lokam*—to the planet; *param*—supreme; *arka-maṇḍalam*—the sun globe; *vrajanti*—go; *nirbhidya*—piercing; *yam*—to which; *ūrdhva-retasaḥ*—those who do not discharge semina at any time.

TRANSLATION

When Dhruva Mahārāja saw the Yakṣas coming forward, he immediately took his arrows and cut the enemies to pieces. Separating their arms, legs, heads and bellies from their bodies, he delivered the Yakṣas to the planetary system which is situated above the sun-globe and which is attainable only by first-class brahmacārīs who have never discharged their semina.

PURPORT

To be killed by the Lord or by His devotees is auspicious for non-devotees. The Yakṣas were killed indiscriminately by Dhruva Mahārāja, but they attained the planetary system which was only attainable for *brahmacārīs* who had never discharged their semina. As the impersonalist *jñānīs* or the demons who are killed by the Lord attain Brahmaloka, or Satyaloka, so persons who are killed by a devotee of the Lord also attain Satyaloka. To reach the Satyaloka planetary system described here, one has to be elevated above the sun globe. Killing, therefore, is not always bad. If the killing is done by the Supreme Personality of Godhead or His devotee or in great sacrifices, it is for the benefit of the entity killed in that way. Material so-called nonviolence is very insignificant in comparison to killing done by the Supreme Personality of Godhead or His devotees. Even when a king or the state government kills a person who is a murderer, that killing is for the benefit of the murderer, for thus he may become cleared of all sinful reactions.

An important word in this verse is *ūrdhva-retasaḥ,* which means *brahmacārīs* who have never discharged semina. Celibacy is so important that even though one does not undergo any austerities, penances or ritualistic ceremonies prescribed in the *Vedas*, if one simply keeps himself a pure *brahmacārī,* not discharging his semina, the result is that after death he goes to the Satyaloka. Generally, sex life is the cause of all miseries in the material world. In the Vedic civilization sex life is restricted in various ways. Out of the whole population of the social structure, only the *gṛhasthas* are allowed restricted sex life. All others refrain from sex. The people of this age especially do not know the value of not discharging semina. As such, they are variously entangled with material qualities and suffer an existence of struggle only. The word *ūrdhva-retasaḥ* especially indicates the Māyāvādī *sannyāsīs*, who undergo strict principles of austerity. But in the *Bhagavad-gītā* the Lord says that even if one goes up to Brahmaloka, he again comes back. (*Ābrahma-bhuvanāl lokāḥ punar āvartino 'rjuna.* Bg. 8.16) Therefore, actual *mukti* or liberation can be attained only by devotional service, because by devotional service one can go above Brahmaloka, or to the spiritual world, wherefrom he never comes back. Māyāvādī *sannyāsīs* are very proud of becoming liberated, but actual liberation is not possible unless one is in touch with the Supreme Lord in devotional service. It is said, *hariṁ vinā na sṛtiṁ taranti:* without Kṛṣṇa's mercy, no one can have liberation.

TEXT 6

तान् हन्यमानानभिवीक्ष्य गुह्यका-
ननागसश्चित्ररथेन भूरिशः ।
औत्तानपादिं कृपया पितामहो
मनुर्जगादोपगतः सहर्षिभिः ॥ ६ ॥

tān hanyamānān abhivīkṣya guhyakān
anāgasaś citra-rathena bhūriśaḥ
auttānapādiṁ kṛpayā pitāmaho
manur jagādopagataḥ saharṣibhiḥ

tān—those Yakṣas; *hanyamānān*—being killed; *abhivīkṣya*—seeing; *guhyakān*—the Yakṣas; *anāgasaḥ*—offenseless; *citra-rathena*—by Dhruva Mahārāja, who had a beautiful chariot; *bhūriśaḥ*—greatly; *auttānapādim*—unto the son of Uttānapāda; *kṛpayā*—out of mercy; *pitāmahaḥ*—the grandfather; *manuḥ*—Svāyambhuva Manu; *jagāda*—gave instructions; *upagataḥ*—approached; *saha ṛṣibhiḥ*—with great sages.

TRANSLATION

When Svāyambhuva Manu saw that his grandson Dhruva Mahārāja was killing so many of the Yakṣas who were not actually offenders, out of his great compassion he approached Dhruva with great sages to give him good instruction.

PURPORT

Dhruva Mahārāja attacked Alakāpurī, the city of the Yakṣas, because his brother was killed by one of them. Actually only one of the citizens, not all of them, was guilty of killing his brother Uttama. Dhruva Mahārāja, of course, took a very serious step when his brother was killed by the Yakṣas. War was declared, and the fighting was going on. This sometimes happens in present days also—for one man's fault a whole state is sometimes attacked. This kind of wholesale attack is not approved by Manu, the father and lawgiver of the human race. He therefore wanted to stop his grandson Dhruva from continuing to kill the Yakṣa citizens who were not offenders.

TEXT 7

मनुरुवाच
अलं वत्सातिरोषेण तमोद्वारेण पाप्मना ।
येन पुण्यजनानेतानवधीस्त्वमनागसः ॥ ७ ॥

manur uvāca
alaṁ vatsātiroṣeṇa
tamo-dvāreṇa pāpmanā
yena puṇya-janān etān
avadhīs tvam anāgasaḥ

manuḥ uvāca—Manu said; *alam*—enough; *vatsa*—my dear boy; *atiroṣeṇa*—with excessive anger; *tamaḥ-dvāreṇa*—the path of ignorance; *pāpmanā*—

sinful; *yena*—by which; *puṇya-janān*—the Yakṣas; *etān*—all these; *avadhīḥ*—you have killed; *tvam*—you; *anāgasaḥ*—offenseless.

TRANSLATION

Lord Manu said: My dear son, please stop. It is not good to become unnecessarily angry—it is the path to hellish life. Now you are going beyond the limit by killing Yakṣas who are actually not offenders.

PURPORT

In this verse the word *atiroṣeṇa* means "with unnecessary anger." When Dhruva Mahārāja went beyond the limits of necessary anger, his grandfather, Svāyambhuva Manu, immediately came to protect him from further sinful action. From this we can understand that killing is not bad, but when killing is done unnecessarily or when an offenseless person is killed, such killing opens the path to hell. Dhruva Mahārāja was saved from such sinful action because he was a great devotee.

A *kṣatriya* is allowed to kill only for maintenance of the law and order of the state; he is not allowed to kill or commit violence without reason. Violence is certainly a path leading to a hellish condition of life, but it is also required for maintenance of the law and order of the state. Here Lord Manu prohibited Dhruva Mahārāja from killing the Yakṣas because only one of them was punishable for killing his brother Uttama; all of the Yakṣa citizens were not punishable. We find in modern warfare, however, that attacks are made upon innocent citizens who are without fault. According to the law of Manu, such warfare is a most sinful activity. Furthermore, at the present moment civilized nations are unnecessarily maintaining many slaughterhouses for killing innocent animals. When a nation is attacked by its enemies, the wholesale slaughter of the citizens should be taken as a reaction to their own sinful activities—that is nature's law.

TEXT 8

नास्मत्कुलोचितं तात कर्मैतत्सद्विगर्हितम् ।
वधो यदुपदेवानामारब्धस्तेऽकृतैनसाम् ॥ ८ ॥

nāsmat-kulocitaṁ tāta
karmaitat sad-vigarhitam
vadho yad upadevānām
ārabdhas te 'kṛtainasām

na—not; *asmat-kula*—our family; *ucitam*—befitting; *tāta*—my dear son; *karma*—action; *etat*—this; *sat*—by authorities on religion; *vigarhitam*—forbidden; *vadhaḥ*—the killing; *yat*—which; *upadevānām*—of the Yakṣas; *ārabdhaḥ*—was undertaken; *te*—by you; *akṛta-enasām*—of those who are sinless.

TRANSLATION

My dear son, the killing of the sinless Yakṣas which you have undertaken is not at all approved by authorities, and it does not befit our family, which is supposed to know the laws of religion and irreligion.

TEXT 9

नन्वेकस्यापराधेन प्रसङ्गाद् बहवो हताः ।
भ्रातुर्वधाभितप्तेन त्वयाङ्ग भ्रातृवत्सल ॥ ९ ॥

nanv ekasyāparādhena
prasaṅgād bahavo hatāḥ
bhrātur vadhābhitaptena
tvayāṅga bhrātṛ-vatsala

nanu—certainly; *ekasya*—of one (Yakṣa); *aparādhena*—with the offense; *prasaṅgāt*—because of their association; *bahavaḥ*—many; *hatāḥ*—have been killed; *bhrātuḥ*—of your brother; *vadha*—by the death; *abhitaptena*—being aggrieved; *tvayā*—by you; *aṅga*—my dear son; *bhrātṛ-vatsala*—affectionate to your brother.

TRANSLATION

My dear son, it has been proved that you are very much affectionate towards your brother and are greatly aggrieved at his being killed by the Yakṣas, but just consider—for one Yakṣa's offense, you have killed many others, who are innocent.

TEXT 10

नायं मार्गो हि साधूनां हृषीकेशानुवर्तिनाम् ।
यदात्मानं पराग्गृह्य पशुवद्भूतवैशसम् ॥१०॥

nāyaṁ mārgo hi sādhūnāṁ
hṛṣīkeśānuvartinām
yad ātmānaṁ parāg gṛhya
paśuvad bhūta-vaiśasam

na—never; *ayam*—this; *mārgaḥ*—path; *hi*—certainly; *sādhūnām*—of honest persons; *hṛṣīkeśa*—of the Supreme Personality of Godhead; *anuvartinām*—

following the path; *yat*—which; *ātmānam*—self; *parāk*—the body; *gṛhya*—thinking to be; *paśu-vat*—like animals; *bhūta*—of living entities; *vaiśasam*—killing.

TRANSLATION

One should not accept the body as the self and thus, like the animals, kill the bodies of others. It is especially forbidden by saintly persons who follow the path of devotional service to the Supreme Personality of Godhead.

PURPORT

The words *sādhūnāṁ hṛṣīkeśānuvartinām* are very significant. *Sādhu* means a saintly person. But who is a saintly person? A saintly person is he who follows the path of rendering service unto the Supreme Personality of Godhead, Hṛṣīkeśa. In the *Nārada-pañcarātra* it is said, *hṛṣīkeṇa hṛṣīkeśa-sevanaṁ bhaktir ucyate:* the process of rendering favorable service to the Supreme Personality of Godhead with one's senses is called *bhakti,* or devotional service. Therefore, why should a person who is already engaged in the service of the Lord engage himself in personal sense gratification? Dhruva Mahārāja is advised here by Lord Manu that he is a pure servitor of the Lord. Why should he unnecessarily engage, like the animals, in the bodily concept of life? An animal thinks that the body of another animal is his food; therefore, in the bodily concept of life, one animal attacks another. A human being, especially one who is a devotee of the Lord, should not act like this. *Sādhu,* a saintly devotee, is not supposed to kill animals unnecessarily.

TEXT 11

सर्वभूतात्मभावेन भूतावासं हरिं भवान् ।
आराध्याप दुराराध्यं विष्णोस्तत्परमं पदम् ॥११॥

sarva-bhūtātma-bhāvena
bhūtāvāsaṁ hariṁ bhavān
ārādhyāpa durārādhyaṁ
viṣṇos tat paramaṁ padam

sarva-bhūta—in all living entities; *ātma*—upon the Supersoul; *bhāvena*—with meditation; *bhūta*—of all existence; *āvāsam*—the abode; *harim*—Lord Hari; *bhavān*—you; *ārādhya*—by worshiping; *āpa*—have achieved; *dur-ārādhyam*—very difficult to propitiate; *viṣṇoḥ*—of Lord Viṣṇu; *tat*—that; *paramam*—supreme; *padam*—situation.

TRANSLATION

It is very difficult to achieve the spiritual abode of Hari in the Vaikuṇṭha planets, but you are so fortunate that you are already destined to go to that abode by worshiping Him as the supreme abode of all living entities.

PURPORT

The material bodies of all living entities cannot exist unless sheltered by the spirit soul and the Supersoul. The spirit soul is dependent on the Supersoul, who is present even within the atom. Therefore, since anything material or spiritual is completely dependent on the Supreme Lord, the Supreme Lord is referred to here as *bhūtāvāsa*. Dhruva Mahārāja, as a *kṣatriya*, could have argued with his grandfather, Manu, when Manu requested him to stop fighting. But even though Dhruva could have argued that as a *kṣatriya* it was his duty to fight with the enemy, still he was informed that since every living entity is a residence of the Supreme Lord and can be considered a temple of the Lord, the unnecessary killing of any living entity is not permitted.

**स त्वं हरेरनुध्यातस्तत्पुंसामपि सम्मतः ।
कथं त्ववद्यं कृतवाननुशिक्षन् सतां व्रतम् ॥१२॥**

sa tvaṁ harer anudhyātas
tat-puṁsām api sammataḥ
kathaṁ tv avadyaṁ kṛtavān
anuśikṣan satāṁ vratam

saḥ—that person; *tvam*—you; *hareḥ*—by the Supreme Lord; *anudhyātaḥ*—being always remembered; *tat*—His; *puṁsām*—by the devotees; *api*—also; *sammataḥ*—esteemed; *katham*—why; *tu*—then; *avadyam*—abominable (act); *kṛtavān*—you have undertaken; *anuśikṣan*—setting the example; *satām*—of saintly persons; *vratam*—a vow.

TRANSLATION

Because you are a pure devotee of the Lord, the Lord is always thinking of you, and you are also recognized by all His confidential devotees. Your life is meant for exemplary behavior. I am, therefore, surprised—why have you undertaken such an abominable task?

PURPORT

Dhruva Mahārāja was a pure devotee and was accustomed to always thinking of the Lord. Reciprocally, the Lord always thinks of those pure devotees who think of Him only, twenty-four hours a day. As a pure devotee does not know anything beyond the Lord, so the Lord does not know anything beyond His pure devotee. Svāyambhuva Manu pointed out this fact to Dhruva Mahārāja: "You are not only a pure devotee, but you are recognized by all pure devotees of the Lord. You should always act in such an exemplary way that others may learn from you. Under the circumstances, it is surprising that you have killed so many faultless Yakṣas."

TEXT 13

तितिक्षया करुणया मैत्र्या चाखिलजन्तुषु ।
समत्वेन च सर्वात्मा भगवान् सम्प्रसीदति ॥१३॥

titikṣayā karuṇayā
maitryā cākhila-jantuṣu
samatvena ca sarvātmā
bhagavān samprasīdati

titikṣayā—by tolerance; *karuṇayā*—by mercy; *maitryā*—by friendship; *ca*—also; *akhila*—universal; *jantuṣu*—unto the living entities; *samatvena*—by equilibrium; *ca*—also; *sarva-ātmā*—the Supersoul; *bhagavān*—Personality of Godhead; *samprasīdati*—becomes very satisfied.

TRANSLATION

The Lord is very satisfied with His devotee when the devotee greets other people with tolerance, mercy, friendship and equality.

PURPORT

It is the duty of an advanced devotee in the second stage of devotional perfection to act in accordance with this verse. There are three stages of devotional life. In the lowest stage, a devotee is simply concerned with the Deity in the temple, and he worships the Lord with great devotion, according to rules and regulations. In the second stage the devotee is cognizant of his relationship with the Lord, his relationship with fellow devotees, his relationship with persons who are innocent and his relationship with persons who are envious. Sometimes devotees are ill-treated by envious persons. It is advised that an advanced devotee should be tolerant; he should show complete mercy to persons who are ignorant or innocent. A preacher-devotee is meant to show mercy to innocent persons whom he can elevate to devotional service. Everyone, by constitutional position, is an eternal servant of God. Therefore, a devotee's business is to awaken everyone's Kṛṣṇa consciousness. That is his mercy. As for a devotee's treatment of other devotees who are his equals, he should maintain friendship with them. His general view should be to see every living entity as part of the Supreme Lord. Different living entities appear in different forms of dress, but according to the instruction of the *Bhagavad-gītā,* a learned person sees all living entities equally. Such treatment by the devotee is very much appreciated by the Supreme Lord. It is said, therefore, that a saintly person is always tolerant and merciful, he is a friend for everyone, never an enemy to anyone, and is peaceful. These are some of the good qualities of a devotee.

TEXT 14

सम्प्रसन्ने भगवति पुरुषः प्राकृतैर्गुणैः ।
विमुक्तो जीवनिर्मुक्तो ब्रह्म निर्वाणमृच्छति ॥१४॥

samprasanne bhagavati
puruṣaḥ prākṛtair guṇaiḥ
vimukto jīva-nirmukto
brahma nirvāṇam ṛcchati

samprasanne—upon satisfaction; *bhagavati*—of the Supreme Personality of Godhead; *puruṣaḥ*—a person; *prākṛtaiḥ*—from the material; *guṇaiḥ*—modes of nature; *vimuktaḥ*—being liberated; *jīva-nirmuktaḥ*—freed from the subtle body also; *brahma*—unlimited; *nirvāṇam*—spiritual bliss; *ṛcchati*—achieves.

TRANSLATION

One who actually satisfies the Supreme Personality of Godhead during his lifetime becomes liberated from the gross and subtle material conditions. Thus being freed from all material modes of nature, he achieves unlimited spiritual bliss.

PURPORT

In the previous verse it has been explained that one should treat all living entities with tolerance, mercy, friendship and equality. By such behavior one satisfies the Supreme Personality of Godhead, and upon His satisfaction the devotee immediately becomes free from all material conditions. The Lord also confirms this in the *Bhagavad-gītā*: "Anyone who sincerely and seriously engages in My service immediately becomes situated in the transcendental stage wherein he can enjoy unlimited spiritual bliss." Everyone in this material world is struggling hard in order to achieve blissful life. Unfortunately, people do not know how to achieve it. Atheists do not believe in God, and certainly they do not please Him. Here it is clearly said that upon pleasing the Supreme Personality of Godhead one immediately attains to the spiritual platform and enjoys unlimited blissful life. To become free from material existence means to become free from the influence of material nature.

The word *samprasanne,* which is used in this verse, means "being satisfied." A person should act in such a way that the Lord is satisfied by the activity; it is not that he himself is to be satisfied. Of course, when the Lord is satisfied, the devotee automatically becomes satisfied. This is the secret of the process of *bhakti-yoga.* Outside of *bhakti-yoga,* everyone is trying to satisfy himself. No one is trying to satisfy the Lord. *Karmīs* grossly try to satisfy their senses, but even those who are elevated on the platform of knowledge also try to satisfy themselves, in a subtle form. *Karmīs* try to satisfy themselves by sense gratification, and *jñānīs* try to satisfy themselves by subtle activities or mental speculation and thinking themselves to be God. *Yogīs* also try to satisfy themselves by thinking that they can achieve different mystic perfections. But only devotees try to satisfy the Supreme Personality of Godhead. The devotees' process of self-realization is completely different from the processes of the *karmīs, jñānīs* and *yogīs.* Everyone else is trying to satisfy himself, whereas the devotee tries only to satisfy the Lord. The devotional process is completely different from the others; by working to please the Lord by engaging his senses in His loving service, the devotee is immediately situated on the transcendental platform, and he enjoys unlimited blissful life.

TEXT 15

भूतैः पञ्चभिरारब्धैर्योषित्पुरुष एव हि ।
तयोर्व्यवायात्सम्भूतिर्योषित्पुरुषयोरिह ॥१५॥

bhūtaiḥ pañcabhir ārabdhair
yoṣit puruṣa eva hi
tayor vyavāyāt sambhūtir
yoṣit-puruṣayor iha

bhūtaiḥ—by the material elements; *pañcabhiḥ*—five; *ārabdhaiḥ*—developed; *yoṣit*—woman; *puruṣaḥ*—man; *eva*—just so; *hi*—certainly; *tayoḥ*—of them; *vyavāyāt*—by sexual life; *sambhūtiḥ*—the further creation; *yoṣit*—of women; *puruṣayoḥ*—and of men; *iha*—in this material world.

TRANSLATION

The creation of the material world begins with the five elements, and thus everything, including the body of a man or a woman, is created of the five elements. By the sexual life of a man and woman, the number of men and women in this material world is further increased.

PURPORT

When Svāyambhuva Manu saw that Dhruva Mahārāja understood the philosophy of Vaiṣṇavism, and yet was still dissatisfied because of his brother's death, he gave him an explanation of how this material body is created by the five elements of material nature. In the *Bhagavad-gītā* it is also confirmed, *prakṛteḥ kriyamāṇāni:* everything is created, maintained and annihilated by the material modes of nature. In the background, of course, there is the direction of the Supreme Personality of Godhead. This is also confirmed in the *Bhagavad-gītā (mayādhyakṣeṇa).* In the Ninth Chapter, Kṛṣṇa says, "Under My superintendence material nature is acting." Svāyambhuva Manu wanted to impress on Dhruva Mahārāja that the death of the material body of his brother was not actually the Yakṣas' fault; it was an action of the material nature. The Supreme Personality of Godhead has immense varieties of potencies, and they act in different gross and subtle ways.

It is by such powerful potencies that the universe is created, although grossly it appears to be no more than the five elements—earth, water, fire, air and ether. Similarly, the bodies of all species of living entities, whether human beings or demigods, animals or birds, are also created by the same five elements, and by sexual union they expand into more and more living entities. That is the way of creation, maintenance and annihilation. One should not be disturbed by the waves of material nature in this process. Dhruva Mahārāja was indirectly advised not to be afflicted by the death of his brother because our relationship with the body is completely material. The real self, spirit soul, is never annihilated or killed by anyone.

TEXT 16

एवं प्रवर्तते सर्गः स्थितिः संयम एव च ।
गुणव्यतिकराद्राजन् मायया परमात्मनः ॥१६॥

evaṁ pravartate sargaḥ
sthitiḥ saṁyama eva ca
guṇa-vyatikarād rājan
māyayā paramātmanaḥ

evam—thus; *pravartate*—occurs; *sargaḥ*—creation; *sthitiḥ*—maintenance; *saṁyamaḥ*—annihilation; *eva*—certainly; *ca*—and; *guṇa*—of the modes; *vyatikarāt*—by interaction; *rājan*—O King; *māyayā*—by the illusory energy; *paramātmanaḥ*—of the Supreme Personality of Godhead.

TRANSLATION

Manu continued: My dear King Dhruva, it is simply by the illusory material energy of the Supreme Personality of Godhead and by the interaction of the three modes of material nature that creation, maintenance and annihilation take place.

PURPORT

First, creation takes place with the ingredients of the five elements of material nature. Then, by the interaction of the modes of material nature, maintenance also takes place. When a child is born, the parents immediately see to its maintenance. This tendency for maintenance of offspring is present not only in human society, but in animal society as well. Even tigers care for their cubs, although their propensity is to eat other animals. By the interaction of the material modes of nature, creation, maintenance and also annihilation take place inevitably. But at the same time we should know that all is conducted under the superintendence of the Supreme Personality of Godhead. Everything is going on under that process. Creation is the action of the *rajo-guṇa,* the mode of passion; maintenance is the action of *sattva-guṇa,* the mode of goodness; and annihilation is the action of *tamo-guṇa,* the mode of ignorance. We can see that those who are situated in the mode of goodness live longer than those who are situated in the *tamo-guṇa* or *rajo-guṇa*. In other words, if one is elevated to the mode of goodness, he is elevated to a higher planetary system where the duration of life is very great. *Ūrdhvaṁ gacchanti sattva-sthāḥ:* Great *ṛṣis,* sages and *sannyāsīs* who maintain themselves in *sattva-guṇa,* or the mode of material goodness, are elevated to a higher planetary system. Those who are transcendental even to the material modes of nature are situated in the mode of pure goodness; they attain eternal life in the spiritual world.

TEXT 17

निमित्तमात्रं तत्रासीन्निर्गुणः पुरुषर्षभः ।
व्यक्ताव्यक्तमिदं विश्वं यत्र भ्रमति लोहवत् ॥१७॥

nimitta-mātraṁ tatrāsīn
nirguṇaḥ puruṣarṣabhaḥ
vyaktāvyaktam idaṁ viśvaṁ
yatra bhramati lohavat

nimitta-mātram—remote cause; *tatra*—then; *āsīt*—was; *nirguṇaḥ*—uncontaminated; *puruṣa-ṛṣabhaḥ*—the Supreme Person; *vyakta*—manifested; *avyaktam*—unmanifested; *idam*—this; *viśvam*—world; *yatra*—where; *bhramati*—moves; *loha-vat*—like iron.

TRANSLATION

My dear Dhruva, the Supreme Personality of Godhead is uncontaminated by the material modes of nature. He is the remote cause of the creation of this material cosmic manifestation. When He gives the impetus, many other causes and effects are produced, and thus the whole universe moves, just as iron moves by the integrated force of a magnet.

PURPORT

How the external energy of the Supreme Personality of Godhead works within this material world is explained in this verse. Everything is happening by the energy of the Supreme Lord. The atheistic philosophers who do not agree to accept the Supreme Personality of Godhead as the original cause of creation think that the material world moves by the action and reaction of different material elements. A simple example of the interaction of elements occurs when we mix soda and acid and the movement of effervescence is produced. But one cannot produce life by such interaction of chemicals. There are 8,400,000 different species of life, with different wishes and different actions. How the material force is working cannot be explained just on the basis of chemical reaction. A suitable example in this connection is that of the potter and the potter's wheel. The potter's wheel rotates, and several varieties of earthen pots come out. There are many causes for the earthen pots, but the original cause is the potter who sets a force on the wheel. That force comes by his superintendence. The same idea is explained in *Bhagavad-gītā*—behind all material action and reaction there is Kṛṣṇa, the Supreme Personality of Godhead. Kṛṣṇa says that everything depends on His energy and yet He is not everywhere. The pot is produced under certain conditions of action and reaction of material energy, but the potter is not in the pot. In a similar way, the material creation is set up by the Lord, but He remains aloof. As stated in the *Vedas*, He simply glanced over it, and the agitation of matter immediately began.

In *Bhagavad-gītā* it is also said that the Lord impregnates the material energy with the part and parcel *jīvas*, and thus the different forms and different activities immediately ensue. Because of the different desires and karmic activities of the *jīva* soul, different types of bodies in different species are produced. In Darwin's theory there is no acceptance of the living entity as spirit soul, and therefore his explanation of evolution is incomplete. Varieties of phenomena occur within this universe on account of the action and reaction of the three material modes, but the original creator, or the cause, is the Supreme Personality of Godhead, who is mentioned here as *nimitta-mātram,* the remote cause. He simply pushes the wheel with His energy. According to the Māyāvādī philosophers, the Supreme Brahman has transformed Himself into many varieties of forms, but that is not the fact. He is always transcendental to the action and reaction of the material *guṇas*, although He is the cause of all causes. Lord Brahmā says, therefore, in the *Brahma-saṁhitā: īśvaraḥ paramaḥ kṛṣṇaḥ sac-cid-ānanda-vigrahaḥ/ anādir ādir govindaḥ sarva-kāraṇa-kāraṇam.* There are many causes and effects, but the original cause is Śrī Kṛṣṇa.

TEXT 18

स खल्विदं भगवान् कालशक्त्या
गुणप्रवाहेण विभक्तवीर्यः ।
करोत्यकर्तैव निहन्त्यहन्ता
चेष्टा विभूम्नः खलु दुर्विभाव्या ॥१८॥

sa khalv idaṁ bhagavān kāla-śaktyā
guṇa-pravāheṇa vibhakta-vīryaḥ
karoty akartaiva nihanty ahantā
ceṣṭā vibhūmnaḥ khalu durvibhāvyā

saḥ—the; *khalu*—however; *idam*—this (universe); *bhagavān*—Personality of Godhead; *kāla*—of time; *śaktyā*—by the force; *guṇa-pravāheṇa*—by the interaction of the modes of nature; *vibhakta*—divided; *vīryaḥ*—(whose) potencies; *karoti*—acts upon; *akartā*—the non-doer; *eva*—although; *nihanti*—kills; *ahantā*—non-killer; *ceṣṭā*—the energy; *vibhūmnaḥ*—of the Lord; *khalu*—certainly; *durvibhāvyā*—inconceivable.

TRANSLATION

The Supreme Personality of Godhead, by His inconceivable supreme energy, time, causes the interaction of the three modes of material nature, and thus varieties of energy become manifest. It appears that He is acting, but He is not the actor. He is killing, but He is not the killer. Thus it is understood that only by His inconceivable power is everything happening.

PURPORT

The word *durvibhāvyā* means inconceivable by our tiny brain, and *vibhakta-vīryaḥ* means divided in varieties of potencies. This is the right explanation of the display of creative energies in the material world. We can better understand the mercy of God by an example: a government state is always supposed to be merciful, but sometimes, in order to keep law and order, the government employs its police force, and thus punishment is meted out to the rebellious citizens. Similarly, the Supreme Personality of Godhead is always merciful and full of transcendental qualities, but certain individual souls have forgotten their relationship with Kṛṣṇa and have endeavored to lord it over material nature. As a result of their endeavor, they are involved in varieties of material interaction. It is incorrect to argue, however, that because energy issues from the Supreme Personality of Godhead, He is therefore the actor. In the previous verse, the word *nimitta-mātram* indicates that the Supreme Lord is completely aloof from the action and reaction of this material world. How is everything being done? The word "inconceivable" has been used. It is not within the power of one's small brain to comprehend; unless one accepts the inconceivable power and energy of the Lord, one cannot make any progress. The forces which act are certainly set up by the Supreme Personality of Godhead, but He is always aloof from their action and reaction. The varieties of energies produced by the interaction of material nature produce the varieties of species of life and their resultant happiness and unhappiness.

How the Lord acts is nicely explained in *Viṣṇu Purāṇa:* fire is situated in one place, while the heat and light produced by the fire act in many different ways. Another example given is that the electric powerhouse is situated in one place, but by its energies many different types of machinery move. The production is never identical with the original source of the energy, but the original source of energy, being the prime factor, is simultaneously one and different from the product. Therefore, Lord Caitanya's philosophy, *acintya-bhedābheda-tattva,* is the perfect way of understanding. In this material world, the Lord incarnates in three forms—as Brahmā, Viṣṇu and Śiva—by which He takes charge of the three modes of material nature. By His incarnation of Brahmā He creates, as the incarnation of Viṣṇu He maintains, and by His incarnation of Śiva, He also annihilates. But the original source of Brahmā, Viṣṇu and Śiva—Garbhodakaśāyī Viṣṇu—is always apart from these actions and reactions of material nature.

TEXT 19

सोऽनन्तोऽन्तकरः कालोऽनादिरादिकृदव्ययः।
जनं जनेन जनयन्मारयन्मृत्युनान्तकम् ॥१९॥

so 'nanto 'nta-karaḥ kālo
'nādir ādi-kṛd avyayaḥ
janaṁ janena janayan
mārayan mṛtyunāntakam

saḥ—He; *anantaḥ*—infinite; *anta-karaḥ*—annihilator; *kālaḥ*—time; *anādiḥ*—without beginning; *ādi-kṛt*—beginning of everything; *avyayaḥ*—without decrease; *janam*—living entities; *janena*—by living entities; *janayan*—causing to be born; *mārayan*—killing; *mṛtyunā*—by death; *anta-kam*—killers.

TRANSLATION

My dear Dhruva, the Supreme Personality of Godhead is ever existing. In the form of time, He is the killer of everything. He has no beginning, although He is the beginning of everything, nor is He ever exhaustible, although everything is exhausted in due course of time. The living entities are created through the agency of the father, and they are killed through the agency of death, but He is perpetually free of birth and death.

PURPORT

The supreme authority and inconceivable power of the Supreme Personality of Godhead can be minutely studied from this verse. He is always unlimited. That means that He has no creation or end. He is, however, death (in the form of time), as described in *Bhagavad-gītā*. Kṛṣṇa says, "I am death. I take away everything at the end of life." Eternal time is also without beginning, but it is the creator of all creatures. The example is given of touchstone, which creates many valuable stones and jewels but does not decrease in power. Similarly, creation occurs many times, everything is maintained, and, after a time, everything is annihilated—but the original creator, the Supreme Lord, remains untouched and undiminished in power. The secondary creation is made by Brahmā, but Brahmā is created by the Supreme Godhead. Lord Śiva annihilates the whole creation, but at the end he is also annihilated by Viṣṇu. Lord Viṣṇu remains. In the Vedic hymns it is stated that in the beginning there is only Viṣṇu and that He alone remains at the end.

An example can help us to understand the inconceivable potency of the Supreme Lord. In the recent history of warfare the Supreme Personality of Godhead created a Hitler and, before that, a Napoleon Bonaparte, and they each killed many living entities in war. But in the end Bonaparte and Hitler were also killed. People are still very much interested in writing and reading books about Hitler and Bonaparte and how they killed so many people in war. Year after year many books are published for public reading regarding Hitler's killing thousands of Jews in confinement. But no one is researching who killed Hitler and who created such a gigantic killer of human beings. The devotees of the Lord are not much interested in the study of the flickering history of the world. They are interested only in He who is the original creator, maintainer and annihilator. That is the purpose of the Kṛṣṇa consciousness movement.

TEXT 20

न वै स्वपक्षोऽस्य विपक्ष एव वा
परस्य मृत्योर्विशतः समं प्रजाः ।
तं धावमानमनुधावन्त्यनीशा
यथा रजांस्यनिलं भूतसङ्घाः ॥२०॥

na vai sva-pakṣo 'sya vipakṣa eva vā
parasya mṛtyor viśataḥ samaṁ prajāḥ
taṁ dhāvamānam anu dhāvanty anīśā
yathā rajāṁsy anilaṁ bhūta-saṅghāḥ

na—not; *vai*—however; *sva-pakṣaḥ*—ally; *asya*—of the Supreme Personality of Godhead; *vipakṣaḥ*—enemy; *eva*—certainly; *vā*—or; *parasya*—of the Supreme; *mṛtyoḥ*—in the form of time; *viśataḥ*—entering; *samam*—equally; *prajāḥ*—living entities; *tam*—Him; *dhāvamānam*—moving; *anu dhāvanti*—

follow behind; *anīśāḥ*—dependent living entities; *yathā*—as; *rajāṁsi*—particles of dust; *anilam*—the wind; *bhūta-saṅghāḥ*—other material elements.

TRANSLATION

The Supreme Personality of Godhead, in His feature of eternal time, is present in the material world and is neutral towards everyone. No one is His ally, and no one is His enemy. Within the jurisdiction of the time element, everyone enjoys or suffers the result of his own karma, or fruitive activities. As, when the wind blows, small particles of dust fly in the air, so, according to one's particular karma, one suffers or enjoys material life.

PURPORT

Although the Supreme Personality of Godhead is the original cause of all causes, He is not responsible for anyone's material sufferings or enjoyment. There is no such partiality on the part of the Supreme Lord. The less intelligent accuse the Supreme Lord of being partial and claim that this is why one enjoys in this material world and another suffers. But this verse specifically says that there is no such partiality on the part of the Supreme Lord. Living entities, however, are never independent. As soon as they declare their independence of the supreme controller, they are immediately put into this material world to try their luck freely, as far as possible. When the material world is created for such misguided living entities, they create their own *karma*, fruitive activities, and take advantage of the time elements, and thereby they create their own fortune or misfortune. Everyone is created, everyone is maintained, and everyone is ultimately killed. As far as these three things are concerned, the Lord is equal to everyone, it is according to his *karma* that a person suffers and enjoys. The living entity's higher or lower position, his suffering and enjoying, are due to his own *karma*. The exact word used in this connection is *anīśāḥ*, which means "dependent on their own *karma.*" The example is given that the government gives everyone the facilities for governmental action and management, but by one's own choice he creates a situation which obliges him to exist under different types of consciousness. The example given in this verse is that when the wind blows, particles of dust float in the air. Gradually lightning occurs, and then torrents of rain follow, and thus the rainy season creates a situation of varieties in the forest. God is very kind—He gives everyone an equal chance—but by the resultant actions of one's own *karma* he suffers or enjoys this material world.

TEXT 21

आयुषोऽपचयं जन्तोस्तथैवोपचयं विभुः ।
उभाभ्यां रहितः स्वस्थो दुःस्थस्य विदधात्यसौ ॥२१॥

āyuṣo 'pacayaṁ jantos
tathaivopacayaṁ vibhuḥ
ubhābhyāṁ rahitaḥ sva-stho
duḥsthasya vidadhāty asau

āyuṣaḥ—of duration of life; *apacayam*—diminution; *jantoḥ*—of the living entities; *tathā*—similarly; *eva*—also; *upacayam*—increase; *vibhuḥ*—the Supreme Personality of Godhead; *ubhābhyām*—from both of them; *rahitaḥ*—free; *sva-sthaḥ*—always situated in His transcendental position; *duḥsthasya*—of the living entities under the laws of *karma; vidadhāti*—awards; *asau*—He.

TRANSLATION

The Supreme Personality of Godhead, Viṣṇu, is all-powerful, and He awards the results of one's fruitive activities. Thus, although one living entity's duration of life is very small whereas that of another is very great, He is always in His transcendental position, and there is no question of lessening or increasing His duration of life.

PURPORT

Both the mosquito and Lord Brahmā are living entities in the material world; both are minute sparks and are part of the Supreme Lord. The very short duration of life of the mosquito and the very long lifetime of Lord Brahmā are both awarded by the Supreme Personality of Godhead according to the results of their *karma*. But in the *Brahma-saṁhitā* we find it said, *karmāṇi nirdahati:* the Lord diminishes or vanquishes the reactions of devotees. The same fact is explained in *Bhagavad-gītā, yajñārthāt karmaṇo 'nyatra:* one should perform *karma* only for the purpose of satisfying the Supreme Lord, otherwise one is bound by the action and reaction of *karma*. Under the laws of *karma* a living entity wanders within the universe under the rule of eternal time, and sometimes he becomes a mosquito and sometimes Lord Brahmā. To a sane man this business is not very fruitful. *Bhagavad-gītā* (9.25) gives a warning to the living entities: *yānti deva-vratā devān*—those who are addicted to the worship of the demigods go to the planets of the demigods, and those who are addicted to worship of the *pitās*, forefathers, go to the *pitās*. Those who are inclined to material activities remain in the material sphere. But persons who engage in devotional service reach the abode of the Supreme Personality of Godhead, where there is neither birth nor death nor different varieties of life under the influence of the law of *karma.* The best interest of the living entity is to engage himself in devotional service and go back home, back to Godhead. Śrīla Bhaktivinoda Ṭhākura advised: "My friend, you are being washed away in material nature's waves of time. Please try to understand that you are the eternal servant of the Lord. Then everything will stop, and you will be eternally happy."

TEXT 22

केचित्कर्म वदन्त्येनं स्वभावमपरे नृप ।
एके कालं परे दैवं पुंसः काममुतापरे ॥२२॥

kecit karma vadanty enaṁ
svabhāvam apare nṛpa
eke kālaṁ pare daivaṁ
puṁsaḥ kāmam utāpare

kecit—some; *karma*—fruitive activities; *vadanti*—explain; *enam*—that; *svabhāvam*—nature; *apare*—others; *nṛpa*—my dear King Dhruva; *eke*—some; *kālam*—time; *pare*—others; *daivam*—fate; *puṁsaḥ*—of the living entity; *kāmam*—desire; *uta*—also; *apare*—others.

TRANSLATION

The differentiation among varieties of life and their suffering and enjoyment is explained by some to be the result of karma. Others say it is due to nature, others due to time, others due to fate, and still others say that it is due to desire.

PURPORT

There are different types of philosophers—*mīmāṁsakas*, atheists, astronomers, sexualists and so many other classifications of mental speculators. The real conclusion is that it is our work only that binds us within this material world in different varieties of life. How these varieties have sprung up is explained in the *Vedas*: it is due to the desire of the living entity. The living entity is not a dead stone; he has different varieties of desire, or *kāma.* The *Vedas* say, *kāmo 'kārṣīt.* The living entities are originally parts of the Lord, like sparks of a fire, but they have dropped to this material world, attracted by a desire to lord it over nature. That is a fact. Every living entity is trying to lord it over the material resources to the best of his ability.

This *kāma*, or desire, cannot be annihilated. There are some philosophers who say that if one gives up his desires, he again becomes liberated. But it is not at all possible to give up desire because desire is a symptom of the living entity. If there were no desire, then the living entity would be a dead stone. Śrīla Narottama dāsa Ṭhākura, therefore, advises that one turn his desire to serve the Supreme Personality of Godhead. Then desire becomes purified. And when one's desires are purified, he becomes liberated from all material contamination. The conclusion is that the different philosophers' theories to explain the varieties of life and their pleasure and pain are all imperfect. The real explanation is that we are eternal servants of God and that as soon as we forget this relationship, we are thrown into the material world, where we create our different activities and suffer or enjoy the result. We are drawn in this material world by desire, but the same desire must be purified and employed in the devotional service of the Lord. Then our disease of wandering in the universe under different forms and conditions will end.

TEXT 23

अव्यक्तस्याप्रमेयस्य नानाशक्त्युदयस्य च ।
न वै चिकीर्षितं तात को वेदाथ स्वसम्भवम् ॥२३॥

avyaktasyāprameyasya
nānā-śakty-udayasya ca
na vai cikīrṣitaṁ tāta
ko vedātha sva-sambhavam

avyaktasya—of the unmanifested; *aprameyasya*—of the Transcendence; *nānā*—various; *śakti*—energies; *udayasya*—of He who gives rise to; *ca*—also; *na*—never; *vai*—certainly; *cikīrṣitam*—the plan; *tāta*—my dear boy; *kaḥ*—who; *veda*—can know; *atha*—therefore; *sva*—own; *sambhavam*—origin.

TRANSLATION

The Absolute Truth, Transcendence, is never subjected to the understanding of imperfect sense endeavor, nor is He subject to direct experience. He is the master of varieties of energies, like the full material energy, and no one can understand His plans or actions; therefore it should be concluded that although He is the original cause of all causes, no one can know Him by mental speculation.

PURPORT

The question may be raised, "Since there are so many varieties of philosophers theorizing in different ways, which of them is correct?" The answer is that the Absolute Truth, Transcendence, is never subject to direct experience or mental speculation. The mental speculator may be called Dr. Frog. The story is that a frog in a three-foot well wanted to calculate the length and breadth of the Atlantic Ocean on the basis of his knowledge of his own well. But it was an impossible task for Dr. Frog. A person may be a great academician, scholar or professor, but he cannot speculate and expect to understand the Absolute Truth because his senses are limited. The cause of all causes, the Absolute Truth, can be known from the Absolute Truth Himself, and not by our ascending process to reach Him. When the sun is not visible at night or when it is covered by a cloud in the day, it is not possible to uncover it, either by bodily or mental strength or by scientific instruments, although the sun is there in the sky. No one can say that he has discovered a torchlight so powerful that if one goes on a roof and focuses the torchlight on the night sky, the sun will then be seen. There is no such torchlight, nor is it possible.

The word *avyakta*, unmanifested, in this verse indicates that the Absolute Truth cannot be manifested by any strain of so-called scientific advancement of knowledge. Transcendence is not the subject matter of direct experience. The Absolute Truth may be known in the same way as the sun covered by a cloud or covered by night, for when the sun rises in the morning, in its own way, then everyone can see the sun, everyone can see the world, and everyone can see himself. This understanding of self-realization is called *ātma-tattva.* Unless, however, one comes to this point of understanding *ātma-tattva,* one remains in the darkness in which he was born. Under the circumstances, no one can understand the plan of the Supreme Personality of Godhead. The Lord is equipped with varieties of energies, as stated in the Vedic literature (*parāsya śaktir vividhaiva śrūyate*). He is equipped with the energy of eternal time. He has not only the material energy which we see and experience, but He has also many reserve energies that He can manifest in due course of time when necessary. The material scientist can simply study the partial understanding of the varieties of energies; he can take up one of the energies and try to understand it with limited knowledge, but still it is not possible to understand the Absolute Truth in full by dint of material science. No material scientist can foretell what is going to happen in the future. The *bhakti-yoga* process is, however, completely different from so-called scientific advancement of knowledge.

A devotee completely surrenders unto the Supreme, and He reveals Himself by His causeless mercy. As stated in *Bhagavad-gītā, dadāmi buddhi-yogaṁ tam*. The Lord says, "I give him intelligence." What is that intelligence? *Yena mām upayānti te*. He gives him the intelligence to cross over the ocean of nescience and come back home, back to Godhead. In conclusion, the cause of all causes, the Absolute Truth or Supreme Brahman, cannot be understood by philosophical speculation, but He reveals Himself to His devotee because the devotee fully surrenders unto His lotus feet. *Bhagavad-gītā* is therefore to be accepted as a revealed scripture spoken by the Absolute Truth Himself when He descended to this planet. If any intelligent man wants to know what God is, he should study this transcendental literature under the guidance of a bona fide spiritual master. Then it is very easy to understand Kṛṣṇa as He is.

TEXT 24

न चैते पुत्रक भ्रातुर्हन्तारो धनदानुगाः ।
विसर्गादानयोस्तात पुंसो दैवं हि कारणम् ॥२४॥

na caite putraka bhrātur
hantāro dhana-dānugāḥ
visargādānayos tāta
puṁso daivaṁ hi kāraṇam

na—never; *ca*—also; *ete*—all these; *putraka*—my dear son; *bhrātuḥ*—of your brother; *hantāraḥ*—killers; *dhana-da*—of Kuvera; *anugāḥ*—followers; *visarga*—of birth; *ādānayoḥ*—of death; *tāta*—my dear son; *puṁsaḥ*—of a living entity; *daivam*—the supreme; *hi*—certainly; *kāraṇam*—the cause.

TRANSLATION

My dear son, those Yakṣas, who are descendants of Kuvera, are not actually the killers of your brother; the birth and death of every living entity is caused by the Supreme, who is certainly the cause of all causes.

TEXT 25

स एव विश्वं सृजति स एवावति हन्ति च ।
अथापि ह्यनहंकारान्नाज्यते गुणकर्मभिः ॥२५॥

sa eva viśvaṁ sṛjati
sa evāvati hanti ca
athāpi hy anahaṅkārān
nājyate guṇa-karmabhiḥ

saḥ—He; *eva*—certainly; *viśvam*—the universe; *sṛjati*—creates; *saḥ*—He; *eva*—certainly; *avati*—maintains; *hanti*—annihilates; *ca*—also; *athāpi*—moreover; *hi*—certainly; *anahaṅkārāt*—from being without ego; *na*—not; *ajyate*—becomes entangled; *guṇa*—by the modes of material nature; *karmabhiḥ*—by activities.

TRANSLATION

The Supreme Personality of Godhead creates this material world, maintains it, and annihilates it in due course of time, but because He is transcendental to such activities, He is never affected by ego in such action or by the modes of material nature.

PURPORT

In this verse the word *anahaṅkāra* means "without ego." The conditioned soul has a false ego, and as a result of his *karma* he gets different types of bodies in this material world. Sometimes he gets the body of a demigod, and he thinks that body to be his identity. Similarly, when he gets the body of a dog he identifies his self with that body. But for the Supreme Personality of Godhead there is no such distinction between the body and the soul. *Bhagavad-gītā*, therefore, certifies that anyone who thinks of Kṛṣṇa as an ordinary human being is without knowledge of His transcendental nature and is a great fool. The Lord says, *na māṁ karmāṇi limpanti*: He is not affected by anything He does because He is never contaminated by the material modes of nature. That we have a material body proves that we are infected by the three material modes of nature. The Lord says to Arjuna, "You and I had many, many births previously, but I remember everything, whereas you do not." That is the difference between the living entity, or conditioned soul, and the Supreme Soul. The Supersoul, the Supreme Personality of Godhead, has no material body, and because He has no material body, He is not affected by any work that He executes. There are many Māyāvādī philosophers who consider that Kṛṣṇa's body is the effect of a concentration of the material mode of goodness, and they distinguish Kṛṣṇa's soul from Kṛṣṇa's body. The real situation, however, is that the body of the conditioned soul, even if he has a large accumulation of material goodness, is material, whereas Kṛṣṇa's body is never material; it is transcendental. Kṛṣṇa has no false ego, for He does not identify Himself with the false and temporary body. His body is always eternal; He descends on this world in His own original spiritual body. This is explained in *Bhagavad-gītā* as *paraṁ bhāvam*. The words *paraṁ bhāvaṁ divyam* are especially significant in understanding Kṛṣṇa's personality.

TEXT 26

एष भूतानि भूतात्मा भूतेशो भूतभावनः ।
स्वशक्त्या मायया युक्तः सृजत्यत्ति च पाति च ॥२६॥

eṣa bhūtāni bhūtātmā
bhūteśo bhūta-bhāvanaḥ
sva-śaktyā māyayā yuktaḥ
sṛjaty atti ca pāti ca

eṣaḥ—this; *bhūtāni*—all created beings; *bhūta-ātmā*—the Supersoul of all living entities; *bhūta-īśaḥ*—the controller of everyone; *bhūta-bhāvanaḥ*—the maintainer of everyone; *sva-śaktyā*—through His energy; *māyayā*—the external energy; *yuktaḥ*—through such agency; *sṛjati*—creates; *atti*—annihilates; *ca*—and; *pāti*—maintains; *ca*—and.

TRANSLATION

The Supreme Personality of Godhead is the Supersoul of all living entities. He is the controller and maintainer of everyone; through the agency of His external energy, He creates, maintains and annihilates everyone.

PURPORT

There are two kinds of energies in the matter of creation. The Lord creates this material world through His external, material energy, whereas the spiritual world is a manifestation of His internal energy. He is always associated with the internal energy, but He is always aloof from the material energy. Therefore in *Bhagavad-gītā* the Lord says, *mat-sthāni sarva-bhūtāni na cāhaṁ teṣv avasthitaḥ:* "All living entities are living on Me or on My energy, but I am not everywhere." (Bg. 9.4) He is personally always situated in the spiritual world. In the material world also, wherever the Supreme Lord is personally present is to be understood as the spiritual world. For example, the Lord is worshiped in the temple by pure devotees. The temple is therefore to be understood as the spiritual world.

TEXT 27

तमेव मृत्युममृतं तात दैवं
सर्वात्मनोपेहि जगत्परायणम् ।

यस्मै बलिं विश्वसृजो हरन्ति
गावो यथा वै नसि दामयन्त्रिताः ॥२७॥

tam eva mṛtyum amṛtaṁ tāta daivaṁ
sarvātmanopehi jagat-parāyaṇam
yasmai baliṁ viśva-sṛjo haranti
gāvo yathā vai nasi dāma-yantritāḥ

tam—unto Him; *eva*—certainly; *mṛtyum*—death; *amṛtam*—immortality; *tāta*—my dear son; *daivam*—the Supreme; *sarva-ātmanā*—in all respects; *upehi*—surrender; *jagat*—of the world; *parāyaṇam*—ultimate goal; *yasmai*—unto whom; *balim*—offerings; *viśva-sṛjaḥ*—all the demigods like Brahmā; *haranti*—bear; *gāvaḥ*—bulls; *yathā*—as; *vai*—without fail; *nasi*—in the nose; *dāma*—by a rope; *yantritāḥ*—controlled.

TRANSLATION

My dear boy Dhruva, please surrender unto the Supreme Personality of Godhead, who is the ultimate goal of the progress of the world. Everyone, including the demigods headed by Lord Brahmā, is working under His control, just as a bull, prompted by a rope in its nose, is controlled by its owner.

PURPORT

The material disease is to declare independence from the supreme controller. Factually, our material existence begins when we forget the supreme controller and wish to lord it over material nature. Everyone in the material world is trying his best to become the supreme controller—individually, nationally, socially and in many other ways. Dhruva Mahārāja was advised to stop fighting by his grandfather, who was concerned that Dhruva was adhering to a personal ambition to fight to annihilate the whole race of Yakṣas. In this verse, therefore, Svāyambhuva Manu seeks to eradicate the last tinge of false ambition in Dhruva by explaining the position of the supreme controller. The words *mṛtyum amṛtam,* "death and immortality," are significant. In *Bhagavad-gītā* the Lord says, "I am ultimate death, who takes away everything from the demons." The demons' business is to continually struggle for existence as lords over material nature. The demons repeatedly meet death after death and create a network of involvement in the material world. The Lord is death for the demons, but for devotees He is *amṛta,* eternal life. Devotees who render continuous service to the Lord have already attained immortality, for whatever they are doing in this life they will continue to do in the next. They will simply change their material bodies for spiritual bodies. Unlike the demons, they no longer have to change material bodies. The Lord, therefore, is simultaneously death and immortality. He is death for demons and immortality for devotees. He is the ultimate goal of everyone because He is the cause of all causes. Dhruva Mahārāja was advised to surrender unto Him in all respects, without keeping any personal ambition. One may put forward the argument, "Why are the demigods worshiped?" The answer is given here that demigods are worshiped by less intelligent men. The demigods themselves accept sacrifices for the ultimate satisfaction of the Supreme Personality of Godhead.

TEXT 28

यः पञ्चवर्षो जननीं त्वं विहाय
मातुः सपत्न्या वचसा भिन्नमर्मा ।
वनं गतस्तपसा प्रत्यगक्ष-
माराध्य लेभे मूर्ध्नि पदं त्रिलोक्याः ॥२८॥

yaḥ pañca-varṣo jananīṁ tvaṁ vihāya
mātuḥ sapatnyā vacasā bhinna-marmā
vanaṁ gatas tapasā pratyag-akṣam
ārādhya lebhe mūrdhni padaṁ tri-lokyāḥ

yaḥ—one who; *pañca-varṣaḥ*—five years old; *jananīm*—mother; *tvam*—you; *vihāya*—leaving aside; *mātuḥ*—of the mother; *sa-patnyāḥ*—of the co-wife; *vacasā*—by the words; *bhinna-marmā*—aggrieved at heart; *vanam*—to the forest; *gataḥ*—went; *tapasā*—by austerity; *pratyak-akṣam*—the Supreme Lord; *ārādhya*—worshiping; *lebhe*—achieved; *mūrdhni*—on the top; *padam*—the position; *tri-lokyāḥ*—of the three worlds.

TRANSLATION

My dear Dhruva, at the age of only five years you were very grievously afflicted by the words of your mother's co-wife, and you very boldly gave up the protection of your mother and went to the forest to engage in the yogic process for realization of the Supreme Personality of Godhead. As a result of this you have already achieved the topmost position in all the three worlds.

PURPORT

Manu was very proud that Dhruva Mahārāja was one of the descendants in his family because at the age of only five years Dhruva began meditating upon the Supreme Personality of Godhead and within six months he was able to see the Supreme Lord face to face. Factually, Dhruva Mahārāja is the glory of the Manu dynasty, or the human family. The human family begins from Manu. The Sanskrit word for man is *manuṣya,* which means "descendant of Manu." Dhruva Mahārāja is not only the glory of the family of Svāyambhuva Manu, but he is the glory of the entire human society. Because Dhruva Mahārāja had already surrendered to the Supreme Godhead, he was especially requested not to do anything unbefitting a surrendered soul.

TEXT 29

तमेनमङ्गात्मनि मुक्तविग्रहे
व्यपाश्रितं निर्गुणमेकमक्षरम् ।
आत्मानमन्विच्छ विमुक्तमात्मदृग्
यस्मिन्निदं भेदमसत्प्रतीयते ॥२९॥

tam enam aṅgātmani mukta-vigrahe
vyapāśritaṁ nirguṇam ekam akṣaram
ātmānam anviccha vimuktam ātma-dṛg
yasminn idaṁ bhedam asat pratīyate

tam—Him; *enam*—that; *aṅga*—my dear Dhruva; *ātmani*—in the mind; *mukta-vigrahe*—free from anger; *vyapāśritam*—situated; *nirguṇam*—transcendental; *ekam*—one; *akṣaram*—the infallible Brahman; *ātmānam*—the self; *anviccha*—try to find out; *vimuktam*—uncontaminated; *ātma-dṛk*—facing toward the Supersoul; *yasmin*—in which; *idam*—this; *bhedam*—differentiation; *asat*—unreal; *pratīyate*—appears to be.

TRANSLATION

My dear Dhruva, please, therefore, turn your attention to the Supreme Person, who is the infallible Brahman. Face the Supreme Personality of Godhead in your original position, and thus, by self-realization, you will find this material differentiation to be merely flickering.

PURPORT

The living entities have three kinds of vision, according to their positions in self-realization. According to the bodily concept of life, one sees differentiation in terms of varieties of bodies. The living entity actually passes through many varieties of material forms, but despite all such changes of body, he is eternal. When living entities, therefore, are viewed in the bodily concept of life, one appears to be different from another. Lord Manu wanted to change the vision of Dhruva Mahārāja, who was looking upon the Yakṣas as different from him or as his enemies. Factually no one is an enemy or a friend. Everyone is passing through different types of bodies under the law of *karma*, but as soon as one is situated in his spiritual identity, he does not see differentiation in terms of this law. In other words, as stated in the *Bhagavad-gītā*, *brahma-bhūtaḥ prasannātmā na śocati na kāṅkṣati/samaḥ sarveṣu bhūteṣu mad-bhaktiṁ labhate parām* (Bg. 18.54). A devotee, who is already liberated, does not see differentiation in terms of the outward body; he sees all living entities as spirit souls, eternal servants of the Lord. Dhruva Mahārāja was advised by Lord Manu to see with that vision. He was specifically advised to do so because he was a great devotee and should not have looked upon other living entities with ordinary vision. Indirectly Manu pointed out to Dhruva Mahārāja that out of material affection Dhruva thought of his brother as his kin and the Yakṣas as his enemies. Such observation of differentiation subsides as soon as one is situated in his original position as an eternal servant of the Lord.

TEXT 30

त्वं प्रत्यगात्मनि तदा भगवत्यनन्त
आनन्दमात्र उपपन्नसमस्तशक्तौ ।
भक्तिं विधाय परमां शनकैरविद्या-
ग्रन्थिं विभेत्स्यसि ममाहमिति प्ररूढम् ॥३०॥

tvaṁ pratyag-ātmani tadā bhagavaty ananta
ānanda-mātra upapanna-samasta-śaktau
bhaktiṁ vidhāya paramāṁ śanakair avidyā-
granthiṁ vibhetsyasi mamāham iti prarūḍham

tvam—you; *pratyak-ātmani*—unto the Supersoul; *tadā*—at that time; *bhagavati*—unto the Supreme Personality of Godhead; *anante*—who is unlimited; *ānanda-mātre*—reservoir of all pleasure; *upapanna*—possessed of; *samasta*—all; *śaktau*—potencies; *bhaktim*—devotional service; *vidhāya*—by rendering; *paramām*—supreme; *śanakaiḥ*—very soon; *avidyā*—of illusion; *granthim*—the knot; *vibhetsyasi*—you will undo; *mama*—my; *aham*—I; *iti*—thus; *prarūḍham*—firmly fixed.

TRANSLATION

Thus regaining your natural position and rendering service unto the Supreme Lord, who is the all-powerful reservoir of all pleasure and who

lives in all living entities as the Supersoul, you will very soon forget the illusory understanding of "I" and "my."

PURPORT

Dhruva Mahārāja was already a liberated person because at the age of five years he had seen the Supreme Personality of Godhead. But even though liberated, he was, for the time being, afflicted by the illusion of *māyā*, thinking himself the brother of Uttama in the bodily concept of life. The whole material world is working on the basis of "I" and "mine." This is the root of attraction to the material world. If one is attracted by this root of illusory conceptions—"I" and "mine"—he will have to remain within this material world in different exalted or nasty positions. By the grace of Lord Kṛṣṇa, the sages and Lord Manu reminded Dhruva Mahārāja that he should not continue this material conception of "I" and "mine." Simply by devotional service unto the Lord his illusion could be eradicated without difficulty.

TEXT 31

संयच्छ रोषं भद्रं ते प्रतीपं श्रेयसां परम् ।
श्रुतेन भूयसा राजन्नगदेन यथाऽऽमयम् ॥३१॥

saṁyaccha roṣaṁ bhadraṁ te
pratīpaṁ śreyasāṁ param
śrutena bhūyasā rājann
agadena yathāmayam

saṁyaccha—just control; *roṣam*—anger; *bhadram*—all good fortune; *te*—to you; *pratīpam*—enemy; *śreyasām*—of all goodness; *param*—the foremost; *śrutena*—by hearing; *bhūyasā*—constantly; *rājan*—my dear King; *agadena*—by medicinal treatment; *yathā*—as; *āmayam*—disease.

TRANSLATION

My dear King, just consider what I have said to you, which will act as medicinal treatment upon disease. Control your anger, for anger is the foremost enemy on the path of spiritual realization. I wish all good fortune for you. Please follow my instructions.

PURPORT

Dhruva Mahārāja was a liberated soul, and actually he was not angry with anyone. But because he was the ruler, it was his duty to become angry for some time in order to keep law and order in the state. His brother, Uttama, was without fault, yet he was killed by one of the Yakṣas. It was the duty of Dhruva Mahārāja to kill the offender (life for life) because he was the king. When the challenge came, Dhruva Mahārāja fought vehemently and punished the Yakṣas sufficiently. But anger is such that if one increases it, it increases unlimitedly. In order that Dhruva Mahārāja's kingly anger not exceed the limit, Manu was kind enough to check his grandson. Dhruva Mahārāja could understand the purpose of his grandfather, and he immediately stopped the fighting. The words *śrutena bhūyasā,* by constantly hearing, are very important in this verse. By constantly hearing about devotional service, one can check the force of anger, which is detrimental to the process of devotional service. Śrīla Parīkṣit Mahārāja said that the constant hearing of the pastimes of the Lord is the panacea for all material diseases. Everyone, therefore, should hear about the Supreme Personality of Godhead constantly. By hearing one can always remain in equilibrium, and thus his progress in spiritual life will not be hampered.

Dhruva Mahārāja's becoming angry with the miscreants was quite appropriate. There is a short story in this connection about a snake who became a devotee upon instruction by Nārada, who instructed him not to bite any more. Since ordinarily a snake's business is to fatally bite other living entities, as a devotee he was forbidden to do so. Unfortunately, people took advantage of this nonviolence on the part of the snake, especially the children, who began to throw stones at him. He did not bite anyone, however, because it was the instruction of his spiritual master. After a while, when the snake met his spiritual master, Nārada, he complained, "I have given up the bad habit of biting innocent living entities, but they are mistreating me by throwing stones at me." Upon hearing this, Nārada Muni instructed him, "Don't bite, but do not forget to expand your hood as if you were going to bite. Then they will go away." Similarly, a devotee is always nonviolent; he is qualified with all good characteristics. But, in the common world, when there is mischief made by others, he should not forget to become angry, at least for the time being, in order to drive away the miscreants.

TEXT 32

येनोपसृष्टात्पुरुषाल्लोक उद्विजते भृशम् ।
न बुधस्तद्वशं गच्छेदिच्छन्नभयमात्मनः ॥३२॥

yenopasṛṣṭāt puruṣāl
loka udvijate bhṛśam
na budhas tad-vaśaṁ gacched
icchann abhayam ātmanaḥ

yena—by which; *upasṛṣṭāt*—being overwhelmed; *puruṣāt*—by the person; *lokaḥ*—everyone; *udvijate*—becomes terrified; *bhṛśam*—greatly; *na*—never; *budhaḥ*—a learned person; *tat*—of anger; *vaśam*—under the control; *gacchet*—should go; *icchan*—desiring; *abhayam*—fearlessness, liberation; *ātmanaḥ*—of the self.

TRANSLATION

A person who desires liberation from this material world should not fall under the control of anger because when bewildered by anger one becomes a source of dread for all others.

PURPORT

A devotee or saintly person should not be dreadful to others, nor should anyone be a source of dread to him. If one treats others with non-enmity, then no one will become his enemy. There is the example, however, of Jesus Christ, who had enemies, and they crucified him. The demonic are always present, and they find fault even in saintly persons. But a saintly person never becomes angry, even if there is very great provocation.

TEXT 33

हेलनं गिरिशभ्रातुर्धनदस्य त्वया कृतम् ।
यज्जघ्निवान् पुण्यजनान् भ्रातृघ्नानित्यमर्षितः ॥३३॥

helanaṁ giriśa-bhrātur
dhanadasya tvayā kṛtam
yaj jaghnivān puṇya-janān
bhrātṛ-ghnān ity amarṣitaḥ

helanam—disrespectful behavior; *giriśa*—of Lord Śiva; *bhrātuḥ*—the brother; *dhana-dasya*—to Kuvera; *tvayā*—by you; *kṛtam*—was performed; *yat*—because; *jaghnivān*—you have killed; *puṇya-janān*—the Yakṣas; *bhrātṛ*—of your brother; *ghnān*—killers; *iti*—thus (thinking); *amarṣitaḥ*—angry.

TRANSLATION

My dear Dhruva, you thought that the Yakṣas killed your brother, and therefore you have killed great numbers of them. But by this action you have agitated the mind of Lord Śiva's brother, Kuvera, who is the treasurer of the demigods. Please note that your actions have been very disrespectful to Kuvera and Lord Śiva.

PURPORT

Lord Manu stated that Dhruva Mahārāja had been offensive to Lord Śiva and his brother Kuvera because the Yakṣas belonged to Kuvera's family. They were not ordinary persons. As such, they have been described as *puṇya-jana,* pious men. Somehow or other the mind of Kuvera had been agitated, and Dhruva Mahārāja was advised to pacify him.

TEXT 34

तं प्रसादय वत्साशु संनत्या प्रश्रयोक्तिभिः ।
न यावन्महतां तेजः कुलं नोऽभिभविष्यति ॥३४॥

taṁ prasādaya vatsāśu
sannatyā praśrayoktibhiḥ
na yāvan mahatāṁ tejaḥ
kulaṁ no 'bhibhaviṣyati

tam—him; *prasādaya*—pacify; *vatsa*—my son; *āśu*—immediately; *sannatyā*—by offering obeisances; *praśrayā*—by respectful behavior; *uktibhiḥ*—by gentle words; *na yāvat*—before; *mahatām*—of great personalities; *tejaḥ*—wrath; *kulam*—family; *naḥ*—our; *abhibhaviṣyati*—will affect.

TRANSLATION

For this reason, my son, you should immediately pacify Kuvera with gentle words and prayers, and thus his wrath may not affect our family.

PURPORT

In our common dealings we should maintain friendship with everyone and certainly with such exalted demigods as Kuvera. Our behavior should be such that no one should become angry and thereby commit a wrong to individuals, families or society.

TEXT 35

**एवं स्वायम्भुवः पौत्रमनुशास्य मनुर्ध्रुवम् ।
तेनाभिवन्दितः साकमृषिभिः स्वपुरं ययौ ॥३५॥**

evaṁ svāyambhuvaḥ pautram
anuśāsya manur dhruvam
tenābhivanditaḥ sākam
ṛṣibhiḥ sva-puraṁ yayau

evam—thus; *svāyambhuvaḥ*—Lord Svāyambhuva Manu; *pautram*—to his grandson; *anuśāsya*—after giving instruction; *manuḥ*—Lord Manu; *dhruvam*—to Dhruva Mahārāja; *tena*—by him; *abhivanditaḥ*—being offered obeisances to; *sākam*—together; *ṛṣibhiḥ*—with the sages; *sva-puram*—to his own abode; *yayau*—went.

TRANSLATION

Thus Svāyambhuva Manu, after giving instruction to Dhruva Mahārāja, his grandson, received respectful obeisances from him. Then Lord Manu and the great sages went back to their respective homes.

Thus end the Bhaktivedanta purports of the Fourth Canto, Eleventh Chapter, of the Śrīmad-Bhāgavatam, *entitled "Svāyambhuva Manu Advises Dhruva Mahārāja to Stop Fighting."*

CHAPTER TWELVE

Dhruva Mahārāja Goes Back to Godhead

TEXT 1

मैत्रेय उवाच
ध्रुवं निवृत्तं प्रतिबुद्ध्य वैशसा-
दपेतमन्युं भगवान् धनेश्वरः ।
तत्रागतश्चारणयक्षकिन्नरैः
संस्तूयमानो न्यवदत्कृताञ्जलिम् ॥ १ ॥

maitreya uvāca
dhruvaṁ nivṛttaṁ pratibuddhya vaiśasād
apeta-manyuṁ bhagavān dhaneśvaraḥ
tatrāgataś cāraṇa-yakṣa-kinnaraiḥ
saṁstūyamāno nyavadat kṛtāñjalim

maitreyaḥ uvāca—Maitreya said; *dhruvam*—Dhruva Mahārāja; *nivṛttam*—ceased; *pratibuddhya*—having learned; *vaiśasāt*—from killing; *apeta*—subsided; *manyum*—anger; *bhagavān*—Kuvera; *dhana-īśvaraḥ*—master of the treasury; *tatra*—there; *āgataḥ*—appeared; *cāraṇa*—by the Cāraṇas; *yakṣa*—Yakṣas; *kinnaraiḥ*—and by the Kinnaras; *saṁstūyamānaḥ*—being worshiped; *nyavadat*—spoke; *kṛta-añjalim*—to Dhruva with folded hands.

TRANSLATION

The great sage Maitreya said: My dear Vidura, Dhruva Mahārāja's anger subsided, and he completely ceased killing Yakṣas. When Kuvera, the most blessed master of the treasury, learned this news, he appeared before him. While being worshiped by Yakṣas, Kinnaras and Cāraṇas, he spoke to Dhruva Mahārāja, who stood before him with folded hands.

TEXT 2

धनद उवाच
भो भोः क्षत्रियदायाद परितुष्टोऽस्मि तेऽनघ ।
यत्त्वं पितामहादेशाद्वैरं दुस्त्यजमत्यजः ॥ २ ॥

dhanada uvāca
bho bhoḥ kṣatriya-dāyāda
parituṣṭo 'smi te 'nagha
yat tvaṁ pitāmahādeśād
vairaṁ dustyajam atyajaḥ

dhana-daḥ uvāca—the master of the treasury (Kuvera) said; *bhoḥ bhoḥ*—O; *kṣatriya-dāyāda*—O son of a *kṣatriya; parituṣṭaḥ*—very glad; *asmi*—I am; *te*—with you; *anagha*—O sinless one; *yat*—because; *tvam*—you; *pitāmaha*—of your grandfather; *ādeśāt*—under the instruction; *vairam*—enmity; *dustyajam*—difficult to avoid; *atyajaḥ*—have given up.

TRANSLATION

The master of the treasury, Kuvera said, O sinless son of a kṣatriya, I am very glad to know that under the instruction of your grandfather you have given up your enmity, although it is very difficult to avoid. I am very pleased with you.

TEXT 3

न भवानवधीद्यक्षान्न यक्षा भ्रातरं तव ।
काल एव हि भूतानां प्रभुरप्ययभावयोः ॥ ३ ॥

na bhavān avadhīd yakṣān
na yakṣā bhrātaraṁ tava
kāla eva hi bhūtānāṁ
prabhur apyaya-bhāvayoḥ

na—not; *bhavān*—you; *avadhīt*—killed; *yakṣān*—the Yakṣas; *na*—not; *yakṣāḥ*—the Yakṣas; *bhrātaram*—brother; *tava*—your; *kālaḥ*—time; *eva*—certainly; *hi*—for; *bhūtānām*—of living entities; *prabhuḥ*—the Supreme Lord; *apyaya-bhāvayoḥ*—of annihilation and generation.

TRANSLATION

Actually, you have not killed the Yakṣas, nor have they killed your brother, for the ultimate cause of generation and annihilation is the eternal time feature of the Supreme Lord.

PURPORT

When the master of the treasury addressed him as sinless, Dhruva Mahārāja, considering himself responsible for killing so many Yakṣas, might have thought himself otherwise. Kuvera, however, assured him that factually he did not kill any of the Yakṣas; therefore, he was not at all sinful. He did his duty as a king, as it is ordered by the laws of nature. "Nor should you think that your brother was killed by the Yakṣas," said Kuvera. "He died or was killed in due course of time by the laws of nature. Eternal time, one of the features of the Lord, is ultimately responsible for annihilation and generation. You are not responsible for such actions."

TEXT 4

अहं त्वमित्यपार्था धीरज्ञानात्पुरुषस्य हि ।
स्वाप्नीवाभात्यतद्ध्यानाद्यया बन्धविपर्ययौ ॥ ४ ॥

ahaṁ tvam ity apārthā dhīr
ajñānāt puruṣasya hi
svāpnīvābhāty atad-dhyānād
yayā bandha-viparyayau

aham—I; *tvam*—you; *iti*—thus; *apārthā*—misconceived; *dhīḥ*—intelligence; *ajñānāt*—from ignorance; *puruṣasya*—of a person; *hi*—certainly; *svāpni*—a dream; *iva*—like; *ābhāti*—appears; *a-tat-dhyānāt*—from the bodily concept of life; *yayā*—by which; *bandha*—bondage; *viparyayau*—and misery.

TRANSLATION

Misidentification of oneself and others as "I" and "you" on the basis of the bodily concept of life is a product of ignorance. This bodily concept is the cause of repeated birth and death, and it makes us go on continuously in material existence.

PURPORT

The conception of "I" and "you," *ahaṁ tvam,* as separate from one another, is due to our forgetfulness of our eternal relationship with the Supreme Personality of Godhead. The Supreme Person, Kṛṣṇa, is the central point, and all of us are His parts and parcels, just as hands and legs are parts and parcels of the whole body. When we actually come to this understanding of being eternally related to the Supreme Lord, this distinction, which is based on the bodily concept of life, cannot exist. The same example can be cited herewith: the hand is the hand, and the leg is the leg, but when both of them engage in the service of the whole body, there is no such distinction as hands and legs, for all of them belong to the whole body, and all the parts working together constitute the whole body. Similarly, when the living entities are in Kṛṣṇa consciousness, there is no such distinction as "I" and "you" because everyone is engaged in the service of the Lord. Since the Lord is absolute, the services are also absolute; even though the hand is working one way and the leg is working in another way, since the purpose is the Supreme Personality of Godhead, they are all one. This is not to be confused with the statement by the Māyāvādī philosopher that "everything is one." Real knowledge is that hand is hand, leg is leg, body is body, and yet all together they are one. As soon as the living entity thinks that he is independent, his conditional material existence begins. The conception of independent existence is, therefore, like a dream. One has to be in Kṛṣṇa consciousness, his original position. Then he can be freed from material bondage.

TEXT 5

तद्गच्छ ध्रुव भद्रं ते भगवन्तमधोक्षजम् ।
सर्वभूतात्मभावेन सर्वभूतात्मविग्रहम् ॥ ५ ॥

tad gaccha dhruva bhadraṁ te
bhagavantam adhokṣajam
sarva-bhūtātma-bhāvena
sarva-bhūtātma-vigraham

tat—therefore; *gaccha*—come; *dhruva*—Dhruva; *bhadram*—good fortune; *te*—unto you; *bhagavantam*—unto the Supreme Personality of Godhead; *adhokṣajam*—who is beyond the concepts of material senses; *sarva-bhūta*—all living entities; *ātma-bhāvena*—by thinking of them as one; *sarva-bhūta*—in all living entities; *ātma*—the Supersoul; *vigraham*—having form.

TRANSLATION

My dear Dhruva, come forward. May the Lord always grace you with good fortune. The Supreme Personality of Godhead, who is beyond our sensual perception, is the Supersoul of all living entities, and thus all entities are one, without distinction. Begin, therefore, to render service unto the transcendental form of the Lord, who is the ultimate shelter of all living entities.

PURPORT

Here the word *vigraham,* "having specific form," is very significant, for it indicates that the Absolute Truth is ultimately the Supreme Personality of Godhead. That is explained in the *Brahma-saṁhitā. Sac-cid-ānanda-vigrahaḥ:* He has form, but His form is different from any kind of material form. The living entities are the marginal energy of the supreme form. As such, they are not different from the supreme form, but at the same time they are not equal to the supreme form. Dhruva Mahārāja is advised herewith to render service unto the supreme form. That will include service to other individual forms. For example, a tree has a form, and when water is poured on the root of the tree, the other forms—the leaves, twigs, flowers and fruits—are automatically watered. The Māyāvāda conception that because the Absolute Truth is everything He must be formless is rejected here. Rather, it is confirmed that the Absolute Truth has form, and yet He is all-pervading. Nothing is independent from Him.

TEXT 6

भजस्व भजनीयाङ्घ्रिमभवाय भवच्छिदम् ।
युक्तं विरहितं शक्त्या गुणमय्याऽऽत्ममायया ॥ ६ ॥

bhajasva bhajanīyāṅghrim
abhavāya bhava-cchidam
yuktaṁ virahitaṁ śaktyā
guṇa-mayyātma-māyayā

bhajasva—engage in devotional service; *bhajanīya*—worthy to be worshiped; *aṅghrim*—unto Him whose lotus feet; *abhavāya*—for deliverance from material existence; *bhava-chidam*—who cuts the knot of material entanglement; *yuktam*—attached; *virahitam*—aloof; *śaktyā*—to His potency; *guṇa-mayyā*—consisting of the modes of material nature; *ātma-māyayā*—by His inconceivable potency.

TRANSLATION

Engage yourself fully, therefore, in the devotional service of the Lord, for only He can deliver us from this entanglement of materialistic existence. Although the Lord is attached to His material potency, He is aloof from her activities. Everything in this material world is happening by the inconceivable potency of the Supreme Personality of Godhead.

PURPORT

In continuation of the previous verse, it is specifically mentioned here that Dhruva Mahārāja should engage himself in devotional service. Devotional service cannot be rendered to the impersonal Brahman feature of the Supreme Personality of Godhead. Whenever the word "*bhajasva*" appears, meaning "engage yourself in devotional service," there must be the servant, service and the served. The Supreme Personality of Godhead is served, the mode of activities to please Him is called service, and one who renders such service is called the servant. Another significant feature in this verse is that only the Lord, and no one else, is to be served. That is confirmed in the *Bhagavad-gītā, (mām ekaṁ śaraṇaṁ vraja).* There is no need to serve the demigods, who are just like the hands and legs of the Supreme Lord. When the Supreme Lord is served, the hands and legs of the Supreme Lord are automatically served. There is no need of separate service. As stated in *Bhagavad-gītā, teṣām ahaṁ samuddhartā mṛtyu-saṁsāra-sāgarāt.* (Bg.12.7) This means that the Lord, in order to show specific favor to the devotee, directs the devotee from within in such a way that ultimately he is delivered from the entanglement of material existence. No one but the Supreme Lord can help the living entity to be delivered from the entanglement of this material world. The material energy is a manifestation of one of the Supreme Personality of Godhead's varieties of potencies *(parāsya śaktir vividhaiva śrūyate).* This material energy is one of the Lord's potencies, as much as heat and light are potencies of fire. The material energy is not different from the Supreme Godhead, but at the same time He has nothing to do with the material energy. The living entity, who is of the marginal energy, is entrapped by the material energy on the basis of his desire to lord it over the material world. The Lord is aloof from this, but when the same living entity engages himself in the devotional service of the Lord, then he becomes attached to this service. This situation is called *yuktam.* For devotees the Lord is present even in the material energy. This is the inconceivable potency of the Lord. Material energy acts in the three modes of material qualities, which produce the action and reaction of material existence. Those who are not devotees become involved in such activities, whereas devotees, who are dovetailed with the Supreme Personality of Godhead, are freed from such action and reaction of the material energy. The Lord is therefore described herewith as *bhava-cchidam,* one who can give deliverance from the entanglement of material existence.

TEXT 7

वृणीहि कामं नृप यन्मनोगतं
मत्तस्त्वमौत्तानपदेऽविशङ्कितः ।
वरं वरार्होऽम्बुजनाभपादयो-
रनन्तरं त्वां वयमङ्ग शुश्रुम ॥ ७ ॥

vṛṇīhi kāmaṁ nṛpa yan manogataṁ
mattas tvam auttānapade 'viśaṅkitaḥ
varaṁ varārho 'mbuja-nābha-pādayor
anantaraṁ tvāṁ vayam aṅga śuśruma

vṛṇīhi—please ask; *kāmam*—desire; *nṛpa*—O King; *yat*—whatever; *manaḥ-gatam*—within your mind; *mattaḥ*—from me; *tvam*—you; *auttānapade*—O son of Mahārāja Uttānapāda; *aviśaṅkitaḥ*—without hesitation; *varam*—benediction; *vara-arhaḥ*—worthy to take benediction; *ambuja*—lotus flower; *nābha*—whose navel; *pādayoḥ*—at His lotus feet; *anantaram*—constantly; *tvām*—about you; *vayam*—we; *aṅga*—dear Dhruva; *śuśruma*—have heard.

TRANSLATION

My dear Dhruva Mahārāja, son of Mahārāja Uttānapāda, we have heard that you are constantly engaged in transcendental loving service to the Supreme Personality of Godhead, who is known for His lotus navel. You are therefore worthy to take all benediction from us. Please, therefore, ask whatever benediction you want from me without hesitation.

PURPORT

Dhruva Mahārāja, the son of King Uttānapāda, was already known throughout the universe as a great devotee of the Lord, constantly thinking of His lotus feet. Such a pure, uncontaminated devotee of the Lord is worthy to have all the benedictions that can be offered by the demigods. He doesn't have to worship the demigods separately for such benediction. Kuvera is the treasurer of the demigods, and he is personally offering whatever benediction Dhruva Mahārāja would like to have from him. Śrīla Bilvamaṅgala Ṭhākura stated, therefore, that for persons who engage in the devotional service of the Lord, all material benedictions wait like maid-servants. Mukti-devī is just waiting at the door of the devotee to offer liberation, or more than that, at any time. To be a devotee is therefore an exalted position. Simply by rendering transcendental loving service unto the Supreme Personality of Godhead one can have all the benedictions of the world without separate endeavor. Lord Kuvera said to Dhruva Mahārāja that he had heard that he was always in *samādhi,* or thinking of the lotus feet of the Lord. In other words, he knew that for Dhruva Mahārāja there was nothing desirable within the three material worlds. He knew that Dhruva would ask for nothing but to remember the lotus feet of the Supreme Lord constantly.

TEXT 8

मैत्रेय उवाच
स राजराजेन वराय चोदितो
ध्रुवो महाभागवतो महामतिः ।
हरौ स वव्रेऽचलितां स्मृतिं यया
तरत्ययत्नेन दुरत्ययं तमः ॥ ८ ॥

maitreya uvāca
sa rāja-rājena varāya codito
dhruvo mahā-bhāgavato mahā-matiḥ
harau sa vavre 'calitāṁ smṛtiṁ yayā
taraty ayatnena duratyayaṁ tamaḥ

maitreyaḥ uvāca—the great sage Maitreya said; *saḥ*—he; *rāja-rājena*—by the king of kings (Kuvera); *varāya*—for benediction; *coditaḥ*—being asked; *dhruvaḥ*—Dhruva Mahārāja; *mahā-bhāgavataḥ*—a first-class pure devotee; *mahā-matiḥ*—most intelligent or thoughtful; *harau*—unto the Supreme Personality of Godhead; *saḥ*—he; *vavre*—asked; *acalitām*—unflinching; *smṛtim*—remembrance; *yayā*—by which; *tarati*—crosses over; *ayatnena*—without difficulty; *duratyayam*—unsurpassable; *tamaḥ*—nescience.

TRANSLATION

The great sage Maitreya continued: My dear Vidura, when thus asked to accept a benediction from Kuvera the Yakṣarāja [King of the Yakṣas], Dhruva Mahārāja, that most elevated pure devotee, who was an intelligent and thoughtful king, begged from him that he might have unflinching faith in and remembrance of the Supreme Personality of Godhead, for thus a person can cross over the ocean of nescience very easily, although it is very difficult for others to cross.

PURPORT

According to the opinion of expert followers of Vedic rites, there are different types of benedictions in terms of religiosity, economic development, sense gratification and liberation. These four principles are known as *catur-vargas.* Of all the *catur-vargas,* the benediction of liberation is considered to be the highest in this material world. To be enabled to cross over material nescience is known as the highest *puruṣārtha,* or benediction for the human being. But Dhruva Mahārāja wanted a benediction which surpasses even the highest *puruṣārtha,* liberation. He wanted the benediction that he might constantly remember the lotus feet of the Lord. This stage of life is called *pañca-puruṣārtha.* When a devotee comes to the platform of *pañca-puruṣārtha,* simply engaging in devotional service to the Lord, the fourth *puruṣārtha,* liberation, becomes very insignificant in his eyes. Śrīla Prabodhānanda Sarasvatī has stated in this connection that for a devotee liberation is a hellish condition of life; as for sense gratification, which is available in the heavenly planets, the devotee considers it to be a will-o'-the-wisp, having no value in life. *Yogīs* endeavor to control the senses, but for a devotee, controlling the senses is no difficulty at all. The senses are compared to serpents, but for a devotee the serpents' poison teeth are broken. Thus Śrīla Prabodhānanda Sarasvatī has analyzed all kinds of benedictions available in this world, and he clearly declares that for a pure devotee they are all of no significance. Dhruva Mahārāja was also a *mahā-bhāgavata,* or a first-class pure devotee, and his intelligence was very great *(mahā-matiḥ).* Unless one is very intelligent, one cannot take to devotional service or Kṛṣṇa consciousness. Naturally, anyone who is a first-class devotee must be a first-class intelligent person and therefore not interested in any kind of benediction within this material world. Dhruva Mahārāja was offered benediction by the king of the kings. Kuvera, the treasurer of the demigods, whose only business is to supply immense riches to persons within this materialistic world, is described as the king of kings because unless benedicted by Kuvera one cannot become a king. The king of the kings personally offered Dhruva Mahārāja any amount of riches, but he declined. He is described, therefore, as *mahā-matih,* very thoughtful or highly intellectual.

TEXT 9

तस्य प्रीतेन मनसा तां दत्त्वैडविडस्ततः ।
पश्यतोऽन्तर्दधे सोऽपि स्वपुरं प्रत्यपद्यत ॥ ९ ॥

tasya prītena manasā
tāṁ dattvaiḍaviḍas tataḥ
paśyato 'ntardadhe so 'pi
sva-puraṁ pratyapadyata

tasya—with Dhruva; *prītena*—being very pleased; *manasā*—with such a mentality; *tām*—that remembrance; *dattvā*—having given; *aiḍaviḍaḥ*—Kuvera, son of Iḍaviḍā; *tataḥ*—thereafter; *paśyataḥ*—while Dhruva was looking on; *antardadhe*—disappeared; *saḥ*—he (Dhruva); *api*—also; *sva-puram*—to his city; *pratyapadyata*—returned.

TRANSLATION

The son of Iḍaviḍā, Lord Kuvera, was very pleased, and happily he gave Dhruva Mahārāja the benediction he wanted. Thereafter he disappeared from Dhruva's presence, and Dhruva Mahārāja also returned to his capital city.

PURPORT

Kuvera, who is known as the son of Iḍaviḍā, was very pleased with Dhruva Mahārāja because he did not ask him for anything materially enjoyable. Kuvera is one of the demigods, so one may put forward the argument, "Why did Dhruva Mahārāja take benediction from a demigod?" The answer is that for a Vaiṣṇava there is no objection in taking benediction from a demigod if it is favorable for advancing Kṛṣṇa consciousness. The *gopīs,* for example, worshiped Kātyāyanī, the demigoddess, but the only benediction they wanted from the goddess was to have Kṛṣṇa as their husband. A Vaiṣṇava is not interested in asking any benediction from the demigods, nor is he interested in asking benediction from the Supreme Personality of Godhead. It is said in the *Bhāgavatam* that liberation can be offered by the Supreme Person, but even if a pure devotee is offered liberation by the Supreme Lord, he refuses to accept it. Dhruva Mahārāja did not ask Kuvera for transference to the spiritual world, which is called liberation; he simply asked that wherever he would remain—whether in the spiritual or material world—he would always remember the Supreme Personality of Godhead. A Vaiṣṇava is always respectful to everyone. So when Kuvera offered him a benediction, he did not refuse it. But he wanted something which would be favorable to his advancement in Kṛṣṇa consciousness.

TEXT 10

अथायजत यज्ञेशं क्रतुभिर्भूरिदक्षिणैः ।
द्रव्यक्रियादेवतानां कर्म कर्मफलप्रदम् ॥१०॥

athāyajata yajñeśaṁ
kratubhir bhūri-dakṣiṇaiḥ
dravya-kriyā-devatānāṁ
karma karma-phala-pradam

atha—thereafter; *ayajata*—he worshiped; *yajña-īśam*—the master of sacrifices; *kratubhiḥ*—by sacrificial ceremonies; *bhūri*—great; *dakṣiṇaiḥ*—by charities; *dravya-kriyā-devatānām*—of (sacrifices including various) paraphernalia, activities, and demigods; *karma*—the objective; *karma-phala*—the result of activities; *pradam*—who awards.

TRANSLATION

As long as he remained at home, Dhruva Mahārāja performed many great ceremonial sacrifices in order to please the enjoyer of all sacrifices, the Supreme Personality of Godhead. Prescribed ceremonial sacrifices are especially meant to please Lord Viṣṇu, who is the objective of all such sacrifices and who awards the resultant benedictions.

PURPORT

In *Bhagavad-gītā* (Bg.3.9) it is said, *yajñārthāt karmaṇo 'nyatra loko 'yaṁ karma-bandhanaḥ:* one should act or work only in order to please the Supreme Lord, otherwise he becomes entangled in the resultant reactions. According to the four divisions of *varṇa* and *āśrama, kṣatriyas* and *vaiśyas* are especially advised to perform great ceremonial sacrifices and to distribute their accumulated money very liberally. Dhruva Mahārāja, as a king and ideal *kṣatriya,* performed many such sacrifices, giving very liberally in charity. *Kṣatriyas* and *vaiśyas* are supposed to earn their money and accumulate great riches. Sometimes they do it by acting sinfully. *Kṣatriyas* are meant to rule over a country; Dhruva Mahārāja, for example, in the course of ruling, had to fight and kill many Yakṣas. Such action is necessary for *kṣatriyas.* A *kṣatriya* should not be a coward, and he should not be nonviolent; to rule over the country he has to act violently.

Kṣatriyas and the *vaiśyas* are therefore especially advised to give in charity at least fifty percent of their accumulated wealth. In *Bhagavad-gītā* it is recommended that even though one enters the renounced order of life, he still cannot give up the performance of *yajña, dāna,* and *tapasya.* They are never to be given up. *Tapasya* is meant for the renounced order of life; those who are retired from worldly activities should perform *tapasya,* penances and austerities. Those who are in the material world, the *kṣatriyas* and the *vaiśyas*, must give in charity. *Brahmacārīs,* in the beginning of their lives, should perform different kinds of *yajñas.*

Dhruva Mahārāja, as an ideal king, practically emptied his treasury by giving in charity. A king is not meant to simply realize taxes from the citizens and accumulate wealth to spend in sense gratification. World monarchy has failed ever since kings began to satisfy their personal senses with the taxes accumulated from the citizens. Of course, whether the system is monarchy or democracy, the same corruption is still going on. At the present moment there are different parties in the democratic government, but everyone is busy trying to keep their posts or trying to keep their political party in power. They have very little time to think of the welfare of the citizens, whom they oppress with heavy taxes in the form of income tax, sales tax and many other taxes—people sometimes have eighty to ninety percent of their income taken away, and these taxes are lavishly spent for the high salaries drawn by the officers and rulers. Formerly, the taxes accumulated from the citizens were spent for performing great sacrifices as enjoined in the Vedic literature. At the present moment, however, almost all forms of sacrifice are not at all possible; therefore, it is recommended in the *śāstras* that people should perform *saṅkīrtana-yajña.* Any householder, regardless of his position, can perform this *saṅkīrtana-yajña* without expenditure. All the family members can sit down together and simply clap their hands and chant the Hare Kṛṣṇa *mahā-mantra.* Somehow or other, everyone can manage to perform such a *yajña* and distribute *prasāda* to the people in general. That is quite sufficient for this age of Kali. The Kṛṣṇa consciousness movement is based on this principle: chant the Hare Kṛṣṇa *mantra* every moment, as much as possible, both inside and outside of the temples, and, as far as possible, distribute *prasāda.* This process can be accelerated with the cooperation of state administrators and those who are producing the country's wealth. Simply by liberal distribution of *prasāda* and *saṅkīrtana,* the whole world can become peaceful and prosperous.

Generally in all the material sacrifices recommended in the Vedic literature there are offerings to the demigods. This demigod worship is especially meant for less intelligent men. Actually, the result of such sacrifice goes to the Supreme Personality of Godhead, Nārāyaṇa. Lord Kṛṣṇa says in *Bhagavad-gītā, bhoktāraṁ yajña-tapasām:* He is actually the enjoyer of all sacrifices (Bg. 5.29). His name is, therefore, Yajñapuruṣa.

Although he was a great devotee and had nothing to do with these sacrifices, still, to set an example to his people, Dhruva Mahārāja performed many sacrifices and gave all his wealth in charity. For as long as he lived as a householder, he never spent a farthing for his sense gratification. In this verse the word *karma-phala-pradam* is very significant. The Lord awards everyone different kinds of *karma* as the individual living entities desire; He is the Supersoul present within the heart of everyone, and He is so kind and liberal that He gives everyone full facilities to perform whatever acts one wants. Then the result of the action is also enjoyed by the living entity. If anyone wants to enjoy or lord it over material nature, the Lord gives him full facilities, but he becomes entangled in the resultant reactions. Similarly, if anyone wants to engage himself fully in devotional service, the Lord gives him full facilities, and the devotee enjoys the results. The Lord is therefore known as *karma-phala-prada.*

TEXT 11

सर्वात्मन्यच्युतेऽसर्वे तीव्रौघां भक्तिमुद्वहन् ।
ददर्शात्मनि भूतेषु तमेवावस्थितं विभुम् ॥११॥

sarvātmany acyute 'sarve
tīvraughāṁ bhaktim udvahan
dadarśātmani bhūteṣu
tam evāvasthitaṁ vibhum

sarva-ātmani—unto the Supersoul; *acyute*—infallible; *asarve*—without any limit; *tīvra-oghām*—with unrelenting force; *bhaktim*—devotional service; *udvahan*—rendering; *dadarśa*—he saw; *ātmani*—in the Supreme Spirit; *bhūteṣu*—in all living entities; *tam*—Him; *eva*—only; *avasthitam*—situated; *vibhum*—all-powerful.

TRANSLATION

Dhruva Mahārāja rendered devotional service unto the Supreme, the reservoir of everything, with unrelenting force. While carrying out his devotional service to the Lord, he could see that everything is situated in Him only and that He is situated in all living entities. The Lord is called acyuta because He never fails in His prime duty, to give protection to His devotees.

PURPORT

Dhruva Mahārāja not only performed many sacrifices, but he carried on his transcendental occupation, engagement in the devotional service of the Lord. The ordinary *karmīs* who want to enjoy the results of fruitive activities are concerned only with sacrifices and ritualistic ceremonies as enjoined in the Vedic *śāstras*. Although Dhruva Mahārāja performed many sacrifices in order to be an exemplary king, he was constantly engaged in devotional service. The Lord always protects His surrendered devotee. A devotee can see that the Lord is situated in everyone's heart, as stated in the *Bhagavad-gītā* (*īśvaraḥ sarva-bhūtānāṁ hṛd-deśe 'rjuna tiṣṭhati*). Ordinary persons cannot understand how the Supreme Lord is situated in everyone's heart, but a devotee can actually see Him. Not only can he see Him outwardly, but he can see, with spiritual vision, that everything is resting in the Supreme Personality of Godhead, as described in *Bhagavad-gītā (mat-sthāni sarva-bhūtāni)*. That is the vision of a *mahā-bhāgavata*. He sees everything others see, but instead of seeing merely the trees, the mountains, the cities or the sky, he sees only his worshipable Supreme Personality of Godhead in everything, because everything is resting in Him only. This is the vision of the *mahā-bhāgavata.* In summary, a *mahā-bhāgavata,* a highly elevated pure devotee, sees the Lord everywhere as well as within the heart of everyone. This is possible for devotees who have developed elevated devotional service to the Lord. As stated in the *Brahma-saṁhitā, premāñjana-cchurita-bhakti-vilocanena:* only those who have smeared their eyes with the ointment of love of Godhead can see everywhere the Supreme Lord face to face; it is not possible by imagination or so-called meditation (Bs. 5.38).

TEXT 12

तमेवं शीलसम्पन्नं ब्रह्मण्यं दीनवत्सलम् ।
गोप्तारं धर्मसेतूनां मेनिरे पितरं प्रजाः ॥१२॥

tam evaṁ śīla-sampannaṁ
brahmaṇyaṁ dīna-vatsalam
goptāraṁ dharma-setūnāṁ
menire pitaraṁ prajāḥ

tam—him; *evam*—thus; *śīla*—with godly qualities; *sampannam*—endowed; *brahmaṇyam*—respectful to the *brāhmaṇas; dīna*—to the poor; *vatsalam*—kind; *goptāram*—protector; *dharma-setūnām*—of religious principles; *menire*—thought; *pitaram*—father; *prajāḥ*—the citizens.

TRANSLATION

Dhruva Mahārāja was endowed with all the godly qualities; he was very respectful to the devotees of the Supreme Lord and very kind to the poor and innocent, and he protected religious principles. With all these qualifications, he was considered to be the direct father of all the citizens.

PURPORT

The personal qualities of Dhruva Mahārāja described herein are the exemplary qualities of a saintly king. Not only a king but also the leaders of a modern democratic or impersonal government must be qualified with all these godly characteristics. Then the citizens of the state can be happy. It is clearly stated here that the citizens thought of Dhruva Mahārāja as their father; as a child, depending on the able father, is completely satisfied, so the citizens of the state, being protected by the state or the king, should remain satisfied in every respect. At the present moment, however, there is no guarantee by the government of even the primary necessities of life in the state, namely, the protection of the lives and property of the citizens.

One word is very significant in this connection: *brahmaṇyam.* Dhruva Mahārāja was very devoted to the *brāhmaṇas,* who engage in the study of the *Vedas* and thereby know the Supreme Personality of Godhead. They are always busy propagating Kṛṣṇa consciousness. The state should be very respectful to societies that distribute God consciousness all over the world, but, unfortunately, at the present moment there is no state or government support given to such movements. As for good qualities, it is very difficult to find anyone in state administration with any good qualities. The administrators simply sit in their administrative posts and say "no" to every request, as if they were paid to say "no" to the citizens. Another word, *dīna-vatsalam,* is very significant also. The state head should be very kind to the innocent. Unfortunately in this age the state agents and the presidents draw good salaries from the state, and they pose themselves as very pious, but they allow the running of slaughterhouses where innocent animals are killed. If we try to compare the godly qualities of Dhruva Mahārāja to the qualities of modern statesmen, we can see that there is no actual comparison. Dhruva Mahārāja was present in the Satya-yuga, as will be clear from the next verses. He was the ideal king in Satya-yuga. The government administration in the present age (Kali-yuga) is bereft of all godly qualities. Considering all these points, the people today have no alternative but to take to Kṛṣṇa consciousness for protection of religion, life and property.

TEXT 13

षट्त्रिंशद्वर्षसाहस्रं शशास क्षितिमण्डलम् ।
भोगैः पुण्यक्षयं कुर्वन्नभोगैरशुभक्षयम् ॥१३॥

ṣaṭ-triṁśad-varṣa-sāhasraṁ
śaśāsa kṣiti-maṇḍalam
bhogaiḥ puṇya-kṣayaṁ kurvann
abhogair aśubha-kṣayam

ṣaṭ-triṁśat—thirty-six; *varṣa*—years; *sāhasram*—thousand; *śaśāsa*—ruled; *kṣiti-maṇḍalam*—the earth planet; *bhogaiḥ*—by enjoyment; *puṇya*—of reactions of pious activities; *kṣayam*—diminution; *kurvan*—doing; *abhogaiḥ*—by austerities; *aśubha*—of inauspicious reactions; *kṣayam*—diminution.

TRANSLATION

Dhruva Mahārāja ruled over this planet for 36,000 years; he diminished the reactions of pious activities by enjoyment, and by practicing austerities he diminished inauspicious reactions.

PURPORT

That Dhruva Mahārāja ruled over the planet for 36,000 years means that he was present in the Satya-yuga because in the Satya-yuga people used to live for 100,000 years. In the next *yuga,* Tretā, people used to live for 10,000 years, and in the next *yuga,* Dvāpara, for 1,000 years. In the present age, the Kali-yuga, the maximum duration of life is 100 years. With the change of the *yugas,* the duration of life and memory, the quality of kindness—all good qualities—diminish. There are two kinds of activities, namely pious and impious. By executing pious activities one can gain facilities for higher material enjoyment, but due to impious activities one has to undergo severe distress. A devotee, however, is not interested in enjoyment or affected by distress. When he is prosperous he knows, "I am diminishing the results of my pious activities," and when he is in distress he knows, "I am diminishing the reactions of my impious activities." A devotee is not concerned with enjoyment or distress; he simply desires to execute devotional service. It is said in the *Śrīmad-Bhāgavatam* that devotional service should be *apratihatā,* not checked by the material conditions of happiness or distress. The devotee undergoes processes of austerity such as observing Ekādaśī and similar other fasting days and restraining from illicit sex life, intoxication, gambling and meat-eating. Thus he becomes purified from the reactions of his past impious life, and because he engages in devotional service, which is the most pious activity, he enjoys life without separate endeavor.

TEXT 14

एवं बहुसवं कालं महात्माविचलेन्द्रियः ।
त्रिवर्गौपयिकं नीत्वा पुत्रायादान्नृपासनम् ॥१४॥

evaṁ bahu-savaṁ kālaṁ
mahātmāvicalendriyaḥ
trivargaupayikaṁ nītvā
putrāyādān nṛpāsanam

evam—thus; *bahu*—many; *savam*—years; *kālam*—time; *mahātmā*—great soul; *avicala-indriyaḥ*—without being disturbed by sense agitation;

tri-varga—three kinds of worldly activities; *aupayikam*—favorable for executing; *nītvā*—having passed; *putrāya*—to his son; *adāt*—he handed over; *nṛpa-āsanam*—the royal throne.

TRANSLATION

The self-controlled great soul Dhruva Mahārāja thus passed many, many years favorably executing three kinds of worldly activities, namely religiosity, economic development and satisfaction of all material desires. Thereafter he handed over the charge of the royal throne to his son.

PURPORT

Perfection of materialistic life is suitably attained by the process of observing religious principles. This leads automatically to successful economic development, and thus there is no difficulty in satisfying all material desires, but since, as a king, he had to keep up his status quo or it would not have been possible to rule over the people in general, he did it perfectly. But as soon as he saw that his son was grown up and could take charge of the royal throne, he immediately handed over the charge and retired from all material engagements.

One word used here is very significant—*avicalendriya,* which means that neither was he disturbed by the agitation of the senses nor was his sense power diminished, although in years he was a very old man. Since he ruled over the world for 36,000 years, naturally one may conclude that he became very, very old, but factually his senses were very young—and yet he was not interested in sense gratification. In other words, he remained self-controlled. He performed his duties perfectly according to the materialistic way. That is the way of behavior of great devotees. Śrīla Raghunātha dāsa Gosvāmī, one of the direct disciples of Lord Caitanya, was the son of a very rich man. Although he had no interest in enjoying material happiness, when he was entrusted to do something in managing the state, he did it perfectly. Śrīla Gaurasundara advised him, "From within, keep yourself and your mind completely aloof, but externally execute the material duties just as they need to be done." This transcendental position can be achieved by devotees only, as described in the *Bhagavad-gītā:* while others, such as *yogīs*, try to control their senses by force, devotees, even though possessing full sense powers, do not use them because they engage in higher transcendental activities.

TEXT 15

मन्यमान इदं विश्वं मायारचितमात्मनि ।
अविद्यारचितस्वप्नगन्धर्वनगरोपमम् ॥१५॥

manyamāna idaṁ viśvaṁ
māyā-racitam ātmani
avidyā-racita-svapna-
gandharva-nagaropamam

manyamānaḥ—realizing; *idam*—this; *viśvam*—universe; *māyā*—by the external energy; *racitam*—manufactured; *ātmani*—unto the living entity; *avidyā*—by illusion; *racita*—manufactured; *svapna*—a dream; *gandharva-nagara*—phantasmagoria; *upamam*—like.

TRANSLATION

Śrīla Dhruva Mahārāja realized that this cosmic manifestation bewilders living entities like a dream or phantasmagoria because it is a creation of the illusory external energy of the Supreme Lord.

PURPORT

In the deep forest sometimes it appears that there are big palaces and nice cities. That is technically called *gandharva-nagara.* Similarly, in dreams also we create many false things out of imagination. A self-realized person or a devotee knows well that this material cosmic manifestation is a temporary illusory representation appearing to be truth. It is like phantasmagoria. But behind this shadow creation there is reality—the spiritual world. A devotee is interested in the spiritual world, not its shadow. Since he has realization of the supreme truth, a devotee is not interested in this temporary shadow of truth. This is confirmed in the *Bhagavad-gītā (paraṁ dṛṣṭvā nivartate).*

TEXT 16

आत्मस्त्र्यपत्यसुहृदो बलमृद्धकोश-
मन्तःपुरं परिविहारभुवश्च रम्याः ।
भूमण्डलं जलधिमेखलमाकलय्य
कालोपसृष्टमिति स प्रययौ विशालाम् ॥१६॥

ātma-stry-apatya-suhṛdo balam ṛddha-kośam
antaḥ-puraṁ parivihāra-bhuvaś ca ramyāḥ
bhū-maṇḍalaṁ jaladhi-mekhalam ākalayya
kālopasṛṣṭam iti sa prayayau viśālām

ātma—body; *strī*—wives; *apatya*—children; *suhṛdaḥ*—friends; *balam*—influence, army; *ṛddha-kośam*—rich treasury; *antaḥ-puram*—female residential quarters; *parivihāra-bhuvaḥ*—pleasure-grounds; *ca*—and; *ramyāḥ*—beautiful; *bhū-maṇḍalam*—the complete earth; *jala-dhi*—by oceans; *mekhalam*—bound; *ākalayya*—considering; *kāla*—by time; *upasṛṣṭam*—created; *iti*—thus; *saḥ*—he; *prayayau*—went; *viśālām*—to Badarikāśrama.

TRANSLATION

Thus Dhruva Mahārāja, at the end, left his kingdom, which extended all over the earth and was bounded by the great oceans. He considered his body, his wife, his children, his friends, his army, his rich treasury, his very comfortable palaces and his many enjoyable pleasure-grounds to be creations of the illusory energy. Thus in due course of time he retired to the forest known as Badarikāśrama in the Himalayas.

PURPORT

In the beginning of his life, when he went to the forest in search of the Supreme Personality of Godhead, Dhruva Mahārāja realized that all bodily conceptions of pleasure are products of the illusory energy. In the very beginning, of course, he was after the kingdom of his father, and in order to get it he went to search for the Supreme Lord. But he later realized that everything is the creation of the illusory energy. From the acts of Śrīla Dhruva Mahārāja we can understand that somehow or other if one becomes Kṛṣṇa conscious—it does not matter what his motivation is in the beginning—he will eventually realize the real truth by the grace of the Lord. In the beginning, Dhruva Mahārāja was interested in the kingdom of his father, but later on he became a great devotee, *mahā-bhāgavata,* and had no interest in material enjoyment. The perfection of life can be achieved only by devotees. Even if one completes only a minute percentage of devotional service and then falls down from his immature position, he is better than a person who fully engages in the fruitive activities of this material world.

TEXT 17

तस्यां विशुद्धकरणः शिववार्विगाह्य
बद्ध्वाऽऽसनं जितमरुन्मनसाऽऽहृताक्षः ।

स्थूले दधार भगवत्प्रतिरूप एतद्
ध्यायंस्तदव्यवहितो व्यसृजत्समाधौ ॥१७॥

tasyāṁ viśuddha-karaṇaḥ śiva-vār vigāhya
baddhvāsanaṁ jita-marun manasāhṛtākṣaḥ
sthūle dadhāra bhagavat-pratirūpa etad
dhyāyaṁs tad avyavahito vyasṛjat samādhau

tasyām—in Badarikāśrama; *viśuddha*—purified; *karaṇaḥ*—his senses; *śiva*—pure; *vāḥ*—water; *vigāhya*—bathing in; *baddhvā*—having fixed; *āsanam*—sitting position; *jita*—controlled; *marut*—breathing process; *manasā*—by the mind; *āhṛta*—withdrawn; *akṣaḥ*—his senses; *sthūle*—physical; *dadhāra*—he concentrated; *bhagavat-pratirūpe*—on the exact form of the Lord; *etat*—the mind; *dhyāyan*—meditating upon; *tat*—that; *avyavahitaḥ*—without stopping; *vyasṛjat*—he entered; *samādhau*—into trance.

TRANSLATION

In Badarikāśrama Dhruva Mahārāja's senses became completely purified because he bathed regularly in the crystal-clear purified water. He fixed his sitting position and by yogic practice controlled the breathing process and the air of life; in this way his senses were completely withdrawn. Then he concentrated his mind on the arcā-vigraha form of the Lord, which is the exact replica of the Lord, and thus meditating upon Him he entered into complete trance.

PURPORT

Here is a description of the *aṣṭāṅga-yoga* system, to which Dhruva Mahārāja was already accustomed. *Aṣṭāṅga-yoga* was never meant to be practiced in a fashionable city. Dhruva Mahārāja went to Badarikāśrama, and in a solitary place, alone, he practiced *yoga.* He concentrated his mind on the *arcā-vigraha,* the worshipable Deity of the Lord, which exactly represents the Supreme Lord, and thus thinking constantly of that Deity, he became absorbed in trance. Worship of the *arcā-vigraha* is not idol worship. The *arcā-vigraha* is an incarnation of the Lord in a form appreciable by a devotee. Therefore devotees engage in the temple in the service of the Lord as *arcā-vigraha,* a form made of *sthūla* (material) objects such as stone, metal, wood, jewels or paint. All of these are called *sthūla*, or physical representations. Since the devotees follow the regulative principles of worship, even though the Lord is there in His physical form, He is non-different from His original spiritual form. Thus the devotee gets the benefit of achieving the ultimate goal of life, that is to say, becoming always absorbed in thought of the Lord. This incessant thought of the Lord, as prescribed in the *Bhagavad-gītā,* makes one the topmost *yogī.*

TEXT 18

भक्तिं हरौ भगवति प्रवहन्नजस्र-
मानन्दबाष्पकलया मुहुरर्द्यमानः ।
विक्लिद्यमानहृदयः पुलकाचिताङ्गो
नात्मानमस्मरदसाविति मुक्तलिङ्गः ॥१८॥

bhaktiṁ harau bhagavati pravahann ajasram
ānanda-bāṣpa-kalayā muhur ardyamānaḥ
viklidyamāna-hṛdayaḥ pulakācitāṅgo
nātmānam asmarad asāv iti mukta-liṅgaḥ

bhaktim—devotional service; *harau*—unto Hari; *bhagavati*—the Supreme Personality of Godhead; *pravahan*—constantly engaging in; *ajasram*—always; *ānanda*—blissful; *bāṣpa-kalayā*—by a stream of tears; *muhuḥ*—again and again; *ardyamānaḥ*—being overcome; *viklidyamāna*—melting; *hṛdayaḥ*—his heart; *pulaka*—standing of hairs; *ācita*—covered; *aṅgaḥ*—his body; *na*—not; *ātmānam*—body; *asmarat*—he remembered; *asau*—he; *iti*—thus; *mukta-liṅgaḥ*—free from the subtle body.

TRANSLATION

Due to his transcendental bliss, incessant tears flowed from his eyes, his heart melted, and there was shivering and standing of the hairs all over his body. Thus transformed, in a trance of devotional service, Dhruva Mahārāja completely forgot his bodily existence, and thus he immediately became liberated from material bondage.

PURPORT

Due to constant engagement in devotional service—hearing, chanting, remembering, worshiping the Deity, etc., as prescribed in nine varieties—there are different symptoms which appear in the body of a devotee. These eight bodily transformations, which indicate that a devotee is already liberated within himself, are called *aṣṭa-sāttvika-vikāra.* When a devotee completely forgets his bodily existence, he is to be understood as liberated. He is no longer encaged in the body. The example is given that when a coconut becomes completely dry, the coconut pulp within the coconut shell separates from the bondage of the shell and the outer covering. By moving the dry coconut, one can hear that the pulp within is no longer attached to the shell or to the covering. Similarly, when one is fully absorbed in devotional service, he is completely disconnected from the two material coverings, the subtle and gross bodies. Dhruva Mahārāja actually attained this stage of life by constantly discharging devotional service. He is already described as a *mahā-bhāgavata,* for unless one becomes a *mahā-bhāgavata,* or a first-class pure devotee, these symptoms are not visible. Lord Caitanya exhibited all these symptoms. Ṭhākura Haridāsa also exhibited them, and there are many pure devotees who manifested such bodily symptoms. They are not to be imitated, but when one is actually advanced, these symptoms are exhibited. At that time it is to be understood that a devotee is materially free. Of course, from the beginning of devotional service the path of liberation immediately opens, just as the coconut taken from the tree immediately begins to dry; it simply takes some time for the shell and pulp to separate from one another.

An important word in this verse is *mukta-liṅgaḥ. Mukta* means liberated, and *liṅga* means the subtle body. When a man dies, he quits the gross body, but the subtle body of mind, intelligence and ego carries him to a new body. While existing in the present body, the same subtle body carries him from one stage of life to another (for example, from childhood to boyhood) by mental development. The mental condition of a baby is different from that of a boy, the mental condition of a boy is different from that of a young man, and the mental condition of a young man is different from that of an old man. So at death the process of changing bodies takes place due to the subtle body; the mind, intelligence and ego carry the soul from one gross body to another. This is called transmigration of the soul. But there is another stage, when one becomes liberated even from the subtle body; at that time the living entity is competent and fully prepared to be transferred to the transcendental or spiritual world.

The description of the bodily symptoms of Śrī Dhruva Mahārāja makes it apparent that he became perfectly fit to be transferred to the spiritual world. One can experience the distinction between the subtle and gross bodies even daily; in a dream, one's gross body is lying on the bed while the subtle body carries the soul, the living entity, to another atmosphere. But because the gross body has to be continued, the subtle body comes back and settles in the present gross body. Therefore one has to become free from the subtle body also. This freedom is known as *mukta-liṅga.*

TEXT 19

स ददर्श विमानाग्र्यं नभसोऽवतरद् ध्रुवः ।
विभ्राजयद्दश दिशो राकापतिमिवोदितम् ॥१९॥

sa dadarśa vimānāgryaṁ
nabhaso 'vatarad dhruvaḥ
vibhrājayad daśa diśo
rākāpatim ivoditam

saḥ—he; *dadarśa*—saw; *vimāna*—an airplane; *agryam*—very beautiful; *nabhasaḥ*—from the sky; *avatarat*—descending; *dhruvaḥ*—Dhruva Mahārāja; *vibhrājayat*—illuminating; *daśa*—ten; *diśaḥ*—directions; *rākā-patim*—the full moon; *iva*—like; *uditam*—visible.

TRANSLATION

As soon as the symptoms of his liberation were manifest, he saw a very beautiful airplane coming down from the sky, as if the brilliant full moon were coming down, illuminating all the ten directions.

PURPORT

There are different levels of acquired knowledge—direct knowledge, knowledge received from authorities, transcendental knowledge, knowledge beyond the senses, and finally spiritual knowledge. When one surpasses the stage of acquiring knowledge by the descending process, he is immediately situated on the transcendental platform. Dhruva Mahārāja, being liberated from the material concept of life, was situated in transcendental knowledge and could perceive the presence of a transcendental airplane which was as brilliant as the full moonlight. This is not possible in the stages of direct or indirect perception of knowledge. Such knowledge is a special favor of the Supreme Personality of Godhead. One can, however, rise to this platform of knowledge by the gradual process of advancing in devotional service, or Kṛṣṇa consciousness.

TEXT 20

तत्रानु देवप्रवरौ चतुर्भुजौ
श्यामौ किशोरावरुणाम्बुजेक्षणौ ।
स्थिताववष्टभ्य गदां सुवाससौ
किरीटहाराङ्गदचारुकुण्डलौ ॥२०॥

tatrānu deva-pravarau catur-bhujau
śyāmau kiśorāv aruṇāmbujekṣaṇau
sthitāv avaṣṭabhya gadāṁ suvāsasau
kirīṭa-hārāṅgada-cāru-kuṇḍalau

tatra—there; *anu*—then; *deva-pravarau*—two very beautiful demigods; *catuḥ-bhujau*—with four arms; *śyāmau*—blackish; *kiśorau*—quite young; *aruṇa*—reddish; *ambuja*—lotus flower; *īkṣaṇau*—with eyes; *sthitau*—situated; *avaṣṭabhya*—holding; *gadām*—clubs; *su-vāsasau*—with nice garments; *kirīṭa*—helmets; *hāra*—necklaces; *aṅgada*—bracelets; *cāru*—beautiful; *kuṇḍalau*—with earrings.

TRANSLATION

Dhruva Mahārāja saw two very beautiful associates of Lord Viṣṇu in the plane. They had four hands and a blackish bodily luster; they were very youthful, and their eyes were just like reddish lotus flowers. They held clubs in their hands, and they were dressed in very attractive garments with helmets and were decorated with necklaces, bracelets and earrings.

PURPORT

The inhabitants of Viṣṇuloka are of the same bodily feature as Lord Viṣṇu, and they also hold club, conchshell, lotus flower and disc. In this verse it is distinctly stated that they had four hands and were nicely dressed; the description of their bodily decorations corresponds exactly to that of Viṣṇu. So the two uncommon personalities who descended from the airplane came directly from Viṣṇuloka, or the planet where Lord Viṣṇu lives.

TEXT 21

विज्ञाय तावुत्तमगायकिङ्करा-
वभ्युत्थितः साध्वसविस्मृतक्रमः ।
ननाम नामानि गृणन्मधुद्विषः
पार्षत्प्रधानाविति संहताञ्जलिः ॥२१॥

vijñāya tāv uttamagāya-kiṅkarāv
abhyutthitaḥ sādhvasa-vismṛta-kramaḥ
nanāma nāmāni gṛṇan madhu-dviṣaḥ
pārṣat-pradhānāv iti saṁhatāñjaliḥ

vijñāya—after understanding; *tau*—them; *uttama-gāya*—of Lord Viṣṇu (of excellent renown); *kiṅkarau*—two servants; *abhyutthitaḥ*—stood up; *sādhvasa*—by being puzzled; *vismṛta*—forgot; *kramaḥ*—proper behavior; *nanāma*—

offered obeisances; *nāmāni*—names; *gṛṇan*—chanting; *madhu-dviṣaḥ*—of the Lord (the enemy of Madhu); *pārṣat*—associates; *pradhānau*—chief; *iti*—thus; *saṁhata*—respectfully joined; *añjaliḥ*—with folded hands.

TRANSLATION

Dhruva Mahārāja, seeing that these uncommon personalities were direct servants of the Supreme Personality of Godhead, immediately stood up. But, being puzzled, in hastiness he forgot how to receive them in the proper way. Therefore, he simply offered obeisances with folded hands and chanted and glorified the holy names of the Lord.

PURPORT

Chanting of the holy names of the Lord is perfect in every way. When Dhruva Mahārāja saw the Viṣṇudūtas, the direct associates of Lord Viṣṇu, four-handed and nicely decorated, he could understand who they were, but for the time being he was puzzled. But simply by chanting the holy name of the Lord, the Hare Kṛṣṇa *mantra,* he could satisfy the uncommon guests who had all of a sudden arrived before him. The chanting of the holy name of the Lord is perfect; even though one does not know how to please Lord Viṣṇu or His associates, simply by sincerely chanting the holy name of the Lord, everything becomes perfect. A devotee, therefore, either in danger or in happiness, constantly chants the Hare Kṛṣṇa *mantra.* When he is in danger he is immediately relieved, and when he is in a position to see Lord Viṣṇu or His associates directly, by chanting this *mahā-mantra* he can please the Lord. This is the absolute nature of the *mahā-mantra.* Either in danger or in happiness, it can be chanted without limitation.

TEXT 22

तं कृष्णपादाभिनिविष्टचेतसं
बद्धाञ्जलिं प्रश्रयनम्रकन्धरम् ।
सुनन्दनन्दावुपसृत्य सस्मितं
प्रत्यूचतुः पुष्करनाभसम्मतौ ॥२२॥

taṁ kṛṣṇa-pādābhiniviṣṭa-cetasaṁ
baddhāñjaliṁ praśraya-namra-kandharam
sunanda-nandāv upasṛtya sasmitaṁ
pratyūcatuḥ puṣkara-nābha-sammatau

tam—him; *kṛṣṇa*—of Lord Kṛṣṇa; *pāda*—of the lotus feet; *abhiniviṣṭa*—absorbed in thought; *cetasam*—whose heart; *baddha-añjalim*—with folded hands; *praśraya*—very humbly; *namra*—bowed; *kandharam*—whose neck; *sunanda*—Sunanda; *nandau*—and Nanda; *upasṛtya*—approaching; *sa-smitam*—smilingly; *pratyūcatuḥ*—addressed; *puṣkara-nābha*—of Lord Viṣṇu, who has a lotus navel; *sammatau*—confidential servants.

TRANSLATION

Dhruva Mahārāja was always absorbed in thinking of the lotus feet of Lord Kṛṣṇa. His heart was full with Kṛṣṇa. When the two confidential servants of the Supreme Lord, who were named Nanda and Sunanda, approached him, smiling happily, Dhruva stood with folded hands, bowing humbly. They then addressed him as follows.

PURPORT

In this verse the word *puṣkara-nābha-sammatau* is significant. Kṛṣṇa, or Lord Viṣṇu, is known for His lotus eyes, lotus navel, lotus feet and lotus palms. Here He is called *puṣkara-nābha,* which means the Supreme Personality of Godhead who has a lotus navel, and *sammatau* means two confidential or very obedient servants. The materialistic way of life differs from the spiritual way of life in that one is disobedience and one is obedience to the will of the Supreme Lord. All living entities are part and parcel of the Supreme Lord, and they are supposed to be always agreeable to the order of the Supreme Person; that is perfect oneness.

In the Vaikuṇṭha world all the living entities are in oneness with the Supreme Godhead because they never defy His orders. Here in the material world, however, they are not *sammata,* agreeable, but always *asammata,* disagreeable. This human form of life is a chance to be trained to be agreeable to the orders of the Supreme Lord. To bring about this training in society is the mission of the Kṛṣṇa consciousness movement. As stated in the *Bhagavad-gītā,* the laws of material nature are very strict; no one can overcome the stringent laws of material nature. But one who becomes a surrendered soul and agrees to the order of the Supreme Lord can easily overcome those stringent laws. The example of Dhruva Mahārāja is very fitting. Simply by becoming agreeable to the orders of the Supreme Personality of Godhead and by developing love of Godhead, Dhruva got the chance to personally meet the confidential servants of Lord Viṣṇu face to face. What is possible for Dhruva Mahārāja is possible for everyone. Anyone who very seriously engages in devotional service can obtain, in due course of time, the same perfection of the human form of life.

TEXT 23

सुनन्दनन्दावूचतुः
भो भो राजन् सुभद्रं ते वाचं नोऽवहितः शृणु ।
यः पञ्चवर्षस्तपसा भवान्देवमतीतृपत् ॥२३॥

sunanda-nandāv ūcatuḥ
bho bho rājan subhadraṁ te
vācaṁ no 'vahitaḥ śṛṇu
yaḥ pañca-varṣas tapasā
bhavān devam atītṛpat

sunanda-nandau ūcatuḥ—Sunanda and Nanda said; *bhoḥ bhoḥ rājan*—O dear King; *su-bhadram*—good fortune; *te*—unto you; *vācam*—words; *naḥ*—our; *avahitaḥ*—attentively; *śṛṇu*—hear; *yaḥ*—who; *pañca-varṣaḥ*—five years old; *tapasā*—by austerity; *bhavān*—yourself; *devam*—the Supreme Personality of Godhead; *atītṛpat*—greatly satisfied.

TRANSLATION

The two confidential associates of Lord Viṣṇu, Nanda and Sunanda, said: Dear King, let there be all good fortune unto you. Please attentively hear what we shall say. When you were only five years old, you underwent severe austerities, and you thereby greatly satisfied the Supreme Personality of Godhead.

PURPORT

What was possible for Dhruva Mahārāja is possible for anyone. Any five-year-old child can be trained, and within a very short time his life will become successful by realization of Kṛṣṇa consciousness. Unfortunately, this training is lacking all over the world. It is necessary for the leaders of the Kṛṣṇa consciousness movement to start educational institutions in different parts of the world to train children, starting at the age of five years. Thus such children will not become hippies or spoiled children of society, but they can all become devotees of the Lord. The face of the world will then change automatically.

TEXT 24

तस्याखिलजगद्धातुरावां देवस्य शार्ङ्गिणः ।
पार्षदाविह सम्प्राप्तौ नेतुं त्वां भगवत्पदम् ॥२४॥

tasyākhila-jagad-dhātur
āvāṁ devasya śārṅgiṇaḥ
pārṣadāv iha samprāptau
netuṁ tvāṁ bhagavat-padam

tasya—His; *akhila*—entire; *jagat*—universe; *dhātuḥ*—creator; *āvām*—we; *devasya*—of the Supreme Personality of Godhead; *śārṅgiṇaḥ*—who has the bow named Śārṅga; *pārṣadau*—associates; *iha*—now; *samprāptau*—approached; *netum*—to take; *tvām*—you; *bhagavat-padam*—to the position of the Supreme Personality of Godhead.

TRANSLATION

We are representatives of the Supreme Personality of Godhead, the creator of the whole universe, who carries in His hand the bow named Śārṅga. We have been specifically deputed to take you to the spiritual world.

PURPORT

In *Bhagavad-gītā* the Lord says that simply by knowing His transcendental pastimes (whether within this material world or in the spiritual world), anyone who understands factually who He is, how He appears and how He acts can be immediately fit for transfer to the spiritual world. This principle stated in the *Bhagavad-gītā* operated in the case of King Dhruva. Throughout his life he tried to understand the Supreme Personality of Godhead by austerity and penances. Now, the mature result was that Dhruva Mahārāja became fit to be carried to the spiritual world, accompanied by the confidential associates of the Lord.

TEXT 25

सुदुर्जयं विष्णुपदं जितं त्वया
यत्सूरयोऽप्राप्य विचक्षते परम् ।
आतिष्ठ तच्चन्द्रदिवाकरादयो
ग्रहर्क्षतारा: परियन्ति दक्षिणम् ॥२५॥

sudurjayaṁ viṣṇu-padaṁ jitaṁ tvayā
yat sūrayo 'prāpya vicakṣate param
ātiṣṭha tac candra-divākarādayo
graharkṣa-tārāḥ pariyanti dakṣiṇam

sudurjayam—very difficult to achieve; *viṣṇu-padam*—planet known as Vaikuṇṭhaloka or Viṣṇuloka; *jitam*—conquered; *tvayā*—by you; *yat*—which; *sūrayaḥ*—great demigods; *aprāpya*—without achieving; *vicakṣate*—simply see; *param*—supreme; *ātiṣṭha*—please come; *tat*—that; *candra*—the moon; *divākara*—sun; *ādayaḥ*—and others; *graha*—the nine planets (Mercury, Venus, Earth, Mars, Jupiter, Saturn, Uranus, Neptune, and Pluto); *ṛkṣa-tārāḥ*—stars; *pariyanti*—circumambulate; *dakṣiṇam*—to the right.

TRANSLATION

To achieve Viṣṇuloka is very difficult, but by your austerity you have conquered. Even the great ṛṣis and demigods cannot achieve this position. Simply to see the supreme abode [the Viṣṇu planet], the sun and moon and all the other planets, stars, lunar mansions, and solar systems are circumambulating it. Now please come; you are welcome to go there.

PURPORT

Even in this material world the so-called scientists, philosophers and mental speculators strive to merge into the spiritual sky, but they can never go there. But a devotee, by executing devotional service, not only realizes what the spiritual world actually is, but he factually goes there to live an eternal life of bliss and knowledge. The Kṛṣṇa consciousness movement is so potent that by adopting these principles of life and developing love of God one can very easily go back home, back to Godhead. Here the practical example is the case of Dhruva Mahārāja. While the scientist and philosopher go to the moon but are disappointed in their attempts to stay there and live, the devotee makes an easy journey to other planets and ultimately goes back to Godhead. Devotees have no interest in seeing other planets, but while going back to Godhead, they see all of them as passing phases, just as one who is going to a distant place passes through many small stations.

TEXT 26

अनास्थितं ते पितृभिरन्यैरप्यङ्ग कर्हिचित् ।
आतिष्ठ जगतां वन्द्यं तद्विष्णोः परमं पदम् ॥२६॥

anāsthitaṁ te pitṛbhir
anyair apy aṅga karhicit
ātiṣṭha jagatāṁ vandyaṁ
tad viṣṇoḥ paramaṁ padam

anāsthitam—never achieved; *te*—your; *pitṛbhiḥ*—by forefathers; *anyaiḥ*—by others; *api*—even; *aṅga*—O Dhruva; *karhicit*—at any time; *ātiṣṭha*—please come and live there; *jagatām*—by the inhabitants of the universe; *vandyam*—worshipable; *tat*—that; *viṣṇoḥ*—of Lord Viṣṇu; *paramam*—supreme; *padam*—situation.

TRANSLATION

Dear King Dhruva, neither your forefathers nor anyone else before you ever achieved such a transcendental planet. The planet known as Viṣṇuloka, where Lord Viṣṇu personally resides, is the highest of all. It is worshipable by the inhabitants of all other planets within the universe. Please come with us and live there eternally.

PURPORT

When Dhruva Mahārāja went to perform austerities he was very determined to achieve a post never dreamed of by his forefathers. His father was Uttānapāda, his grandfather was Manu, and his great-grandfather was Lord Brahmā. So Dhruva wanted a kingdom even greater than Lord Brahmā could achieve, and he requested Nārada Muni to give him facility for achieving it. The associates of Lord Viṣṇu reminded him that not only his forefathers but everyone else before him was unable to attain Viṣṇuloka, the planet where Lord Viṣṇu resides. This is because everyone within this material world is either a *karmī, jñānī,* or a *yogī,* but there are hardly any pure devotees. The transcendental planet known as Viṣṇuloka is especially meant for devotees, not for *karmīs, jñānīs* or *yogīs.* Great *ṛṣis* or demigods can hardly approach Brahmaloka, and, as stated in *Bhagavad-gītā,* Brahmaloka is not a permanent residence. Lord Brahmā's duration of life is so long that it is difficult to estimate even the duration of one day in his life, and yet Lord Brahmā also dies, as do the residents of his planet. *Bhagavad-gītā* says, *ābrahma-bhuvanāl lokāḥ punar āvartino 'rjuna*: except for those who go to Viṣṇuloka, everyone is subjected to the four principles of material life, namely birth, death, old age and disease (Bg. 8.16). The Lord says, *yad gatvā na nivartante tad dhāma paramaṁ mama*: the planet from which, once going, no one returns, is My supreme abode (Bg. 15.6). Dhruva Mahārāja was reminded, "You are going in our company to that planet from which no one returns to this material world." Material scientists are attempting to go to the moon and other planets, but they cannot imagine going to the topmost planet, Brahmaloka, for it is beyond their imaginations. By material calculation, traveling at the speed of light it would take forty thousand years to reach the topmost planet. By mechanical processes we are unable to reach the topmost planet of this universe, but the process called *bhakti-yoga*, as executed by Mahārāja Dhruva, can give one the facility not only to reach other planets within this universe, but also to reach beyond this universe to the Viṣṇuloka planets. We have outlined this in our small booklet *Easy Journey to Other Planets.*

TEXT 27

एतद्विमानप्रवरमुत्तमश्लोकमौलिना ।
उपस्थापितमायुष्मन्नधिरोढुं त्वमर्हसि ॥२७॥

etad vimāna-pravaram
uttama-śloka-maulinā
upasthāpitam āyuṣmann
adhiroḍhuṁ tvam arhasi

etat—this; *vimāna*—airplane; *pravaram*—unique; *uttamaśloka*—the Supreme Personality of Godhead; *maulinā*—by the head of all living entities; *upasthāpitam*—sent; *āyuṣman*—O immortal one; *adhiroḍhum*—to board; *tvam*—you; *arhasi*—are worthy.

TRANSLATION

O immortal one, this unique airplane has been sent by the Supreme Personality of Godhead, who is worshiped by selected prayers and who is the chief of all living entities. You are quite worthy to board such a plane.

PURPORT

According to astronomical calculation, along with the Pole Star there is another star, which is called Śiśumāra, where Lord Viṣṇu, who is in charge of the maintenance of this material world, resides. Śiśumāra or Dhruvaloka can never be reached by anyone but the Vaiṣṇavas, as will be described by the following *ślokas.* The associates of Lord Viṣṇu brought the special airplane for Dhruva Mahārāja and then informed him that Lord Viṣṇu had especially sent this airplane.

The Vaikuṇṭha airplane does not move by mechanical arrangement. There are three processes for moving in outer space. One of the processes is known to the modern scientist. It is called *kapota-vāyu. Ka* means outer space, and *pota* means ship. There is a second process also called *kapota-vāyu. Kapota* means pigeon. One can train pigeons to carry one into outer space. The third process is very subtle. It is called *ākāśa-patana.* This *ākāśa-patana* system is also material. Just as the mind can fly anywhere one likes without mechanical arrangement, so the *ākāśa-patana* airplane can fly at the speed of mind. Beyond this *ākāśa-patana* system is the Vaikuṇṭha process, which is completely spiritual. The airplane sent by Lord Viṣṇu to carry Dhruva Mahārāja to Śiśumāra was a completely spiritual, transcendental airplane. Material scientists can neither see such vehicles nor imagine how they fly in the air. The material scientist has no information about the spiritual sky, although it is mentioned in the *Bhagavad-gītā (paras tasmāt tu bhāvo 'nyaḥ).*

TEXT 28

मैत्रेय उवाच
निशम्य वैकुण्ठनियोज्यमुख्ययो-
र्मधुच्युतं वाचमुरुक्रमप्रियः ।
कृताभिषेकः कृतनित्यमङ्गलो
मुनीन् प्रणम्याशिषमभ्यवादयत् ॥२८॥

maitreya uvāca
niśamya vaikuṇṭha-niyojya-mukhyayor
madhu-cyutaṁ vācam urukrama-priyaḥ
kṛtābhiṣekaḥ kṛta-nitya-maṅgalo
munīn praṇamyāśiṣam abhyavādayat

maitreyaḥ uvāca—the great sage Maitreya said; *niśamya*—after hearing; *vaikuṇṭha*—of the Lord; *niyojya*—associates; *mukhyayoḥ*—of the chief; *madhu-cyutam*—like pouring honey; *vācam*—speeches; *urukrama-priyaḥ*—Dhruva Mahārāja, who was very dear to the Lord; *kṛta-abhiṣekaḥ*—took his sacred bath; *kṛta*—performed; *nitya-maṅgalaḥ*—his daily spiritual duties; *munīn*—to the sages; *praṇamya*—having offered obeisances; *āśiṣam*—blessings; *abhyavādayat*—accepted.

TRANSLATION

The great sage Maitreya continued: Mahārāja Dhruva was very dear to the Supreme Personality of Godhead. When he heard the sweet speeches of the Lord's chief associates in the Vaikuṇṭha planet, he immediately took his sacred bath, dressed himself with suitable ornaments, and performed his daily spiritual duties. Thereafter he offered his respectful obeisances to the great sages present there and accepted their blessings.

PURPORT

We should mark how dutiful Dhruva Mahārāja was in his devotional service, even at the time he left this material world. He was constantly alert in the performance of devotional duties. Every devotee should take his bath early in the morning and decorate his body with *tilaka.* In Kaliyuga one can hardly acquire gold or jeweled ornaments, but the twelve *tilaka* marks on the body are sufficient as auspicious decorations to purify the body. Since Dhruva Mahārāja was living at that time at Badarikāśrama, there were other great sages there. He did not become puffed up because the airplane sent by Lord Viṣṇu was waiting for him; as a humble Vaiṣṇava, he accepted blessings from all the sages before riding on the plane brought by the chief of the Vaikuṇṭha associates.

TEXT 29

परीत्याभ्यर्च्य धिष्ण्याग्र्यं पार्षदावभिवन्द्य च ।
इयेष तदधिष्ठातुं बिभ्रद्रूपं हिरण्मयम् ॥२९॥

parītyābhyarcya dhiṣṇyāgryaṁ
pārṣadāv abhivandya ca
iyeṣa tad adhiṣṭhātuṁ
bibhrad rūpaṁ hiraṇmayam

parītya—having circumambulated; *abhyarcya*—having worshiped; *dhiṣṇya-agryam*—the transcendental airplane; *pārṣadau*—unto the two associates; *abhivandya*—having offered obeisances; *ca*—also; *iyeṣa*—he attempted; *tat*—that plane; *adhiṣṭhātum*—to board; *bibhrat*—illuminating; *rūpam*—his form; *hiraṇmayam*—golden.

TRANSLATION

Before getting aboard, Dhruva Mahārāja worshiped the airplane, circumambulated it, and also offered obeisances to the associates of Viṣṇu. In the meantime he became as brilliant and illuminating as molten gold. He was thus completely prepared to board the transcendental plane.

PURPORT

In the absolute world, the plane as well as the associates of Lord Viṣṇu and Lord Viṣṇu Himself are all spiritual. There is no material contamination. In quality, everything there is one. As Lord Viṣṇu is worshipable, so also are His associates, His paraphernalia, His airplane and His abode, for everything of Viṣṇu's is as good as Lord Viṣṇu. Dhruva Mahārāja knew all this very well, as a pure Vaiṣṇava, and he offered his respects to the associates and to the plane before riding in it. But in the meantime, his body changed into spiritual existence, and therefore it was illuminating like molten gold. In this way he also became one with the other paraphernalia of Viṣṇuloka.

Māyāvādī philosophers cannot imagine how this oneness can be achieved even in different varieties. Their idea of oneness is that there is no variety. Therefore they have become impersonalists. As Śiśumāra, Viṣṇuloka or Dhruvaloka are completely different from this material world, so a Viṣṇu temple within this world is also completely different from this material world. As soon as we are in a temple we should know very well that we are situated differently from the material world. In the temple, Lord Viṣṇu, His throne, His room and everything associated with the temple are transcendental. The three modes, *sattva-guṇa, rajo-guṇa* and *tamo-guṇa,* have no entrance into the temple. It is said, therefore, that to live in the forest is in the mode of goodness, to live in the city is in the mode of passion, and to live in a brothel, liquor shop or slaughterhouse is in the mode of ignorance. But to live in the temple means to live in Vaikuṇṭhaloka. Everything in the temple is as worshipable as Lord Viṣṇu or Kṛṣṇa.

TEXT 30

तदोत्तानपदः पुत्रो ददर्शान्तकमागतम् ।
मृत्योर्मूर्ध्नि पदं दत्त्वा आरुरोहाद्भुतं गृहम् ॥३०॥

tadottānapadaḥ putro
dadarśāntakam āgatam
mṛtyor mūrdhni padaṁ dattvā
ārurohādbhutaṁ gṛham

tadā—then; *uttānapadaḥ*—of King Uttānapāda; *putraḥ*—son; *dadarśa*—could see; *antakam*—death personified; *āgatam*—approached him; *mṛtyoḥ mūrdhni*—on the head of death; *padam*—feet; *dattvā*—placing; *āruroha*—got up; *adbhutam*—wonderful; *gṛham*—on the airplane which resembled a big house.

TRANSLATION

When Dhruva Mahārāja was attempting to get on the transcendental plane, he saw death personified approach him. Not caring for death, how-

ever, he took advantage of the opportunity to put his feet on the head of death, and thus he got up on the airplane, which was as big as a house.

PURPORT

To take the passing away of a devotee and the passing away of a nondevotee as one and the same is completely misleading. While ascending the transcendental airplane, Dhruva Mahārāja suddenly saw death personified before him, but he was not afraid. Instead of death's giving him trouble, Dhruva Mahārāja took advantage of death's presence and put his feet on the head of death. People with a poor fund of knowledge do not know the difference between the death of a devotee and the death of a nondevotee. In this connection, an example can be given: a cat carries its kittens in its mouth, and it also catches a rat in its mouth. Superficially, the catching of the rat and the kitten appear to be one and the same, but actually they are not. When the cat catches the rat in its mouth it means death for the rat, whereas when the cat catches the kitten, the kitten enjoys it. When Dhruva Mahārāja boarded the airplane, he took advantage of the arrival of death personified, who came to offer him obeisances; putting his feet on the head of death, he got up on the unique airplane, which is described here to be as big as a house *(gṛham).*

There are many other similar instances in *Bhāgavata* literature. It is stated that when Kardama Muni created an airplane to carry his wife, Devahūti, all over the universe, the airplane was like a big city, carrying many houses, lakes and gardens. Modern scientists have manufactured big airplanes, but they are packed with passengers, who experience all sorts of discomforts while riding in them.

Material scientists are not even perfect in manufacturing a material airplane. In order to compare with the plane used by Kardama or the plane sent from Viṣṇuloka, they must manufacture an airplane equipped like a big city, with all the comforts of life—lakes, gardens, parks, etc. Their plane must be able to fly in outer space and hover and visit all other planets. If they invent such a plane they will not have to make different space stations for fuel to travel into outer space. Such a plane would have an unlimited supply of fuel, or, like the plane from Viṣṇuloka, would fly without it.

TEXT 31

तदा दुन्दुभयो नेदुर्मृदङ्गपणवादयः ।
गन्धर्वमुख्याः प्रजगुः पेतुः कुसुमवृष्टयः ॥३१॥

tadā dundubhayo nedur
mṛdaṅga-paṇavādayaḥ
gandharva-mukhyāḥ prajaguḥ
petuḥ kusuma-vṛṣṭayaḥ

tadā—at that time; *dundubhayaḥ*—kettledrums; *neduḥ*—resounded; *mṛdaṅga*—drums; *paṇava*—small drums; *ādayaḥ*—etc.; *gandharva-mukhyāḥ*—the chief residents of Gandharvaloka; *prajaguḥ*—sang; *petuḥ*—showered; *kusuma*—flowers; *vṛṣṭayaḥ*—like rains.

TRANSLATION

At that time drums and kettledrums resounded from the sky, the chief Gandharvas began to sing, and other demigods showered flowers like torrents of rain upon Dhruva Mahārāja.

TEXT 32

स च स्वर्लोकमारोक्ष्यन् सुनीतिं जननीं ध्रुवः ।
अन्वस्मरदगं हित्वा दीनां यास्ये त्रिविष्टपम् ॥३२॥

sa ca svarlokam ārokṣyan
sunītiṁ jananīṁ dhruvaḥ
anvasmarad agaṁ hitvā
dīnāṁ yāsye tri-viṣṭapam

saḥ—He; *ca*—also; *svar-lokam*—to the celestial planet; *ārokṣyan*—about to ascend; *sunītim*—Sunīti; *jananīm*—mother; *dhruvaḥ*—Dhruva Mahārāja; *anvasmarat*—immediately remembered; *agam*—difficult to attain; *hitvā*—leaving behind; *dīnām*—poor; *yāsye*—I shall go; *tri-viṣṭapam*—to the Vaikuṇṭha planet.

TRANSLATION

Dhruva was seated in the transcendental airplane, which was just about to start, when he remembered his poor mother, Sunīti. He thought to himself, "How shall I go alone to the Vaikuṇṭha planet and leave behind my poor mother?"

PURPORT

Dhruva had a feeling of obligation to his mother, Sunīti. It was Sunīti who gave him the clue which had enabled him to now be personally carried to the Vaikuṇṭha planet by the associates of Lord Viṣṇu. He now remembered her and wanted to take her with him. Actually, Dhruva Mahārāja's mother, Sunīti, was his *patha-pradarśaka-guru. Patha-pradarśaka-guru* means the *guru* or the spiritual master who shows the way. Such a *guru* is sometimes called *śikṣā-guru.* Although Nārada Muni was his *dīkṣā-guru* (initiating spiritual master), Sunīti, his mother, was the first who gave him instruction on how to achieve the favor of the Supreme Personality of Godhead. It is the duty of the *śikṣā-guru* or *dīkṣā-guru* to instruct the disciple in the right way, and it depends on the disciple to execute the process. According to śāstric injunctions, there is no difference between *śikṣā-guru* and *dīkṣā-guru,* and generally the *śikṣā-guru* later on becomes the *dīkṣā-guru.* Sunīti, however, being a woman, and specifically his mother, could not become Dhruva Mahārāja's *dīkṣā-guru.* Still, he was not less obliged to Sunīti. There was no question of carrying Nārada Muni to Vaikuṇṭhaloka, but Dhruva Mahārāja thought of his mother.

Whatever plan the Supreme Personality of Godhead contemplates immediately fructifies. Similarly, a devotee who is completely dependent on the Supreme Lord can also fulfill his wishes by the grace of the Lord. The Lord fulfills His wishes independently, but a devotee fulfills his wishes simply by being dependent on the Supreme Personality of Godhead. Therefore as soon as Dhruva Mahārāja thought of his poor mother, he was assured by the associates of Viṣṇu that Sunīti was also going to Vaikuṇṭhaloka in another plane. Dhruva Mahārāja had thought that he was going alone to Vaikuṇṭhaloka, leaving behind his mother, which was not very auspicious because people would criticize him for going alone to Vaikuṇṭhaloka and not carrying with him Sunīti, who had given him so much. But Dhruva also considered that he was not personally the Supreme. Therefore, if Kṛṣṇa fulfilled his desires, only then would it be possible. Kṛṣṇa could immediately understand his mind, and He told him that his mother was also going with him. This incident proves that a pure devotee like Dhruva Mahārāja can fulfill all his desires; by the grace of the Lord, he becomes exactly like the Lord, and thus whenever he thinks of anything, his wish is immediately fulfilled.

TEXT 33

इति व्यवसितं तस्य व्यवसाय सुरोत्तमौ ।
दर्शयामासतुर्देवीं पुरो यानेन गच्छतीम् ॥३३॥

iti vyavasitaṁ tasya
vyavasāya surottamau
darśayām āsatur devīṁ
puro yānena gacchatīm

iti—thus; *vyavasitam*—contemplation; *tasya*—of Dhruva; *vyavasāya*—understanding; *sura-uttamau*—the two chief associates; *darśayām āsatuḥ*—showed (to him); *devīm*—exalted Sunīti; *puraḥ*—before; *yānena*—by airplane; *gacchatīm*—going forward.

TRANSLATION

The great associates of Vaikuṇṭhaloka, Nanda and Sunanda, could understand the mind of Dhruva Mahārāja, and thus they showed him that his mother, Sunīti, was going forward in another plane.

PURPORT

This incident proves that the *śikṣā* or *dīkṣā-guru* who has a disciple who strongly executes devotional service like Dhruva Mahārāja can be carried by the disciple even though the instructor is not as advanced. Although Sunīti was an instructor to Dhruva Mahārāja, she could not go to the forest because she was a woman, nor could she execute austerities and penances as Dhruva Mahārāja did. Still, Dhruva Mahārāja was able to take his mother with him. Similarly, Prahlāda Mahārāja also delivered his atheistic father, Hiraṇyakaśipu. The conclusion is that a disciple or an offspring who is a very strong devotee can carry with him to Vaikuṇṭhaloka either his father, mother or *śikṣā* or *dīkṣā-guru.* Śrīla Bhaktisiddhānta Sarasvatī Ṭhākura used to say, "If I could perfectly deliver even one soul back home, back to Godhead, I would think my mission—propagating Kṛṣṇa consciousness—to be successful." The Kṛṣṇa consciousness movement is spreading now all over the world, and sometimes I think that even though I am crippled in many ways, if one of my disciples becomes as strong as Dhruva Mahārāja, then he will be able to carry me with him to Vaikuṇṭhaloka.

TEXT 34

तत्र तत्र प्रशंसद्भिः पथि वैमानिकैः सुरैः ।
अवकीर्यमाणो ददृशे कुसुमैः क्रमशो ग्रहान् ॥३४॥

tatra tatra praśaṁsadbhiḥ
pathi vaimānikaiḥ suraiḥ
avakīryamāṇo dadṛśe
kusumaiḥ kramaśo grahān

tatra tatra—here and there; *praśaṁsadbhiḥ*—by persons engaged in the praise of Dhruva Mahārāja; *pathi*—on the path; *vaimānikaiḥ*—carried by different types of airplanes; *suraiḥ*—by the demigods; *avakīryamāṇaḥ*—

being covered; *dadṛśe*—could see; *kusumaiḥ*—by flowers; *kramaśaḥ*—one after another; *grahān*—all the planets of the solar system.

TRANSLATION

While Dhruva Mahārāja was passing through space, he gradually saw all the planets of the solar system, and on the path he saw all the demigods in their airplanes showering flowers upon him like rain.

PURPORT

There is a Vedic version, *yasmin vijñāte sarvam evaṁ vijñātaṁ bhavanti,* which means that by knowing the Supreme Personality of Godhead, everything becomes known to the devotee. Similarly, by going to the planet of the Supreme Personality of Godhead, one can know all the other planetary systems on the path to Vaikuṇṭha. We should remember that Dhruva Mahārāja's body was different from our bodies. While boarding the Vaikuṇṭha airplane, his body changed to a completely spiritual golden hue. No one can surpass the higher planets in a material body, but when one gets a spiritual body he can travel not only to the higher planetary system of this material world, but he can go even to the still higher planetary system known as Vaikuṇṭhaloka. It is well known that Nārada Muni travels everywhere, both in the spiritual and material worlds.

It should be noted also that while Sunīti was going to Vaikuṇṭhaloka she also changed her body into spiritual form. Like Śrī Sunīti, every mother should train her child to become a devotee like Dhruva Mahārāja. Sunīti instructed her son, even at the age of five years, to be unattached to worldly affairs and to go to the forest to search out the Supreme Lord. She never desired that her son remain at home comfortably without ever undertaking austerities and penances to achieve the favor of the Supreme Personality of Godhead. Every mother, like Sunīti, must take care of her son and train him to become a *brahmacārī* from the age of five years and to undergo austerities and penances for spiritual realization. The benefit will be that if her son becomes a strong devotee like Dhruva, certainly not only will he be transferred back home, back to Godhead, but she will also be transferred with him to the spiritual world, even though she may be unable to undergo austerities and penances in executing devotional service.

TEXT 35

त्रिलोकीं देवयानेन सोऽतिव्रज्य मुनीनपि ।
परस्ताद्यद् ध्रुवगतिर्विष्णोः पदमथाभ्यगात् ॥३५॥

tri-lokīṁ deva-yānena
so 'tivrajya munīn api
parastād yad dhruva-gatir
viṣṇoḥ padam athābhyagāt

tri-lokīm—the three planetary systems; *deva-yānena*—by the transcendental airplane; *saḥ*—Dhruva; *ativrajya*—having surpassed; *munīn*—great sages; *api*—even; *parastāt*—beyond; *yat*—which; *dhruva-gatiḥ*—Dhruva, who attained permanent life; *viṣṇoḥ*—of Lord Viṣṇu; *padam*—abode; *atha*—then; *abhyagāt*—achieved.

TRANSLATION

Dhruva Mahārāja thus surpassed the seven planetary systems of the great sages who are known as saptarṣi. Beyond that region, he achieved the transcendental situation of permanent life in the planet where Lord Viṣṇu lives.

PURPORT

The airplane was piloted by the two chief associates of Lord Viṣṇu, namely Sunanda and Nanda. Only such spiritual astronauts can pilot their airplane beyond the seven planets and arrive in the region of eternal blissful life. It is confirmed in the *Bhagavad-gītā* also *(paras tasmāt tu bhāvo 'nyaḥ)* that beyond this planetary system begins the spiritual sky, where everything is permanent and blissful. The planets there are known as Viṣṇuloka or Vaikuṇṭhaloka. Only there can one get an eternal blissful life of knowledge. Below Vaikuṇṭhaloka is the material universe, where Lord Brahmā and others in Brahmaloka can live until the annihilation of this universe; but that life is not permanent. That is also confirmed in the *Bhagavad-gītā (ābrahma-bhuvanāl lokāḥ).* Even if one goes to the topmost planet, one cannot achieve eternal life. Only by arriving in Vaikuṇṭhaloka can one live an eternally blissful life.

TEXT 36

यद् भ्राजमानं स्वरुचैव सर्वतो
लोकास्त्रयो ह्यनु विभ्राजन्त एते ।
यन्नाव्रजञ्जन्तुषु येऽननुग्रहा
व्रजन्ति भद्राणि चरन्ति येऽनिशम् ॥३६॥

yad bhrājamānaṁ sva-rucaiva sarvato
lokās trayo hy anu vibhrājanta ete
yan nāvrajañ jantuṣu ye 'nanugrahā
vrajanti bhadrāṇi caranti ye 'niśam

yat—which planet; *bhrājamānam*—illuminating; *sva-rucā*—by self-effulgence; *eva*—only; *sarvataḥ*—everywhere; *lokāḥ*—planetary systems; *trayaḥ*—three; *hi*—certainly; *anu*—thereupon; *vibhrājante*—give off light; *ete*—these; *yat*—which planet; *na*—not; *avrajat*—have reached; *jantuṣu*—to living entities; *ye*—those who; *ananugrahāḥ*—not merciful; *vrajanti*—reach; *bhadrāṇi*—welfare activities; *caranti*—engage in; *ye*—those who; *aniśam*—constantly.

TRANSLATION

The self-effulgent Vaikuṇṭha planets, by whose illumination alone all the illuminating planets within this material world give off reflected light, cannot be reached by those who are not merciful to other living entities. Only persons who constantly engage in welfare activities for other living entities can reach the Vaikuṇṭha planets.

PURPORT

Here is a description of two aspects of the Vaikuṇṭha planets. The first is that in the Vaikuṇṭha sky there is no need of the sun and moon. This is confirmed by the *Upaniṣads* as well as *Bhagavad-gītā (na tad bhāsayate sūryo na śaśāṅko na pāvakaḥ).* In the spiritual world the Vaikuṇṭhalokas are themselves illuminated; there is therefore no need of sun, moon or electric light. It is, in fact, the illumination of the Vaikuṇṭhalokas which is reflected in the material sky. Only by this reflection are the suns in the material universes illuminated; after the illumination of the sun, all the stars and moons are illuminated. In other words, all the luminaries in the material sky borrow illumination from Vaikuṇṭhaloka. From this material world, however, people can be transferred to the Vaikuṇṭhaloka, if they incessantly engage in welfare activities for all other living entities. Such incessant welfare activities can really be performed only in Kṛṣṇa consciousness. There is no other philanthropic work within this material world but Kṛṣṇa consciousness which can engage a person twenty-four hours a day.

A Kṛṣṇa conscious being is always engaged in planning how to take all the suffering humanity back home, back to Godhead. Even if one is not successful in reclaiming all the fallen souls back to Godhead, still, because he is Kṛṣṇa conscious, his path to Vaikuṇṭhaloka is open. He personally becomes qualified to enter the Vaikuṇṭhalokas, and if anyone follows such a devotee, he also enters into Vaikuṇṭhaloka. Others, who engage in envious activities, are known as *karmīs. Karmīs* are envious of one another. Simply for sense gratification, they can kill thousands of innocent animals. *Jñānīs* are not as sinful as *karmīs,* but they do not try to reclaim others back to Godhead. They perform austerities for their own liberation. *Yogīs* are also engaged in self-aggrandizement by trying to attain mystic powers. But devotees, Vaiṣṇavas, who are servants of the Lord, come forward in the actual field of work in Kṛṣṇa consciousness to reclaim fallen souls. Only Kṛṣṇa conscious persons are eligible to enter into the spiritual world. That is clearly stated in this verse and is confirmed in the *Bhagavad-gītā,* wherein the Lord says that there is no one dearer to Him than those who preach the gospel of *Bhagavad-gītā* to the world.

TEXT 37

शान्ताः समदृशः शुद्धाः सर्वभूतानुरञ्जनाः ।
यान्त्यञ्जसाच्युतपदमच्युतप्रियबान्धवाः ॥३७॥

śāntāḥ samadṛśaḥ śuddhāḥ
sarva-bhūtānurañjanāḥ
yānty añjasācyuta-padam
acyuta-priya-bāndhavāḥ

śāntāḥ—peaceful; *samadṛśaḥ*—equipoised; *śuddhāḥ*—cleansed, purified; *sarva*—all; *bhūta*—living entities; *anurañjanāḥ*—pleasing; *yānti*—go; *añjasā*—easily; *acyuta*—of the Lord; *padam*—to the abode; *acyuta-priya*—with devotees of the Lord; *bāndhavāḥ*—friends.

TRANSLATION

Persons who are peaceful, equipoised, cleansed and purified, and who know the art of pleasing all other living entities, keep friendship only with devotees of the Lord; they alone can very easily achieve the perfection of going back home, back to Godhead.

PURPORT

The description of this verse fully indicates that only devotees are eligible to enter into the kingdom of Godhead. The first point stated is that devotees are peaceful, for they have no demands for their personal sense gratification. They are simply dedicated to the service of the Lord. *Karmīs* cannot be peaceful because they have immense demands for sense gratification. As for *jñānīs,* they cannot be peaceful because they are too busy trying to attain liberation or merge into the existence of the Supreme.

Similarly, *yogīs* are also restless to get mystic power. But a devotee is peaceful because he is fully surrendered to the Supreme Personality of Godhead and thinks of himself as completely helpless; just as a child feels complete peace in depending on the parent, so a devotee is completely peaceful, for he depends on the mercy of the Supreme Personality of Godhead.

A devotee is equipoised. He sees everyone on the same transcendental platform. A devotee knows that although a conditioned soul has a particular type of body according to his past fruitive activities, factually everyone is part of the Supreme Lord. A devotee sees all living entities with spiritual vision and does not discriminate on the platform of the bodily concept of life. Such qualities develop only in the association of devotees. Without the association of devotees, one cannot advance in Kṛṣṇa consciousness. Therefore, we have established the International Society for Krishna Consciousness. Factually, whoever lives in this society automatically develops Kṛṣṇa consciousness. Devotees are dear to the Supreme Personality of Godhead, and the Supreme Personality of Godhead is only dear to devotees. On this platform only can one make progress in Kṛṣṇa consciousness. Persons in Kṛṣṇa consciousness, or devotees of the Lord, can please everyone, as is evident in the Kṛṣṇa consciousness movement. We invite everyone, without discrimination; we request everyone to sit down and chant the Hare Kṛṣṇa *mantra* and take as much *prasāda* as we can supply—and thus everyone is pleased with us. This is the qualification. *Sarva-bhūtānurañjanāḥ.* As for purification, no one can be more pure than devotees. Anyone who once utters the name of Viṣṇu immediately becomes purified, inside and outside *(yaḥ smaret puṇḍarīkākṣam).* Since a devotee constantly chants the Hare Kṛṣṇa *mantra,* no contamination of the material world can touch him. He is, therefore, actually purified. *Muci haya śuci haya yadi kṛṣṇa bhaje.* It is said that even a cobbler or person born in the family of a cobbler can be elevated to the position of a *brāhmaṇa (śuci)* if he takes to Kṛṣṇa consciousness. Any person who is purely Kṛṣṇa conscious and who engages in chanting the Hare Kṛṣṇa *mantra* is the purest in the whole universe.

TEXT 38

इत्युत्तानपदः पुत्रो ध्रुवः कृष्णपरायणः ।
अभूत्त्रयाणां लोकानां चूडामणिरिवामलः ॥३८॥

ity uttānapadaḥ putro
dhruvaḥ kṛṣṇa-parāyaṇaḥ
abhūt trayāṇāṁ lokānāṁ
cūḍā-maṇir ivāmalaḥ

iti—thus; *uttānapadaḥ*—of Mahārāja Uttānapāda; *putraḥ*—the son; *dhruvaḥ*—Dhruva Mahārāja; *kṛṣṇa-parāyaṇaḥ*—fully Kṛṣṇa conscious; *abhūt*—became; *trayāṇām*—of the three; *lokānām*—worlds; *cūḍā-maṇiḥ*—the summit jewel; *iva*—like; *amalaḥ*—purified.

TRANSLATION

In this way, the fully Kṛṣṇa conscious Dhruva Mahārāja, the exalted son of Mahārāja Uttānapāda, attained the summit of the three statuses of planetary systems.

PURPORT

The exact Sanskrit terminology for Kṛṣṇa consciousness is here mentioned: *kṛṣṇa-parāyaṇaḥ. Parāyaṇa* means going forward. Anyone who is going forward to the goal of Kṛṣṇa is called *kṛṣṇa-parāyaṇa,* or fully Kṛṣṇa conscious. The example of Dhruva Mahārāja indicates that every Kṛṣṇa conscious person can expect to reach the topmost summit of all three planetary systems within the universe. A Kṛṣṇa conscious person can occupy an exalted position beyond the imagination of any ambitious materialist.

TEXT 39

गम्भीरवेगोऽनिमिषं ज्योतिषां चक्रमाहितम् ।
यस्मिन् भ्रमति कौरव्य मेढ्यामिव गवां गणः ॥३९॥

gambhīra-vego 'nimiṣaṁ
jyotiṣāṁ cakram āhitam
yasmin bhramati kauravya
meḍhyām iva gavāṁ gaṇaḥ

gambhīra-vegaḥ—with great force and speed; *animiṣam*—unceasingly; *jyotiṣām*—of luminaries; *cakram*—sphere; *āhitam*—connected; *yasmin*—around which; *bhramati*—encircles; *kauravya*—O Vidura; *meḍhyām*—a central pole; *iva*—as; *gavām*—of bulls; *gaṇaḥ*—a herd.

TRANSLATION

Saint Maitreya continued: My dear Vidura, descendant of Kuru, as a herd of bulls circumambulates a central pole on their right side, so all the luminaries within the universal sky unceasingly circumambulate the abode of Dhruva Mahārāja with great force and speed.

PURPORT

Each and every planet within the universe travels at a very high speed. From a statement in *Śrīmad-Bhāgavatam* it is understood that even the sun travels 16,000 miles in a second, and from *Brahmā-saṁhitā* we understand from the *śloka, yac-cakṣur eṣa savitā sakala-grahāṇām,* that the sun is considered to be the eye of the Supreme Personality of Godhead, Govinda, and it also has a specific orbit within which it circles. Similarly, all other planets have their specific orbits. But together all of them encircle the Pole Star, or Dhruvaloka, where Dhruva Mahārāja is situated at the summit of the three worlds. We can only imagine how highly exalted the actual position of a devotee is, and certainly we cannot even conceive how exalted is the position of the Supreme Personality of Godhead.

TEXT 40

महिमानं विलोक्यास्य नारदो भगवानृषिः ।
आतोद्यं वितुदञ् श्लोकान् सत्रेऽगायत्प्रचेतसाम् ॥४०॥

mahimānaṁ vilokyāsya
nārado bhagavān ṛṣiḥ
ātodyaṁ vitudañ ślokān
satre 'gāyat pracetasām

mahimānam—glories; *vilokya*—observing; *asya*—of Dhruva Mahārāja; *nāradaḥ*—the great sage Nārada; *bhagavān*—equally exalted like the Supreme Personality of Godhead; *ṛṣiḥ*—the saint; *ātodyam*—the string instrument, *vīṇā; vitudan*—playing on; *ślokān*—verses; *satre*—in the sacrificial arena; *agāyat*—chanted; *pracetasām*—of the Pracetās.

TRANSLATION

After observing the glories of Dhruva Mahārāja, the great sage Nārada, playing his vīṇā, went to the sacrificial arena of the Pracetās and very happily chanted the following three verses.

PURPORT

The great sage Nārada was the spiritual master of Dhruva Mahārāja. Certainly he was very glad to see his glories. As a father is very happy to see the son's advancement in every respect, so the spiritual master is very happy to observe the ascendancy of his disciple.

TEXT 41

नारद उवाच

नूनं सुनीतेः पतिदेवताया-
स्तपःप्रभावस्य सुतस्य तां गतिम् ।
दृष्ट्वाभ्युपायानपि   वेदवादिनो
नैवाधिगन्तुं प्रभवन्ति किं नृपाः ॥४१॥

nārada uvāca
nūnaṁ sunīteḥ pati-devatāyās
tapaḥ-prabhāvasya sutasya tāṁ gatim
dṛṣṭvābhyupāyān api veda-vādino
naivādhigantuṁ prabhavanti kiṁ nṛpāḥ

nāradaḥ uvāca—Nārada said; nūnam—certainly; sunīteḥ—of Sunīti; pati-devatāyāḥ—very much attached to her husband; tapaḥ-prabhāvasya—by the influence of austerity; sutasya—of the son; tām—that; gatim—position; dṛṣṭvā—observing; abhyupāyān—the means; api—although; veda-vādinaḥ—strict followers of the Vedic principles or the so-called Vedāntists; na—never; eva—certainly; adhigantum—to attain; prabhavanti—are eligible; kim—what to speak of; nṛpāḥ—ordinary kings.

TRANSLATION

The great sage Nārada said: Simply by the influence of his spiritual advancement and powerful austerity, Dhruva Mahārāja, the son of Sunīti, who was devoted to her husband, acquired an exalted position not possible even for the so-called Vedāntists or strict followers of the Vedic principles to attain, not to speak of ordinary human beings.

PURPORT

In this verse the word veda-vādinaḥ is very significant. Generally, a person who strictly follows the Vedic principles is called veda-vādī. There are also so-called Vedāntists who advertise themselves as followers of Vedānta philosophy but who misinterpret Vedānta. This expression is also found in the Bhagavad-gītā: veda-vāda-ratāḥ, which means persons who are attached to the Vedas without understanding the purport of the Vedas. Such persons may go on talking about the Vedas or may execute austerities in their own way, but it is not possible for them to attain to such an exalted position as Dhruva Mahārāja. As far as ordinary kings are concerned, it is not at all possible. The specific mention of kings is significant because formerly kings were also *rājarṣis*, for the kings were as good as great sages. Dhruva Mahārāja was a king, and at the same time he was as learned as a great sage. But without devotional service, neither a great king, a *kṣatriya*, nor a great *brāhmaṇa* strictly adhering to the Vedic principles can be elevated to the exalted position attained by Dhruva Mahārāja.

TEXT 42

यः पञ्चवर्षो गुरुदारवाक्शरै-
भिन्नेन यातो हृदयेन दूयता ।
वनं मदादेशकरोऽजितं प्रभुं
जिगाय तद्भक्तगुणैः पराजितम् ॥४२॥

yaḥ pañca-varṣo guru-dāra-vāk-śarair
bhinnena yāto hṛdayena dūyatā
vanaṁ mad-ādeśa-karo 'jitaṁ prabhuṁ
jigāya tad-bhakta-guṇaiḥ parājitam

yaḥ—he who; *pañca-varṣaḥ*—at the age of five years; *guru-dāra*—of the wife of his father; *vāk-śaraiḥ*—by the harsh words; *bhinnena*—being very much aggrieved; *yātaḥ*—went; *hṛdayena*—because his heart; *dūyatā*—very much pained; *vanam*—to the forest; *mat-ādeśa*—according to my instruction; *karaḥ*—acting; *ajitam*—unconquerable; *prabhum*—the Supreme Personality of Godhead; *jigāya*—he defeated; *tat*—His; *bhakta*—of devotees; *guṇaiḥ*—with the qualities; *parājitam*—conquered.

TRANSLATION

The great sage Nārada continued: Just see how Dhruva Mahārāja, aggrieved at the harsh words of his stepmother, went to the forest at the age of only five years and under my direction underwent austerity. Although the Supreme Personality of Godhead is unconquerable, still he defeated Him with the specific qualifications possessed by the Lord's devotees.

PURPORT

The Supreme Godhead is unconquerable; no one can conquer the Lord. But He voluntarily accepts subordination to the devotional qualities of His devotees. For example, Lord Kṛṣṇa accepted subordination to the control of mother Yaśodā because she was a great devotee. The Lord likes to be under the control of His devotees. In the *Caitanya-caritāmṛta* it is said that everyone comes before the Lord and offers Him exalted prayers, but the Lord does not feel as pleased when offered such prayers as He does when a devotee, out of pure love, chastises Him as a subordinate. The Lord forgets His exalted position and willingly submits to His pure devotee. Dhruva Mahārāja conquered the Supreme Lord because at a very tender age, only five years old, he underwent all the austerities of devotional service. This devotional service was of course executed under the direction of a great sage, Nārada. This is the first principle of devotional service—*ādau gurv-āśrayam.* In the beginning one must accept a bona fide spiritual master, and if a devotee follows strictly the direction of the spiritual master, as Dhruva Mahārāja followed the instruction of Nārada Muni, then it is not difficult for him to achieve the favor of the Lord.

The sum total of devotional qualities is development of unalloyed love for Kṛṣṇa. This unalloyed love for Kṛṣṇa can be achieved simply by hearing about Kṛṣṇa. Lord Caitanya accepted this principle—that if one in any position submissively hears the transcendental message spoken by Kṛṣṇa or about Kṛṣṇa, then gradually he develops the quality of unalloyed love, and by that love only he can conquer the unconquerable. The Māyāvādī philosophers aspire to become one with the Supreme Lord, but a devotee surpasses that position. A devotee not only becomes one in quality with the Supreme Lord, but he sometimes becomes the father, mother or master of the Lord. Arjuna also, by his devotional service, made Lord Kṛṣṇa his chariot driver; he ordered the Lord, "Put my chariot here," and the Lord executed his order. These are some examples of how a devotee can acquire the exalted position of conquering the unconquerable.

TEXT 43

यः क्षत्रबन्धुर्भुवि तस्याधिरूढ-
मन्वारुरुक्षेदपि वर्षपूगैः ।
षट्पञ्चवर्षो यदहोभिरल्पैः
प्रसाद्य वैकुण्ठमवाप तत्पदम् ॥४३॥

yaḥ kṣatra-bandhur bhuvi tasyādhirūḍham
anv ārurukṣed api varṣa-pūgaiḥ
ṣaṭ-pañca-varṣo yad ahobhir alpaiḥ
prasādya vaikuṇṭham avāpa tat-padam

yaḥ—one who; *kṣatra-bandhuḥ*—the son of a *kṣatriya; bhuvi*—on the earth; *tasya*—of Dhruva; *adhirūḍham*—the exalted position; *anu*—after; *ārurukṣet*—can aspire to attain; *api*—even; *varṣa-pūgaiḥ*—after many years; *ṣaṭ-pañca-varṣaḥ*—five or six years old; *yat*—which; *ahobhiḥ alpaiḥ*—after a few days; *prasādya*—after pleasing; *vaikuṇṭham*—the Lord; *avāpa*—attained; *tat-padam*—His abode.

TRANSLATION

Dhruva Mahārāja attained an exalted position at the age of only five or six years, after undergoing austerity for six months. Alas, a great kṣatriya cannot achieve such a position even after undergoing austerities for many, many years.

PURPORT

Dhruva Mahārāja is described herein as *kṣatra-bandhuḥ,* which indicates that he was not fully trained as a *kṣatriya* because he was only five years old; he was not a mature *kṣatriya.* A *kṣatriya* or *brāhmaṇa* has to take training. A boy born in the family of a *brāhmaṇa* is not immediately a *brāhmaṇa,* but he has to take up the training and the purificatory process.

The great sage Nārada Muni was very proud of having a devotee disciple like Dhruva Mahārāja. He had many other disciples, but he was very pleased with Dhruva Mahārāja because in one lifetime, by dint of his severe penances and austerities, he had achieved Vaikuṇṭha, which was never achieved by any other king's son or *rājarṣi* throughout the whole universe. There is the instance of the great King Bharata Mahārāja, who was also a great devotee, but he attained Vaikuṇṭhaloka in three lives. In the first life, although he executed austerities in the forest, he became a victim of too much affection for a small deer, and in his next life he had to take birth as a deer. Although he had a deer's body, he remembered his spiritual position, but he still had to wait until the next life for perfection. In the next life he took birth as Jaḍa Bharata. Of course, in that life he was completely freed from all material entanglement, and he attained perfection and was elevated to Vaikuṇṭhaloka. The lesson from the life of Dhruva Mahārāja is that if one likes, one can attain Vaikuṇṭhaloka in one life, without waiting for many other lives. My Guru Mahārāja, Śrī Śrīmad Bhaktisiddhānta Sarasvatī Gosvāmī Prabhupāda, used to say that every one of his disciples could attain Vaikuṇṭhaloka in this life, without waiting for another life to execute devotional service. One simply has to become as serious and sincere as Dhruva Mahārāja; then it is quite possible to attain Vaikuṇṭhaloka and go back home, back to Godhead, in one life.

TEXT 44

मैत्रेय उवाच
एतत्तेऽभिहितं सर्वं यत्पृष्टोऽहमिह त्वया ।
ध्रुवस्योद्दामयशसश्चरितं सम्मतं सताम् ॥४४॥

maitreya uvāca
etat te 'bhihitaṁ sarvaṁ
yat pṛṣṭo 'ham iha tvayā
dhruvasyoddāma-yaśasaś
caritaṁ sammataṁ satām

maitreyaḥ uvāca—the great sage Maitreya said; *etat*—this; *te*—unto you; *abhihitam*—described; *sarvam*—everything; *yat*—what; *pṛṣṭaḥ aham*—I was asked; *iha*—here; *tvayā*—by you; *dhruvasya*—of Dhruva Mahārāja; *uddāma*—greatly uplifting; *yaśasaḥ*—whose reputation; *caritam*—character; *sammatam*—approved; *satām*—by great devotees.

TRANSLATION

The great sage Maitreya continued: My dear Vidura, whatever you have asked from me about the great reputation and character of Dhruva Mahārāja I have explained to you in all detail. Great saintly persons and devotees very much like to hear about Dhruva Mahārāja.

PURPORT

Śrīmad-Bhāgavatam means everything in relationship with the Supreme Personality of Godhead. Whether we hear the pastimes and activities of the Supreme Lord or we hear about the character, reputation and activities of His devotees, they are all one and the same. Neophyte devotees simply try to understand the pastimes of the Lord and are not very interested to hear about the activities of His devotees, but such discrimination should not be indulged in by any real devotee. Sometimes less intelligent men try to hear about the *rāsa* dance of Kṛṣṇa and do not take care to hear about other portions of *Śrīmad-Bhāgavatam,* which they completely avoid. There are professional *Bhāgavata* reciters who abruptly go to the *rāsa-līlā* chapters of *Śrīmad-Bhāgavatam* as if other portions of *Śrīmad-Bhāgavatam* were useless. This kind of discrimination and abrupt adoption of the *rāsa-līlā* pastimes of the Lord is not approved by the *ācāryas.* A sincere devotee should read every chapter and every word of *Śrīmad-Bhāgavatam*, for the beginning verses describe that it is the ripened fruit of all Vedic literature. Devotees should not try to avoid even a word of *Śrīmad-Bhāgavatam.* The great sage

Maitreya therefore affirmed herein that the *Bhāgavatam* is *sammataṁ satām*, approved by great devotees.

TEXT 45

धन्यं यशस्यमायुष्यं पुण्यं स्वस्त्ययनं महत् ।
स्वर्ग्यं ध्रौव्यं सौमनस्यं प्रशस्यमघमर्षणम् ॥४५॥

dhanyaṁ yaśasyam āyuṣyaṁ
puṇyaṁ svasty-ayanaṁ mahat
svargyaṁ dhrauvyaṁ saumanasyaṁ
praśasyam agha-marṣaṇam

dhanyam—bestowing wealth; *yaśasyam*—bestowing reputation; *āyuṣyam*—increasing duration of life; *puṇyam*—sacred; *svasti-ayanam*—creating auspiciousness; *mahat*—great; *svargyam*—bestowing achievement of heavenly planets; *dhrauvyam*—or Dhruvaloka; *saumanasyam*—pleasing to the mind; *praśasyam*—glorious; *agha-marṣaṇam*—counteracting all kinds of sinful activities.

TRANSLATION

By hearing the narration of Dhruva Mahārāja one can fulfill desires for wealth, reputation and increased duration of life. It is so auspicious that one can even go to a heavenly planet or can attain Dhruvaloka, which was achieved by Dhruva Mahārāja, just by hearing about him. The demigods also become pleased because it is so glorious, and it is so powerful that it can counteract all the results of one's sinful actions.

PURPORT

There are different types of men in this world, not all of them pure devotees. Some are *karmīs*, desiring to acquire vast wealth. There are also persons who are only after reputation. Some desire to be elevated to the heavenly planets or to go to Dhruvaloka, and others want to please the demigods to get material profits. Herein it is recommended by Maitreya that every one of them can hear the narration about Dhruva Mahārāja and thus get their desired goal. It is recommended that the devotees (*akāma*), the *karmīs (sarva-kāma)* and the *jñānīs* who desire to be liberated (*mokṣa-kāma*) should all worship the Supreme Personality of Godhead to acquire their desired goals of life. Similarly, if anyone hears about the activities of the Lord's devotee, he can achieve the same result. There is no difference between the activities and character of the Supreme Personality of Godhead and His pure devotees.

TEXT 46

श्रुत्वैतच्छ्रद्धयाभीक्ष्णमच्युतप्रियचेष्टितम् ।
भवेद्भक्तिर्भगवति यया स्यात्क्लेशसंक्षयः ॥४६॥

śrutvaitac chraddhayābhīkṣṇam
acyuta-priya-ceṣṭitam
bhaved bhaktir bhagavati
yayā syāt kleśa-saṅkṣayaḥ

śrutvā—by hearing; *etat*—this; *śraddhayā*—with faith; *abhīkṣṇam*—repeatedly; *acyuta*—to the Supreme Personality of Godhead; *priya*—dear; *ceṣṭitam*—activities; *bhavet*—develops; *bhaktiḥ*—devotion; *bhagavati*—unto the Supreme Personality of Godhead; *yayā*—by which; *syāt*—must be; *kleśa*—of miseries; *saṅkṣayaḥ*—complete diminution.

TRANSLATION

Anyone who hears the narration of Dhruva Mahārāja, and who repeatedly tries with faith and devotion to understand his pure character, attains the pure devotional platform and executes pure devotional service. By such activities one can diminish the threefold miserable conditions of material life.

PURPORT

Here the word *acyuta-priya* is very significant. Dhruva Mahārāja's character and reputation are great because he is very dear to Acyuta, the Supreme Personality of Godhead. As the pastimes and activities of the Supreme Lord are pleasing to hear, so hearing about His devotees, who are very dear to the Supreme Person, is also pleasing and potent. If one simply reads over and over again about Dhruva Mahārāja by hearing and reading this chapter, he can attain the highest perfection of life in any way he desires; most importantly, he gets the chance to become a great devotee. To become a great devotee means to finish all miserable conditions of materialistic life.

TEXT 47

महत्त्वमिच्छतां तीर्थं श्रोतुः शीलादयो गुणाः ।
यत्र तेजस्तदिच्छूनां मानो यत्र मनस्विनाम् ॥४७॥

mahattvam icchatāṁ tīrthaṁ
śrotuḥ śīlādayo guṇāḥ
yatra tejas tad icchūnāṁ
māno yatra manasvinām

mahattvam—greatness; *icchatām*—for those desiring; *tīrtham*—the process; *śrotuḥ*—of the hearer; *śīla-ādayaḥ*—high character, etc.; *guṇāḥ*—qualities; *yatra*—in which; *tejaḥ*—prowess; *tat*—that; *icchūnām*—for those who desire; *mānaḥ*—adoration; *yatra*—in which; *manasvinām*—for thoughtful men.

TRANSLATION

Anyone who hears this narration of Dhruva Mahārāja acquires exalted qualities like him. For anyone who desires greatness, prowess or influence, here is the process to acquire them, and for thoughtful men who want adoration, here is the proper means.

PURPORT

In the material world everyone is after profit, respectability and reputation, everyone wants the supreme exalted position, and everyone wants to hear about the great qualities of exalted persons. All ambitions which are desirable for great persons can be fulfilled simply by reading and understanding the narration of Dhruva Mahārāja's activities.

TEXT 48

प्रयतः कीर्तयेत्प्रातः समवाये द्विजन्मनाम् ।
सायं च पुण्यश्लोकस्य ध्रुवस्य चरितं महत् ॥४८॥

prayataḥ kīrtayet prātaḥ
samavāye dvijanmanām
sāyaṁ ca puṇya-ślokasya
dhruvasya caritaṁ mahat

prayataḥ—with great care; *kīrtayet*—one should chant; *prātaḥ*—in the morning; *samavāye*—in the association; *dvi-janmanām*—of the twice-born; *sāyam*—in the evening; *ca*—also; *puṇya-ślokasya*—of sacred renown; *dhruvasya*—of Dhruva; *caritam*—character; *mahat*—great.

TRANSLATION

The great sage Maitreya recommended: One should chant of the character and activities of Dhruva Mahārāja both in the morning and in the evening, with great attention and care, in a society of brāhmaṇas or other twice-born persons.

PURPORT

It is said that only in the association of devotees can one understand the importance of the character and pastimes of the Supreme Personality of Godhead or His devotees. In this verse it is especially recommended that Dhruva Mahārāja's character should be discussed in a society of the twice-born, which refers to the qualified *brāhmaṇas, kṣatriyas* and *vaiśyas.* One should especially seek the society of *brāhmaṇas* who are elevated to the position of Vaiṣṇavas. Thus discussion of *Śrīmad-Bhāgavatam*, which describes the character and pastimes of devotees and the Lord, is very quickly effective. The International Society for Krishna Consciousness has been organized for this purpose. In every center of this society—not only in the morning, evening or noon, but practically twenty-four hours a day—there is continuous devotional service going on. Anyone who comes in contact with the Society automatically becomes a devotee. We have actual experience that many *karmīs* and others come to the Society and find a very pleasing and peaceful atmosphere in the temples of ISKCON. In this verse the word *dvijanmanām* means "of the twice-born." Anyone can join the International Society for Krishna Consciousness and be initiated to become twice-born. As recommended by Sanātana Gosvāmī, by the process of initiation and authorized training, any man can become twice-born. The first birth is made possible by the parent, and the second birth is made possible by the spiritual father and Vedic knowledge. Unless one is twice-born one cannot understand the transcendental characteristics of the Lord and His devotees. Study of the *Vedas* is therefore forbidden for *śūdras.* Simply by academic qualifications a *śūdra* cannot understand the transcendental science. At the present moment, throughout the entire world the educational system is geared to produce *śūdras.* A big technologist is no more than a big *śūdra. Kalau śūdra-sambhava:* in the age of Kali, everyone is a *śūdra.* Because the whole population of the world consists only of *śūdras,* there is therefore a decline of spiritual knowledge, and people are unhappy. The Kṛṣṇa consciousness movement has been started especially to create qualified *brāhmaṇas* to broadcast spiritual knowledge all over the world, for thus people may become very happy.

TEXTS 49-50

पौर्णमास्यां सिनीवाल्यां द्वादश्यां श्रवणेऽथवा ।
दिनक्षये व्यतीपाते सङ्क्रमेऽर्कदिनेऽपि वा ॥४९॥
श्रावयेच्छ्रद्दधानानां तीर्थपादपदाश्रयः ।
नेच्छंस्तत्रात्मनाऽऽत्मानं सन्तुष्ट इति सिध्यति॥५०॥

paurṇamāsyāṁ sinīvālyāṁ
dvādaśyāṁ śravaṇe 'thavā
dinakṣaye vyatīpāte
saṅkrame 'rkadine 'pi vā
śrāvayec chraddadhānānāṁ
tīrtha-pāda-padāśrayaḥ
necchaṁs tatrātmanātmānaṁ
santuṣṭa iti sidhyati

paurṇamāsyām—on the full moon; *sinīvālyām*—on the dark moon; *dvādaśyām*—on the day after Ekādaśī; *śravaṇe*—during the Śravaṇa star's appearance; *athavā*—or; *dinakṣaye*—at the end of the *tithi; vyatīpāte*—a particular day of the name; *saṅkrame*—at the end of the month; *arkadine*—on Sunday; *api*—also; *vā*—or; *śrāvayet*—one should recite; *śraddadhānānām*—to a receptive audience; *tīrtha-pāda*—of the Supreme Personality of Godhead; *pada-āśrayaḥ*—taken shelter of the lotus feet; *na icchan*—without desiring remuneration; *tatra*—there; *ātmanā*—by the self; *ātmānam*—the mind; *santuṣṭaḥ*—pacified; *iti*—thus; *sidhyati*—becomes perfect.

TRANSLATION

Persons who have completely taken shelter of the lotus feet of the Lord should recite this narration of Dhruva Mahārāja without taking remuneration. Specifically, recitation is recommended on the full moon or dark moon day, on the day after Ekādaśī, on the appearance of the Sravaṇa star, at the end of a particular tithi, or the occasion of Vyatīpāta, at the end of the month, or on Sunday. Such recitation should of course be performed before a favorable audience. When recitation is performed this way, without professional motive, the reciter and audience become perfect.

PURPORT

Professional reciters may ask money to extinguish the blazing fire within their bellies, but they cannot make any spiritual improvement or become perfect. It is therefore strictly forbidden to recite *Śrīmad-Bhāgavatam* as a profession to earn a livelihood. Only one who is completely surrendered at the lotus feet of the Supreme Personality of Godhead, depending fully on Him for personal maintenance or even for maintenance of his family, can attain perfection by recitation of *Śrīmad-Bhāgavatam,* which is full of narrations of the pastimes of the Lord and His devotees. The process can be summarized as follows: the audience must be faithfully receptive to the *Bhāgavata* message, and the reciter should completely depend on the Supreme Personality of Godhead. *Bhāgavata* recitation must not be a business. If done in the right way, not only does the reciter achieve perfect satisfaction, but the Lord also is very satisfied with the reciter and the audience, and thus both are liberated from material bondage simply by the process of hearing.

TEXT 51

ज्ञानमज्ञाततत्त्वाय यो दद्यात्सत्पथेऽमृतम् ।
कृपालोर्दीननाथस्य देवास्तस्यानुगृह्णते ॥५१॥

jñānam ajñāta-tattvāya
yo dadyāt sat-pathe 'mṛtam
kṛpālor dīna-nāthasya
devās tasyānugṛhṇate

jñānam—knowledge; *ajñāta-tattvāya*—to those who are unaware of the truth; *yaḥ*—one who; *dadyāt*—imparts; *sat-pathe*—on the path of truth; *amṛtam*—immortality; *kṛpāloḥ*—kind; *dīna-nāthasya*—protector of the poor; *devāḥ*—the demigods; *tasya*—to him; *anugṛhṇate*—give blessings.

TRANSLATION

The narration of Dhruva Mahārāja is sublime knowledge for the attainment of immortality. Persons who are unaware of the Absolute Truth can be led to the path of truth. Those who out of transcendental kindness take on the responsibility of becoming master protectors of the poor living entities automatically gain the interest and blessings of the demigods.

PURPORT

Jñānam ajñāta means knowledge which is unknown almost throughout the entire world. No one knows actually what is the Absolute Truth.

Materialists are very proud of their advancement in education, in philosophical speculation and in scientific knowledge, but no one actually knows what the Absolute Truth is. The great sage Maitreya, therefore, recommends that to enlighten people about the Absolute Truth (*tattva*), devotees should preach the teachings of *Śrīmad-Bhāgavatam* throughout the entire world. Śrīla Vyāsadeva especially compiled this great literature of scientific knowledge because people are completely unaware of the Absolute Truth. In the beginning of *Śrīmad-Bhāgavatam,* First Canto, it is said that Vyāsadeva, the learned sage, compiled this great *Bhāgavata Purāṇa* just to stop the ignorance of the mass of people. Because people do not know the Absolute Truth, this *Śrīmad-Bhāgavatam* was specifically compiled by Vyāsadeva under the instruction of Nārada. Generally, even though people are interested in understanding the truth, they take to speculation and reach at most the conception of impersonal Brahman. But very few men actually know the Personality of Godhead.

Recitation of *Śrīmad-Bhāgavatam* is specifically meant to enlighten people about the Absolute Truth, the Supreme Personality of Godhead. Although there is no fundamental difference between impersonal Brahman, localized Paramātmā and the Supreme Person, still factual immortality cannot be obtained unless and until one attains the stage of associating with the Supreme Person. Devotional service, which leads to the association of the Supreme Lord, is actual immortality. Pure devotees, out of compassion for the fallen souls, are *kṛpālu*, very kind to people in general; they distribute this *Bhāgavata* knowledge all over the world. A kindhearted devotee is called *dīna-nātha,* protector of the poor, ignorant mass of people. Lord Kṛṣṇa is also known as *dīna-nātha* or *dīna-bandhu,* the master or actual friend of the poor living entities, and His pure devotee also takes the same position of *dīna-nātha.* The *dīna-nāthas,* or devotees of Lord Kṛṣṇa, who preach the path of devotional service, become the favorites of the demigods. Generally persons are interested in worshiping the demigods, especially Lord Śiva, in order to obtain material benefits, but a pure devotee who engages in preaching the principles of devotional service, as prescribed in the *Śrīmad-Bhāgavatam*, does not need to separately worship the demigods; the demigods are automatically pleased with him and offer all the blessings within their capacity. As by watering the root of a tree the leaves and branches are automatically watered, so, by executing pure devotional service to the Lord, the branches, twigs and leaves of the Lord, known as demigods, are automatically pleased with the devotee, and they offer all benediction.

TEXT 52

इदं मया तेऽभिहितं कुरूद्वह
ध्रुवस्य विख्यातविशुद्धकर्मणः ।
हित्वार्भकः क्रीडनकानि मातु-
र्गृहं च विष्णुं शरणं यो जगाम ॥५२॥

idaṁ mayā te 'bhihitaṁ kurūdvaha
dhruvasya vikhyāta-viśuddha-karmaṇaḥ
hitvārbhakaḥ krīḍanakāni mātur
gṛhaṁ ca viṣṇuṁ śaraṇaṁ yo jagāma

idam—this; *mayā*—by me; *te*—unto you; *abhihitam*—described; *kuru-udvaha*—O great one among the Kurus; *dhruvasya*—of Dhruva; *vikhyāta*—very famous; *viśuddha*—very pure; *karmaṇaḥ*—whose activities; *hitvā*—giving up; *arbhakaḥ*—child; *krīḍanakāni*—toys and playthings; *mātuḥ*—of his mother; *gṛham*—home; *ca*—also; *viṣṇum*—to Lord Viṣṇu; *śaraṇam*—shelter; *yaḥ*—one who; *jagāma*—went.

TRANSLATION

The transcendental activities of Dhruva Mahārāja are well known all over the world, and they are very pure. In childhood Dhruva Mahārāja rejected all kinds of toys and playthings, left the protection of his mother and seriously took shelter of the Supreme Personality of Godhead, Viṣṇu. My dear Vidura, I therefore conclude this narration, for I have described to you all its details.

PURPORT

It is said by Cāṇakya Paṇḍita that life is certainly short for everyone, but if one acts properly, his reputation will remain for a generation. As the Supreme Personality of Godhead, Kṛṣṇa, is everlastingly famous, so the reputation of Lord Kṛṣṇa's devotee is also everlasting. Therefore in describing Dhruva Mahārāja's activities two specific words have been used—*vikhyāta*, very famous, and *viśuddha*, transcendental. Dhruva Mahārāja's leaving home at a tender age and taking shelter of the Supreme Personality of Godhead in the forest is a unique example in this world.

Thus end the Bhaktivedanta purports of the Fourth Canto, Twelfth Chapter, of the Śrīmad-Bhāgavatam, *entitled "Dhruva Mahārāja Goes Back to Godhead."*

CHAPTER THIRTEEN

Description of the Descendants of Dhruva Mahārāja

TEXT 1

सूत उवाच
निशम्य कौषारविणोपवर्णितं
ध्रुवस्य वैकुण्ठपदाधिरोहणम् ।
प्ररूढभावो भगवत्यधोक्षजे
प्रष्टुं पुनस्तं विदुरः प्रचक्रमे ॥ १ ॥

sūta uvāca
niśamya kauṣāraviṇopavarṇitaṁ
dhruvasya vaikuṇṭha-padādhirohaṇam
prarūḍha-bhāvo bhagavaty adhokṣaje
praṣṭuṁ punas taṁ viduraḥ pracakrame

sūtaḥ uvāca—Sūta Gosvāmī said; *niśamya*—after hearing; *kauṣāraviṇā*—by the sage Maitreya; *upavarṇitam*—described; *dhruvasya*—of Mahārāja Dhruva; *vaikuṇṭha-pada*—to the abode of Viṣṇu; *adhirohaṇam*—ascent; *prarūḍha*—increased; *bhāvaḥ*—devotional emotion; *bhagavati*—unto the Supreme Personality of Godhead; *adhokṣaje*—who is beyond the reach of direct perception; *praṣṭum*—to inquire; *punaḥ*—again; *tam*—unto Maitreya; *viduraḥ*—Vidura; *pracakrame*—attempted.

TRANSLATION

Sūta Gosvāmī, continuing to speak to all the ṛṣis, headed by Śaunaka, said: After hearing Maitreya Ṛṣi describe Dhruva Mahārāja's ascent to Lord Viṣṇu's abode, Vidura became very enlightened in devotional emotion, and he inquired from Maitreya as follows.

PURPORT

As evidenced in the topics between Vidura and Maitreya, the activities of the Supreme Personality of Godhead and the devotees are so fascinating that neither the devotee who is describing them nor the devotee who is hearing is at all fatigued by the inquiries and answers. Transcendental subject matter is so nice that no one becomes tired of hearing or speaking. Others, who are not devotees, may think, "How can people devote so much time simply to talks of God?" But devotees are never satisfied or satiated in hearing and speaking about the Supreme Personality of Godhead or about His devotees. The more they hear and talk, the more they become enthusiastic to hear. The chanting of the Hare Kṛṣṇa *mantra* is simply the repetition of three words, *Hare, Kṛṣṇa* and *Rāma,* but still devotees can go on chanting this Hare Kṛṣṇa *mantra* twenty-four hours a day without feeling fatigued.

TEXT 2

विदुर उवाच
के ते प्रचेतसो नाम कस्यापत्यानि सुव्रत ।
कस्यान्ववाये प्रख्याताः कुत्र वा सत्रमासत ॥ २ ॥

vidura uvāca
ke te pracetaso nāma
kasyāpatyāni suvrata
kasyānvavāye prakhyātāḥ
kutra vā satram āsata

viduraḥ uvāca—Vidura inquired; *ke*—who were; *te*—they; *pracetasaḥ*—the Pracetās; *nāma*—of the name; *kasya*—whose; *apatyāni*—sons; *su-vrata*—O Maitreya, who has taken an auspicious vow; *kasya*—whose; *anvavāye*—in the family; *prakhyātāḥ*—famous; *kutra*—where; *vā*—also; *satram*—the sacrifice; *āsata*—was performed.

TRANSLATION

Vidura inquired from Maitreya: O greatly advanced devotee, who were the Pracetās? To which family do they belong? Whose sons were they, and where did they perform the great sacrifices?

PURPORT

The great Nārada's singing, in the previous chapter, of three verses in the sacrificial arena of the Pracetās gave another impetus to Vidura to ask further questions.

TEXT 3

मन्ये महाभागवतं नारदं देवदर्शनम् ।
येन प्रोक्तः क्रियायोगः परिचर्याविधिर्हरेः ॥ ३ ॥

manye mahā-bhāgavataṁ
nāradaṁ deva-darśanam
yena proktaḥ kriyā-yogaḥ
paricaryā vidhir hareḥ

manye—I think; *mahā-bhāgavatam*—greatest of all devotees; *nāradam*—the sage Nārada; *deva*—the Supreme Personality of Godhead; *darśanam*—who met; *yena*—by whom; *proktaḥ*—spoken; *kriyā-yogaḥ*—devotional service; *paricaryā*—for rendering service; *vidhiḥ*—the procedure; *hareḥ*—to the Supreme Personality of Godhead.

TRANSLATION

Vidura continued: I know that the great sage Nārada is the greatest of all devotees. He has compiled the pāñcarātrika procedure of devotional service and has directly met the Supreme Personality of Godhead.

PURPORT

There are two different ways of approaching the Supreme Lord. One is called *bhāgavata-mārga*, or the way of *Śrīmad-Bhāgavatam*, and the other is called *pāñcarātrika-vidhi. Pāñcarātrika-vidhi* is the method of temple worship, and *bhāgavata-vidhi* is the system of nine processes which begin with hearing and chanting. The Kṛṣṇa conscious movement accepts both processes simultaneously and thus enables one to make steady progress on the path of realization of the Supreme Personality of Godhead. This *pāñcarātrika* procedure was first introduced by the great sage Nārada, as referred to here by Vidura.

TEXT 4

स्वधर्मशीलैः पुरुषैर्भगवान् यज्ञपूरुषः ।
इज्यमानो भक्तिमता नारदेनेरितः किल ॥ ४ ॥

sva-dharma-śīlaiḥ puruṣair
bhagavān yajña-pūruṣaḥ
ijyamāno bhaktimatā
nāradeneritaḥ kila

sva-dharma-śīlaiḥ—executing sacrificial duties; *puruṣaiḥ*—by the men; *bhagavān*—Supreme Personality of Godhead; *yajña-pūruṣaḥ*—the enjoyer of all sacrifices; *ijyamānaḥ*—being worshiped; *bhaktimatā*—by the devotee; *nāradena*—by Nārada; *īritaḥ*—described; *kila*—indeed.

TRANSLATION

While all the Pracetās were executing religious rituals and sacrificial ceremonies and thus worshiping the Supreme Personality of Godhead for His satisfaction, the great sage Nārada described the transcendental qualities of Dhruva Mahārāja.

PURPORT

Nārada Muni is always glorifying the pastimes of the Lord. In this verse we see that he not only glorifies the Lord, but he also likes to glorify the devotees of the Lord. The great sage Nārada Muni's mission is to broadcast the devotional service of the Lord. For this purpose he has compiled the *Nārada-pañcarātra,* a directory of devotional service, so that devotees can always take information about how to execute devotional service and thus engage twenty-four hours a day in performing sacrifices for the pleasure of the Supreme Personality of Godhead. As stated in the *Bhagavad-gītā,* the Lord has created four orders of social life, namely *brāhmaṇa, kṣatriya, vaiśya* and *śūdra.* In the *Nārada-pañcarātra* it is very clearly described how each of the social orders can please the Supreme Lord. In the *Bhagavad-gītā* (Bg.18.45) it is stated, *sve sve karmaṇy abhirataḥ saṁsiddhiṁ labhate naraḥ:* by executing one's prescribed duties one can please the Supreme Lord. In the *Śrīmad-Bhāgavatam* also it is stated, *svanuṣṭhitasya dharmasya saṁsiddhir hari-toṣaṇam:* the perfection of duty is to see that by discharging one's specific duties one satisfies the Supreme Personality of Godhead (*Bhāg.*1.2.13). When the Pracetās were performing sacrifices according to this direction, Nārada Muni was satisfied to see these activities, and he also wanted to glorify Dhruva Mahārāja in that sacrificial arena.

TEXT 5

यास्ता देवर्षिणा तत्र वर्णिता भगवत्कथाः ।
मह्यं शुश्रूषवे ब्रह्मन् कार्त्स्न्येनाचष्टुमर्हसि ॥ ५ ॥

yās tā devarṣiṇā tatra
varṇitā bhagavat-kathāḥ
mahyaṁ śuśrūṣave brahman
kārtsnyenācaṣṭum arhasi

yāḥ—which; *tāḥ*—all those; *devarṣiṇā*—by the great sage Nārada; *tatra*—there; *varṇitāḥ*—narrated; *bhagavat-kathāḥ*—preachings pertaining to the activities of the Lord; *mahyam*—unto me; *śuśrūṣave*—very eager to hear; *brahman*—my dear *brāhmaṇa; kārtsnyena*—fully; *ācaṣṭum arhasi*—kindly explain.

TRANSLATION

My dear brāhmaṇa, how did Nārada Muni glorify the Supreme Personality of Godhead, and what pastimes were described in that meeting? I am very eager to hear of them. Kindly explain fully about that glorification of the Lord.

PURPORT

Śrīmad-Bhāgavatam is the record of *bhagavat-kathā*, topics about the pastimes of the Lord. What Vidura was anxious to hear from Maitreya we can also hear five thousand years later, provided we are very eager.

TEXT 6

मैत्रेय उवाच

ध्रुवस्य चोत्कलः पुत्रः पितरि प्रस्थिते वनम् ।
सार्वभौमश्रियं नैच्छदधिराजासनं पितुः ॥ ६ ॥

maitreya uvāca
dhruvasya cotkalaḥ putraḥ
pitari prasthite vanam
sārvabhauma-śriyaṁ naicchad
adhirājāsanaṁ pituḥ

maitreyaḥ uvāca—the great sage Maitreya said; *dhruvasya*—of Dhruva Mahārāja; *ca*—also; *utkalaḥ*—Utkala; *putraḥ*—son; *pitari*—after the father; *prasthite*—departed; *vanam*—for the forest; *sārva-bhauma*—including all lands; *śriyam*—opulence; *na aicchat*—did not desire; *adhirāja*—royal; *āsanam*—throne; *pituḥ*—of the father.

TRANSLATION

The great sage Maitreya replied: My dear Vidura, when Mahārāja Dhruva departed for the forest, his son, Utkala, did not desire to accept the opulent throne of his father, which was meant for the ruler of all the lands of this planet.

TEXT 7

स जन्मनोपशान्तात्मा निःसङ्गः समदर्शनः ।
ददर्श लोके विततमात्मानं लोकमात्मनि ॥ ७ ॥

sa janmanopaśāntātmā
niḥsaṅgaḥ samadarśanaḥ
dadarśa loke vitatam
ātmānaṁ lokam ātmani

saḥ—his son Utkala; *janmanā*—from the very beginning of his birth; *upaśānta*—very well satisfied; *ātmā*—soul; *niḥsaṅgaḥ*—without attachment; *sama-darśanaḥ*—equipoised; *dadarśa*—saw; *loke*—in the world; *vitatam*—spread; *ātmānam*—the Supersoul; *lokam*—all the world; *ātmani*—in the Supersoul.

TRANSLATION

From his very birth, Utkala was fully satisfied and unattached to the world. He was equipoised, for he could see everything resting in the Supersoul and the Supersoul present in everyone's heart.

PURPORT

The symptoms and characteristics of Utkala, the son of Mahārāja Dhruva, are those of a *mahā-bhāgavata*. As stated in the *Bhagavad-gītā* (Bg. 6.30), *yo māṁ paśyati sarvatra sarvaṁ ca mayi paśyati:* a highly advanced devotee sees the Supreme Personality of Godhead everywhere, and He also sees everything resting in the Supreme. It is also confirmed in the *Bhagavad-gītā* (Bg. 9.4), *mayā tatam idaṁ sarvaṁ jagad avyakta-mūrtinā:* Lord Kṛṣṇa is spread all over the universe in His impersonal feature. Everything is resting on Him, but that does not mean that everything is He Himself. A highly advanced *mahā-bhāgavata* devotee sees in this spirit: he sees the same Supersoul, Paramātmā, existing within everyone's heart, regardless of discrimination based on the different material forms of the living entities. He sees everyone as part and parcel of the Supreme Personality of Godhead. The *mahā-bhāgavata* who experiences the Supreme Godhead's presence everywhere is never missing from the sight of the Supreme Lord, nor is the Supreme Lord ever lost from his sight. This is only possible when one is advanced in love of Godhead.

TEXTS 8-9

आत्मानं ब्रह्म निर्वाणं प्रत्यस्तमितविग्रहम् ।
अवबोधरसैकात्म्यमानन्दमनुसन्ततम् ॥ ८ ॥
अव्यवच्छिन्नयोगाग्निदग्धकर्ममलाशयः ।
स्वरूपमवरुन्धानो नात्मनोऽन्यं तदैक्षत ॥ ९ ॥

ātmānaṁ brahma nirvāṇaṁ
pratyastamita-vigraham
avabodha-rasaikātmyam
ānandam anusantatam
avyavacchinna-yogāgni-
dagdha-karma-malāśayaḥ
svarūpam avarundhāno
nātmano 'nyaṁ tadaikṣata

ātmānam—self; *brahma*—spirit; *nirvāṇam*—extinction of material existence; *pratyastam-ita*—ceased; *vigraham*—separation; *avabodha-rasa*—by the mellow of knowledge; *eka-ātmyam*—oneness; *ānandam*—bliss; *anusantatam*—expanded; *avyavacchinna*—continuous; *yoga*—by practice of *yoga; agni*—by the fire; *dagdha*—burned; *karma*—fruitive desires; *mala*—dirty; *āśayaḥ*—in his mind; *svarūpam*—constitutional position; *avarundhānaḥ*—realizing; *na*—not; *ātmanaḥ*—than the Supreme Soul; *anyam*—anything else; *tadā*—then; *aikṣata*—saw.

TRANSLATION

By expansion of his knowledge of the Supreme Brahman, he had already attained liberation from the bondage of the body. This is known as nirvāṇa. He was situated in transcendental bliss, and he continued always in that blissful existence, which expanded more and more. This was possible for him by continual practice of bhakti-yoga, which is compared with fire because it burns away all dirty material things. He was always situated in his constitutional position of self-realization, and he could not see anything else but the Supreme Lord and himself engaged in discharging devotional service.

PURPORT

These two verses explain the verse in the *Bhagavad-gītā, brahma-bhūtaḥ prasannātmā na śocati na kāṅkṣati/ samaḥ sarveṣu bhūteṣu mad-bhaktiṁ labhate parām:* "One who is transcendentally situated at once realizes the Supreme Brahman. He never laments or desires to have anything. He is equally disposed towards every living entity. In that state he achieves pure devotional service unto Me." (Bg. 18.54) This is also explained by Lord Caitanya in His *Śikṣāṣṭaka* in the beginning of the first verse:

ceto-darpaṇa-mārjanaṁ bhava-mahā-dāvāgni-nirvāpaṇaṁ
śreyaḥ kairava-candrikā-vitaraṇaṁ vidyā-vadhū-jīvanam

The *bhakti-yoga* system is the topmost *yoga* system, and in this system the chanting of the holy name of the Lord is the foremost performance of devotional service. By chanting the holy name one can attain the perfection of *nirvāṇa,* or liberation from material existence, and so increase one's blissful life of spiritual existence as described by Lord Caitanya (*ānandāmbudhi-vardhanam*). When one is situated in that position he no longer has any interest in material opulence or even a royal throne and sovereignty over the whole planet. This situation is called *viraktir anyatra syāt.* It is the result of devotional service.

The more one makes advancement in devotional service, the more one becomes detached from material opulence and material activity. This is the spiritual nature, full of bliss. This is also described in *Bhagavad-gītā* (Bg. 2.59). *Paraṁ dṛṣṭvā nivartate:* one ceases to take part in material enjoyment upon tasting superior, blissful life in spiritual existence. By advancement in spiritual knowledge, which is considered to be like blazing fire, all material desires are burned to ashes. The perfection of mystic *yoga* is possible when one is continuously in connection with the Supreme Personality of Godhead by discharging devotional service. A devotee is always thinking of the Supreme Person at every step of his life. Every conditioned soul is full of the reactions of his past life, but all dirty things are immediately burned to ashes if one simply executes devotional service. This is described in the *Nārada-pañcarātra: sarvopādhi-vinirmuktaṁ tat-paratvena nirmalam.*

TEXT 10

जडान्धबधिरोन्मत्तमूकाकृतिरतन्मतिः ।
लक्षितः पथि बालानां प्रशान्तार्चिरिवानलः ॥१०॥

jaḍāndha-badhironmatta-
mūkākṛtir atanmatiḥ
lakṣitaḥ pathi bālānāṁ
praśāntārcir ivānalaḥ

jaḍa—foolish; *andha*—blind; *badhira*—deaf; *unmatta*—mad; *mūka*—dumb; *ākṛtiḥ*—appearance; *a-tat*—not like that; *matiḥ*—his intelligence; *lakṣitaḥ*—he was seen; *pathi*—on the road; *bālānām*—by the less intelligent; *praśānta*—calmed; *arciḥ*—with flames; *iva*—like; *analaḥ*—fire.

TRANSLATION

Utkala appeared to the less intelligent persons on the road to be foolish, blind, dumb, deaf and mad, although actually he was not so. He remained like fire covered with ashes, without blazing flames.

PURPORT

In order to avoid contradiction, botheration and unfavorable situations created by materialistic persons, a great saintly person like Jaḍa Bharata or Utkala remains silent. The less intelligent consider such saintly persons to be mad, deaf or dumb. Factually, an advanced devotee avoids speaking with persons who are not in devotional life, but to those who are in devotional life he speaks in friendship, and he speaks to the innocent for their enlightenment. For all practical purposes, the whole world is full of nondevotees, and so one kind of very advanced devotee is called *bhajanānandī.* Those who are *goṣṭhānandī,* however, preach to increase the number of devotees. But even such preachers also avoid opposing elements who are unfavorably disposed towards spiritual life.

TEXT 11

मत्वा तं जडमुन्मत्तं कुलवृद्धाः समन्त्रिणः ।
वत्सरं भूपतिं चक्रुर्यवीयांसं भ्रमेः सुतम् ॥११॥

matvā taṁ jaḍam unmattaṁ
kula-vṛddhāḥ samantriṇaḥ
vatsaraṁ bhūpatiṁ cakrur
yavīyāṁsaṁ bhrameḥ sutam

matvā—thinking; *tam*—Utkala; *jaḍam*—without intelligence; *unmattam*—mad; *kula-vṛddhāḥ*—elderly members of the family; *sa-mantriṇaḥ*—with the ministers; *vatsaram*—Vatsara; *bhū-patim*—ruler of the world; *cakruḥ*—they made; *yavīyāṁsam*—younger; *bhrameḥ*—of Bhrami; *sutam*—son.

TRANSLATION

For this reason the ministers and all the elderly members of the family thought Utkala to be without intelligence and, in fact, mad. Thus his

younger brother, named Vatsara, who was the son of Bhrami and who was junior to Utkala, was elevated to the royal throne, and he became king of the world.

PURPORT

It appears that although there was monarchy, it was not at all an autocracy. There were senior family members and ministers who could make changes and elect the proper person to the throne, although the throne could be occupied only by the royal family. In modern days also, wherever there is monarchy, sometimes the ministers and elderly members of the family select one member from the royal family to occupy the throne in preference to another.

TEXT 12

स्वर्वीथिर्वत्सरस्येष्टा भार्यासूत षडात्मजान् ।
पुष्पार्णं तिग्मकेतुं च इषमूर्जं वसुं जयम् ॥१२॥

svarvīthir vatsarasyeṣṭā
bhāryāsūta ṣaḍ-ātmajān
puṣpārṇaṁ tigmaketuṁ ca
iṣam ūrjaṁ vasuṁ jayam

svarvīthiḥ—Svarvīthi; *vatsarasya*—of King Vatsara; *iṣṭā*—very dear; *bhāryā*—wife; *asūta*—gave birth to; *ṣaṭ*—six; *ātmajān*—sons; *puṣpārṇam*—Puṣpārṇa; *tigmaketum*—Tigmaketu; *ca*—also; *iṣam*—Iṣa; *ūrjam*—Ūrja; *vasum*—Vasu; *jayam*—Jaya.

TRANSLATION

King Vatsara had a very dear wife whose name was Svarvīthi, and she gave birth to six sons, named Puṣpārṇa, Tigmaketu, Iṣa, Ūrja, Vasu and Jaya.

PURPORT

Vatsara's wife is mentioned here as *iṣṭā,* which means worshipable. In other words it appears that Vatsara's wife had all good qualities; for example, she was always very faithful and obedient and affectionate to her husband. She had all good qualities for managing household affairs. If both the husband and wife are endowed with good qualities and live peacefully, then nice children take birth, and thus the whole family is happy and prosperous.

TEXT 13

पुष्पार्णस्य प्रभा भार्या दोषा च द्वे बभूवतुः ।
प्रातर्मध्यन्दिनं सायमिति ह्यासन् प्रभासुताः ॥१३॥

puṣpārṇasya prabhā bhāryā
doṣā ca dve babhūvatuḥ
prātar madhyandinaṁ sāyam
iti hy āsan prabhā-sutāḥ

puṣpārṇasya—of Puṣpārṇa; *prabhā*—Prabhā; *bhāryā*—wife; *doṣā*—Doṣā; *ca*—also; *dve*—two; *babhūvatuḥ*—were; *prātaḥ*—Prātaḥ; *madhyandinam*—Madhyandinam; *sāyam*—Sāyam; *iti*—thus; *hi*—certainly; *āsan*—were; *prabhā-sutāḥ*—sons of Prabhā.

TRANSLATION

Puṣpārṇa had two wives, named Prabhā and Doṣā. Prabhā had three sons, named Prātaḥ, Madhyandinam and Sāyam.

TEXT 14

प्रदोषो निशिथो व्युष्ट इति दोषासुतास्त्रयः ।
व्युष्टः सुतं पुष्करिण्यां सर्वतेजसमादधे ॥१४॥

pradoṣo niśitho vyuṣṭa
iti doṣā-sutās trayaḥ
vyuṣṭaḥ sutaṁ puṣkariṇyāṁ
sarva-tejasam ādadhe

pradoṣaḥ—Pradoṣa; *niśithaḥ*—Niśitha; *vyuṣṭaḥ*—Vyuṣṭa; *iti*—thus; *doṣā*—of Doṣā; *sutāḥ*—sons; *trayaḥ*—three; *vyuṣṭaḥ*—Vyuṣṭa; *sutam*—son; *puṣkariṇyām*—in Puṣkariṇī; *sarva-tejasam*—named Sarvatejā, all-powerful; *ādadhe*—begot.

TRANSLATION

Doṣā had three sons—Pradoṣa, Niśitha and Vyuṣṭa. Vyuṣṭa's wife was named Puṣkariṇī, and she gave birth to a very powerful son named Sarvatejā.

TEXTS 15-16

स चक्षुः सुतमाकूत्यां पत्न्यां मनुमवाप ह ।
मनोरसूत महिषी विरजान्नड्वला सुतान् ॥१५॥

पुरुं कुत्सं त्रितं द्युम्नं सत्यवन्तमृतं व्रतम् ।
अग्निष्टोममतीरात्रं प्रद्युम्नं शिबिमुल्मुकम् ॥१६॥

sa cakṣuḥ sutam ākūtyāṁ
patnyāṁ manum avāpa ha
manor asūta mahiṣī
virajān naḍvalā sutān

puruṁ kutsaṁ tritaṁ dyumnaṁ
satyavantam ṛtaṁ vratam
agniṣṭomam atīrātraṁ
pradyumnaṁ śibim ulmukam

saḥ—he (Sarvatejā); *cakṣuḥ*—named Cakṣuḥ; *sutam*—son; *ākūtyām*—in Ākūti; *patnyām*—wife; *manum*—Cākṣuṣa Manu; *avāpa*—obtained; *ha*—indeed; *manoḥ*—of Manu; *asūta*—gave birth to; *mahiṣī*—queen; *virajān*—without passion; *naḍvalā*—Naḍvalā; *sutān*—sons; *purum*—Puru; *kutsam*—Kutsa; *tritam*—Trita; *dyumnam*—Dyumna; *satyavantam*—Satyavān; *ṛtam*—Ṛta; *vratam*—Vrata; *agniṣṭomam*—Agniṣṭoma; *atīrātram*—Atīrātra; *pradyumnam*—Pradyumna; *śibim*—Śibi; *ulmukam*—Ulmuka.

TRANSLATION

Sarvatejā's wife, Ākūti, gave birth to a son named Cākṣuṣa, who became the sixth Manu at the end of the Manu millennium. Naḍvalā, the wife of Cākṣuṣa Manu, gave birth to the following faultless sons: Puru, Kutsa, Trita, Dyumna, Satyavān, Ṛta, Vrata, Agniṣṭoma, Atīrātra, Pradyumna, Śibi and Ulmuka.

TEXT 17

उल्मुकोऽजनयत्पुत्रान्पुष्करिण्यां षडुत्तमान् ।
अङ्गं सुमनसं ख्यातिं क्रतुमङ्गिरसं गयम् ॥१७॥

ulmuko 'janayat putrān
puṣkariṇyāṁ ṣaḍ uttamān
aṅgaṁ sumanasaṁ khyātiṁ
kratum aṅgirasaṁ gayam

ulmukaḥ—Ulmuka; *ajanayat*—begot; *putrān*—sons; *puṣkariṇyām*—in Puṣkariṇī, his wife; *ṣaṭ*—six; *uttamān*—very good; *aṅgam*—Aṅga; *sumanasam*—Sumanā; *khyātim*—Khyāti; *kratum*—Kratu; *aṅgirasam*—Aṅgirā; *gayam*—Gaya.

TRANSLATION

Of the twelve sons, Ulmuka begot six sons in his wife Puṣkariṇī. They were all very good sons, and their names were Aṅga, Sumanā, Khyāti, Kratu, Aṅgirā and Gaya.

TEXT 18

सुनीथाङ्गस्य या पत्नी सुषुवे वेनमुल्बणम् ।
यद्दौःशील्यात्स राजर्षिर्निर्विण्णो निरगात्पुरात् ॥१८॥

sunīthāṅgasya yā patnī
suṣuve venam ulbaṇam
yad-dauḥśīlyāt sa rājarṣir
nirviṇṇo niragāt purāt

sunīthā—Sunīthā; *aṅgasya*—of Aṅga; *yā*—she who; *patnī*—the wife; *suṣuve*—gave birth to; *venam*—Vena; *ulbaṇam*—very crooked; *yat*—whose; *dauḥśīlyāt*—on account of bad character; *saḥ*—he; *rāja-ṛṣiḥ*—the saintly King Aṅga; *nirviṇṇaḥ*—very disappointed; *niragāt*—went out; *purāt*—from home.

TRANSLATION

The wife of Aṅga, Sunīthā, gave birth to a son named Vena, who was very crooked. The saintly King Aṅga was very disappointed with his bad character, and he left home and kingdom and went out to the forest.

TEXTS 19-20

यमङ्ग शेपुः कुपिता वाग्वज्रा मुनयः किल ।
गतासोस्तस्य भूयस्ते ममन्थुर्दक्षिणं करम् ॥१९॥
अराजके तदा लोके दस्युभिः पीडिताः प्रजाः ।
जातो नारायणांशेन पृथुराद्यः क्षितीश्वरः ॥२०॥

yam aṅga śepuḥ kupitā
vāg-vajrā munayaḥ kila
gatāsos tasya bhūyas te
mamanthur dakṣiṇaṁ karam

arājake tadā loke
dasyubhiḥ pīḍitāḥ prajāḥ
jāto nārāyaṇāṁśena
pṛthur ādyaḥ kṣitīśvaraḥ

yam—him (Vena) whom; *aṅga*—my dear Vidura; *śepuḥ*—they cursed; *kupitāḥ*—being angry; *vāk-vajrāḥ*—whose words are as strong as a thunderbolt; *munayaḥ*—great sages; *kila*—indeed; *gata-asoḥ tasya*—after he died; *bhūyaḥ*—moreover; *te*—they; *mamanthuḥ*—churned; *dakṣiṇam*—right; *karam*—hand; *arājake*—being without a king; *tadā*—then; *loke*—the world; *dasyubhiḥ*—by rogues and thieves; *pīḍitāḥ*—suffering; *prajāḥ*—all the citizens; *jātaḥ*—advented; *nārāyaṇa*—of the Supreme Personality of Godhead; *aṁśena*—by a partial representation; *pṛthuḥ*—Pṛthu; *ādyaḥ*—original; *kṣiti-īśvaraḥ*—ruler of the world.

TRANSLATION

My dear Vidura, when great sages curse, their words are as invincible as a thunderbolt. Thus when they cursed King Vena out of anger, he died. After his death, since there was no king, all the rogues and thieves flourished, the kingdom became unregulated, and all the citizens suffered greatly. On seeing this, the great sages took the right hand of Vena as a churning rod, and as a result of their churning, Lord Viṣṇu in His partial representation advented as King Pṛthu, the original emperor of the world.

PURPORT

Monarchy is better than democracy because if the monarchy is very strong the regulative principles within the kingdom are upheld very nicely. Even one hundred years ago in the state of Kashmir in India, the king was so strong that if a thief were arrested in his kingdom and brought before him, the king would immediately chop off the hands of the thief. As a result of this severe punishment there were practically no theft cases within the kingdom. Even if someone left something on the street, no one would touch it. The rule was that the things could be taken away only by the proprietor and that no one else would touch them. In the so-called democracy, wherever there is a theft case the police come and take note of the case, but generally the thief is never caught, nor is any punishment offered to him. As a result of incapable government, at the present moment thieves, rogues and cheaters are very prominent all over the world.

TEXT 21

विदुर उवाच

तस्य शीलनिधेः साधोर्ब्रह्मण्यस्य महात्मनः ।
राज्ञः कथमभूद्दुष्टा प्रजा यद्विमना ययौ ॥२१॥

vidura uvāca
tasya śīla-nidheḥ sādhor
brahmaṇyasya mahātmanaḥ
rājñaḥ katham abhūd duṣṭā
prajā yad vimanā yayau

viduraḥ uvāca—Vidura said; *tasya*—of him (Aṅga); *śīla-nidheḥ*—reservoir of good characteristics; *sādhoḥ*—saintly person; *brahmaṇyasya*—lover of brahminical culture; *mahātmanaḥ*—great soul; *rājñaḥ*—of the king; *katham*—how; *abhūt*—it was; *duṣṭā*—bad; *prajā*—son; *yat*—by which; *vimanāḥ*—being indifferent; *yayau*—he left.

TRANSLATION

Vidura inquired from the sage Maitreya: My dear brāhmaṇa, King Aṅga was very gentle. He had high character and was a saintly personality and lover of brahminical culture. How is it that such a great soul got a bad son like Vena, because of whom he became indifferent to his kingdom and left it?

PURPORT

In family life a man is supposed to live happily with father, mother, wife and children, but sometimes, under certain conditions, a father, mother, child or wife becomes an enemy. It is said by Cāṇakya Paṇḍita that a father is an enemy when he is too much in debt, a mother is an enemy if she marries for a second time, a wife is an enemy when she is very beautiful, and a son is an enemy when he is a foolish rascal. In this way, when a family member becomes an enemy it is very difficult to live in family life or remain a householder. Generally such situations occur in the material world. Therefore according to Vedic culture one has to take leave of his family members just after his fiftieth year so that the balance of his life may be completely devoted in search of Kṛṣṇa consciousness.

TEXT 22

किं वांहो वेन उद्दिश्य ब्रह्मदण्डमयूयुजन् ।
दण्डव्रतधरे राज्ञि मुनयो धर्मकोविदाः ॥२२॥

kiṁ vāṁho vena uddiśya
brahma-daṇḍam ayūyujan
daṇḍa-vrata-dhare rājñi
munayo dharma-kovidāḥ

kim—why; *vā*—also; *aṁhaḥ*—sinful activities; *vene*—unto Vena; *uddiśya*—seeing; *brahma-daṇḍam*—curse of a *brāhmaṇa; ayūyujan*—they desired to award; *daṇḍa-vrata-dhare*—who carries the rod of punishment; *rājñi*—unto the king; *munayaḥ*—the great sages; *dharma-kovidāḥ*—completely conversant with religious principles.

TRANSLATION

Vidura also inquired: How is it that the great sages, who were completely conversant with religious principles, desired to curse King Vena, who himself carried the rod of punishment, and thus awarded him the greatest punishment [brahma-śāpa]?

PURPORT

It is understood that the king is able to give punishment to everyone, but in this case it appears that the great sages punished him. The king must have done something very serious, otherwise how could the great sages, who were supposed to be the greatest and most tolerant, still punish him in spite of their elevated religious consciousness? It appears also that the king was not independent of the brahminical culture. Above the king there was the control of the *brāhmaṇas,* and if needed the *brāhmaṇas* would dethrone the king or would kill him, not with any weapon, but with the *mantra* of a *brahma-śāpa.* The *brāhmaṇas* were so powerful that simply by their cursing one would immediately die.

TEXT 23

नावध्येयः प्रजापालः प्रजाभिरघवानपि ।
यदसौ लोकपालानां बिभर्त्योजः स्वतेजसा ॥२३॥

nāvadhyeyaḥ prajā-pālaḥ
prajābhir aghavān api
yad asau loka-pālānāṁ
bibharty ojaḥ sva-tejasā

na—never; *avadhyeyaḥ*—to be insulted; *prajā-pālaḥ*—the king; *prajābhiḥ*—by the citizens; *aghavān*—ever sinful; *api*—even though; *yat*—because; *asau*—he; *loka-pālānām*—of many kings; *bibharti*—maintains; *ojaḥ*—prowess; *sva-tejasā*—by personal influence.

TRANSLATION

It is the duty of all citizens in a state never to insult the king, even though he sometimes appears to have done something very sinful. Because

of his prowess, the king is always more influential than all other ruling chiefs.

PURPORT

According to Vedic civilization the king is supposed to be the representative of the Supreme Personality of Godhead. He is called *nara-nārāyaṇa,* indicating that Nārāyaṇa, the Supreme Personality of Godhead, appears in human society as the king. It is etiquette that neither a *brāhmaṇa* nor a *kṣatriya* king is ever insulted by the citizens; even though a king appears to be sinful, the citizens should not insult him. But in the case of Vena it appears that he was cursed by the *nara-devatās;* therefore, it was concluded that his sinful activities were very grievous.

TEXT 24

एतदाख्याहि मे ब्रह्मन् सुनीथात्मजचेष्टितम् ।
श्रद्दधानाय भक्ताय त्वं परावरवित्तमः ॥२४॥

etad ākhyāhi me brahman
sunīthātmaja-ceṣṭitam
śraddadhānāya bhaktāya
tvaṁ parāvara-vittamaḥ

etat—all these; *ākhyāhi*—please describe; *me*—unto me; *brahman*—O great *brāhmaṇa; sunīthā-ātmaja*—of the son of Sunīthā, Vena; *ceṣṭitam*—activities; *śraddadhānāya*—faithful; *bhaktāya*—unto your devotee; *tvam*—you; *para-avara*—with past and future; *vit-tamaḥ*—well conversant.

TRANSLATION

Vidura requested Maitreya: My dear brāhmaṇa, you are well conversant with all subjects, both past and future. Therefore I wish to hear from you all the activities of King Vena. I am your faithful devotee, so please explain this.

PURPORT

Vidura accepted Maitreya as his spiritual master. A disciple always inquires from the spiritual master, and the spiritual master answers the question, provided the disciple is very gentle and devoted. Śrīla Viśvanātha Cakravartī Ṭhākura said that by the mercy of the spiritual master one is benedicted with the mercy of the Supreme Lord. The spiritual master is not inclined to disclose all the secrets of transcendental science unless the disciple is very submissive and devoted. As stated in the *Bhagavad-gītā*, the process of receiving knowledge from the spiritual master entails submission, inquiry and service.

TEXT 25

मैत्रेय उवाच
अङ्गोऽश्वमेधं राजर्षिराजहार महाक्रतुम् ।
नाजग्मुर्देवतास्तस्मिन्नाहूता ब्रह्मवादिभिः ॥२५॥

maitreya uvāca
aṅgo 'śvamedhaṁ rājarṣir
ājahāra mahā-kratum
nājagmur devatās tasminn
āhūtā brahma-vādibhiḥ

maitreyaḥ uvāca—Maitreya answered; *aṅgaḥ*—King Aṅga; *aśvamedham*—*aśvamedha* sacrifice; *rāja-ṛṣiḥ*—the saintly king; *ājahāra*—executed; *mahā-kratum*—great sacrifice; *na*—not; *ajagmuḥ*—came; *devatāḥ*—the demigods; *tasmin*—in that sacrifice; *āhūtāḥ*—being invited; *brahma-vādibhiḥ*—by the *brāhmaṇas* expert in executing sacrifices.

TRANSLATION

Śrī Maitreya replied: My dear Vidura, once the great King Aṅga arranged to perform the great sacrifice known as aśvamedha. All the expert brāhmaṇas present knew how to invite the demigods, but in spite of their efforts, no demigods participated or appeared in that sacrifice.

PURPORT

A Vedic sacrifice is not an ordinary performance. The demigods used to participate in such sacrifices, and the animals sacrificed in such performances were reincarnated with new life. In this age of Kali there are no powerful *brāhmaṇas* who can invite the demigods or give renewed life to animals. Formerly, the *brāhmaṇas* well conversant in Vedic *mantras* could show the potency of the *mantras,* but in this age, because there are no such *brāhmaṇas,* all such sacrifices are forbidden. The sacrifice in which horses were offered was called *aśvamedha.* Sometimes cows were sacrificed (*gavālambha*), not for eating purposes, but to give them new life in order to show the potency of the *mantra.* In this age, therefore, the only practical *yajña* is *saṅkīrtana-yajña* or chanting of the Hare Kṛṣṇa *mantra* twenty-four hours a day.

TEXT 26

तमूचुर्विस्मितास्तत्र यजमानमथर्त्विजः ।
हवींषि हूयमानानि न ते गृह्णन्ति देवताः ॥२६॥

tam ūcur vismitās tatra
yajamānam athartvijaḥ
havīṁṣi hūyamānāni
na te gṛhṇanti devatāḥ

tam—unto King Aṅga; *ūcuḥ*—said; *vismitāḥ*—in wonder; *tatra*—there; *yajamānam*—to the institutor of the sacrifice; *atha*—then; *ṛtvijaḥ*—the priests; *havīṁṣi*—offerings of clarified butter; *hūyamānāni*—being offered; *na*—not; *te*—they; *gṛhṇanti*—accept; *devatāḥ*—the demigods.

TRANSLATION

The priests engaged in the sacrifice then informed King Aṅga: O King, we are properly offering the clarified butter in the sacrifice, but despite all our efforts the demigods do not accept it.

TEXT 27

राजन् हवींष्यदुष्टानि श्रद्धयाऽऽसादितानि ते ।
छन्दांस्ययातयामानि योजितानि धृतव्रतैः ॥२७॥

rājan havīṁṣy aduṣṭāni
śraddhayāsāditāni te
chandāṁsy ayāta-yāmāni
yojitāni dhṛta-vrataiḥ

rājan—O King; *havīṁṣi*—sacrificial offerings; *aduṣṭāni*—not polluted; *śraddhayā*—with great faith and care; *āsāditāni*—collected; *te*—your; *chandāṁsi*—the *mantras; ayāta-yāmāni*—not deficient; *yojitāni*—properly executed; *dhṛta-vrataiḥ*—by qualified *brāhmaṇas.*

TRANSLATION

O King, we know that the paraphernalia to perform the sacrifice is well collected by you with great faith and care and is not polluted. Our chanting of the Vedic hymns also is not deficient in any way because all the brāhmaṇas and priests present here are expert and are executing the performances properly.

PURPORT

It is the practice of the *brāhmaṇas* conversant with the science to pronounce a Vedic *mantra* in the right accent. The combination of the *mantra* and Sanskrit words must be chanted with the right pronunciation, otherwise it will not be successful. In this age the *brāhmaṇas* are neither well versed in the Sanskrit language nor very pure in practical life. But by chanting the Hare Kṛṣṇa *mantra* one can attain the highest benefit of sacrificial performances. Even if the Hare Kṛṣṇa *mantra* is not chanted properly, still it has so much potency that the chanter gains the effect.

TEXT 28

न विदामेह देवानां हेलनं वयमण्वपि ।
यन्न गृह्णन्ति भागान् स्वान् ये देवाः कर्मसाक्षिणः ॥२८॥

na vidāmeha devānāṁ
helanaṁ vayam aṇv api
yan na gṛhṇanti bhāgān svān
ye devāḥ karma-sākṣiṇaḥ

na—not; *vidāma*—can find; *iha*—in this connection; *devānām*—of the demigods; *helanam*—insult, neglect; *vayam*—we; *aṇu*—minute; *api*—even; *yat*—because of which; *na*—not; *gṛhṇanti*—accept; *bhāgān*—shares; *svān*—own; *ye*—who; *devāḥ*—the demigods; *karma-sākṣiṇaḥ*—witnesses for the sacrifice.

TRANSLATION

Dear King, we do not find any reason that the demigods should feel insulted or neglected in any way, but still the demigods who are witnesses for the sacrifice do not accept their shares. We do not know why it is so.

PURPORT

It is indicated herein that if there is negligence on the part of the priest, the demigods do not accept their share in sacrifices. Similarly, in devotional service there are offenses known as *sevā-aparādha.* Those who are engaged in worshiping the Deity, Rādhā and Kṛṣṇa in the temple, should avoid such offenses in service. The offenses in service are described in *The Nectar of Devotion.* If we simply make a show of offering services to the Deity but do not care for the *sevā-aparādha,* certainly the Rādhā-Kṛṣṇa Deity will not accept offerings from such nondevotees. Devotees engaged in temple worship should not, therefore, manufacture their own methods, but should strictly follow the regulative principles of cleanliness, and then offerings will be accepted.

TEXT 29

मैत्रेय उवाच

अङ्गो द्विजवचः श्रुत्वा यजमानः सुदुर्मनाः ।
तत्प्रष्टुं व्यसृजद्वाचं सदस्यांस्तदनुज्ञया ॥२९॥

maitreya uvāca
aṅgo dvija-vacaḥ śrutvā
yajamānaḥ sudurmanāḥ
tat praṣṭuṁ vyasṛjad vācaṁ
sadasyāṁs tad-anujñayā

maitreyaḥ uvāca—the great sage Maitreya answered; *aṅgaḥ*—King Aṅga; *dvija-vacaḥ*—the *brāhmaṇas* words; *śrutvā*—after hearing; *yajamānaḥ*—performer of the sacrifice; *sudurmanāḥ*—very much aggrieved in mind; *tat*—about that; *praṣṭum*—in order to inquire; *vyasṛjat vācam*—he spoke; *sadasyān*—to the priests; *tat*—their; *anujñayā*—taking permission.

TRANSLATION

Maitreya explained that King Aṅga, after hearing the statements of the priests, was greatly aggrieved. At that time he took permission from the priests to break his silence and inquired from all the priests who were present in the sacrificial arena.

TEXT 30

नागच्छन्त्याहुता देवा न गृह्णन्ति ग्रहानिह ।
सदसस्पतयो ब्रूत किमवद्यं मया कृतम् ॥३०॥

nāgacchanty āhutā devā
na gṛhṇanti grahān iha
sadasas patayo brūta
kim avadyaṁ mayā kṛtam

na—not; *āgacchanti*—are coming; *āhutāḥ*—being invited; *devāḥ*—the demigods; *na*—not; *gṛhṇanti*—are accepting; *grahān*—shares; *iha*—in the sacrifice; *sadasaḥ patayaḥ*—My dear priests; *brūta*—kindly tell me; *kim*—what; *avadyam*—offense; *mayā*—by me; *kṛtam*—was committed.

TRANSLATION

King Aṅga addressed the priestly order: My dear priests, kindly tell me what offense I have committed. Although invited, the demigods are neither taking part in the sacrifice nor accepting their shares.

TEXT 31

सदसस्पतय ऊचुः
नरदेवेह भवतो नाघं तावन्मनाक् स्थितम् ।
अस्त्येकं प्राक्तनमघं यदिहेदृक् त्वमप्रजः ॥३१॥

sadasas pataya ūcuḥ
nara-deveha bhavato
nāghaṁ tāvan manāk sthitam
asty ekaṁ prāktanam aghaṁ
yad ihedṛk tvam aprajaḥ

sadasaḥ patayaḥ ūcuḥ—the head priests said; *nara-deva*—O King; *iha*—in this life; *bhavataḥ*—of you; *na*—not; *agham*—sinful activity; *tāvat manāk*—even very slight; *sthitam*—situated; *asti*—there is; *ekam*—one; *prāktanam*—in the previous birth; *agham*—sinful activity; *yat*—by which; *iha*—in this life; *īdṛk*—like this; *tvam*—you; *aprajaḥ*—without any son.

TRANSLATION

The head priests said: O King, in this life we do not find any sinful activity, even within your mind, so you are not in the least offensive. But we can see that in your previous life you performed sinful activities due to which, in spite of your having all qualifications, you have no son.

PURPORT

The purpose of marrying is to beget a son because a son is necessary to deliver his father and forefathers from any hellish conditional life in which they may be. Cāṇakya Paṇḍita, therefore, says, *putra-hīnaṁ gṛhaṁ śūnyam:* without a son, married life is simply abominable. King Aṅga was a very pious king in this life, but because of his previous sinful activity he could not get a son. It is concluded, therefore, that if a person does not get a son it is due to his past sinful life.

TEXT 32

तथा साधय भद्रं ते आत्मानं सुप्रजं नृप ।
इष्टस्ते पुत्रकामस्य पुत्रं दास्यति यज्ञभुक् ॥३२॥

tathā sādhaya bhadraṁ te
ātmānaṁ suprajaṁ nṛpa
iṣṭas te putra-kāmasya
putraṁ dāsyati yajña-bhuk

tathā—therefore; *sādhaya*—execute the sacrifice to get; *bhadram*—good fortune; *te*—to you; *ātmānam*—your own; *su-prajam*—good son; *nṛpa*—O King; *iṣṭaḥ*—being worshiped; *te*—by you; *putra-kāmasya*—desiring to have a son; *putram*—a son; *dāsyati*—He will deliver; *yajña-bhuk*—the Lord, the enjoyer of the sacrifice.

TRANSLATION

O King, we wish all good fortune for you. You have no son, but if you pray at once to the Supreme Lord and ask for a son, and if you execute the sacrifice for that purpose, the enjoyer of the sacrifice, the Supreme Personality of Godhead, will fulfill your desire.

TEXT 33

तथा स्वभागधेयानि ग्रहीष्यन्ति दिवौकसः ।
यद्यज्ञपुरुषः साक्षादपत्याय हरिर्वृतः ॥३३॥

tathā sva-bhāga-dheyāni
grahīṣyanti divaukasaḥ
yad yajña-puruṣaḥ sākṣād
apatyāya harir vṛtaḥ

tathā—thereupon; *sva-bhāga-dheyāni*—their shares in the sacrifice; *grahīṣyanti*—will accept; *diva-okasaḥ*—all the demigods; *yat*—because; *yajña-puruṣaḥ*—the enjoyer of all sacrifices; *sākṣāt*—directly; *apatyāya*—for the purpose of a son; *hariḥ*—the Supreme Personality of Godhead; *vṛtaḥ*—is invited.

TRANSLATION

When Hari, the supreme enjoyer of all sacrifices, is invited to fulfill your desire for a son, all the demigods will come with Him and take their shares in the sacrifice.

PURPORT

Whenever a sacrifice is performed, it is meant for satisfying Lord Viṣṇu, the enjoyer of the fruits of all sacrifices; and when Lord Viṣṇu agrees to come to a sacrificial arena, all the demigods naturally follow their master, and their shares are offered in such sacrifices. The conclusion is that the sacrifices performed are meant for Lord Viṣṇu, not for the demigods.

TEXT 34

तांस्तान् कामान् हरिर्दद्याद्यान् यान् कामयते जनः ।
आराधितो यथैवैष तथा पुंसां फलोदयः ॥३४॥

tāṁs tān kāmān harir dadyād
yān yān kāmayate janaḥ
ārādhito yathaivaiṣa
tathā puṁsāṁ phalodayaḥ

tān tān—those; *kāmān*—desired objects; *hariḥ*—the Lord; *dadyāt*—will award; *yān yān*—whatsoever; *kāmayate*—desires; *janaḥ*—the person; *ārādhitaḥ*—being worshiped; *yathā*—as; *eva*—certainly; *eṣaḥ*—the Lord; *tathā*—similarly; *puṁsām*—of men; *phala-udayaḥ*—the result.

TRANSLATION

The performer of the sacrifices [under karma-kāṇḍa activities] achieves the fulfillment of the desire for which he worships the Lord.

PURPORT

In the *Bhagavad-gītā* the Lord says that He awards benediction to the worshiper according to his desire. The Supreme Personality of Godhead gives all living entities conditioned within this material world full freedom to act in their own way. But to His devotee He says that instead of working in that way, it is better to surrender unto Him, for He will take charge of the devotee. That is the difference between a devotee and a fruitive actor. The fruitive actor enjoys only the fruits of his own activities, but a devotee, being under the guidance of the Supreme Lord, simply advances in devotional service to achieve the ultimate goal of life—to go back home, back to Godhead. The significant word in this verse is *kāmān,* which means sense gratificatory desires. A devotee is devoid of all *kāmān.* He is *anyābhilāṣitā-śūnya*: a devotee is always devoid of all desires for sense gratification. His only aim is to satisfy or gratify the senses of the Lord. That is the difference between a *karmī* and a devotee.

TEXT 35

इति व्यवसिता विप्रास्तस्य राज्ञः प्रजातये ।
पुरोडाशं निरवपन् शिपिविष्टाय विष्णवे ॥३५॥

iti vyavasitā viprās
tasya rājñaḥ prajātaye
puro-ḍāśaṁ niravapan
śipi-viṣṭāya viṣṇave

iti—thus; *vyavasitāḥ*—having decided; *viprāḥ*—the *brāhmaṇas; tasya*—his; *rājñaḥ*—of the king; *prajātaye*—for the purpose of getting a son; *puraḥ-ḍāśam*—the paraphernalia of sacrifice; *niravapan*—offered; *śipi-viṣṭāya*—to the Lord, who is situated in the sacrificial fire; *viṣṇave*—to Lord Viṣṇu.

TRANSLATION

Thus for the sake of a son for King Aṅga, they decided to offer oblations to Lord Viṣṇu, who is situated in the hearts of all living entities.

PURPORT

According to sacrificial rituals, animals are sometimes sacrificed in the *yajña* arena. Such animals are sacrificed not to kill them but to give them new life. Such action was an experiment to observe whether the Vedic *mantras* were being properly pronounced. Sometimes small animals are killed in a medical laboratory to investigate therapeutic effect. In a medical clinic the animals are not revived, but in the *yajña* arena, when animals were sacrificed, they were again given life by the potency of Vedic *mantras*. The word *śipi-viṣṭāya* appears in this verse. *Śipi* means the flames of the sacrifice. In the sacrificial fire if the oblations are offered into the flames, then Lord Viṣṇu is situated there in the form of the flames. Therefore Lord Viṣṇu is known as Śipiviṣṭa.

TEXT 36

तस्मात्पुरुष उत्तस्थौ हेममाल्यमलाम्बरः ।
हिरण्मयेन पात्रेण सिद्धमादाय पायसम् ॥३६॥

tasmāt puruṣa uttasthau
hema-māly amalāmbaraḥ
hiraṇmayena pātreṇa
siddham ādāya pāyasam

tasmāt—from that fire; *puruṣaḥ*—a person; *uttasthau*—appeared; *hema-mālī*—with a golden garland; *amala-ambaraḥ*—in white garments;

hiraṇmayena—golden; *pātreṇa*—with a pot; *siddham*—cooked; *ādāya*—carrying; *pāyasam*—rice boiled in milk.

TRANSLATION

As soon as the oblation was offered in the fire, a person appeared from the fire altar wearing a golden garland and white dress. He was carrying a golden pot filled with rice boiled in milk.

TEXT 37

स विप्रानुमतो राजा गृहीत्वाञ्जलिनौदनम् ।
अवघ्राय मुदा युक्तः प्रादात्पत्न्या उदारधीः ॥३७॥

sa viprānumato rājā
gṛhītvāñjalinaudanam
avaghrāya mudā yuktaḥ
prādāt patnyā udāra-dhīḥ

saḥ—he; *vipra*—of the *brāhmaṇas; anumataḥ*—taking permission; *rājā*—the King; *gṛhītvā*—taking; *añjalinā*—in his joined palms; *odanam*—rice boiled in milk; *avaghrāya*—after smelling; *mudā*—with great delight; *yuktaḥ*—fixed; *prādāt*—offered; *patnyai*—to his wife; *udāra-dhīḥ*—liberal-minded.

TRANSLATION

The King was very liberal, and after taking permission from the priests, he took the preparation in his joined palms, and after smelling it he offered a portion to his wife.

PURPORT

The word *udāra-dhīḥ* is significant in this connection. The wife of the King, Sunīthā, was not fit to accept this benediction, yet the King was so liberal that without hesitation he offered to his wife the boiled rice in milk *prasāda* received from the *yajña-puruṣa*. Of course everything is designed by the Supreme Personality of Godhead. As will be explained in later verses, this incident was not very favorable for the King. Since the King was very liberal, the Supreme Personality of Godhead, in order to increase his detachment from this material world, willed that a cruel son be born of the Queen so that the King would have to leave home. As stated above, Lord Viṣṇu fulfills the desires of the *karmīs* as they desire, but the Lord fulfills the desire of a devotee in a different way so that the devotee may gradually come to Him. This is confirmed in the *Bhagavad-gītā (dadāmi buddhi-yogaṁ taṁ yena mām upayānti te).* The Lord gives the devotee the opportunity to make progress further and further so that he may come back home, back to Godhead.

TEXT 38

सा तत्पुंसवनं राज्ञी प्राश्य वै पत्युरादधे ।
गर्भं काल उपावृत्ते कुमारं सुषुवेऽप्रजा ॥३८॥

sā tat puṁ-savanaṁ rājñī
prāśya vai patyur ādadhe
garbhaṁ kāla upāvṛtte
kumāraṁ suṣuve 'prajā

sā—she; *tat*—that food; *puṁ-savanam*—which produces a male child; *rājñī*—the Queen; *prāśya*—eating; *vai*—indeed; *patyuḥ*—from the husband; *ādadhe*—conceived; *garbham*—pregnancy; *kāle*—when the due time; *upāvṛtte*—appeared; *kumāram*—a son; *suṣuve*—gave birth to; *aprajā*—having no son.

TRANSLATION

Although the Queen had no son, after eating that food, which had the power to produce a male child, she became pregnant from her husband, and in due course of time she gave birth to a son.

PURPORT

Among the ten kinds of purificatory processes, one is *puṁ-savanam,* in which the wife is offered some *prasāda,* or remnants of foodstuff offered to Lord Viṣṇu, so that after sexual intercourse with her husband she may conceive a child.

TEXT 39

स बाल एव पुरुषो मातामहमनुव्रतः ।
अधर्मांशोद्भवं मृत्युं तेनाभवदधार्मिकः ॥३९॥

sa bāla eva puruṣo
mātā-maham anuvrataḥ
adharmāṁśodbhavaṁ mṛtyuṁ
tenābhavad adhārmikaḥ

saḥ—that; *bālaḥ*—child; *eva*—certainly; *puruṣaḥ*—male; *mātā-maham*—maternal grandfather; *anuvrataḥ*—a follower of; *adharma*—of irreligion;

aṁśa—from a portion; *udbhavam*—who appeared; *mṛtyum*—death; *tena*—by this; *abhavat*—he became; *adhārmikaḥ*—irreligious.

TRANSLATION

That boy was born partially in the dynasty of irreligion. His grandfather was death personified, and the boy grew up as his follower; he became a greatly irreligious person.

PURPORT

The child's mother, Sunīthā, was the daughter of death personified. Generally the daughter receives the qualifications of her father, and the son acquires those of the mother. So, according to the axiomatic truth that things equal to the same thing are equal to one another, the child born of King Aṅga became the follower of his maternal grandfather. According to *smṛti-śāstra,* a child generally follows the principles of his maternal uncle's house. *Narāṇāṁ mātula-karma* means that a child generally follows the qualities of his maternal family. If the maternal family is very corrupt or sinful, the child, even though born of a good father, becomes a victim of the maternal family. According to Vedic civilization, therefore, before the marriage takes place an account is taken of both the boy's and girl's families. If according to astrological calculation the combination is perfect, then marriage takes place. Sometimes, however, there is a mistake, and family life becomes frustrating.

It appears that King Aṅga did not get a very good wife in Sunīthā because she was the daughter of death personified. Sometimes the Lord arranges an unfortunate wife for His devotee so that gradually, due to family circumstances, the devotee becomes detached from his wife and home and makes progress in devotional life. It appears that by the arrangement of the Supreme Personality of Godhead, King Aṅga, although a pious devotee, got an unfortunate wife like Sunīthā and later on a bad child like Vena. But the result was that he got complete freedom from the entanglement of family life and left home to go back to Godhead.

TEXT 40

स शरासनमुद्यम्य मृगयुर्वनगोचरः ।
हन्त्यसाधुर्मृगान् दीनान् वेनोऽसावित्यरौज्जनः ॥४०॥

sa śarāsanam udyamya
mṛgayur vana-gocaraḥ
hanty asādhur mṛgān dīnān
veno 'sāv ity arauj janaḥ

saḥ—that boy of the name Vena; *śarāsanam*—his bow; *udyamya*—taking up; *mṛgayuḥ*—the hunter; *vana-gocaraḥ*—going into the forest; *hanti*—used to kill; *asādhuḥ*—being very cruel; *mṛgān*—deer; *dīnān*—poor; *venaḥ*—Vena; *asau*—there he is; *iti*—thus; *araut*—would cry; *janaḥ*—all the people.

TRANSLATION

After fixing his bow and arrow, the cruel boy used to go to the forest and unnecessarily kill innocent deer, and as soon as he came all the people would cry, "Here comes cruel Vena! Here comes cruel Vena!"

PURPORT

Kṣatriyas are allowed to hunt in the forest for the purpose of learning the killing art, not to kill animals for eating or for any other purpose. The *kṣatriya* kings were sometimes expected to cut off the head of a culprit in the state. For this reason the *kṣatriyas* were allowed to hunt in the forest. Because this son of King Aṅga, Vena, was born of a bad mother, he was very cruel, and he used to go to the forest and unnecessarily kill the animals. All the neighboring inhabitants would be frightened by his presence, and they would call, "Here comes Vena! Here comes Vena!" So from the beginning of his life he was fearful to the citizens.

TEXT 41

आक्रीडे क्रीडतो बालान् वयस्यानतिदारुणः ।
प्रसह्य निरनुक्रोशः पशुमारममारयत् ॥४१॥

ākrīḍe krīḍato bālān
vayasyān atidāruṇaḥ
prasahya niranukrośaḥ
paśu-māram amārayat

ākrīḍe—in the playground; *krīḍataḥ*—while playing; *bālān*—boys; *vayasyān*—of his age; *atidāruṇaḥ*—very cruel; *prasahya*—by force; *niranukrośaḥ*—merciless; *paśu-māram*—as if slaughtering animals; *amārayat*—killed.

TRANSLATION

The boy was so cruel that while playing with young boys of his age he would kill them very mercilessly, as if they were animals meant for slaughter.

TEXT 42

तं विचक्ष्य खलं पुत्रं शासनैर्विविधैर्नृपः ।
यदा न शासितुं कल्पो भृशमासीत्सुदुर्मनाः ॥४२॥

taṁ vicakṣya khalaṁ putraṁ
śāsanair vividhair nṛpaḥ
yadā na śāsituṁ kalpo
bhṛśam āsīt sudurmanāḥ

tam—him; *vicakṣya*—observing; *khalam*—cruel; *putram*—son; *śāsanaiḥ*—by punishments; *vividhaiḥ*—different kinds of; *nṛpaḥ*—the King; *yadā*—when; *na*—not; *śāsitum*—to bring under control; *kalpaḥ*—was able; *bhṛśam*—greatly; *āsīt*—became; *sudurmanāḥ*—aggrieved.

TRANSLATION

After seeing the cruel and merciless behavior of his son Vena, King Aṅga punished him in different ways to reform him, but he was unable to bring him to the path of gentleness. He thus became greatly aggrieved.

TEXT 43

प्रायेणाभ्यर्चितो देवो येऽप्रजा गृहमेधिनः ।
कदपत्यभृतं दुःखं ये न विन्दन्ति दुर्भरम् ॥४३॥

prāyeṇābhyarcito devo
ye 'prajā gṛha-medhinaḥ
kad-apatya-bhṛtaṁ duḥkhaṁ
ye na vindanti durbharam

prāyeṇa—probably; *abhyarcitaḥ*—was worshiped; *devaḥ*—the Lord; *ye*—they who; *aprajāḥ*—without a son; *gṛha-medhinaḥ*—persons living at home; *kad-apatya*—by a bad son; *bhṛtam*—caused; *duḥkham*—unhappiness; *ye*—they who; *na*—not; *vindanti*—suffer; *durbharam*—unbearable.

TRANSLATION

The King thought to himself: Persons who have no son are certainly fortunate. They must have worshiped the Lord in their previous lives so that they would not have to suffer the unbearable unhappiness caused by a bad son.

TEXT 44

यतः पापीयसी कीर्तिरधर्मश्च महान्नृणाम् ।
यतो विरोधः सर्वेषां यत आधिरनन्तकः ॥४४॥

yataḥ pāpīyasī kīrtir
adharmaś ca mahān nṛṇām
yato virodhaḥ sarveṣāṁ
yata ādhir anantakaḥ

yataḥ—on account of a bad son; *pāpīyasī*—sinful; *kīrtiḥ*—reputation; *adharmaḥ*—irreligion; *ca*—also; *mahān*—great; *nṛṇām*—of men; *yataḥ*—from which; *virodhaḥ*—quarrel; *sarveṣām*—of all people; *yataḥ*—from which; *ādhiḥ*—anxiety; *anantakaḥ*—endless.

TRANSLATION

A sinful son causes a person's reputation to vanish. His irreligious activities at home cause irreligion and quarrel among everyone, and this creates only endless anxiety.

PURPORT

It is said that a married couple must have a son, otherwise their family life is void. But a son born without good qualities is as good as a blind eye. A blind eye has no use for seeing, but it is simply unbearably painful. The King therefore thought himself very unfortunate to have such a bad son.

TEXT 45

कस्तं प्रजापदेशं वै मोहबन्धनमात्मनः ।
पण्डितो बहु मन्येत यदर्थाः क्लेशदा गृहाः ॥४५॥

kas taṁ prajāpadeśaṁ vai
moha-bandhanam ātmanaḥ
paṇḍito bahu manyeta
yad-arthāḥ kleśadā gṛhāḥ

kaḥ—who; *tam*—him; *prajā-apadeśam*—son in name only; *vai*—certainly; *moha*—of illusion; *bandhanam*—bondage; *ātmanaḥ*—for the soul; *paṇḍitaḥ*—intelligent man; *bahu manyeta*—would value; *yat-arthāḥ*—because of whom; *kleśa-dāḥ*—painful; *gṛhāḥ*—home.

TRANSLATION

Who, if he is considerate and intelligent, would desire such a worthless son? Such a son is nothing but a bondage of illusion for the living entity, and he makes one's home miserable.

TEXT 46

कदपत्यं वरं मन्ये सदपत्याच्छुचां पदात् ।
निर्विद्येत गृहान्मर्त्यो यत्क्लेशनिवहा गृहाः ॥४६॥

kad-apatyaṁ varaṁ manye
sad-apatyāc chucāṁ padāt
nirvidyeta gṛhān martyo
yat kleśa-nivahā gṛhāḥ

kad-apatyam—bad son; *varam*—better; *manye*—I think; *sat-apatyāt*—than a good son; *śucām*—of grief; *padāt*—the source; *nirvidyeta*—becomes detached; *gṛhāt*—from home; *martyaḥ*—a mortal man; *yat*—because of whom; *kleśa-nivahāḥ*—hellish; *gṛhāḥ*—home.

TRANSLATION

Then the King thought: A bad son is better than a good son because a good son creates an attachment for home, whereas a bad son does not. A bad son creates a hellish home from which an intelligent man naturally becomes very easily detached.

PURPORT

The King began to think in terms of attachment and detachment from one's material home. According to Prahlāda Mahārāja, the material home is compared to a blind well. If a man falls down into a blind well, it is very difficult to get out of it and begin life again. Prahlāda Mahārāja has advised that one should give up this blind well of home life as soon as possible and go to the forest to take shelter of the Supreme Personality of Godhead. According to Vedic civilization, this giving up of home with *vānaprastha* and *sannyāsa* is compulsory. But people are so attached to their homes that even up to the point of death they do not like to retire from home life. King Aṅga, therefore, thinking in terms of detachment, accepted his bad son as a good impetus for detachment from home life. He therefore considered his bad son his friend since he was helping him to become detached from his home. Ultimately one has to learn how to detach oneself from attachment to material life; therefore, if a bad son, by his bad behavior, helps a householder to go away from home, it is a boon.

TEXT 47

एवं स निर्विण्णमना नृपो गृहा-
न्निशीथ उत्थाय महोदयोदयात् ।

अलब्धनिद्रोऽनुपलक्षितो नृभि-
हित्वा गतो वेनसुवं प्रसुप्ताम् ॥४७॥

evaṁ sa nirviṇṇa-manā nṛpo gṛhān
niśītha utthāya mahodayodayāt
alabdha-nidro 'nupalakṣito nṛbhir
hitvā gato vena-suvaṁ prasuptām

evam—thus; *saḥ*—he; *nirviṇṇa-manāḥ*—being indifferent in mind; *nṛpaḥ*—King Aṅga; *gṛhāt*—from home; *niśīthe*—in the dead of night; *utthāya*—getting up; *mahā-udaya-udayāt*—opulent by the blessings of great souls; *alabdha-nidraḥ*—being without sleep; *anupalakṣitaḥ*—without being seen; *nṛbhiḥ*—by people in general; *hitvā*—giving up; *gataḥ*—went off; *vena-suvam*—the mother of Vena; *prasuptām*—sleeping deeply.

TRANSLATION

Thinking like that, King Aṅga could not sleep at night. He became completely indifferent to household life. Once, therefore, in the dead of night, he got up from bed and left Vena's mother [his wife], who was sleeping deeply. He gave up all attraction for his greatly opulent kingdom, and, unseen by anyone, he very silently gave up his home and opulence and proceeded toward the forest.

PURPORT

In this verse the word *mahodayodayāt* indicates that by the blessings of a great soul one becomes materially opulent. But when one gives up attachment to material wealth, that should be considered an even greater blessing from the great souls. It was not a very easy task for the King to give up his opulent kingdom and young faithful wife, but it was certainly a great blessing of the Supreme Personality of Godhead that he could give up the attachment and go out to the forest without being seen by anyone. There are many instances of great souls leaving home in this way in the dead of night, giving up attachment for home, wife and money.

TEXT 48

विज्ञाय निर्विद्य गतं पतिं प्रजाः
पुरोहितामात्यसुहृद्गणादयः ।
विचिक्युरुर्व्यामतिशोककातरा
यथा निगूढं पुरुषं कुयोगिनः ॥४८॥

vijñāya nirvidya gataṁ patiṁ prajāḥ
purohitāmātya-suhṛd-gaṇādayaḥ
vicikyur urvyām atiśoka-kātarā
yathā nigūḍhaṁ puruṣaṁ kuyoginaḥ

vijñāya—after understanding; *nirvidya*—being indifferent; *gatam*—had left; *patim*—the King; *prajāḥ*—all the citizens; *purohita*—priests; *āmātya*—ministers; *suhṛt*—friends; *gaṇa-ādayaḥ*—and people in general; *vicikyuḥ*—searched; *urvyām*—on the earth; *atiśoka-kātarāḥ*—being greatly aggrieved; *yathā*—just as; *nigūḍham*—concealed; *puruṣam*—the Supersoul; *ku-yoginaḥ*—inexperienced mystics.

TRANSLATION

When it was understood that the King had indifferently left home, all the citizens, priests, ministers, friends, and people in general were greatly aggrieved. They began to search for him all over the world, just as a less experienced mystic searches out the Supersoul within himself.

PURPORT

The example of searching for the Supersoul within the heart by the less intelligent mystics is very instructive. The Absolute Truth is understood in three different features, namely impersonal Brahman, localized Paramātmā, and the Supreme Personality of Godhead. Such *kuyoginaḥ*, or less intelligent mystics, can by mental speculation reach the point of the impersonal Brahman, but they cannot find the Supersoul who is sitting within each living entity. When the King left, it was certain that he was staying somewhere else, but because they did not know how to find him they were frustrated like the less intelligent mystics.

TEXT 49

अलक्षयन्तः पदवीं प्रजापते-
र्हतोद्यमाः प्रत्युपसृत्य ते पुरीम् ।
ऋषीन् समेतानभिवन्द्य साश्रवो
न्यवेदयन् पौरव भर्तृविप्लवम् ॥४९॥

alakṣayantaḥ padavīṁ prajāpater
hatodyamāḥ pratyupasṛtya te purīm
ṛṣīn sametān abhivandya sāśravo
nyavedayan paurava bhartṛ-viplavam

alakṣayantaḥ—not finding; *padavīm*—any trace; *prajāpateḥ*—of King Aṅga; *hata-udyamāḥ*—having become disappointed; *pratyupasṛtya*—after returning; *te*—those citizens; *purīm*—to the city; *ṛṣīn*—the great sages; *sametān*—assembled; *abhivandya*—after making respectful obeisances; *sa-aśravaḥ*—with tears in their eyes; *nyavedayan*—informed; *paurava*—O Vidura; *bhartṛ*—of the king; *viplavam*—the absence.

TRANSLATION

When the citizens could not find any trace of the King after searching for him everywhere, they were very disappointed, and they returned to the city, where all the great sages of the country assembled because of the King's absence. With tears in their eyes the citizens offered respectful obeisances and informed them in full detail that they were unable to find the King anywhere.

Thus end the Bhaktivedanta purports of the Fourth Canto, Thirteenth Chapter, of the Śrīmad-Bhāgavatam, *entitled "Description of the Descendants of Dhruva Mahārāja."*

CHAPTER FOURTEEN

The Story of King Vena

TEXT 1

मैत्रेय उवाच
भृग्वादयस्ते मुनयो लोकानां क्षेमदर्शिनः ।
गोप्तर्यसति वै नृणां पश्यन्तः पशुसाम्यताम् ॥ १ ॥

maitreya uvāca
bhṛgv-ādayas te munayo
lokānāṁ kṣema-darśinaḥ
goptary asati vai nṛṇāṁ
paśyantaḥ paśu-sāmyatām

maitreyaḥ uvāca—the great sage Maitreya continued; *bhṛgu-ādayaḥ*—headed by Bhṛgu; *te*—all of them; *munayaḥ*—the great sages; *lokānām*—of the people; *kṣema-darśinaḥ*—who always aspire for the welfare; *goptari*—the King; *asati*—being absent; *vai*—certainly; *nṛṇām*—of all the citizens; *paśyantaḥ*—having understood; *paśu-sāmyatām*—existence on the level of the animals.

TRANSLATION

The great sage Maitreya continued: O great hero Vidura, the great sages, headed by Bhṛgu, were always thinking of the welfare of the people in general. When they saw that in the absence of King Aṅga there was no one to protect the interests of the people, they understood that without a ruler the people would become independent and nonregulated.

PURPORT

In this verse the significant word is *kṣema-darśinaḥ*, which refers to those who are always looking after the welfare of the people in general. However, all the great sages headed by Bhṛgu were always thinking of how to elevate all the people of the universe to the spiritual platform. Indeed, they advised the kings of every planet to rule the people with that ultimate goal of life in mind. The great sages used to advise the head of the state, or the king, and he used to rule the populace in accordance with their instruction. After the disappearance of King Aṅga, there was no one to follow the instructions of the great sages. Consequently all the citizens became unruly, so much so that they could be compared to animals. As described in *Bhagavad-gītā* (Bg. 4.13), human society must be divided into four orders according to quality and work. In every society there must be an intelligent class, administrative class, productive class and worker class. In modern democracy these scientific divisions are turned topsy-turvy, and by vote *śūdras,* or workers, are chosen for administrative posts. Having no knowledge of the ultimate goal of life, such persons whimsically enact laws without knowledge of life's purpose. The result is that no one is happy.

TEXT 2

वीरमातरमाहूय सुनीथां ब्रह्मवादिनः ।
प्रकृत्यसम्मतं वेनमभ्यषिञ्चन् पतिं भुवः ॥ २ ॥

vīra-mātaram āhūya
sunīthāṁ brahma-vādinaḥ
prakṛty-asammataṁ venam
abhyaṣiñcan patiṁ bhuvaḥ

vīra—of Vena; *mātaram*—mother; *āhūya*—calling; *sunīthām*—of the name Sunīthā; *brahma-vādinaḥ*—the great sages learned in the *Vedas; prakṛti*—by the ministers; *asammatam*—not approved of; *venam*—Vena; *abhyaṣiñcan*—enthroned; *patim*—the master; *bhuvaḥ*—of the world.

TRANSLATION

The great sages then called for the Queen Mother, Sunīthā, and with her permission they installed Vena on the throne as master of the world. All the ministers, however, disagreed with this.

TEXT 3

श्रुत्वा नृपासनगतं वेनमत्युग्रशासनम् ।
निलिल्युर्दस्यवः सद्यः सर्पत्रस्ता इवाखवः ॥ ३ ॥

śrutvā nṛpāsana-gataṁ
venam aty-ugra-śāsanam
nililyur dasyavaḥ sadyaḥ
sarpa-trastā ivākhavaḥ

śrutvā—after hearing; *nṛpa*—of the King; *āsana-gatam*—ascended to the throne; *venam*—Vena; *ati*—very; *ugra*—severe; *śāsanam*—punisher; *nililyuḥ*—hid themselves; *dasyavaḥ*—all the thieves; *sadyaḥ*—immediately; *sarpa*—from snakes; *trastāḥ*—being afraid; *iva*—like; *ākhavaḥ*—rats.

TRANSLATION

It was already known that Vena was very severe and cruel; therefore as soon as all the thieves and rogues in the state heard of his ascendance to the royal throne, they became very much afraid of him. Indeed, they hid themselves here and there as rats hide themselves from snakes.

PURPORT

When the government is very weak, rogues and thieves flourish. Similarly, when the government is very strong, all the thieves and rogues disappear or hide themselves. Of course Vena was not a very good king, but he was known to be cruel and severe. Thus the state at least became freed from thieves and rogues.

TEXT 4

स आरूढनृपस्थान उन्नद्धोऽष्टविभूतिभिः ।
अवमेने महाभागान् स्तब्धः सम्भावितः स्वतः॥ ४ ॥

sa ārūḍha-nṛpa-sthāna
unnaddho 'ṣṭa-vibhūtibhiḥ
avamene mahā-bhāgān
stabdhaḥ sambhāvitaḥ svataḥ

saḥ—King Vena; *ārūḍha*—ascended to; *nṛpa-sthānaḥ*—the seat of the king; *unnaddhaḥ*—very proud; *aṣṭa*—eight; *vibhūtibhiḥ*—by opulences; *avamene*—began to insult; *mahā-bhāgān*—great personalities; *stabdhaḥ*—inconsiderate; *sambhāvitaḥ*—considered great; *svataḥ*—by himself.

TRANSLATION

When the King ascended to the throne, he became all-powerful with eight kinds of opulences. Consequently he became too proud. By virtue of his false prestige, he considered himself to be greater than anyone. Thus he began to insult great personalities.

PURPORT

In this verse the word *aṣṭa-vibhūtibhiḥ*, meaning by eight opulences, is very important. The king is supposed to possess eight kinds of opulences.

By dint of mystic *yoga* practice, kings generally acquired these eight kinds of opulences. These kings were called *rājarṣis,* kings who were also great sages. By practicing mystic *yoga,* a *rājarṣi* could become smaller than the smallest, greater than the greatest, and could get whatever he desired. A *rājarṣi* could also create a kingdom, bring everyone under his control and rule them. These were some of the opulences of a king. King Vena, however, was not practiced in *yoga,* but he became very proud of his royal position nonetheless. Because he was not very considerate, he began to misuse his power and insult great personalities.

TEXT 5

एवं मदान्ध उत्सिक्तो निरङ्कुश इव द्विपः ।
पर्यटन् रथमास्थाय कम्पयन्निव रोदसी ॥ ५ ॥

evaṁ madāndha utsikto
niraṅkuśa iva dvipaḥ
paryaṭan ratham āsthāya
kampayann iva rodasī

evam—thus; *mada-andhaḥ*—being blind with power; *utsiktaḥ*—proud; *niraṅkuśaḥ*—uncontrolled; *iva*—like; *dvipaḥ*—an elephant; *paryaṭan*—traveling; *ratham*—a chariot; *āsthāya*—having mounted; *kampayan*—causing to tremble; *iva*—indeed; *rodasī*—the sky and earth.

TRANSLATION

When he became overly blind due to his opulences, King Vena mounted a chariot and, like an uncontrolled elephant, began to travel through the kingdom causing the sky and earth to tremble wherever he went.

TEXT 6

न यष्टव्यं न दातव्यं न होतव्यं द्विजाः क्वचित् ।
इति न्यवारयद्धर्मं भेरीघोषेण सर्वशः ॥ ६ ॥

na yaṣṭavyaṁ na dātavyaṁ
na hotavyaṁ dvijāḥ kvacit
iti nyavārayad dharmaṁ
bherī-ghoṣeṇa sarvaśaḥ

na—not; *yaṣṭavyam*—any sacrifices can be performed; *na*—not; *dātavyam*—any charity can be given; *na*—not; *hotavyam*—any clarified butter can be offered; *dvijāḥ*—O twice-born; *kvacit*—at any time; *iti*—thus; *nyavārayat*—he stopped; *dharmam*—the procedures of religious principles; *bherī*—of kettledrums; *ghoṣeṇa*—with the sound; *sarvaśaḥ*—everywhere.

TRANSLATION

All the twice-born [brāhmaṇas] were forbidden henceforward to perform any sacrifice, and they were also forbidden to give charity or offer clarified butter. Thus King Vena sounded kettledrums throughout the countryside. In other words, he stopped all kinds of religious rituals.

PURPORT

What was committed by King Vena many years ago is at present being carried out by atheistic governments all over the world. The world situation is so tense that at any moment governments may issue declarations to stop religious rituals. Eventually the world situation will become so degraded that it will be impossible for pious men to live on the planet. Therefore sane people should execute Kṛṣṇa consciousness very seriously so that they can go back home, back to Godhead, without having to further suffer the miserable conditions predominant in this universe.

TEXT 7

वेनस्यावेक्ष्य मुनयो दुर्वृत्तस्य विचेष्टितम् ।
विमृश्य लोकव्यसनं कृपयोचुः स्म सत्रिणः ॥ ७ ॥

venasyāvekṣya munayo
durvṛttasya viceṣṭitam
vimṛśya loka-vyasanaṁ
kṛpayocuḥ sma satriṇaḥ

venasya—of King Vena; *āvekṣya*—after observing; *munayaḥ*—all great sages; *durvṛttasya*—of the great rogue; *viceṣṭitam*—activities; *vimṛśya*—considering; *loka-vyasanam*—danger to the people in general; *kṛpayā*—out of compassion; *ūcuḥ*—talked; *sma*—in the past; *satriṇaḥ*—the performers of sacrifices.

TRANSLATION

Therefore all the great sages assembled together, and, after observing cruel Vena's atrocities, concluded that a great danger and catastrophe was approaching the people of the world. Thus out of compassion they began to talk amongst themselves, for they themselves were the sacrificial performers.

PURPORT

Before King Vena was enthroned, all the great sages were very much anxious to see to the welfare of society. When they saw that King Vena was most irresponsible, cruel and atrocious, they again began to think of the welfare of the people. It should be understood that sages, saintly persons and devotees are not unconcerned with the people's welfare. Ordinary *karmīs* are busy acquiring money for sense gratification, and ordinary *jñānīs* are socially aloof when they speculate on liberation, but actual devotees and saintly persons are always anxious to see how the people can be made happy both materially and spiritually. Therefore the great sages began to consult one another on how to get out of the dangerous atmosphere created by King Vena.

TEXT 8

अहो उभयतः प्राप्तं लोकस्य व्यसनं महत् ।
दारुण्युभयतो दीप्ते इव तस्करपालयोः ॥ ८ ॥

aho ubhayataḥ prāptaṁ
lokasya vyasanaṁ mahat
dāruṇy ubhayato dīpte
iva taskara-pālayoḥ

aho—alas; *ubhayataḥ*—from both directions; *prāptam*—received; *lokasya*—of the people in general; *vyasanam*—danger; *mahat*—great; *dāruṇi*—a log; *ubhayataḥ*—from both sides; *dīpte*—burning; *iva*—like; *taskara*—from thieves and rogues; *pālayoḥ*—and from the king.

TRANSLATION

When the great sages consulted one another, they saw that the people were in a dangerous position from both directions. When a fire blazes on both ends of a log, the ants in the middle are in a very dangerous situation. Similarly, at that time the people in general were in a dangerous position due to an irresponsible king on one side and thieves and rogues on the other.

TEXT 9

अराजकभयादेष कृतो राजातदर्हणः ।
ततोऽप्यासीद्भयं त्वद्य कथं स्यात्स्वस्ति देहिनाम् ॥ ९ ॥

arājaka-bhayād eṣa
kṛto rājātad-arhaṇaḥ
tato 'py āsīd bhayaṁ tv adya
kathaṁ syāt svasti dehinām

arājaka—being without a king; *bhayāt*—out of fear of; *eṣaḥ*—this Vena; *kṛtaḥ*—was made; *rājā*—the king; *a-tat-arhaṇaḥ*—though not qualified for it; *tataḥ*—from him; *api*—also; *āsīt*—there was; *bhayam*—danger; *tu*—then; *adya*—now; *katham*—how; *syāt*—can there be; *svasti*—happiness; *dehinām*—of the people in general.

TRANSLATION

Thinking to save the state from irregularity, the sages began to consider that it was due to a political crisis that they made Vena king although he was not qualified. But alas, now the people were being disturbed by the king himself. Under such circumstances, how could the people be happy?

PURPORT

In *Bhagavad-gītā* (Bg.18.5) it is stated that even in the renounced order one should not give up sacrifice, charity and penance. The *brahmacārīs* must perform sacrifices, the *gṛhasthas* must give in charity, and those in the renounced order of life (the *vānaprasthas* and *sannyāsīs*) must practice penance and austerities. These are the procedures by which everyone can be elevated to the spiritual platform. When the sages and saintly persons saw that King Vena had stopped all these functions, they became concerned about the people's progress. Saintly people preach God consciousness or Kṛṣṇa consciousness because they are anxious to save the general populace from the dangers of animalistic life. There must be a good government to see that the citizens are actually executing their religious rituals, and thieves and rogues must be curbed. When this is done, the people can advance peacefully in spiritual consciousness and make their lives successful.

TEXT 10

अहेरिव पयःपोषः पोषकस्याप्यनर्थभृत् ।
वेनः प्रकृत्यैव खलः सुनीथागर्भसम्भवः ॥१०॥

aher iva payaḥ-poṣaḥ
poṣakasyāpy anartha-bhṛt
venaḥ prakṛtyaiva khalaḥ
sunīthā-garbha-sambhavaḥ

aheḥ—of a snake; *iva*—like; *payaḥ*—with milk; *poṣaḥ*—the maintaining; *poṣakasya*—of the maintainer; *api*—even; *anartha*—against the interest; *bhṛt*—becomes; *venaḥ*—King Vena; *prakṛtyā*—by nature; *eva*—certainly; *khalaḥ*—mischievous; *sunīthā*—of Sunīthā, Vena's mother; *garbha*—the womb; *sambhavaḥ*—born of.

TRANSLATION

The sages began to think within themselves: Because he was born in the womb of Sunīthā, King Vena is by nature very mischievous. Supporting this mischievous king is exactly like maintaining a snake with milk. Now he has become a source of all difficulties.

PURPORT

Saintly persons are generally aloof from social activities and the materialistic way of life. King Vena was supported by the saintly persons just to protect the citizens from the hands of rogues and thieves, but after his ascendance to the throne, he became a source of trouble to the sages. Saintly people are especially interested in performing sacrifices and austerities for the advancement of spiritual life, but Vena, instead of being obliged because of the saints' mercy, turned out to be their enemy because he prohibited them from executing their ordinary duties. A serpent who is maintained with milk and bananas simply stores poison in his teeth and awaits the day to bite his master.

TEXT 11

निरूपितः प्रजापालः स जिघांसति वै प्रजाः ।
तथापि सान्त्वयेमामुं नास्मांस्तत्पातकं स्पृशेत् ॥११॥

nirūpitaḥ prajā-pālaḥ
sa jighāṁsati vai prajāḥ
tathāpi sāntvayemāmuṁ
nāsmāṁs tat-pātakaṁ spṛśet

nirūpitaḥ—appointed; *prajā-pālaḥ*—the king; *saḥ*—he; *jighāṁsati*—desires to harm; *vai*—certainly; *prajāḥ*—the citizens; *tathāpi*—nevertheless; *sāntvayema*—we should pacify; *amum*—him; *na*—not; *asmān*—us; *tat*—his; *pātakam*—sinful result; *spṛśet*—may touch.

TRANSLATION

We appointed this Vena king of the state in order to give protection to the citizens, but now he has become the enemy of the citizens. Despite

all these discrepancies, we should at once try to pacify him. By doing so, we may not be touched by the sinful results caused by him.

PURPORT

The saintly sages elected King Vena to become king, but he proved to be mischievous; therefore the sages were very much afraid of incurring sinful reaction. The law of *karma* even prohibits a person to associate with a mischievous individual. By electing Vena to the throne, the saintly sages certainly associated with him. Ultimately King Vena became so mischievous that the saintly sages actually became afraid of becoming contaminated by his activities. Thus before taking any action against him, the sages tried to pacify and correct him so that he might turn from his mischief.

TEXT 12

तद्विद्वद्भिरसद्वृत्तो वेनोऽस्माभिः कृतो नृपः ।
सान्त्वितो यदि नो वाचं न ग्रहीष्यत्यधर्मकृत् ।
लोकधिक्कारसन्दग्धं दहिष्यामः स्वतेजसा ॥१२॥

tad-vidvadbhir asad-vṛtto
veno 'smābhiḥ kṛto nṛpaḥ
sāntvito yadi no vācaṁ
na grahīṣyaty adharma-kṛt
loka-dhik-kāra-sandagdhaṁ
dahiṣyāmaḥ sva-tejasā

tat—his mischievous nature; *vidvadbhiḥ*—aware of; *asat-vṛttaḥ*—impious; *venaḥ*—Vena; *asmābhiḥ*—by us; *kṛtaḥ*—was made; *nṛpaḥ*—king; *sāntvitaḥ*—(in spite of) being pacified; *yadi*—if; *naḥ*—our; *vācam*—words; *na*—not; *grahīṣyati*—he will accept; *adharma-kṛt*—the most mischievous; *loka-dhik-kāra*—by public condemnation; *sandagdham*—burned; *dahiṣyāmaḥ*—we shall burn; *sva-tejasā*—by our prowess.

TRANSLATION

The saintly sages continued thinking: Of course we are completely aware of his mischievous nature. Yet nevertheless we enthroned Vena. If we cannot persuade King Vena to accept our advice, he will be condemned by the public, and we will join them. Thus by our prowess we shall burn him to ashes.

PURPORT

Saintly persons are not interested in political matters, yet they are always thinking of the welfare of the people in general. Consequently they sometimes have to come down to the political field and take steps to correct the misguided government or royalty. However, in Kali-yuga, saintly persons are not as powerful as they previously were. They used to be able to burn any sinful man to ashes by virtue of their spiritual prowess. Now saintly persons have no such power due to the influence of the age of Kali. Indeed, the *brāhmaṇas* do not even have the power to perform sacrifices in which animals are put into a fire to attain a new life. Under these circumstances, instead of actively taking part in politics, saintly persons should engage in chanting the *mahā-mantra,* Hare Kṛṣṇa. By the grace of Lord Caitanya, by simply chanting this Hare Kṛṣṇa *mahā-mantra,* the general populace can derive all benefits without political implications.

TEXT 13

एवमध्यवसायैनं मुनयो गूढमन्यवः ।
उपव्रज्याब्रुवन् वेनं सान्त्वयित्वा च सामभिः ॥१३॥

evam adhyavasāyainaṁ
munayo gūḍha-manyavaḥ
upavrajyābruvan venaṁ
sāntvayitvā ca sāmabhiḥ

evam—thus; *adhyavasāya*—having decided; *enam*—him; *munayaḥ*—the great sages; *gūḍha-manyavaḥ*—concealing their anger; *upavrajya*—having approached; *abruvan*—spoke; *venam*—to King Vena; *sāntvayitvā*—after pacifying; *ca*—also; *sāmabhiḥ*—with sweet words.

TRANSLATION

The great sages, having thus decided, approached King Vena. Concealing their real anger, they pacified him with sweet words and then spoke as follows.

TEXT 14

मुनय ऊचुः
नृपवर्य निबोधैतद्यत्ते विज्ञापयाम भोः ।
आयुःश्रीबलकीर्तीनां तव तात विवर्धनम् ॥१४॥

munaya ūcuḥ
nṛpa-varya nibodhaitad
yat te vijñāpayāma bhoḥ
āyuḥ-śrī-bala-kīrtīnāṁ
tava tāta vivardhanam

munayaḥ ūcuḥ—the great sages said; *nṛpa-varya*—O best of the kings; *nibodha*—kindly try to understand; *etat*—this; *yat*—which; *te*—to you; *vijñāpayāma*—we shall instruct; *bhoḥ*—O King; *āyuḥ*—duration of life; *śrī*—opulences; *bala*—strength; *kīrtīnām*—good reputation; *tava*—your; *tāta*—dear son; *vivardhanam*—which will increase.

TRANSLATION

The great sages said: Dear King, we have come to give you good advice. Kindly hear us with great attention. By doing so, your duration of life, your opulence, strength and reputation will increase.

PURPORT

According to Vedic civilization, in a monarchy the king is advised by saintly persons and sages. By taking their advice, he can become the greatest executive power, and everyone in his kingdom will be happy, peaceful and prosperous. The great kings were very responsible in taking the instructions given by great saintly personalities. The kings used to accept the instructions given by great sages like Parāśara, Vyāsadeva, Nārada, Devala, Asita, etc. In other words, they would first accept the authority of saintly persons and then execute their monarchical power. Unfortunately, in the present age of Kali, the head of government does not follow the instructions given by the saintly persons; therefore neither the citizens nor the men of government are very happy. Their duration of life is shortened, and almost everyone is wretched and bereft of bodily strength and spiritual power. If citizens want to be happy and prosperous in this democratic age, they should not elect rascals and fools who have no respect for saintly persons.

TEXT 15

धर्म आचरितः पुंसां वाङ्मनःकायबुद्धिभिः ।
लोकान् विशोकान् वितरत्यथानन्त्यमसङ्गिनाम् ।१५।

dharma ācaritaḥ puṁsāṁ
vāṅ-manaḥ-kāya-buddhibhiḥ
lokān viśokān vitaraty
athānantyam asaṅginām

dharmaḥ—religious principles; *ācaritaḥ*—executed; *puṁsām*—to persons; *vāk*—by words; *manaḥ*—mind; *kāya*—body; *buddhibhiḥ*—and by intelligence; *lokān*—the planets; *viśokān*—without misery; *vitarati*—bestow; *atha*—certainly; *ānantyam*—unlimited happiness, liberation; *asaṅginām*—to those free from material influence.

TRANSLATION

Those who live according to religious principles and who follow them by words, mind, body and intelligence, are elevated to the heavenly kingdom, which is devoid of all miseries. Being thus rid of the material influence, they achieve unlimited happiness in life.

PURPORT

The saintly sages herein instruct that the king or head of government should set an example by living a religious life. As stated in *Bhagavad-gītā*, religion means worshiping the Supreme Personality of Godhead. One should not simply make a show of religious life, but one should perform devotional service perfectly with words, mind, body and good intelligence. By doing so, not only will the king or government head rid himself of the contamination of the material modes of nature, but the general public will also, and they will all become gradually elevated to the kingdom of God and go back home, back to Godhead. The instructions given herein serve as a summary of how the head of government should execute his ruling power and thus attain happiness not only in this life but also in the life after death.

TEXT 16

स ते मा विनशेद्वीर प्रजानां क्षेमलक्षणः ।
यस्मिन् विनष्टे नृपतिरैश्वर्यादवरोहति ॥१६॥

sa te mā vinaśed vīra
prajānāṁ kṣema-lakṣaṇaḥ
yasmin vinaṣṭe nṛpatir
aiśvaryād avarohati

saḥ—that spiritual life; *te*—by you; *mā*—don't; *vinaśet*—let it be spoiled; *vīra*—O hero; *prajānām*—of the people; *kṣema-lakṣaṇaḥ*—the cause of prosperity; *yasmin*—which; *vinaṣṭe*—being spoiled; *nṛpatiḥ*—the king; *aiśvaryāt*—from opulence; *avarohati*—falls down.

TRANSLATION

The sages continued: O great hero, for this reason you should not be the cause of spoiling the spiritual life of the general populace. If their spiritual life is spoiled because of your activities, you will certainly fall down from your opulent and royal position.

PURPORT

Formerly, in practically all parts of the world, there were monarchies, but gradually as monarchy declined from the ideal life of religion to the godless life of sense gratification, monarchies all over the world were abolished. However, simply abolishing monarchy and replacing it with democracy is not sufficient unless the government men are religious and follow the footsteps of great religious personalities.

TEXT 17

राजन्नसाध्वमात्येभ्यश्चोरादिभ्यः प्रजा नृपः ।
रक्षन् यथा बलिं गृह्णन्निह प्रेत्य च मोदते ॥१७॥

rājann asādhv-amātyebhyaś
corādibhyaḥ prajā nṛpaḥ
rakṣan yathā baliṁ gṛhṇann
iha pretya ca modate

rājan—O King; *asādhu*—mischievous; *amātyebhyaḥ*—from ministers; *cora-ādibhyaḥ*—from thieves and rogues; *prajāḥ*—the citizens; *nṛpaḥ*—the king; *rakṣan*—protecting; *yathā*—accordingly as; *balim*—taxes; *gṛhṇan*—accepting; *iha*—in this world; *pretya*—after death; *ca*—also; *modate*—enjoys.

TRANSLATION

The saintly persons continued: When the king protects the citizens from the disturbances of mischievous ministers as well as from thieves and rogues, he can, by virtue of such pious activities, accept taxes given by his subjects. Thus a pious king can certainly enjoy himself in this world as well as in the life after death.

PURPORT

The duty of a pious king is described very nicely in this verse. His first and foremost duty is to give protection to the citizens from thieves and rogues as well as from ministers who are no better than thieves and rogues. Formerly, ministers were appointed by the king and were not elected. Consequently, if the king was not very pious or strict, the ministers would become thieves and rogues and exploit the innocent citizens. It is the king's duty to see that there is no increase of thieves and rogues either in the government secretariat or in the departments of public affairs. If a king cannot give protection to citizens from thieves and rogues both in the government service and in public affairs, he has no right to exact taxes from them. In other words, the king or the government that taxes can levy taxes from the citizens only if the king or government is able to give protection to the citizens from thieves and rogues.

In the Twelfth Canto of *Śrīmad-Bhāgavatam* there is a description of these thieves and rogues in government service. As stated: *prajās te bhakṣayiṣyanti mlecchā rājanya-rūpiṇaḥ* (*Bhāg.* 12.1.42). "These proud *mlecchas* [persons who are less than *śūdras*], representing themselves as kings, will tyrannize their subjects, and their subjects, on the other hand, will cultivate the most vicious practices. Thus practicing evil habits and behaving foolishly, the subjects will be like their rulers." The idea is that in the democratic days of Kali-yuga, the general population will fall down to the standard of *śūdras.* As stated *(kalau śūdra-sambhava),* practically the whole population of the world will be *śūdra.* A *śūdra* is a fourth-class man who is only fit to work for the three higher social castes. Being fourth-class men, *śūdras* are not very intelligent. Since the population is fallen in these democratic days, they can only elect a person in their category, but a government cannot run very well when it is run by *śūdras.* The second class of men, known as *kṣatriyas,* are especially meant for governing a country under the direction of saintly persons *(brāhmaṇas)* who are supposed to be very intelligent. In other ages—in Satya-yuga, Tretā-yuga and Dvāpara-yuga—the general populace was not so degraded, and the head of government was never elected. The king was the supreme executive personality, and if he caught any ministers stealing like thieves and rogues, he would at once have them killed or dismissed from service. As it was the duty of the king to kill thieves and rogues, it was similarly his duty to immediately kill dishonest ministers in government service. By such strict vigilance, the king could run the government very well, and the citizens would be happy to have such a king. The conclusion is that unless the king is perfectly able to give protection to the citizens from rogues and thieves, he has no right to levy taxes from the citizens for his own sense gratification. However, if he gives all protection to the citizens and levies taxes on them, he can live very happily and peacefully in this life, and at the end of this life be elevated to the heavenly kingdom or even to the Vaikuṇṭhas, where he would be happy in all respects.

TEXT 18

यस्य राष्ट्रे पुरे चैव भगवान् यज्ञपूरुषः ।
इज्यते स्वेन धर्मेण जनैर्वर्णाश्रमान्वितैः ॥१८॥

yasya rāṣṭre pure caiva
bhagavān yajña-pūruṣaḥ
ijyate svena dharmeṇa
janair varṇāśramānvitaiḥ

yasya—whose; *rāṣṭre*—in the state or kingdom; *pure*—in the cities; *ca*—also; *eva*—certainly; *bhagavān*—the Supreme Personality of Godhead; *yajña-pūruṣaḥ*—who is the enjoyer of all sacrifices; *ijyate*—is worshiped; *svena*—their own; *dharmeṇa*—by occupation; *janaiḥ*—by the people; *varṇa-āśrama*—the system of eight social orders; *anvitaiḥ*—who follow.

TRANSLATION

The king is supposed to be pious in whose state and cities the general populace strictly observes the system of eight social orders of varṇa and āśrama, and where all citizens engage in worshiping the Supreme Personality of Godhead by their particular occupations.

PURPORT

The state's duty and the citizen's duty are very nicely explained in this verse. The activities of the government head, or king, as well as the activities of the citizens, should be so directed that ultimately everyone engages in devotional service to the Supreme Personality of Godhead. The king, or government head, is supposed to be the representative of the Supreme Personality of Godhead and is therefore supposed to see that things go on nicely and that the citizens are situated in the scientific social order comprised of four *varṇas* and four *āśramas*. In the *Viṣṇu Purāṇa* it is stated that unless people are educated or situated in the scientific social order comprised of four *varṇas (brāhmaṇa, kṣatriya, vaiśya* and *śūdra)* and four *āśramas* (*brahmacarya, gṛhastha, vānaprastha* and *sannyāsa*) society can never be considered real human society, nor can it make any advancement toward the ultimate goal of human life. It is the duty of the government to see that things go on in terms of *varṇa* and *āśrama*. As stated herein, *bhagavān yajña-pūruṣaḥ*—the Supreme Personality of Godhead, Kṛṣṇa, is the *yajña-pūruṣa.* As stated in *Bhagavad-gītā: bhoktāraṁ yajña-tapasām* (Bg. 5.29). Kṛṣṇa is the ultimate purpose of all sacrifice. He is also the enjoyer of all sacrifices; therefore He is known as *yajña-pūruṣa.* The word *yajña-pūruṣa* indicates Lord Viṣṇu or Lord Kṛṣṇa, or any Personality of Godhead in the category of *viṣṇu-tattva*. In perfect human society, people are situated in the orders of *varṇa* and *āśrama* and are engaged in worshiping Lord Viṣṇu by their respective activities. Every citizen engaged in an occupation renders service by the resultant actions of his activities. That is the perfection of life. As stated in *Bhagavad-gītā:*

yataḥ pravṛttir bhūtānāṁ
yena sarvam idaṁ tatam
sva-karmaṇā tam abhyarcya
siddhiṁ vindati mānavaḥ

"By worship of the Lord, who is the source of all beings and who is all-pervading, man can, in the performance of his own duty, attain perfection." (Bg. 18.46)

Thus the *brāhmaṇas, kṣatriyas, śūdras* and *vaiśyas* must execute their prescribed duties as these duties are stated in the *śāstras.* In this way everyone can satisfy the Supreme Personality of Godhead, Viṣṇu. The king, or government head, has to see that the citizens are thus engaged. In other words, the state or the government must not deviate from its duty by declaring that the state is a secular one which has no interest in whether or not the people advance in *varṇāśrama-dharma.* Today people engaged in government service and people who rule over the citizens have no respect for the *varṇāśrama-dharma.* They complacently feel that the state is secular. In such a government, no one can be happy. The people must follow the *varṇāśrama-dharma,* and the king must see that they are following it nicely.

TEXT 19

तस्य राज्ञो महाभाग भगवान् भूतभावनः ।
परितुष्यति विश्वात्मा तिष्ठतो निजशासने ॥१९॥

tasya rājño mahā-bhāga
bhagavān bhūta-bhāvanaḥ
parituṣyati viśvātmā
tiṣṭhato nija-śāsane

tasya—with him; *rājñaḥ*—the king; *mahā-bhāga*—O noble one; *bhagavān*—the Supreme Personality of Godhead; *bhūta-bhāvanaḥ*—who is the original cause of the cosmic manifestation; *parituṣyati*—becomes satisfied; *viśva-ātmā*—the Supersoul of the entire universe; *tiṣṭhataḥ*—being situated; *nija-śāsane*—in his own governing situation.

TRANSLATION

O noble one, if the king sees that the Supreme Personality of Godhead, the original cause of the cosmic manifestation and the Supersoul within everyone, is worshiped, the Lord will be satisfied.

PURPORT

It is a fact that the government's duty is to see that the Supreme Personality of Godhead is satisfied by the activities of the people as well as by the activities of the government. There is no possibility of happiness if the government or citizenry have no idea of Bhagavān, the Supreme Personality of Godhead, who is the original cause of the cosmic manifestation, or if they have no knowledge of *bhūta-bhāvana,* who is *viśvātmā,* or the Supersoul, the soul of everyone's soul. The conclusion is that without engaging in devotional service, neither the citizens nor the government can be happy in any way. At the present moment neither the king nor the governing body is interested in seeing that the people are engaged in the devotional service of the Supreme Personality of Godhead. Rather, they are more interested in advancing the machinery of sense gratification. Consequently they are becoming more and more implicated in the complex machinery of the stringent laws of nature. People should be freed from the entanglement of the three modes of material nature, and the only process by which this is possible is surrender unto the Supreme Personality of Godhead. This is advised in *Bhagavad-gītā.* Unfortunately neither the government nor the people in general have any idea of this; they are simply interested in sense gratification and in being happy in this life. The word *nija-śāsane* (in his own governmental duty) indicates that both the government and the citizens are responsible for the execution of *varṇāśrama-dharma.* Once the populace is situated in the *varṇāśrama-dharma,* there is every possibility of real life and prosperity both in this world and in the next.

TEXT 20

तस्मिंस्तुष्टे किमप्राप्यं जगतामीश्वरेश्वरे ।
लोकाः सपाला ह्येतस्मै हरन्ति बलिमादृताः ॥२०॥

tasmiṁs tuṣṭe kim aprāpyaṁ
jagatām īśvareśvare
lokāḥ sapālā hy etasmai
haranti balim ādṛtāḥ

tasmin—when He; *tuṣṭe*—is satisfied; *kim*—what; *aprāpyam*—impossible to achieve; *jagatām*—of the universe; *īśvara-īśvare*—controller of the controllers; *lokāḥ*—the inhabitants of the planets; *sa-pālāḥ*—with their presiding deities; *hi*—for this reason; *etasmai*—unto Him; *haranti*—offer; *balim*—paraphernalia for worship; *ādṛtāḥ*—with great pleasure.

TRANSLATION

The Supreme Personality of Godhead is worshiped by the great demigods, controllers of universal affairs. When He is satisfied, nothing is impossible to achieve. For this reason all the demigods, presiding deities of different planets, as well as the inhabitants of their planets, take great pleasure in offering all kinds of paraphernalia for His worship.

PURPORT

All Vedic civilization is summarized in this verse: all living entities, either on this planet or on other planets, have to satisfy the Supreme Personality of Godhead by their respective duties. When He is satisfied, all necessities of life are automatically supplied. In the *Vedas* it is also stated: *eko bahūnāṁ yo vidadhāti kāmān* (*Kaṭha Up.* 2.2.13). From the *Vedas* we understand that He is supplying everyone's necessities, and we can actually see that the lower animals, the birds and the bees, have no business or profession, yet they are not dying for want of food. They are all living in nature's way, and they all have the necessities of life provided—namely, eating, sleeping, mating and defending.

Human society, however, has artificially created a type of civilization which makes one forgetful of his relationship with the Supreme Personality of Godhead. Modern society even enables one to forget the Supreme Personality of Godhead's grace and mercy. Consequently modern civilized man is always unhappy and in need of things. People do not know that the ultimate goal of life is to approach Lord Viṣṇu and satisfy Him. They have taken this materialistic way of life as everything and have become captivated by materialistic activities. Indeed, their leaders are always encouraging them to follow this path, and the general populace, being ignorant of the laws of God, is following their blind leaders down the path of unhappiness. In order to rectify this world situation, all people should be trained in Kṛṣṇa consciousness and act in accordance with the *varṇāśrama* system. The state should also see that the people are engaged in satisfying the Supreme Personality of Godhead. This is the primary duty of the state. The Kṛṣṇa consciousness movement was started to convince the general populace to adopt the best process by which to satisfy the Supreme Personality of Godhead and thus solve all problems.

TEXT 21

तं सर्वलोकामरयज्ञसंग्रहं
त्रयीमयं द्रव्यमयं तपोमयम् ।

यज्ञैर्विचित्रैर्यजतो भवाय ते
राजन् स्वदेशाननुरोद्धुमर्हसि ॥२१॥

taṁ sarva-lokāmara-yajña-saṅgrahaṁ
trayīmayaṁ dravyamayaṁ tapomayam
yajñair vicitrair yajato bhavāya te
rājan sva-deśān anuroddhum arhasi

tam—Him; *sarva-loka*—in all planets; *amara*—with the predominating deities; *yajña*—sacrifices; *saṅgraham*—who accepts; *trayī-mayam*—the sum total of the three *Vedas; dravya-mayam*—the owner of all paraphernalia; *tapaḥ-mayam*—the goal of all austerity; *yajñaiḥ*—by sacrifices; *vicitraiḥ*—various; *yajataḥ*—worshiping; *bhavāya*—for elevation; *te*—your; *rājan*—O King; *sva-deśān*—your countrymen; *anuroddhum*—to direct; *arhasi*—you ought.

TRANSLATION

Dear King, the Supreme Personality of Godhead, along with the predominating deities, is the enjoyer of the results of all sacrifices in all planets. The Supreme Lord is the sum total of the three Vedas, the owner of everything, and the ultimate goal of all austerity. Therefore your countrymen should engage in performing various sacrifices for your elevation. Indeed, you should always direct them toward the offering of sacrifices.

TEXT 22

यज्ञेन युष्मद्विषये द्विजातिभि-
र्वितायमानेन सुराः कला हरेः ।
स्विष्टाः सुतुष्टाः प्रदिशन्ति वाञ्छितं
तद्धेलनं नार्हसि वीर चेष्टितुम् ॥२२॥

yajñena yuṣmad-viṣaye dvijātibhir
vitāyamānena surāḥ kalā hareḥ
sviṣṭāḥ sutuṣṭāḥ pradiśanti vāñchitaṁ
tad-dhelanaṁ nārhasi vīra ceṣṭitum

yajñena—by sacrifice; *yuṣmat*—your; *viṣaye*—in the kingdom; *dvijātibhiḥ*—by the *brāhmaṇas; vitāyamānena*—being performed; *surāḥ*—all the demigods; *kalāḥ*—expansions; *hareḥ*—of the Personality of Godhead; *su-iṣṭāḥ*—being properly worshiped; *su-tuṣṭāḥ*—very much satisfied; *pradiśanti*—will give;

vāñchitam—desired result; *tat-helanam*—disrespect to them; *na*—not; *arhasi*—you ought; *vīra*—O hero; *ceṣṭitum*—to do.

TRANSLATION

When all the brāhmaṇas engage in performing sacrifices in your kingdom, all the demigods, who are plenary expansions of the Lord, will be very much satisfied by their activities and will give you your desired result. Therefore, O hero, do not stop the sacrificial performances. If you stop them, you will disrespect the demigods.

TEXT 23

वेन उवाच
बालिशा बत यूयं वा अधर्मे धर्ममानिनः ।
ये वृत्तिदं पतिं हित्वा जारं पतिमुपासते ॥२३॥

vena uvāca
bāliśā bata yūyaṁ vā
adharme dharma-māninaḥ
ye vṛtti-daṁ patiṁ hitvā
jāraṁ patim upāsate

venaḥ—King Vena; *uvāca*—replied; *bāliśāḥ*—childish; *bata*—oh; *yūyam*—all of you; *vā*—indeed; *adharme*—in irreligious principles; *dharma-māninaḥ*—accepting as religious; *ye*—all of you who; *vṛtti-dam*—providing maintenance; *patim*—husband; *hitvā*—giving up; *jāram*—paramour; *patim*—husband; *upāsate*—worship.

TRANSLATION

King Vena replied: You are not at all experienced. It is very much regrettable that you are maintaining something which is not religious and are accepting it as religious. Indeed, I think you are giving up your real husband who maintains you and are searching after some paramour to worship.

PURPORT

King Vena was so foolish that he accused the saintly sages of being inexperienced like small children. In other words, he was accusing them of not having perfect knowledge. In this way he could reject their advice and make accusations against them, comparing them with a woman who does not care for her husband who maintains her but goes to satisfy a paramour who does not maintain her. The purpose of this simile is apparent. It is the duty of the *kṣatriyas* to engage the *brāhmaṇas* in different types of religious activities, and the king is supposed to be the maintainer of the *brāhmaṇas*. If the *brāhmaṇas* do not worship the king and go to the demigods, they are as polluted as unchaste women.

TEXT 24

अवजानन्त्यमी मूढा नृपरूपिणमीश्वरम् ।
नानुविन्दन्ति ते भद्रमिह लोके परत्र च ॥२४॥

avajānanty amī mūḍhā
nṛpa-rūpiṇam īśvaram
nānuvindanti te bhadram
iha loke paratra ca

avajānanti—disrespect; *amī*—those (who); *mūḍhāḥ*—being ignorant; *nṛpa-rūpiṇam*—in the form of the king; *īśvaram*—the Personality of Godhead; *na*—not; *anuvindanti*—experience; *te*—they; *bhadram*—happiness; *iha*—in this; *loke*—world; *paratra*—after death; *ca*—also.

TRANSLATION

Those who, out of gross ignorance, do not worship the king, who is actually the Supreme Personality of Godhead, experience happiness neither in this world nor in the world after death.

TEXT 25

को यज्ञपुरुषो नाम यत्र वो भक्तिरीदृशी ।
भर्तृस्नेहविदूराणां यथा जारे कुयोषिताम् ॥२५॥

ko yajña-puruṣo nāma
yatra vo bhaktir īdṛśī
bhartṛ-sneha-vidūrāṇām
yathā jāre kuyoṣitām

kaḥ—who (is); *yajña-puruṣaḥ*—the enjoyer of all sacrifices; *nāma*—by name; *yatra*—unto whom; *vaḥ*—your; *bhaktiḥ*—devotional service; *īdṛśī*—so great; *bhartṛ*—for the husband; *sneha*—affection; *vidūrāṇām*—bereft of; *yathā*—like; *jāre*—unto the paramour; *ku-yoṣitām*—of unchaste women.

TRANSLATION

You are so much devoted to the demigods, but who are they? Indeed, your affection for these demigods is exactly like the affection of an unchaste woman who neglects her married life and gives all attention to her paramour.

TEXTS 26-27

विष्णुर्विरिञ्चो गिरिश इन्द्रो वायुर्यमो रविः ।
पर्जन्यो धनदः सोमः क्षितिरग्निरपाम्पतिः ॥२६॥

एते चान्ये च विबुधाः प्रभवो वरशापयोः ।
देहे भवन्ति नृपतेः सर्वदेवमयो नृपः ॥२७॥

viṣṇur viriñco giriśa
indro vāyur yamo raviḥ
parjanyo dhanadaḥ somaḥ
kṣitir agnir apām-patiḥ

ete cānye ca vibudhāḥ
prabhavo vara-śāpayoḥ
dehe bhavanti nṛpateḥ
sarva-devamayo nṛpaḥ

viṣṇuḥ—Lord Viṣṇu; *viriñcaḥ*—Lord Brahmā; *giriśaḥ*—Lord Śiva; *indraḥ*—Lord Indra; *vāyuḥ*—Vāyu, the director of the air; *yamaḥ*—Yama, the superintendent of death; *raviḥ*—the sun-god; *parjanyaḥ*—the director of rainfall; *dhana-daḥ*—Kuvera, the treasurer; *somaḥ*—the moon-god; *kṣitiḥ*—the predominating deity of the earth; *agniḥ*—the fire-god; *apām-patiḥ*—Varuṇa, the lord of waters; *ete*—all these; *ca*—and; *anye*—others; *ca*—also; *vibudhāḥ*—demigods; *prabhavaḥ*—competent; *vara-śāpayoḥ*—in both benediction and curse; *dehe*—in the body; *bhavanti*—abide; *nṛpateḥ*—of the king; *sarva-deva-mayaḥ*—comprising all demigods; *nṛpaḥ*—the king.

TRANSLATION

Lord Viṣṇu; Lord Brahmā; Lord Śiva; Lord Indra; Vāyu, the master of air; Yama, the superintendent of death; the sun-god; the director of rainfall; Kuvera, the treasurer; the moon-god; the predominating deity of the earth; Agni, the fire-god; Varuṇa, the lord of waters, and all others who are great and competent to bestow benedictions or to curse, all abide in the body of the king. For this reason the king is known as the reservoir of all demigods, who are simply parts and parcels of the king's body.

PURPORT

There are many demons who think of themselves as the Supreme and present themselves as the directors of the sun, moon and other planets. This is all due to false pride. Similarly, King Vena developed the demonic mentality and presented himself as the Supreme Personality of Godhead. Such demons are numerous in this age of Kali, and all of them are condemned by great sages and saintly persons.

TEXT 28

तस्मान्मां कर्मभिर्विप्रा यजध्वं गतमत्सराः ।
बलिं च मह्यं हरत मत्तोऽन्यः कोऽग्रभुक् पुमान् ॥२८॥

tasmān māṁ karmabhir viprā
yajadhvaṁ gata-matsarāḥ
baliṁ ca mahyaṁ harata
matto 'nyaḥ ko 'gra-bhuk pumān

tasmāt—for this reason; *mām*—me; *karmabhiḥ*—by ritualistic activities; *viprāḥ*—O *brāhmaṇas; yajadhvam*—worship; *gata*—without; *matsarāḥ*—being envious; *balim*—paraphernalia for worship; *ca*—also; *mahyam*—unto me; *harata*—bring; *mattaḥ*—than me; *anyaḥ*—other; *kaḥ*—who (is); *agra-bhuk*—the enjoyer of the first oblations; *pumān*—personality.

TRANSLATION

King Vena continued: For this reason, O brāhmaṇas, you should abandon your envy of me, and, by your ritualistic activities, you should worship me and offer me all paraphernalia. If you are intelligent, you should know that there is no personality superior to me, who can accept the first oblations of all sacrifices.

PURPORT

As stated by Kṛṣṇa Himself throughout *Bhagavad-gītā,* there is no truth superior to Him. King Vena was imitating the Supreme Personality of Godhead and was also speaking out of false pride, presenting himself as the Supreme Lord. These are all characteristics of a demonic person.

TEXT 29

मैत्रेय उवाच
इत्थं विपर्ययमतिः पापीयानुत्पथं गतः ।
अनुनीयमानस्तद्याच्ञां न चक्रे भ्रष्टमङ्गलः ॥२९॥

maitreya uvāca
itthaṁ viparyaya-matiḥ
pāpīyān utpathaṁ gataḥ
anunīyamānas tad-yācñām
na cakre bhraṣṭa-maṅgalaḥ

maitreyaḥ uvāca—Maitreya said; *ittham*—thus; *viparyaya-matiḥ*—one who has developed perverse intelligence; *pāpīyān*—most sinful; *utpatham*—from the right path; *gataḥ*—having gone; *anunīyamānaḥ*—being offered all respect; *tat-yācñām*—the request of the sages; *na*—not; *cakre*—accepted; *bhraṣṭa*—bereft of; *maṅgalaḥ*—all good fortune.

TRANSLATION

The great sage Maitreya continued: Thus the King, who became unintelligent due to his sinful life and deviation from the right path, became actually bereft of all good fortune. Thus he could not accept the requests of the great sages, which the sages put before him with great respect, and therefore he was condemned.

PURPORT

The demons certainly cannot have any faith in the words of authorities. In fact, they are always disrespectful to authorities. They manufacture their own religious principles and disobey great personalities like Vyāsa, Nārada, and even the Supreme Personality of Godhead, Kṛṣṇa. As soon as one disobeys authority, he immediately becomes very sinful and loses his good fortune. The King was so puffed up and impudent that he dared disrespect the great saintly personalities, and this brought him ruination.

TEXT 30

इति तेऽसत्कृतास्तेन द्विजाः पण्डितमानिना ।
भग्नायां भव्ययाच्ञायां तस्मै विदुर चुक्रुधुः ॥३०॥

iti te 'sat-kṛtās tena
dvijāḥ paṇḍita-māninā
bhagnāyāṁ bhavya-yācñāyāṁ
tasmai vidura cukrudhuḥ

iti—thus; *te*—all the great sages; *asat-kṛtāḥ*—being insulted; *tena*—by the King; *dvijāḥ*—the *brāhmaṇas; paṇḍita-māninā*—thinking himself to be very learned; *bhagnāyām*—being broken; *bhavya*—auspicious; *yācñāyām*—their request; *tasmai*—at him; *vidura*—O Vidura; *cukrudhuḥ*—became very angry.

TRANSLATION

My dear Vidura, all good fortune unto you. The foolish King, who thought himself to be very learned, thus insulted the great sages, and the sages, being brokenhearted by the King's words, became very angry at him.

TEXT 31

हन्यतां हन्यतामेष पापः प्रकृतिदारुणः ।
जीवञ्जगदसावाशु कुरुते भस्मसाद् ध्रुवम् ॥३१॥

hanyatāṁ hanyatām eṣa
pāpaḥ prakṛti-dāruṇaḥ
jīvañ jagad asāv āśu
kurute bhasmasād dhruvam

hanyatām—kill him; *hanyatām*—kill him; *eṣaḥ*—this king; *pāpaḥ*—representative of sin; *prakṛti*—by nature; *dāruṇaḥ*—most dreadful; *jīvan*—while living; *jagat*—the whole world; *asau*—he; *āśu*—very soon; *kurute*—will make; *bhasmasāt*—into ashes; *dhruvam*—certainly.

TRANSLATION

All the great saintly sages immediately cried: Kill him! Kill him! He is the most dreadful, sinful person. If he lives, he will certainly turn the whole world into ashes in no time.

PURPORT

Saintly persons are generally very kind to all kinds of living entities, but they are not unhappy when a serpent or a scorpion is killed. It is not good for saintly persons to kill, but they are encouraged to kill demons who are exactly like serpents and scorpions. Therefore all the saintly sages decided to kill King Vena, who was so dreadful and dangerous to all human society. We can appreciate the extent to which the saintly sages actually controlled the king. If the king or government becomes demonic, it is the duty of a saintly person to upset the government and replace it with deserving persons who follow the orders and instructions of saintly persons.

TEXT 32

नायमर्हत्यसद्वृत्तो नरदेववरासनम् ।
योऽधियज्ञपतिं विष्णुं विनिन्दत्यनपत्रपः ॥३२॥

nāyam arhaty asad-vṛtto
naradeva-varāsanam

yo 'dhiyajña-patiṁ viṣṇuṁ
vinindaty anapatrapaḥ

na—never; *ayam*—this man; *arhati*—deserves; *asat-vṛttaḥ*—full of impious activities; *nara-deva*—of the worldly king or worldly god; *vara-āsanam*—the exalted throne; *yaḥ*—he who; *adhiyajña-patim*—master of all sacrifices; *viṣṇum*—Lord Viṣṇu; *vinindati*—insults; *anapatrapaḥ*—shameless.

TRANSLATION

The saintly sages continued: This impious, impudent man does not deserve to sit on the throne at all. He is so shameless that he even dared insult the Supreme Personality of Godhead, Lord Viṣṇu.

PURPORT

One should not at any time tolerate blasphemy and insults against Lord Viṣṇu or His devotees. A devotee is generally very humble and meek, and he is reluctant to pick a quarrel with anyone. Nor does he envy anyone. However, a pure devotee immediately becomes fiery with anger when he sees that Lord Viṣṇu or His devotee is insulted. This is the duty of a devotee. Although a devotee maintains an attitude of meekness and gentleness, it is a great fault on his part if he remains silent when the Lord or His devotee is blasphemed.

TEXT 33

को वैनं परिचक्षीत वेनमेकमृतेऽशुभम् ।
प्राप्त ईदृशमैश्वर्यं यदनुग्रहभाजनः ॥३३॥

ko vainaṁ paricakṣīta
venam ekam ṛte 'śubham
prāpta īdṛśam aiśvaryaṁ
yad-anugraha-bhājanaḥ

kaḥ—who; *vā*—indeed; *enam*—the Lord; *paricakṣīta*—would blaspheme; *venam*—King Vena; *ekam*—alone; *ṛte*—but for; *aśubham*—inauspicious; *prāptaḥ*—having obtained; *īdṛśam*—like this; *aiśvaryam*—opulence; *yat*—whose; *anugraha*—mercy; *bhājanaḥ*—receiving.

TRANSLATION

But for King Vena, who is simply inauspicious, who would blaspheme the Supreme Personality of Godhead by whose mercy one is awarded all kinds of fortune and opulence?

PURPORT

When human society individually or collectively becomes godless and blasphemes the authority of the Supreme Personality of Godhead, it is certainly destined for ruination. Such a civilization invites all kinds of bad fortune due to not appreciating the mercy of the Lord.

TEXT 34

इत्थं व्यवसिता हन्तुमृषयो रूढमन्यवः ।
निजघ्नुर्हुङ्कृतैर्वेनं हतमच्युतनिन्दया ॥३४॥

itthaṁ vyavasitā hantum
ṛṣayo rūḍha-manyavaḥ
nijaghnur huṅkṛtair venaṁ
hatam acyuta-nindayā

ittham—thus; *vyavasitāḥ*—decided; *hantum*—to kill; *ṛṣayaḥ*—the sages; *rūḍha*—manifested; *manyavaḥ*—their anger; *nijaghnuḥ*—they killed; *hum-kṛtaiḥ*—by angry words or by sounds of *hum; venam*—King Vena; *hatam*—dead; *acyuta*—against the Supreme Personality of Godhead; *nindayā*—by blasphemy.

TRANSLATION

The great sages, thus manifesting their covert anger, immediately decided to kill the King. King Vena was already as good as dead due to his blasphemy against the Supreme Personality of Godhead. Thus without using any weapons, the sages killed King Vena simply by high-sounding words.

TEXT 35

ऋषिभिः स्वाश्रमपदं गते पुत्रकलेवरम् ।
सुनीथा पालयामास विद्यायोगेन शोचती ॥३५॥

ṛṣibhiḥ svāśrama-padaṁ
gate putra-kalevaram
sunīthā pālayām āsa
vidyā-yogena śocatī

ṛṣibhiḥ—by the sages; *sva-āśrama-padam*—to their own respective hermitages; *gate*—having returned; *putra*—of her son; *kalevaram*—the body; *sunīthā*—Sunīthā, mother of King Vena; *pālayām āsa*—preserved; *vidyā-yogena*—by *mantra* and ingredients; *śocatī*—while lamenting.

TRANSLATION

After all the sages returned to their respective hermitages, the mother of King Vena, Sunīthā, became very much aggrieved because of her son's death. She decided to preserve the dead body of her son by the application of certain ingredients and by chanting mantras [mantra-yogena].

TEXT 36

एकदा मुनयस्ते तु सरस्वत्सलिलाप्लुताः ।
हुत्वाग्नीन् सत्कथाश्चक्रुरुपविष्टाः सरित्तटे ॥३६॥

ekadā munayas te tu
sarasvat-salilāplutāḥ
hutvāgnīn sat-kathāś cakrur
upaviṣṭāḥ sarit-taṭe

ekadā—once upon a time; *munayaḥ*—all those great saintly persons; *te*—they; *tu*—then; *sarasvat*—of the River Sarasvatī; *salila*—in the water; *āplutāḥ*—bathed; *hutvā*—offering oblations; *agnīn*—into the fires; *sat-kathāḥ*—discussions about transcendental subject matters; *cakruḥ*—began to do; *upaviṣṭāḥ*—sitting; *sarit-taṭe*—by the side of the river.

TRANSLATION

Once upon a time, the same saintly persons, after taking their bath in the River Sarasvatī, began to perform their daily duties by offering oblations into the sacrificial fires. After this, sitting on the bank of the river, they began to talk about the transcendental person and His pastimes.

TEXT 37

**वीक्ष्योत्थितांस्तदोत्पातानाहुर्लोकभयङ्करान् ।
अप्यभद्रमनाथाया दस्युभ्यो न भवेद्भुवः ॥३७॥**

vīkṣyotthitāṁs tadotpātān
āhur loka-bhayaṅkarān
apy abhadram anāthāyā
dasyubhyo na bhaved bhuvaḥ

vīkṣya—having seen; *utthitān*—developed; *tadā*—then; *utpātān*—disturbances; *āhuḥ*—they began to say; *loka*—in society; *bhayam-karān*—causing panic; *api*—whether; *abhadram*—misfortune; *anāthāyāḥ*—having no ruler; *dasyubhyaḥ*—from thieves and rogues; *na*—not; *bhavet*—may happen; *bhuvaḥ*—of the world.

TRANSLATION

In those days there were various disturbances in the country that were creating a panic in society. Therefore all the sages began to talk amongst themselves: Since the King is dead and there is no protector in the world, misfortune may befall the people in general on account of rogues and thieves.

PURPORT

Whenever there is a disturbance in the state, or a panic situation, the property and lives of the citizens become unsafe. This is caused by the uprising of various thieves and rogues. At such a time it is to be understood that the ruler, or the government, is dead. All of these misfortunes happened due to the death of King Vena. Thus the saintly persons became very anxious for the safety of the people in general. The conclusion is that even though saintly persons have no business in political affairs, they are nonetheless always compassionate upon the people in general. Thus even though they are always aloof from society, still out of mercy and compassion they consider how the citizens can peacefully execute their rituals and follow the rules and regulations of *varṇāśrama-dharma*. That was the concern of these sages. In this age of Kali, everything is disturbed. Therefore saintly persons should take to the chanting of the Hare Kṛṣṇa *mantra*, as recommended in the *śāstras*. *Harer nāma harer nāma harer nāmaiva kevalaṁ/ kalau nāsty eva nāsty eva nāsty eva gatir anyathā.* Both for spiritual and material prosperity, everyone should devotedly chant the Hare Kṛṣṇa *mantra*.

TEXT 38

एवं मृशन्त ऋषयो धावतां सर्वतोदिशम् ।
पांसुः समुत्थितो भूरिश्चोराणामभिलुम्पताम् ॥३८॥

evaṁ mṛśanta ṛṣayo
dhāvatāṁ sarvato-diśam
pāṁsuḥ samutthito bhūriś
corāṇām abhilumpatām

evam—thus; *mṛśantaḥ*—while considering; *ṛṣayaḥ*—the great saintly persons; *dhāvatām*—running; *sarvataḥ-diśam*—from all directions; *pāṁsuḥ*—dust; *samutthitaḥ*—arose; *bhūriḥ*—much; *corāṇām*—from thieves and rogues; *abhilumpatām*—engaged in plundering.

TRANSLATION

When the great sages were carrying on their discussion in this way, they saw a dust storm arising from all directions. This storm was caused by the running of thieves and rogues who were engaged in plundering the citizens.

PURPORT

Thieves and rogues simply await some political upset in order to take the opportunity to plunder the people in general. To keep thieves and rogues inactive in their profession, a strong government is always required.

TEXTS 39-40

तदुपद्रवमाज्ञाय लोकस्य वसु लुम्पताम् ।
भर्तर्युपरते तस्मिन्नन्योन्यं च जिघांसताम् ॥३९॥
चोरप्रायं जनपदं हीनसत्त्वमराजकम् ।
लोकान्नावारयञ्छक्ता अपि तद्दोषदर्शिनः ॥४०॥

tad upadravam ājñāya
lokasya vasu lumpatām
bhartary uparate tasminn
anyonyaṁ ca jighāṁsatām

cora-prāyaṁ jana-padaṁ
hīna-sattvam arājakam
lokān nāvārayañ chaktā
api tad-doṣa-darśinaḥ

tat—at that time; *upadravam*—the disturbance; *ājñāya*—understanding; *lokasya*—of the people in general; *vasu*—riches; *lumpatām*—by those who were plundering; *bhartari*—the protector; *uparate*—being dead; *tasmin*—King Vena; *anyonyam*—one another; *ca*—also; *jighāṁsatām*—desiring to kill; *cora-prāyam*—full of thieves; *jana-padam*—the state; *hīna*—bereft of; *sattvam*—regulation; *arājakam*—without a king; *lokān*—the thieves and rogues; *na*—not; *avārayan*—they subdued; *śaktāḥ*—able to do so; *api*—although; *tat-doṣa*—the fault of that; *darśinaḥ*—considering.

TRANSLATION

Upon seeing the dust storm, the saintly persons could understand that there were a great deal of irregularities due to the death of King Vena. Without government, the state was devoid of law and order, and consequently there was a great uprising of murderous thieves and rogues who were plundering the riches of the people in general. Although the great sages could subdue the disturbance by their powers—just as they could kill the King—they nonetheless considered it improper on their part to do so. Thus they did not attempt to stop the disturbance.

PURPORT

The saintly persons and great sages killed King Vena out of emergency, but they did not choose to take part in the government in order to subdue the uprising of thieves and rogues, which took place after the death of King Vena. It is not the duty of *brāhmaṇas* and saintly persons to kill, although they may sometimes do so in the case of an emergency. They could kill all the thieves and rogues by the prowess of their *mantras*, but they thought it the duty of *kṣatriya* kings to do so. Thus they reluctantly did not take part in the killing business.

TEXT 41

ब्राह्मणः समदृक् शान्तो दीनानां समुपेक्षकः ।
स्रवते ब्रह्म तस्यापि भिन्नभाण्डात्पयो यथा ॥४१॥

brāhmaṇaḥ sama-dṛk śānto
dīnānāṁ samupekṣakaḥ
sravate brahma tasyāpi
bhinna-bhāṇḍāt payo yathā

brāhmaṇaḥ—a *brāhmaṇa; sama-dṛk*—equipoised; *śāntaḥ*—peaceful; *dīnānām*—the poor; *samupekṣakaḥ*—grossly neglecting; *sravate*—diminishes; *brahma*—spiritual power; *tasya*—his; *api*—certainly; *bhinna-bhāṇḍāt*—from a cracked pot; *payaḥ*—water; *yathā*—just as.

TRANSLATION

The great sages began to think that although a brāhmaṇa is peaceful and impartial because he is equal to everyone, it is still not his duty to neglect poor humans. By such neglect, a brāhmaṇa's spiritual power diminishes, just as water kept in a cracked pot leaks out.

PURPORT

Brāhmaṇas, the topmost section of human society, are mostly devotees. They are generally not aware of the happenings within the material world because they are always busy in their activities for spiritual advancement. Nonetheless, when there is a calamity in human society, they cannot remain impartial. If they do not do something to relieve the distressed condition of human society, it is said that due to such neglect their spiritual knowledge diminishes. Almost all the sages go to the Himalayas for their personal benefit, but Prahlāda Mahārāja said that he did not want liberation alone. He decided to wait until he was able to deliver all the fallen souls of the world.

In their elevated condition, the *brāhmaṇas* are called Vaiṣṇavas. There are two types of *brāhmaṇas*—namely, *brāhmaṇa-paṇḍita* and *brāhmaṇa-vaiṣṇava.* A qualified *brāhmaṇa* is naturally very learned, but when his learning is advanced in understanding the Supreme Personality of Godhead, he becomes a *brāhmaṇa-vaiṣṇava.* Unless one becomes a Vaiṣṇava, one's perfection of brahminical culture is incomplete.

The saintly persons considered very wisely that although King Vena was very sinful, he was nonetheless born in a family descending from Dhruva Mahārāja. Therefore the semina in the family must be protected by the Supreme Personality of Godhead, Keśava. As such, the sages wanted to take some steps to relieve the situation. For want of a king, everything was being disturbed and turned topsy-turvy.

TEXT 42

नाङ्गस्य वंशो राजर्षेरेष संस्थातुमर्हति ।
अमोघवीर्या हि नृपा वंशेऽस्मिन् केशवाश्रयाः ॥४२॥

nāṅgasya vaṁśo rājarṣer
eṣa saṁsthātum arhati
amogha-vīryā hi nṛpā
vaṁśe 'smin keśavāśrayāḥ

na—not; *aṅgasya*—of King Aṅga; *vaṁśaḥ*—family line; *rāja-ṛṣeḥ*—of the saintly King; *eṣaḥ*—this; *saṁsthātum*—to be stopped; *arhati*—ought; *amogha*—without sin, powerful; *vīryāḥ*—their semina; *hi*—because; *nṛpāḥ*—kings; *vaṁśe*—in the family; *asmin*—this; *keśava*—of the Supreme Personality of Godhead; *āśrayāḥ*—under the shelter.

TRANSLATION

The sages decided that the descendants of the family of the saintly King Aṅga should not be stopped because in this family the semina was very powerful and the children were prone to become devotees of the Lord.

PURPORT

The purity of hereditary succession is called *amogha-vīrya.* The pious seminal succession in the twice-born family of the *brāhmaṇas* and *kṣatriyas* especially, as well as in the family of *vaiśyas* also, must be kept very pure by the observation of the purificatory processes beginning with *garbhādhāna-saṁskāra,* which is observed before giving birth to a child. Unless this purificatory process is strictly observed, especially by the *brāhmaṇas,* the family descendants become impure, and gradually sinful activities become visible in the family. Mahārāja Aṅga was very pure because of the purification of semina in the family of Mahārāja Dhruva. However, his semina became contaminated in association with his wife, Sunīthā, who happened to be the daughter of death personified. Because of this polluted semina, King Vena was produced. This was a catastrophe in the family of Dhruva

Mahārāja. All the saintly persons and sages considered this point, and they decided to take action in this manner, as described in the following verses.

TEXT 43

विनिश्चित्यैवमृषयो विपन्नस्य महीपतेः ।
ममन्थुरूरुं तरसा तत्रासीद्बाहुको नरः ॥४३॥

viniścityaivam ṛṣayo
vipannasya mahīpateḥ
mamanthur ūruṁ tarasā
tatrāsīd bāhuko naraḥ

viniścitya—deciding; *evam*—thus; *ṛṣayaḥ*—the great sages; *vipannasya*—dead; *mahī-pateḥ*—of the King; *mamanthuḥ*—churned; *ūrum*—the thighs; *tarasā*—with specific power; *tatra*—thereupon; *āsīt*—was born; *bāhukaḥ*—of the name Bāhuka (dwarf); *naraḥ*—a person.

TRANSLATION

After making a decision, the saintly persons and sages churned the thighs of the dead body of King Vena with great force and according to a specific method. As a result of this churning, a dwarf-like person was born from King Vena's body.

PURPORT

That a person was born by the churning of the thighs of King Vena proves that the spirit soul is individual and separate from the body. The great sages and saintly persons could beget another person from the body of the dead King Vena, but it was not possible for them to bring King Vena back to life. King Vena was gone, and certainly he had taken another body. The saintly persons and sages were only concerned with the body of Vena because it was a result of the seminal succession in the family of Mahārāja Dhruva. Consequently the ingredients by which another body could be produced were there in the body of King Vena. By a certain process, when the thighs of the dead body were churned, another body came out. Although dead, the body of King Vena was perserved by drugs and *mantras* chanted by King Vena's mother. In this way the ingredients for the production of another body were there. When the body of the person named Bāhuka came out of the dead body of King Vena, it was really not very astonishing. It was simply a question of knowing how to do it. From the semina of one body, another body is produced, and the life symptoms are visible due to the soul's taking shelter of this body. One should not think that it was impossible for another body to come out of the dead body of Mahārāja Vena. This was performed by the skillful action of the sages.

TEXT 44

काककृष्णोऽतिह्रस्वाङ्गो ह्रस्वबाहुर्महाहनुः ।
ह्रस्वपान्निम्ननासाग्रो रक्ताक्षस्ताम्रमूर्धजः ॥४४॥

kāka-kṛṣṇo 'tihrasvāṅgo
hrasva-bāhur mahā-hanuḥ
hrasva-pān nimna-nāsāgro
raktākṣas tāmra-mūrdhajaḥ

kāka-kṛṣṇaḥ—as black as a crow; *atihrasva*—very short; *aṅgaḥ*—his limbs; *hrasva*—short; *bāhuḥ*—his arms; *mahā*—big; *hanuḥ*—his jaws; *hrasva*—short; *pāt*—his legs; *nimna*—flat; *nāsa-agraḥ*—the tip of his nose; *rakta*—reddish; *akṣaḥ*—his eyes; *tāmra*—copperlike; *mūrdha-jaḥ*—his hair.

TRANSLATION

This person born from King Vena's thighs was named Bāhuka, and his complexion was as black as a crow's. All the limbs of his body were very short, his arms and legs were short, and his jaws were large. His nose was flat, his eyes were reddish, and his hair copper-colored.

TEXT 45

तं तु तेऽवनतं दीनं किं करोमीति वादिनम् ।
निषीदेत्यब्रुवंस्तात स निषादस्ततोऽभवत् ॥४५॥

taṁ tu te 'vanataṁ dīnaṁ
kiṁ karomīti vādinam
niṣīdety abruvaṁs tāta
sa niṣādas tato 'bhavat

tam—unto him; *tu*—then; *te*—the sages; *avanatam*—bowed down; *dīnam*—meek; *kim*—what; *karomi*—shall I do; *iti*—thus; *vādinam*—inquiring;

niṣīda—just sit down; *iti*—thus; *abruvan*—they replied; *tāta*—my dear Vidura; *saḥ*—he; *niṣādaḥ*—of the name Niṣāda; *tataḥ*—thereafter; *abhavat*—became.

TRANSLATION

He was very submissive and meek, and immediately after his birth he bowed down and inquired, "Sirs, what shall I do?" The great sages replied, "Please sit down [niṣīda]." Thus Niṣāda, the father of the Naiṣāda race, was born.

PURPORT

It is said in the *śāstras* that the head of the body represents the *brāhmaṇas,* the arms represent the *kṣatriyas,* the abdomen represents the *vaiśyas,* and the legs, beginning with the thighs, represent the *śūdras.* The *śūdras* are sometimes called black or *kṛṣṇa.* The *brāhmaṇas* are called *śukla,* or white, and the *kṣatriyas* and the *vaiśyas* are a mixture of black and white. However, those who are extraordinarily white are said to have skin produced out of white leprosy. It may be concluded that white or a golden hue is the color of the higher caste, and black is the complexion of the *śūdras.*

TEXT 46

तस्य वंश्यास्तु नैषादा गिरिकाननगोचराः ।
येनाहरज्जायमानो वेनकल्मषमुल्बणम् ॥४६॥

tasya vaṁśyās tu naiṣādā
giri-kānana-gocarāḥ
yenāharaj jāyamāno
vena-kalmaṣam ulbaṇam

tasya—his (Niṣāda's); *vaṁśyāḥ*—descendants; *tu*—then; *naiṣādāḥ*—called Naiṣādas; *giri-kānana*—the hills and forests; *gocarāḥ*—inhabiting; *yena*—because; *aharat*—he took upon himself; *jāyamānaḥ*—being born; *vena*—of King Vena; *kalmaṣam*—all kinds of sin; *ulbaṇam*—very fearful.

TRANSLATION

After his [Niṣāda's] birth, he immediately took charge of all the resultant actions of King Vena's sinful activities. As such, this Naiṣāda class is always engaged in sinful activities like stealing, plundering and hunting. Consequently they are only allowed to live in the hills and forests.

PURPORT

The Naiṣādas are not allowed to live in cities and towns because they are sinful by nature. As such, their bodies are very ugly, and their occupations are also sinful. We should, however, know that even these sinful men (who are sometimes called *kirātas*) can be delivered from their sinful condition to the topmost Vaiṣṇava platform by the mercy of a pure devotee. Engagement in the transcendental loving devotional service of the Lord can make anyone, however sinful he may be, fit to return home, back to Godhead. One has only to become free from all contamination by the process of devotional service. In this way everyone can become fit to return home, back to Godhead. This is confirmed by the Lord Himself in *Bhagavad-gītā:*

māṁ hi pārtha vyapāśritya
ye 'pi syuḥ pāpa-yonayaḥ
striyo vaiśyās tathā śūdrās
te 'pi yānti parāṁ gatim

"O son of Pṛthā, those who take shelter of Me, though they be of lower birth—women, *vaiśyas* [merchants], as well as *śūdras* [workers]—can approach the supreme destination." (Bg. 9.32)

Thus end the Bhaktivedanta purports of the Fourth Canto, Fourteenth Chapter, of the Śrīmad-Bhāgavatam, *entitled "The Story of King Vena."*

CHAPTER FIFTEEN

King Pṛthu's Appearance and Coronation

TEXT 1

मैत्रेय उवाच

अथ तस्य पुनर्विप्रैरपुत्रस्य महीपतेः ।
बाहुभ्यां मध्यमानाभ्यां मिथुनं समपद्यत ॥ १ ॥

maitreya uvāca
atha tasya punar viprair
aputrasya mahīpateḥ
bāhubhyāṁ mathyamānābhyāṁ
mithunaṁ samapadyata

maitreyaḥ uvāca—Maitreya continued to speak; *atha*—thus; *tasya*—his; *punaḥ*—again; *vipraiḥ*—by the *brāhmaṇas; aputrasya*—without a son; *mahīpateḥ*—of the King; *bāhubhyām*—from the arms; *mathyamānābhyām*—being churned; *mithunam*—a couple; *samapadyata*—took birth.

TRANSLATION

The great sage Maitreya continued: My dear Vidura, thus the brāhmaṇas and the great sages churned the two arms of King Vena's dead body. As a result a male and female couple came out of his arms.

TEXT 2

तद् दृष्ट्वा मिथुनं जातमृषयो ब्रह्मवादिनः ।
ऊचुः परमसन्तुष्टा विदित्वा भगवत्कलाम् ॥ २ ॥

tad dṛṣṭvā mithunaṁ jātam
ṛṣayo brahma-vādinaḥ

ūcuḥ parama-santuṣṭā
viditvā bhagavat-kalām

tat—that; *dṛṣṭvā*—seeing; *mithunam*—couple; *jātam*—born; *ṛṣayaḥ*—the great sages; *brahma-vādinaḥ*—very learned in Vedic knowledge; *ūcuḥ*—said; *parama*—very much; *santuṣṭāḥ*—being pleased; *viditvā*—knowing; *bhagavat*—of the Supreme Personality of Godhead; *kalām*—expansion.

TRANSLATION

The great sages were highly learned in Vedic knowledge. When they saw the male and female born of the arms of Vena's body, they were very pleased, for they could understand that the couple was an expansion of the plenary portion of Viṣṇu, the Supreme Personality of Godhead.

PURPORT

The method adopted by the great sages and scholars, who were learned in Vedic knowledge, was perfect. They removed all the reactions of King Vena's sinful activities by seeing that King Vena first gave birth to Bāhuka, described in the previous chapter. After King Vena's body was thus purified, a male and female came out of it, and the great sages could understand that this was an expansion of Lord Viṣṇu. This expansion, of course, was not *viṣṇu-tattva* but a specifically empowered expansion of Lord Viṣṇu known as *āveśa*.

TEXT 3

ऋषय ऊचुः
एष विष्णोर्भगवतः कला भुवनपालिनी ।
इयं च लक्ष्म्याः सम्भूतिः पुरुषस्यानपायिनी ॥ ३ ॥

ṛṣaya ūcuḥ
eṣa viṣṇor bhagavataḥ
kalā bhuvana-pālinī
iyaṁ ca lakṣmyāḥ sambhūtiḥ
puruṣasyānapāyinī

ṛṣayaḥ ūcuḥ—the sages said; *eṣaḥ*—this male; *viṣṇoḥ*—of Lord Viṣṇu; *bhagavataḥ*—of the Supreme Personality of Godhead; *kalā*—expansion; *bhuvana-pālinī*—who maintains the world; *iyam*—this female; *ca*—also; *lakṣmyāḥ*—of the goddess of fortune; *sambhūtiḥ*—expansion; *puruṣasya*—of the Lord; *anapāyinī*—inseparable.

TRANSLATION

The great sages said: The male is a plenary expansion of the power of Lord Viṣṇu, who maintains the entire universe, and the female is a plenary expansion of the goddess of fortune, who is never separated from the Lord.

PURPORT

The significance of the goddess of fortune's never being separated from the Lord is clearly mentioned herein. People in the material world are very fond of the goddess of fortune, and they want her favor in the form of riches. They should know, however, that the goddess of fortune is inseparable from Lord Viṣṇu. Materialists should understand that the goddess of fortune should be worshiped along with Lord Viṣṇu and should not be regarded separately. Materialists seeking the favor of the goddess of fortune must worship Lord Viṣṇu and Lakṣmī together to maintain material opulence. If a materialist follows the policy of Rāvaṇa, who wanted to separate Sītā from Lord Rāmacandra, the process of separation will vanquish him. Those who are very rich and have taken favor of the goddess of fortune in this world must engage their money in the service of the Lord. In this way they can continue in their opulent position without disturbance.

TEXT 4

अयं तु प्रथमो राज्ञां पुमान् प्रथयिता यशः ।
पृथुर्नाम महाराजो भविष्यति पृथुश्रवाः ॥ ४ ॥

ayaṁ tu prathamo rājñāṁ
pumān prathayitā yaśaḥ
pṛthur nāma mahārājo
bhaviṣyati pṛthu-śravāḥ

ayam—this; *tu*—then; *prathamaḥ*—the first; *rājñām*—of the kings; *pumān*—the male; *prathayitā*—will expand; *yaśaḥ*—reputation; *pṛthuḥ*—Mahārāja Pṛthu; *nāma*—by name; *mahā-rājaḥ*—the great king; *bhaviṣyati*—will become; *pṛthu-śravāḥ*—of wide renown.

TRANSLATION

Of the two, the male will be able to expand his reputation throughout the world. His name will be Pṛthu. Indeed, he will be the first among kings.

PURPORT

There are different types of incarnations of the Supreme Personality of Godhead. In the *śāstras* it is said that Garuḍa, the carrier of Lord Viṣṇu, and Lord Śiva and Ananta are all very powerful incarnations of the Brahman feature of the Lord. Similarly, Śacīpati, or Indra, the King of heaven, is an incarnation of the lusty feature of the Lord. Aniruddha is an incarnation of the Lord's mind. Similarly, King Pṛthu is an incarnation of the ruling force of the Lord. Thus the saintly persons and great sages predicted the future activities of King Pṛthu, who was already explained as a partial incarnation of the plenary expansion of the Lord.

TEXT 5

इयं च सुदती देवी गुणभूषणभूषणा ।
अर्चिर्नाम वरारोहा पृथुमेवावरुन्धती ॥ ५ ॥

iyaṁ ca sudatī devī
guṇa-bhūṣaṇa-bhūṣaṇā
arcir nāma varārohā
pṛthum evāvarundhatī

iyam—this female child; *ca*—and; *su-datī*—who has very nice teeth; *devī*—the goddess of fortune; *guṇa*—by good qualities; *bhūṣaṇa*—ornaments; *bhūṣaṇā*—who beautifies; *arciḥ*—Arci; *nāma*—by name; *vara-ārohā*—very beautiful; *pṛthum*—unto King Pṛthu; *eva*—certainly; *avarundhatī*—being very much attached.

TRANSLATION

The female has such beautiful teeth and beautiful qualities that she will actually beautify the ornaments she wears. Her name will be Arci. In the future she will accept King Pṛthu as her husband.

TEXT 6

एष साक्षाद्धरेरंशो जातो लोकरिरक्षया ।
इयं च तत्परा हि श्रीरनुजज्ञेऽनपायिनी ॥ ६ ॥

eṣa sākṣād dharer aṁśo
jāto loka-rirakṣayā
iyaṁ ca tat-parā hi śrīr
anujajñe 'napāyinī

eṣaḥ—this male; *sākṣāt*—directly; *hareḥ*—of the Supreme Personality of Godhead; *aṁśaḥ*—partial representative; *jātaḥ*—born; *loka*—the entire world; *rirakṣayā*—with a desire to protect; *iyam*—this female; *ca*—also; *tat-parā*—very much attached to him; *hi*—certainly; *śrīḥ*—the goddess of fortune; *anujajñe*—took birth; *anapāyinī*—inseparable.

TRANSLATION

In the form of King Pṛthu, the Supreme Personality of Godhead has appeared through a part of His potency to protect the people of the world. The goddess of fortune is the constant companion of the Lord, and therefore she has incarnated partially as Arci to become King Pṛthu's queen.

PURPORT

In *Bhagavad-gītā* the Lord says that whenever one sees an extraordinary power, he should conclude that a specific partial representation of the Supreme Personality of Godhead is present. There are innumerable such personalities, but not all of them are direct *viṣṇu-tattva* plenary expansions of the Lord. Many living entities are classified among the *śakti-tattvas*. Such incarnations, empowered for specific purposes, are known as *śaktyāveśa-avatāras*. King Pṛthu was such a *śaktyāveśa-avatāra* of the Lord. Similarly, Arci, King Pṛthu's wife, was a *śaktyāveśa-avatāra* of the goddess of fortune.

TEXT 7

मैत्रेय उवाच
प्रशंसन्ति स तं विप्रा गन्धर्वप्रवरा जगुः ।
मुमुचुः सुमनोधाराः सिद्धा नृत्यन्ति स्वःस्त्रियः ॥ ७ ॥

maitreya uvāca
praśaṁsanti sma taṁ viprā
gandharva-pravarā jaguḥ
mumucuḥ sumano-dhārāḥ
siddhā nṛtyanti svaḥ-striyaḥ

maitreyaḥ uvāca—the great saint Maitreya said; *praśaṁsanti sma*—praised, glorified; *tam*—him (Pṛthu); *viprāḥ*—all the *brāhmaṇas; gandharva-pravarāḥ*—the best of the Gandharvas; *jaguḥ*—chanted; *mumucuḥ*—released; *sumanaḥ-dhārāḥ*—showers of flowers; *siddhāḥ*—the personalities from Siddhaloka; *nṛtyanti*—were dancing; *svaḥ*—of the heavenly planets; *striyaḥ*—women (the Apsarās).

TRANSLATION

The great sage Maitreya continued: My dear Vidurajī, at that time all the brāhmaṇas highly praised and glorified King Pṛthu, and the best singers of Gandharvaloka chanted his glories. The inhabitants of Siddhaloka showered flowers, and the beautiful women in the heavenly planets danced in ecstasy.

TEXT 8

शङ्खतूर्यमृदङ्गाद्या नेदुर्दुन्दुभयो दिवि ।
तत्र सर्व उपाजग्मुर्देवर्षिपितॄणां गणाः ॥ ८ ॥

śaṅkha-tūrya-mṛdaṅgādyā
nedur dundubhayo divi
tatra sarva upājagmur
devarṣi-pitṝṇāṁ gaṇāḥ

śaṅkha—conches; *tūrya*—bugles; *mṛdaṅga*—drums; *ādyāḥ*—and so on; *neduḥ*—vibrated; *dundubhayaḥ*—kettledrums; *divi*—in outer space; *tatra*—there; *sarve*—all; *upājagmuḥ*—came; *deva-ṛṣi*—demigods and sages; *pitṝṇām*—of forefathers; *gaṇāḥ*—groups.

TRANSLATION

Conchshells, bugles, drums and kettledrums vibrated in outer space. Great sages, forefathers and personalities from the heavenly planets all came to earth from various planetary systems.

TEXTS 9-10

ब्रह्मा जगद्गुरुर्देवैः सहासृत्य सुरेश्वरैः ।
वैन्यस्य दक्षिणे हस्ते दृष्ट्वा चिह्नं गदाभृतः ॥ ९ ॥
पादयोररविन्दं च तं वै मेने हरेः कलाम् ।
यस्याप्रतिहतं चक्रमंशः स परमेष्ठिनः ॥१०॥

brahmā jagad-gurur devaiḥ
sahāsṛtya sureśvaraiḥ
vainyasya dakṣiṇe haste
dṛṣṭvā cihnaṁ gadābhṛtaḥ

pādayor aravindaṁ ca taṁ
vai mene hareḥ kalām
yasyāpratihataṁ cakram
aṁśaḥ sa parameṣṭhinaḥ

brahmā—Lord Brahmā; *jagat-guruḥ*—the master of the universe; *devaiḥ*—by the demigods; *saha*—accompanied; *āsṛtya*—arriving; *sura-īśvaraiḥ*—with the chiefs of all the heavenly planets; *vainyasya*—of Mahārāja Pṛthu, the son of Vena; *dakṣiṇe*—right; *haste*—on the hand; *dṛṣṭvā*—seeing; *cihnam*—mark; *gadā-bhṛtaḥ*—of Lord Viṣṇu, who carries the club; *pādayoḥ*—on the two feet; *aravindam*—lotus flower; *ca*—also; *tam*—him; *vai*—certainly; *mene*—he understood; *hareḥ*—of the Supreme Personality of Godhead; *kalām*—part of a plenary expansion; *yasya*—whose; *apratihatam*—invincible; *cakram*—disc; *aṁśaḥ*—partial representation; *saḥ*—he; *parameṣṭhinaḥ*—of the Supreme Personality of Godhead.

TRANSLATION

Lord Brahmā, the master of the entire universe, arrived there accompanied by all the demigods and their chiefs. Seeing the lines of Lord Viṣṇu's palm on King Pṛthu's right hand and impressions of lotus flowers on the soles of his feet, Lord Brahmā could understand that King Pṛthu was a partial representation of the Supreme Personality of Godhead. One whose palm bears the sign of a disc, as well as other such lines, should be considered a partial representation or incarnation of the Supreme Lord.

PURPORT

There is a system by which one can detect an incarnation of the Supreme Personality of Godhead. Nowadays it has become a cheap fashion to accept any rascal as an incarnation of God, but from this incident we can see that Lord Brahmā personally examined the hands and feet of King Pṛthu for specific signs. In their prophecies the learned sages and *brāhmaṇas* accepted Pṛthu Mahārāja as a plenary partial expansion of the Lord. During the presence of Lord Kṛṣṇa, however, a king declared himself Vāsudeva, and Lord Kṛṣṇa killed him. Before accepting someone as an incarnation of God, one should verify his identity according to the symptoms mentioned in the *śāstras*. Without these symptoms the pretender is subject to be killed by the authorities for pretending to be an incarnation of God.

TEXT 11

तस्याभिषेक आरब्धो ब्राह्मणैर्ब्रह्मवादिभिः ।
आभिषेचनिकान्यस्मै आजह्रुः सर्वतो जनाः ॥११॥

tasyābhiṣeka ārabdho
brāhmaṇair brahma-vādibhiḥ
ābhiṣecanikāny asmai
ājahruḥ sarvato janāḥ

tasya—his; *abhiṣekaḥ*—coronation; *ārabdhaḥ*—was arranged; *brāhmaṇaiḥ*—by the learned *brāhmaṇas; brahma-vādibhiḥ*—attached to the Vedic rituals; *ābhiṣecanikāni*—various paraphernalia for performing the ceremony; *asmai*—unto him; *ājahruḥ*—collected; *sarvataḥ*—from all directions; *janāḥ*—people.

TRANSLATION

The learned brāhmaṇas, who were very attached to the Vedic ritualistic ceremonies, then arranged for the King's coronation. People from all directions collected all the different paraphernalia for the ceremony. Thus everything was complete.

TEXT 12

सरित्समुद्रा गिरयो नागा गावः खगा मृगाः ।
द्यौः क्षितिः सर्वभूतानि समाजहुरुपायनम् ॥१२॥

sarit-samudrā girayo
nāgā gāvaḥ khagā mṛgāḥ
dyauḥ kṣitiḥ sarva-bhūtāni
samājahrur upāyanam

sarit—the rivers; *samudrāḥ*—the seas; *girayaḥ*—the mountains; *nāgāḥ*—the serpents; *gāvaḥ*—the cows; *khagāḥ*—the birds; *mṛgāḥ*—the animals; *dyauḥ*—the sky; *kṣitiḥ*—the earth; *sarva-bhūtāni*—all living entities; *samājahruḥ*—collected; *upāyanam*—different kinds of presentations.

TRANSLATION

All the rivers, seas, hills, mountains, serpents, cows, birds, animals, heavenly planets, the earthly planet and all other living entities collected various presentations, according to their ability, to offer the King.

TEXT 13

सोऽभिषिक्तो महाराजः सुवासाः साध्वलङ्कृतः ।
पत्न्यार्चिषालङ्कृतया विरेजेऽग्निरिवापरः ॥१३॥

so 'bhiṣikto mahārājaḥ
suvāsāḥ sādhv-alaṅkṛtaḥ
patnyārciṣālaṅkṛtayā
vireje 'gnir ivāparaḥ

saḥ—the King; *abhiṣiktaḥ*—being coronated; *mahārājaḥ*—Mahārāja Pṛthu; *su-vāsāḥ*—exquisitely dressed; *sādhu-alaṅkṛtaḥ*—highly decorated with ornaments; *patnyā*—along with his wife; *arciṣā*—named Arci; *alaṅkṛtayā*—nicely ornamented; *vireje*—appeared; *agniḥ*—fire; *iva*—like; *aparaḥ*—another.

TRANSLATION

Thus the great King Pṛthu, exquisitely dressed with garments and ornaments, was coronated and placed on the throne. The King and his wife, Arci, who was also exquisitely ornamented, appeared exactly like fire.

TEXT 14

तस्मै जहार धनदो हैमं वीर वरासनम् ।
वरुणः सलिलस्रावमातपत्रं शशिप्रभम् ॥१४॥

tasmai jahāra dhanado
haimaṁ vīra varāsanam
varuṇaḥ salila-srāvam
ātapatraṁ śaśi-prabham

tasmai—unto him; *jahāra*—presented; *dhana-daḥ*—the treasurer of the demigods (Kuvera); *haimam*—made of gold; *vīra*—O Vidura; *vara-āsanam*—royal throne; *varuṇaḥ*—the demigod Varuṇa; *salila-srāvam*—dropping particles of water; *ātapatram*—umbrella; *śaśi-prabham*—as brilliant as the moon.

TRANSLATION

The great sage continued: My dear Vidura, Kuvera presented the great King Pṛthu a golden throne. The demigod Varuṇa presented him an umbrella that constantly sprayed fine particles of water and was as brilliant as the moon.

TEXT 15

वायुश्च वालव्यजने धर्मः कीर्तिमयीं स्रजम् ।
इन्द्रः किरीटमुत्कृष्टं दण्डं संयमनं यमः ॥१५॥

vāyuś ca vāla-vyajane
dharmaḥ kīrtimayīṁ srajam
indraḥ kirīṭam utkṛṣṭaṁ
daṇḍaṁ saṁyamanaṁ yamaḥ

vāyuḥ—the demigod of air; *ca*—also; *vāla-vyajane*—two *cāmaras* made of hair; *dharmaḥ*—the King of religion; *kīrti-mayīm*—expanding one's name and fame; *srajam*—garland; *indraḥ*—the King of heaven; *kirīṭam*—helmet; *utkṛṣṭam*—very valuable; *daṇḍam*—sceptor; *saṁyamanam*-for ruling the world; *yamaḥ*—the superintendent of death.

TRANSLATION

The demigod of air, Vāyu, presented King Pṛthu two whisks [cāmaras] of hair; the King of religion, Dharma, presented him a flower garland which would expand his fame; the King of heaven, Indra, presented him a valuable helmet; and the superintendent of death, Yamarāja, presented him a sceptor with which to rule the world.

TEXT 16

ब्रह्मा ब्रह्ममयं वर्म भारती हारमुत्तमम् ।
हरिः सुदर्शनं चक्रं तत्पत्न्यव्याहतां श्रियम् ॥१६॥

brahmā brahmamayaṁ varma
bhāratī hāram uttamam
hariḥ sudarśanaṁ cakraṁ
tat-patny avyāhatāṁ śriyam

brahmā—Lord Brahmā; *brahma-mayam*—made of spiritual knowledge; *varma*—armor; *bhāratī*—the goddess of learning; *hāram*—necklace; *uttamam*—transcendental; *hariḥ*—the Supreme Personality of Godhead; *sudarśanam cakram*—Sudarśana disc; *tat-patnī*—His wife (Lakṣmī); *avyāhatām*—imperishable; *śriyam*—beauty and opulence.

TRANSLATION

Lord Brahmā presented King Pṛthu a protective garment made of spiritual knowledge. Bhāratī [Sarasvatī], the wife of Brahmā, gave him a transcendental necklace. Lord Viṣṇu presented him a Sudarśana disc, and Lord Viṣṇu's wife, the goddess of fortune, gave him imperishable opulences.

PURPORT

All the demigods presented various gifts to King Pṛthu. Hari, an incarnation of the Supreme Personality of Godhead known as Upendra in the heavenly planet, presented the King a Sudarśana disc. It should be understood that this Sudarśana disc is not exactly the same type of Sudarśana disc used by the Personality of Godhead, Kṛṣṇa or Viṣṇu. Since Mahārāja Pṛthu was a partial representation of the Supreme Personality of Godhead's power, the Sudarśana disc given to him represented the partial power of the original Sudarśana disc.

TEXT 17

दशचन्द्रमसिं रुद्रः शतचन्द्रं तथाम्बिका ।
सोमोऽमृतमयानश्वांस्त्वष्टा रूपाश्रयं रथम् ॥१७॥

daśa-candram asiṁ rudraḥ
śata-candraṁ tathāmbikā
somo 'mṛta-mayān aśvāṁs
tvaṣṭā rūpāśrayaṁ ratham

daśa-candram—decorated with ten moons; *asim*—sword; *rudraḥ*—Lord Śiva; *śata-candram*—decorated with one hundred moons; *tathā*—in that manner; *ambikā*—the goddess Durgā; *somaḥ*—the moon demigod; *amṛta-mayān*—made of nectar; *aśvān*—horses; *tvaṣṭā*—the demigod Viśvakarmā; *rūpa-āśrayam*—very beautiful; *ratham*— a chariot.

TRANSLATION

Lord Śiva presented him a sword within a sheath marked with ten moons, and his wife, the goddess Durgā, presented him with a shield marked with one hundred moons. The moon demigod presented him horses made of nectar, and the demigod Viśvakarmā presented him a very beautiful chariot.

TEXT 18

अग्निराजगवं चापं सूर्यो रश्मिमयानिषून् ।
भूः पादुके योगमय्यौ द्यौः पुष्पावलिमन्वहम् ॥१८॥

agnir āja-gavaṁ cāpaṁ
sūryo raśmimayān iṣūn
bhūḥ pāduke yogamayyau
dyauḥ puṣpāvalim anvaham

agniḥ—the demigod of fire; *āja-gavam*—made of the horns of goats and cows; *cāpam*—a bow; *sūryaḥ*—the sun-god; *raśmi-mayān*—brilliant as sunshine; *iṣūn*—arrows; *bhūḥ*—Bhūmi, the predominating goddess of the earth; *pāduke*—two slippers; *yoga-mayyau*—full of mystic power; *dyauḥ*—the demigods in outer space; *puṣpa*—of flowers; *āvalim*—presentation; *anvaham*—day after day.

TRANSLATION

The demigod of fire, Agni, presented him a bow made of the horns of goats and cows. The sun-god presented him arrows as brilliant as sunshine. The predominating deity of Bhūloka presented him slippers full of mystic power. The demigods from outer space brought him presentations of flowers again and again.

PURPORT

This verse describes that the King's slippers were invested with mystic powers (*pāduke yogamayyau*). Thus as soon as the King placed his feet in the slippers they would immediately carry him wherever he desired. Mystic *yogīs* can transfer themselves from one place to another whenever they desire. A similar power was invested in the slippers of King Pṛthu.

TEXT 19

नाट्यं सुगीतं वादित्रमन्तर्धानं च खेचराः ।
ऋषयश्चाशिषः सत्याः समुद्रः शङ्खमात्मजम् ॥१९॥

nāṭyaṁ sugītaṁ vāditram
antardhānaṁ ca khecarāḥ
ṛṣayaś cāśiṣaḥ satyāḥ
samudraḥ śaṅkham ātmajam

nāṭyam—the art of drama; *su-gītam*—the art of singing sweet songs; *vāditram*—the art of playing musical instruments; *antardhānam*—the art of disappearing; *ca*—also; *khe-carāḥ*—demigods traveling in outer space;

ṛṣayaḥ—the great sages; *ca*—also; *āśiṣaḥ*—blessings; *satyāḥ*—infallible; *samudraḥ*—the demigod of the ocean; *śaṅkham*—conchshell; *ātma-jam*—produced from himself.

TRANSLATION

The demigods who always travel in outer space gave King Pṛthu the arts to perform dramas, sing songs, play musical instruments and disappear at his will. The great sages also offered him infallible blessings. The ocean offered him a conchshell produced from the ocean.

TEXT 20

सिन्धवः पर्वता नद्यो रथवीथीर्महात्मनः ।
सूतोऽथ मागधो वन्दी तं स्तोतुमुपतस्थिरे ॥२०॥

sindhavaḥ parvatā nadyo
ratha-vīthīr mahātmanaḥ
sūto 'tha māgadho vandī
taṁ stotum upatasthire

sindhavaḥ—the seas; *parvatāḥ*—the mountains; *nadyaḥ*—the rivers; *ratha-vīthīḥ*—the paths for the chariot to pass; *mahātmanaḥ*—of the great soul; *sūtaḥ*—a professional who offers praises; *atha*—then; *māgadhaḥ*—a professional bard; *vandī*—a professional who offers prayers; *tam*—him; *stotum*—to praise; *upatasthire*—presented themselves.

TRANSLATION

The seas, mountains and rivers gave him room to drive his chariot without impediments, and a sūta, a māgadha and a vandī offered prayers and praises. They all presented themselves before him to perform their respective duties.

TEXT 21

स्तावकांस्तानभिप्रेत्य पृथुर्वैन्यः प्रतापवान् ।
मेघनिर्ह्रादया वाचा प्रहसन्निदमब्रवीत् ॥२१॥

stāvakāṁs tān abhipretya
pṛthur vainyaḥ pratāpavān

megha-nirhrādayā vācā
prahasann idam abravīt

stāvakān—engaged in offering prayers; *tān*—those persons; *abhipretya*—seeing, understanding; *pṛthuḥ*—King Pṛthu; *vainyaḥ*—son of Vena; *pratāpavān*—greatly powerful; *megha-nirhrādayā*—as grave as the thundering of clouds; *vācā*—with a voice; *prahasan*—smiling; *idam*—this; *abravīt*—he spoke.

TRANSLATION

Thus when the greatly powerful King Pṛthu, the son of Vena, saw the professionals before him, to congratulate them he smiled, and with the gravity of the vibrating sounds of clouds he spoke as follows.

TEXT 22

पृथुरुवाच
भोः सूत हे मागध सौम्य वन्दिँ-
ल्लोकेऽधुनास्पष्टगुणस्य मे स्यात् ।
किमाश्रयो मे स्तव एष योज्यतां
मा मय्यभूवन् वितथा गिरो वः ॥२२॥

pṛthur uvāca
bhoḥ sūta he māgadha saumya vandiṁl
loke 'dhunāspaṣṭa-guṇasya me syāt
kim āśrayo me stava eṣa yojyatāṁ
mā mayy abhūvan vitathā giro vaḥ

pṛthuḥ uvāca—King Pṛthu said; *bhoḥ sūta*—O *sūta; he māgadha*—O *māgadha; saumya*—gentle; *vandin*—O devotee offering prayers; *loke*—in this world; *adhunā*—just now; *aspaṣṭa*—not distinct; *guṇasya*—whose qualities; *me*—of me; *syāt*—there may be; *kim*—why; *āśrayaḥ*—shelter; *me*—of me; *stavaḥ*—praise; *eṣaḥ*—this; *yojyatām*—may be applied; *mā*—never; *mayi*—unto me; *abhūvan*—were; *vitathā*—in vain; *giraḥ*—words; *vaḥ*—your.

TRANSLATION

King Pṛthu said: O gentle sūta, māgadha and other devotee offering prayers, the qualities of which you have spoken are not distinct in me. Why then should you praise me for all these qualities when I do not

shelter these features? I do not wish for these words meant for me to go in vain, but it is better that they be offered to someone else.

PURPORT

The prayers and praises by the *sūta, māgadha* and *vandī* all explain the godly qualities of Mahārāja Pṛthu, for he was a *śaktyāveśa* incarnation of the Supreme Personality of Godhead. Because the qualities were not yet manifest, however, King Pṛthu very humbly asked why the devotees should praise him with such exalted words. He did not want anyone to offer him prayers or glorify him unless he possessed the real qualities of which they spoke. The offering of prayers was certainly appropriate, for he was an incarnation of Godhead, but he warned that one should not be accepted as an incarnation of the Personality of Godhead without having the godly qualities. At the present moment there are many so-called incarnations of the Personality of Godhead, but these are merely fools and rascals whom people accept as incarnations of God although they have no godly qualities. King Pṛthu desired that his real characteristics in the future might justify such words of praise. Although there was no fault in the prayers offered, Pṛthu Mahārāja indicated that such prayers should not be offered to an unfit person who pretends to be an incarnation of the Supreme Personality of Godhead.

TEXT 23

तस्मात्परोक्षेऽस्मदुपश्रुतान्यलं-
करिष्यथ स्तोत्रमपीच्यवाचः ।
सत्युत्तमश्लोकगुणानुवादे
जुगुप्सितं न स्तवयन्ति सभ्याः ॥२३॥

tasmāt parokṣe 'smad-upaśrutāny alaṁ
kariṣyatha stotram apīcya-vācaḥ
saty uttamaśloka-guṇānuvāde
jugupsitaṁ na stavayanti sabhyāḥ

tasmāt—therefore; *parokṣe*—in some future time; *asmat*—my; *upaśrutāni*—about the qualities spoken of; *alam*—sufficiently; *kariṣyatha*—you will be able to offer; *stotram*—prayers; *apīcya-vācaḥ*—O gentle reciters; *sati*—being the proper engagement; *uttama-śloka*—of the Supreme Personality of Godhead; *guṇa*—of the qualities; *anuvāde*—discussion; *jugupsitam*—to an abominable person; *na*—never; *stavayanti*—offer prayers; *sabhyāḥ*—persons who are gentle.

TRANSLATION

O gentle reciters, offer such prayers in due course of time, when the qualities of which you have spoken actually manifest themselves in me. The gentle who offer prayers to the Supreme Personality of Godhead do not attribute such qualities to a human being who does not actually have them.

PURPORT

Gentle devotees of the Supreme Personality of Godhead know perfectly well who is God and who is not. Nondevotee impersonalists, however, who have no idea what God is and who never offer prayers to the Supreme Personality of Godhead, are always interested in accepting a human being as God and offering such prayers to him. This is the difference between a devotee and a demon. Demons manufacture their own gods, or a demon himself claims to be God, following in the footsteps of Rāvaṇa and Hiraṇyakaśipu. Although Pṛthu Mahārāja was factually an incarnation of the Supreme Personality of Godhead, he nonetheless rejected those praises because the qualities of the Supreme Person were not yet manifest in him. He wanted to stress that one who does not actually possess these qualities should not try to engage his followers and devotees in offering him glory for them, even though these qualities might be manifest in the future. If a man who does not factually possess the attributes of a great personality engages his followers in praising him with the expectation that such attributes will develop in the future, that sort of praise is actually an insult.

TEXT 24

महद्गुणानात्मनि कर्तुमीशः
कः स्तावकैः स्तावयतेऽसतोऽपि ।
तेऽस्याभविष्यन्निति विप्रलब्धो
जनावहासं कुमतिर्न वेद ॥२४॥

mahad-guṇān ātmani kartum īśaḥ
kaḥ stāvakaiḥ stāvayate 'sato 'pi
te 'syābhaviṣyann iti vipralabdho
janāvahāsaṁ kumatir na veda

mahat—exalted; *guṇān*—the qualities; *ātmani*—in himself; *kartum*—to manifest; *īśaḥ*—competent; *kaḥ*—who; *stāvakaiḥ*—by followers; *stāvayate*—causes to be praised; *asataḥ*—not existing; *api*—although; *te*—they; *asya*—of him; *abhaviṣyan*—might have been; *iti*—thus; *vipralabdhaḥ*—cheated; *jana*—of people; *avahāsam*—insult; *kumatiḥ*—a fool; *na*—does not; *veda*—know.

TRANSLATION

How could an intelligent man competent enough to possess such exalted qualities allow his followers to praise him if he did not actually have them? Praising a man by saying that if he were educated he might have become a great scholar or great personality is nothing but a process of cheating. A foolish person who agrees to accept such praise does not know that such words simply insult him.

PURPORT

Pṛthu Mahārāja was an incarnation of the Supreme Personality of Godhead, as Lord Brahmā and other demigods had already testified when they had presented the King many heavenly gifts. Because he had just been coronated, however, he could not manifest his godly qualities in action. Therefore he was not willing to accept the praise of the devotees. So-called incarnations of Godhead should therefore take lessons from the behavior of King Pṛthu. Demons without godly qualities should not accept false praise from their followers.

TEXT 25

प्रभवो ह्यात्मनः स्तोत्रं जुगुप्सन्त्यपि विश्रुताः ।
ह्रीमन्तः परमोदाराः पौरुषं वा विगर्हितम् ॥२५॥

prabhavo hy ātmanaḥ stotraṁ
jugupsanty api viśrutāḥ
hrīmantaḥ paramodārāḥ
pauruṣaṁ vā vigarhitam

prabhavaḥ—very powerful persons; *hi*—certainly; *ātmanaḥ*—of themselves; *stotram*—praise; *jugupsanti*—do not like; *api*—although; *viśrutāḥ*—very famous; *hrīmantaḥ*—modest; *parama-udārāḥ*—very magnanimous persons; *pauruṣam*—powerful actions; *vā*—also; *vigarhitam*—abominable.

TRANSLATION

As a person with a sense of honor and magnanimity does not like to hear about his abominable actions, a person who is very famous and powerful does not like to hear himself praised.

TEXT 26

वयं त्वविदिता लोके सूताद्यापि वरीमभिः ।
कर्मभिः कथमात्मानं गापयिष्याम बालवत् ॥२६॥

vayaṁ tv aviditā loke
sūtādyāpi varīmabhiḥ
karmabhiḥ katham ātmānaṁ
gāpayiṣyāma bālavat

vayam—we; *tu*—then; *aviditāḥ*—not famous; *loke*—in the world; *sūta-ādya*—O persons headed by the *sūta; api*—just now; *varīmabhiḥ*—great, praiseworthy; *karmabhiḥ*—by actions; *katham*—how; *ātmānam*—unto myself; *gāpayiṣyāma*—I shall engage you in offering; *bāla-vat*—like children.

TRANSLATION

King Pṛthu continued: My dear devotees, headed by the sūta, just now I am not very famous for my personal activities because I have not done anything praiseworthy you could glorify. Therefore how could I engage you in praising my activities exactly like children?

Thus end the Bhaktivedanta purports of the Fifteenth Chapter, Fourth Canto, of the Śrīmad-Bhāgavatam, *entitled "King Pṛthu's Appearance and Coronation."*

CHAPTER SIXTEEN

Praise of King Pṛthu by the Professional Reciters

TEXT 1

मैत्रेय उवाच

इति ब्रुवाणं नृपतिं गायका मुनिचोदिताः ।
तुष्टुवुस्तुष्टमनसस्तद्वागमृतसेवया ॥ १ ॥

maitreya uvāca
iti bruvāṇaṁ nṛpatiṁ
gāyakā muni-coditāḥ
tuṣṭuvus tuṣṭa-manasas
tad-vāg-amṛta-sevayā

maitreyaḥ uvāca—the great sage Maitreya said; *iti*—thus; *bruvāṇam*—speaking; *nṛpatim*—the King; *gāyakāḥ*—the reciters; *muni*—by the sages; *coditāḥ*—having been instructed; *tuṣṭuvuḥ*—praised, satisfied; *tuṣṭa*—being pleased; *manasaḥ*—their minds; *tat*—his; *vāk*—words; *amṛta*—nectarean; *sevayā*—by hearing.

TRANSLATION

The great sage Maitreya continued: While King Pṛthu thus spoke, the humility of his nectarean speeches pleased the reciters very much. Then again they continued to praise the King highly with exalted prayers, as they had been instructed by the great sages.

PURPORT

Here the word *muni-coditāḥ* indicates instructions received from great sages and saintly persons. Although Mahārāja Pṛthu was simply enthroned on the royal seat and was not at that time exhibiting his godly powers, nonetheless the reciters like the *sūta,* the *māgadha* and the *vandī* understood that King Pṛthu was an incarnation of God. They could understand this by the instructions given by the great sages and learned *brāhmaṇas.* We have to understand the incarnations of God by the instructions of authorized persons. We cannot manufacture a God by our own concoctions. As stated by Narottama dāsa Ṭhākura, *sādhu-śāstra-guru:* one has to test all spiritual matters according to the instructions of saintly persons, scriptures and the spiritual master. The spiritual master is one who follows the instructions of his predecessors, namely the *sādhus,* or saintly persons. A bona fide spiritual master does not mention anything not mentioned in the authorized scriptures. Ordinary people have to follow the instructions of *sādhu, śāstra* and *guru.* Those statements made in the *śāstras* and those made by the bona fide *sādhu* or *guru* cannot differ from one another.

Reciters like the *sūta* and the *māgadha* were confidentially aware that King Pṛthu was an incarnation of the Personality of Godhead. Although the King denied such praise because he was not at that time exhibiting his godly qualities, the reciters nonetheless did not stop praising him. Rather, they were very pleased with the King, who, although actually an incarnation of God, was so humble and delightful in his dealings with devotees. In this connection we may note that previously (4.15.21) it was mentioned that King Pṛthu was smiling and was in a pleasant mood while speaking to the reciters. Thus we have to learn from the Lord or His incarnation how to become gentle and humble. The King's behavior was very pleasing to the reciters, and consequently the reciters continued their praise and even foretold the King's future activities, as they had been instructed by the *sādhus* and sages.

TEXT 2

नालं वयं ते महिमानुवर्णने
यो देववर्योऽवततार मायया ।
वेनाङ्गजातस्य च पौरुषाणि ते
वाचस्पतीनामपि बभ्रमुर्धियः ॥ २ ॥

nālaṁ vayaṁ te mahimānuvarṇane
yo deva-varyo 'vatatāra māyayā
venāṅga-jātasya ca pauruṣāṇi te
vācas-patīnām api babhramur dhiyaḥ

na alam—not able; *vayam*—we; *te*—your; *mahima*—glories; *anuvarṇane*—in describing; *yaḥ*—you who; *deva*—the Personality of Godhead; *varyaḥ*—foremost; *avatatāra*—descended; *māyayā*—by His internal potencies or causeless mercy; *vena-aṅga*—from the body of King Vena; *jātasya*—who have appeared; *ca*—and; *pauruṣāṇi*—glorious activities; *te*—of you; *vācaḥ-patīnām*—of great orators; *api*—although; *babhramuḥ*—became bewildered; *dhiyaḥ*—the minds.

TRANSLATION

The reciters continued: Dear King, you are a direct incarnation of the Supreme Personality of Godhead, Lord Viṣṇu, and by His causeless mercy you have descended on this earth. Therefore it is not possible for us to actually glorify your exalted activities. Although you have appeared through the body of King Vena, even great oraters and speakers like Lord Brahmā and other demigods cannot exactly describe the glorious activities of Your Lordship.

PURPORT

In this verse the word *māyayā* means "by your causeless mercy." The Māyāvādī philosophers explain the word *māyā* as meaning "illusion" or "falseness." However, there is another meaning of *māyā*—that is, "causeless mercy." There are two kinds of *māyā*—*yogamāyā* and *mahāmāyā. Mahāmāyā* is an expansion of *yogamāyā,* and both these *māyās* are different expressions of the Lord's internal potencies. As stated in *Bhagavad-gītā,* the Lord appears through His internal potencies (*ātma-māyayā*). We should therefore reject the Māyāvāda explanation that the Lord appears in a body given by the external potency, the material energy. The Lord and His incarnation are fully independent and can appear anywhere and everywhere by virtue of the internal potency. Although born out of the so-called dead body of King Vena, King Pṛthu was still an incarnation of the Supreme Personality of Godhead by the Lord's internal potency. The Lord can appear in any family. Sometimes He appears as a fish incarnation (*matsya-avatāra*), or a boar incarnation (*varāha-avatāra*). Thus the Lord is completely free and independent to appear anywhere and everywhere by His internal potency. It is stated that Ananta, an incarnation of the Lord who has unlimited mouths, cannot reach the end of His glorification of the Lord, although Ananta has been describing the Lord since time immemorial. So what to speak of demigods like Lord Brahmā, Lord Śiva and others? It is said that the Lord is *śiva-viriñci-nutam*—always worshiped by demigods like

Lord Śiva and Lord Brahmā. If the demigods cannot find adequate language to express the glories of the Lord, then what to speak of others? Consequently reciters like the *sūta* and the *māgadha* felt inadequate to speak about King Pṛthu.

By glorifying the Lord with exalted verses, one becomes purified. Although we are unable to offer prayers to the Lord in an adequate fashion, our duty is to make the attempt in order to purify ourselves. It is not that we should stop our glorification because demigods like Lord Brahmā and Lord Śiva cannot adequately glorify the Lord. Rather, as stated by Prahlāda Mahārāja, everyone should glorify the Lord according to his own ability. If we are serious and sincere devotees, the Lord will give us the intelligence to offer prayers properly.

TEXT 3

अथाप्युदारश्रवसः पृथोर्हरेः
कलावतारस्य कथामृतादृताः ।
यथोपदेशं मुनिभिः प्रचोदिताः
श्लाघ्यानि कर्माणि वयं वितन्महि ॥ ३ ॥

athāpy udāra-śravasaḥ pṛthor hareḥ
kalāvatārasya kathāmṛtādṛtāḥ
yathopadeśaṁ munibhiḥ pracoditāḥ
ślāghyāni karmāṇi vayaṁ vitanmahi

athāpi—nevertheless; *udāra*—liberal; *śravasaḥ*—whose fame; *pṛthoḥ*—of King Pṛthu; *hareḥ*—of Lord Viṣṇu; *kalā*—part of a plenary expansion; *avatārasya*—incarnation; *kathā*—words; *amṛta*—nectarean; *ādṛtāḥ*—attentive to; *yathā*—according to; *upadeśam*—instruction; *munibhiḥ*—by the great sages; *pracoditāḥ*—being encouraged; *ślāghyāni*—laudable; *karmāṇi*—activities; *vayam*—we; *vitanmahi*—shall try to spread.

TRANSLATION

Although we are unable to glorify you adequately, we nonetheless have a transcendental taste to glorify your activities. We shall try to glorify you according to the instructions received from authoritative sages and scholars. Whatever we speak, however, is always inadequate and very insignificant. Dear King, because you are a direct incarnation of the Supreme Personality of Godhead, all your activities are liberal and ever laudable.

PURPORT

However expert one may be, he can never describe the glories of the Lord adequately. Nonetheless, those engaged in glorifying the activities of the Lord should try to do so as far as possible. Such an attempt will please the Supreme Personality of Godhead. Lord Caitanya has advised all His followers to go everywhere and preach the message of Lord Kṛṣṇa. Since this message is essentially *Bhagavad-gītā,* the preacher's duty is to study *Bhagavad-gītā* as it is understood by disciplic succession and explained by great sages and learned devotees. One should speak to the general populace in accordance with one's predecessors—*sādhu, guru* and *śāstras.* This simple process is the easiest method by which one can glorify the Lord. Devotional service, however, is the real method, for by devotional service one can satisfy the Supreme Personality of Godhead with just a few words. Without devotional service, volumes of books cannot satisfy the Lord. Even though preachers of the Kṛṣṇa consciousness movement may be unable to describe the glories of the Lord, they can nonetheless go everywhere and request people to chant Hare Kṛṣṇa.

TEXT 4

एष धर्मभृतां श्रेष्ठो लोकं धर्मेऽनुवर्तयन् ।
गोप्ता च धर्मसेतूनां शास्ता तत्परिपन्थिनाम् ॥ ४ ॥

eṣa dharma-bhṛtāṁ śreṣṭho
lokaṁ dharme 'nuvartayan
goptā ca dharma-setūnāṁ
śāstā tat-paripanthinām

eṣaḥ—this King Pṛthu; *dharma-bhṛtām*—of persons executing religious activities; *śreṣṭhaḥ*—the best; *lokam*—the whole world; *dharme*—in religious activities; *anuvartayan*—engaging them properly; *goptā*—the protector; *ca*—also; *dharma-setūnām*—of the principles of religiosity; *śāstā*—the chastiser; *tat-paripanthinām*—of those who are against religious principles.

TRANSLATION

This King, Mahārāja Pṛthu, is the best amongst those who are following religious principles. As such, he will engage everyone in the pursuit of religious principles and give them all protection. He will also be a great chastiser to the irreligious and atheistic.

PURPORT

The duty of the king or the head of the government is described very nicely in this verse. It is the duty of the governmental head to see that people strictly follow a religious life. A king should also be strict in chastising the atheists. In other words, an atheistic or godless government should never be supported by a king or governmental chief. That is the test of good government. In the name of secular government, the king or governmental head remains neutral and allows people to engage in all sorts of irreligious activities. In such a state people cannot be happy despite all economic development. However, in this age of Kali there are no pious kings. Instead, rogues and thieves are elected to head the government. But how can the people be happy without religion and God consciousness? The rogues exact taxes from the citizens for their own sense enjoyment, and in the future the people will be so much harassed that according to *Śrīmad-Bhāgavatam* they will flee from their homes and country and take shelter in the forest. However, in Kali-yuga, democratic government can be captured by Kṛṣṇa conscious people. If this can be done, the general populace can be made very happy.

TEXT 5

एष वै लोकपालानां बिभर्त्येकस्तनौ तनूः ।
काले काले यथाभागं लोकयोरुभयोर्हितम् ॥ ५ ॥

eṣa vai loka-pālānāṁ
bibharty ekas tanau tanūḥ
kāle kāle yathā-bhāgaṁ
lokayor ubhayor hitam

eṣaḥ—this King; *vai*—certainly; *loka-pālānām*—of all the demigods; *bibharti*—bears; *ekaḥ*—alone; *tanau*—in his body; *tanūḥ*—the bodies; *kāle kāle*—in due course of time; *yathā*—according to; *bhāgam*—proper share; *lokayoḥ*—of planetary systems; *ubhayoḥ*—both; *hitam*—welfare.

TRANSLATION

This King alone, in his own body, will be able in due course of time to maintain all living entities and keep them in a pleasant condition by manifesting himself as different demigods to perform various departmental activities. Thus he will maintain the upper planetary system by inducing

the populace to perform Vedic sacrifices. In due course of time he will also maintain this earthly planet by discharging proper rainfall.

PURPORT

The demigods in charge of the various departmental activities that maintain this world are but assistants to the Supreme Personality of Godhead. When an incarnation of Godhead descends on this planet, demigods like the sun-god, the moon-god, or the King of heaven, Indra, all join Him. Consequently the incarnation of Godhead is able to act for the departmental demigods to keep the planetary systems in order. The protection of the earthly planet is dependent on proper rainfall, and as stated in *Bhagavad-gītā* and other scriptures, sacrifices are performed to please those demigods who are in charge of rainfall.

annād bhavanti bhūtāni
parjanyād anna-sambhavaḥ
yajñād bhavati parjanyo
yajñaḥ karma-samudbhavaḥ

"All living bodies subsist on food grains, which are produced from rains. Rains are produced by performance of *yajña* [sacrifice], and *yajña* is born of prescribed duties." (Bg. 3.14)

Thus the proper execution of *yajña,* sacrifice, is required. As indicated herein, King Pṛthu alone would induce all the citizens to engage in such sacrificial activities so that there would not be scarcity or distress. In Kali-yuga, however, in the so-called secular state, the executive branch of government is in the charge of so-called kings and presidents who are all fools and rascals ignorant of the intricacies of nature's causes and ignorant of the principles of sacrifice. Such rascals simply make various plans, which always fail, and the people subsequently suffer disturbances. To counteract this situation, the *śāstras* advise: *harer nāma harer nāma harer nāmaiva kevalam/ kalau nāsty eva nāsty eva nāsty eva gatir anyathā*. Thus in order to counteract this unfortunate situation in government, the general populace is advised to chant the *mahā-mantra:* Hare Kṛṣṇa, Hare Kṛṣṇa, Kṛṣṇa Kṛṣṇa, Hare Hare/ Hare Rāma, Hare Rāma, Rāma Rāma, Hare Hare.

TEXT 6

वसु काल उपादत्ते काले चायं विमुञ्चति ।
समः सर्वेषु भूतेषु प्रतपन् सूर्यवद्विभुः ॥ ६ ॥

vasu kāla upādatte
kāle cāyaṁ vimuñcati
samaḥ sarveṣu bhūteṣu
pratapan sūryavad vibhuḥ

vasu—riches; *kāle*—in due course of time; *upādatte*—exacts; *kāle*—in due course of time; *ca*—also; *ayam*—this King Pṛthu; *vimuñcati*—returns; *samaḥ*—equal; *sarveṣu*—to all; *bhūteṣu*—living entities; *pratapan*—shining; *sūrya-vat*—like the sun-god; *vibhuḥ*—powerful.

TRANSLATION

This King Pṛthu will be as powerful as the sun-god, and just as the sun-god equally distributes his sunshine to everyone, King Pṛthu will distribute his mercy equally. Similarly, just as the sun-god evaporates water for eight months and, during the rainy season, returns it profusely, similarly this King will also exact taxes from the citizens and return these monies in times of need.

PURPORT

The process of tax exaction is very nicely explained in this verse. Tax exaction is not meant for the sense gratification of the so-called administrative heads. Tax revenues should be distributed to the citizens in times of need, during emergencies such as famine or flood. Tax revenues should never be distributed amongst governmental servants in the form of high salaries and various other allowances. In Kali-yuga, however, the position of the citizens is very horrible because taxes are exacted in so many forms and are spent for the personal comforts of the administrators.

The example of the sun in this verse is very appropriate. The sun is many millions of miles away from the earth, and although the sun does not actually touch the earth, it manages to distribute land all over the planet by exacting water from the oceans and seas, and it also manages to make that land fertile by distributing water during the rainy season. As an ideal king, Pṛthu would execute all this business in the village and state as expertly as the sun.

TEXT 7

तितिक्षत्यक्रमं वैन्य उपर्याक्रमतामपि ।
भूतानां करुणः शश्वदार्तानां क्षितिवृत्तिमान् ॥ ७ ॥

titikṣaty akramaṁ vainya
upary ākramatām api
bhūtānāṁ karuṇaḥ śaśvad
ārtānāṁ kṣiti-vṛttimān

titikṣati—tolerates; *akramam*—offense; *vainyaḥ*—the son of King Vena; *upari*—on his head; *ākramatām*—of those who are trampling; *api*—also; *bhūtānām*—to all living entities; *karuṇaḥ*—very kindhearted; *śaśvat*—always; *ārtānām*—to the aggrieved; *kṣiti-vṛtti-mān*—accepting the profession of the earth.

TRANSLATION

This King Pṛthu will be very, very kind to all citizens. Even though a poor person may trample over the King's head by violating the rules and regulations, the King, out of his causeless mercy, will be forgetful and forgiving. As a protector of the world, he will be as tolerant as the earth itself.

PURPORT

King Pṛthu is herein compared to the earthly planet as far as his tolerance is concerned. Although the earth is always trampled upon by men and animals, it still gives food to them by producing grains, fruits and vegetables. As an ideal king, Mahārāja Pṛthu is compared to the earthly planet, for even though some citizens might violate the rules and regulations of the state, he would still be tolerant and maintain them with fruits and grains. In other words, it is the duty of the king to look after the comforts of the citizens, even at the cost of his own personal convenience. This is not the case, however, in Kali-yuga, for in Kali-yuga the kings and heads of state enjoy life at the cost of taxes exacted from the citizens. Such unfair taxation makes the people dishonest, and the people try to hide their income in so many ways. Eventually the state will not be able to collect taxes and consequently will not be able to meet its huge military and administrative expenses. Everything will collapse, and there will be chaos and disturbance all over the state.

TEXT 8

देवेऽवर्षत्यसौ देवो नरदेववपुर्हरिः ।
कृच्छ्रप्राणाः प्रजा ह्येष रक्षिष्यत्यञ्जसेन्द्रवत् ॥ ८ ॥

deve 'varṣaty asau devo
naradeva-vapur hariḥ

kṛcchra-prāṇāḥ prajā hy eṣa
rakṣiṣyaty añjasendravat

deve—when the demigod (Indra); *avarṣati*—does not supply rains; *asau*—that; *devaḥ*—Mahārāja Pṛthu; *nara-deva*—of the king; *vapuḥ*—having the body; *hariḥ*—the Supreme Personality of Godhead; *kṛcchra-prāṇāḥ*—suffering living entities; *prajāḥ*—the citizens; *hi*—certainly; *eṣaḥ*—this; *rakṣiṣyati*—will protect; *añjasā*—very easily; *indra-vat*—like King Indra.

TRANSLATION

When there is no rainfall and the citizens are in great danger due to the scarcity of water, this royal personality of Godhead will be able to supply rains exactly like the heavenly King Indra. Thus he will very easily be able to protect the citizens from drought.

PURPORT

King Pṛthu is very appropriately compared to the sun and the demigod Indra. King Indra of the heavenly planets is in charge of distributing water over the earth and other planetary systems. It is indicated that King Pṛthu would arrange for the distribution of rainfall personally if Indra failed to discharge his duty properly. It is, however, indicated that sometimes the King of heaven, Indra, would become angry at the inhabitants of the earth if they did not offer sacrifices to appease him. However, being an incarnation of the Supreme Personality of Godhead, King Pṛthu did not depend on the mercy of the heavenly King. It is foretold herein that if there would be a scarcity of rain, King Pṛthu would manage to counteract the deficiency by virtue of his godly powers. Such powers were also exhibited by Lord Kṛṣṇa when He was present in Vṛndāvana. Indeed, when Indra poured incessant water on Vṛndāvana for seven days, the inhabitants were protected by Kṛṣṇa, who raised Govardhana Hill over their heads as a great umbrella. Thus Lord Kṛṣṇa is also known as *govardhana-dhārī.*

TEXT 9

आप्याययत्यसौ लोकं वदनामृतमूर्तिना ।
सानुरागावलोकेन विशदस्मितचारुणा ॥ ९ ॥

āpyāyayaty asau lokaṁ
vadanāmṛta-mūrtinā

sānurāgāvalokena
viśada-smita-cāruṇā

āpyāyayati—enhances; *asau*—he; *lokam*—the whole world; *vadana*—by his face; *amṛta-mūrtinā*—moonlike; *sa-anurāga*—affectionate; *avalokena*—with glances; *viśada*—bright; *smita*—smiling; *cāruṇā*—beautiful.

TRANSLATION

This King, Pṛthu Mahārāja, by virtue of his affectionate glances and beautiful full face, which is always smiling with great affection for the citizens, will enhance everyone's peaceful life.

TEXT 10

अव्यक्तवर्त्मैष निगूढकार्यो
गम्भीरवेधा उपगुप्तवित्तः ।
अनन्तमाहात्म्यगुणैकधामा
पृथुः प्रचेता इव संवृतात्मा ॥१०॥

avyakta-vartmaiṣa nigūḍha-kāryo
gambhīra-vedhā upagupta-vittaḥ
ananta-māhātmya-guṇaika-dhāmā
pṛthuḥ pracetā iva saṁvṛtātmā

avyakta—nonmanifested; *vartmā*—his policies; *eṣaḥ*—this King; *nigūḍha*—confidential; *kāryaḥ*—his activities; *gambhīra*—grave, secret; *vedhāḥ*—his accomplishing; *upagupta*—secretly kept; *vittaḥ*—his treasury; *ananta*—unlimited; *māhātmya*—of glories; *guṇa*—of good qualities; *eka-dhāmā*—the only reservoir; *pṛthuḥ*—King Pṛthu; *pracetāḥ*—Varuṇa, the King of the seas; *iva*—like; *saṁvṛta*—covered; *ātmā*—self.

TRANSLATION

The reciters continued: No one will be able to understand the policies the King will follow. His activities will also be very confidential, and it will not be possible for anyone to know how he will make every activity successful. His treasury will always remain unknown to everyone. He will be the reservoir of unlimited glories and good qualities, and his position will be maintained and covered just as Varuṇa, the deity of the seas, is covered all around by water.

PURPORT

There is a predominating deity for all the material elements, and Varuṇa, or Pracetā, is the predominating deity of the seas and the oceans. From outward appearances the seas and oceans appear devoid of life, but a person acquainted with the sea knows that within the water exist many varieties of life. The king of that underwater kingdom is Varuṇa. Just as no one can understand what is going on beneath the sea, no one could understand what policy King Pṛthu was following to make everything successful. Indeed, King Pṛthu's path of diplomacy was very grave. His success was made possible because he was a reservior of unlimited glorified qualities.

The word *upagupta-vittaḥ* is very significant in this verse. It indicates that no one would know the extent of the riches King Pṛthu would confidentially keep. The idea is that not only the king but everyone should keep his hard earned money confidentially and secretly so that in due course of time the money can be spent for good practical purposes. In Kali-yuga, however, the king or government has no well-protected treasury, and the only means of circulation is currency notes made of paper. Thus in times of distress the government will artificially inflate the currency by simply printing papers, and this artificially raises the price of commodities, and the general condition of the citizens becomes very precarious. Thus keeping one's money very secretly is an old practice, for we find this practice present even during the reign of Mahārāja Pṛthu. Just as the king has the right to keep his treasury confidential and secret, the people should also keep their individual earnings a secret. There is no fault in such dealings. The main point is that everyone should be trained in the system of *varṇāśrama-dharma* so that the money is spent only for good causes and nothing else.

TEXT 11

दुरासदो दुर्विषह आसन्नोऽपि विदूरवत् ।
नैवाभिभवितुं शक्यो वेनारण्युत्थितोऽनलः ॥११॥

durāsado durviṣaha
āsanno 'pi vidūravat
naivābhibhavitum śakyo
venārany-utthito 'nalaḥ

durāsadaḥ—unapproachable; *durviṣahaḥ*—unbearable; *āsannaḥ*—being approached; *api*—although; *vidūra-vat*—as if far away; *na*—never; *eva*—

certainly; *abhibhavitum*—to be overcome; *śakyaḥ*—able; *vena*—King Vena; *araṇi*—the wood that produces fire; *utthitaḥ*—being born of; *analaḥ*—fire.

TRANSLATION

King Pṛthu was born of the dead body of King Vena as fire is produced from araṇi wood. Thus King Pṛthu will always remain just like fire, and his enemies will not be able to approach him. Indeed, he will be unbearable to his enemies, for although staying very near him, they will never be able to approach him but will have to remain as if far away. No one will be able to overcome the strength of King Pṛthu.

PURPORT

Araṇi wood is a kind of fuel used to ignite fire by friction. At the time of performing sacrifices, one can ignite a fire from *araṇi* wood. Although born of his dead father, King Pṛthu would still remain just like fire. Just as fire is not easily approached, similarly King Pṛthu would be unapproachable by his enemies, even though they would appear to be very near him.

TEXT 12

अन्तर्बहिश्च भूतानां पश्यन् कर्माणि चारणैः ।
उदासीन इवाध्यक्षो वायुरात्मेव देहिनाम् ॥१२॥

antar bahiś ca bhūtānām
paśyan karmāṇi cāraṇaiḥ
udāsīna ivādhyakṣo
vāyur ātmeva dehinām

antaḥ—internally; *bahiḥ*—externally; *ca*—and; *bhūtānām*—of living entities; *paśyan*—seeing; *karmāṇi*—activities; *cāraṇaiḥ*—by spies; *udāsīnaḥ*—neutral; *iva*—like; *adhyakṣaḥ*—the witness; *vāyuḥ*—the air of life; *ātmā*—the living force; *iva*—like; *dehinām*—of all the embodied.

TRANSLATION

King Pṛthu will be able to see all the internal and external activities of every one of his citizens. Still no one will be able to know his system of espionage, and he himself will remain neutral regarding all matters of glorification or vilification paid to him. He will be exactly like air, the life force

within the body, which is exhibited internally and externally but is always neutral to all affairs.

TEXT 13

नादण्ड्यं दण्डयत्येष सुतमात्मद्विषामपि ।
दण्डयत्यात्मजमपि दण्ड्यं धर्मपथे स्थितः ॥१३॥

nādaṇḍyaṁ daṇḍayaty eṣa
sutam ātma-dviṣām api
daṇḍayaty ātma-jam api
daṇḍyaṁ dharma-pathe sthitaḥ

na—not; *adaṇḍyam*—not punishable; *daṇḍayati*—punishes; *eṣaḥ*—this King; *sutam*—the son; *ātma-dviṣām*—of his enemies; *api*—even; *daṇḍayati*—he punishes; *ātma-jam*—his own son; *api*—even; *daṇḍyan*—punishable; *dharma-pathe*—on the path of piety; *sthitaḥ*—being situated.

TRANSLATION

Since this King will always remain on the path of piety, he will be neutral to both his son and the son of his enemy. If the son of his enemy is not punishable, he will not punish him, but if his son is punishable, he will immediately punish him.

PURPORT

These are the characteristics of an impartial ruler. It is the duty of a ruler to punish the criminal and give protection to the innocent. King Pṛthu was so neutral that if his own son were punishable, he would not hesitate to punish him. On the other hand, if the son of his enemy were innocent, he would not engage in some intrigue in order to punish him.

TEXT 14

अस्याप्रतिहतं चक्रं पृथोरामानसाचलात् ।
वर्तते भगवानर्को यावत्तपति गोगणैः ॥१४॥

asyāpratihataṁ cakraṁ
pṛthor āmānasācalāt
vartate bhagavān arko
yāvat tapati go-gaṇaiḥ

asya—of this King; *apratihatam*—not being impeded; *cakram*—the circle of influence; *pṛthoḥ*—of King Pṛthu; *ā-mānasa-acalāt*—up to the Mānasa mountain; *vartate*—remains; *bhagavān*—the most powerful; *arkaḥ*—sun-god; *yāvat*—just as; *tapati*—shines; *go-gaṇaiḥ*—with rays of light.

TRANSLATION

Just as the sun-god expands his shining rays up to the Arctic region without impedance, the influence of King Pṛthu will cover all tracts of land up to the Arctic region and will remain undisturbed as long as he lives.

PURPORT

Although the Arctic region is not visible to ordinary persons, the sun nonetheless shines there without impediment. Just as no one can check the sunshine from spreading all over the universe, no one could check the influence and reign of King Pṛthu, which would remain undisturbed as long as he lived. The conclusion is that the sunshine and the sun-god cannot be separated, nor can King Pṛthu and his ruling strength be separated. His rule over everyone would continue without disturbance. Thus the King could not be separated from his ruling power.

TEXT 15

रञ्जयिष्यति यल्लोकमयमात्मविचेष्टितैः ।
अथामुमाहू राजानं मनोरञ्जनकैः प्रजाः ॥१५॥

rañjayiṣyati yal lokam
ayam ātma-viceṣṭitaiḥ
athāmum āhū rājānam
mano-rañjanakaiḥ prajāḥ

rañjayiṣyati—will please; *yat*—because; *lokam*—the entire world; *ayam*—this King; *ātma*—personal; *viceṣṭitaiḥ*—by activities; *atha*—therefore; *amum*—him; *āhuḥ*—they call; *rājānam*—the King; *manaḥ-rañjanakaiḥ*—very pleasing to the mind; *prajāḥ*—the citizens.

TRANSLATION

This King will please everyone by his practical activities, and all of his citizens will remain very satisfied. Because of this the citizens will take great satisfaction in accepting him as their ruling king.

TEXT 16

दृढव्रतः सत्यसन्धो ब्रह्मण्यो वृद्धसेवकः ।
शरण्यः सर्वभूतानां मानदो दीनवत्सलः ॥१६॥

dṛḍha-vrataḥ satya-sandho
brahmaṇyo vṛddha-sevakaḥ
śaraṇyaḥ sarva-bhūtānām
mānado dīna-vatsalaḥ

dṛḍha-vrataḥ—firmly determined; _satya-sandhaḥ_—always situated in truth; _brahmaṇyaḥ_—a lover of the brahminical culture; _vṛddha-sevakaḥ_—a servitor of the old men; _śaraṇyaḥ_—to be taken shelter of; _sarva-bhūtānām_—of all living entities; _māna-daḥ_—one who gives respect to all; _dīna-vatsalaḥ_—very kind to the poor and helpless.

TRANSLATION

The King will be firmly determined and always situated in truth. He will be a lover of the brahminical culture and will render all service to old men and give shelter to all surrendered souls. Giving respect to all, he will always be merciful to the poor and innocent.

PURPORT

The word *vṛddha-sevakaḥ* is very significant. *Vṛddha* means "old men." There are two kinds of old men: one is old by age, and another is old by knowledge. This Sanskrit word indicates that one can be older by the advancement of knowledge. King Pṛthu was very respectful to the *brāhmaṇas,* and he protected them. He also protected persons advanced in age. Whatever the King would decide to do, no one would be able to stop. That is called *dṛḍha-saṅkalpa* or *dṛḍha-vrata.*

TEXT 17

मातृभक्तिः परस्त्रीषु पत्न्यामर्ध इवात्मनः ।
प्रजासु पितृवत्स्निग्धः किङ्करो ब्रह्मवादिनाम् ॥१७॥

mātṛ-bhaktiḥ para-strīṣu
patnyām ardha ivātmanaḥ
prajāsu pitṛvat snigdhaḥ
kiṅkaro brahma-vādinām

mātṛ-bhaktiḥ—respectful as one is to his mother; *para-strīṣu*—to other women; *patnyām*—to his own wife; *ardhaḥ*—half; *iva*—like; *ātmanaḥ*—of his body; *prajāsu*—unto the citizens; *pitṛ-vat*—like a father; *snigdhaḥ*—affectionate; *kiṅkaraḥ*—servant; *brahma-vādinām*—of the devotees who preach the glories of the Lord.

TRANSLATION

The King will respect all women as if they were his own mother, and he will treat his own wife as the other half of his body. He will be just like an affectionate father to his citizens, and he will treat himself as the most obedient servant of the devotees who always preach the glories of the Lord.

PURPORT

A learned man treats all women except his wife as his mother, looks on others' property as garbage in the street, and treats others as he would treat his own self. These are the symptoms of a learned person as described by Cāṇakya Paṇḍita. This should be the standard for education. Education does not mean having academic degrees only. One should execute what he has learned in his personal life. These learned characteristics were verily manifest in the life of King Pṛthu. Although he was king, he treated himself as a servant of the Lord's devotees. According to Vedic etiquette, if a devotee came to a king's palace, the king would immediately offer his own seat to him. The word *brahma-vādinām* is very significant. *Brahma-vādī* refers to the devotees of the Lord. Brahman, Paramātmā and Bhagavān are different terms for the Supreme Brahman, and the Supreme Brahman is Lord Kṛṣṇa. This is accepted in *Bhagavad-gītā* by Arjuna (*paraṁ brahma paraṁ dhāma,* Bg. 10.12). Thus the word *brahma-vādinām* refers to the devotees of the Lord. The state should always serve the devotees of the Lord, and the ideal state should conduct itself according to the instructions of the devotee. Because King Pṛthu followed this principle, he is highly praised.

TEXT 18

देहिनामात्मवत्प्रेष्ठः सुहृदां नन्दिवर्धनः ।
मुक्तसङ्गप्रसङ्गोऽयं दण्डपाणिरसाधुषु ॥१८॥

dehinām ātmavat-preṣṭhaḥ
suhṛdāṁ nandi-vardhanaḥ
mukta-saṅga-prasaṅgo 'yaṁ
daṇḍa-pāṇir asādhuṣu

dehinām—to all living entities having a body; *ātma-vat*—as himself; *preṣṭhaḥ*—considering as dear; *suhṛdām*—of his friends; *nandi-vardhanaḥ*—increasing pleasures; *mukta-saṅga*—with persons devoid of all material contamination; *prasaṅgaḥ*—intimately associated; *ayam*—this King; *daṇḍa-pāṇiḥ*—a chastising hand; *asādhuṣu*—to the criminals.

TRANSLATION

The King will consider all embodied living entities as dear as his own self, and he will always be increasing the pleasures of his friends. He will intimately associate with liberated persons, and he will be a chastising hand to all impious persons.

PURPORT

The word *dehinām* refers to those who are embodied. The living entities are embodied in different forms, which number 8,400,000 species. All of these were treated by the King in the same way he would treat himself. In this age, however, so-called kings and presidents do not treat all other living entities as their own self. Most of them are meat-eaters, and even though they may not be meat-eaters and may pose themselves to be very religious and pious, they still allow cow slaughter within their state. Such sinful heads of state cannot actually be popular at any time. Another significant word in this verse is *mukta-saṅga-prasaṅgaḥ*, which indicates that the King was always associating with liberated persons.

TEXT 19

अयं तु साक्षाद्भगवांस्त्र्यधीशः
कूटस्थ आत्मा कलयावतीर्णः ।
यस्मिन्नविद्यारचितं निरर्थकं
पश्यन्ति नानात्वमपि प्रतीतम् ॥१९॥

ayaṁ tu sākṣād bhagavāṁs try-adhīśaḥ
kūṭastha ātmā kalayāvatīrṇaḥ
yasminn avidyā-racitaṁ nirarthakaṁ
paśyanti nānātvam api pratītam

ayam—this King; *tu*—then; *sākṣāt*—directly; *bhagavān*—the Supreme Personality of Godhead; *tri-adhīśaḥ*—the master of the three planetary systems; *kūṭasthaḥ*—without any change; *ātmā*—the Supersoul; *kalayā*—by a partial plenary expansion; *avatīrṇaḥ*—descended; *yasmin*—in whom; *avidyā-racitam*—created by nescience; *nirarthakam*—without meaning; *paśyanti*—they see; *nānātvam*—material variegatedness; *api*—certainly; *pratītam*—understood.

TRANSLATION

This King is the master of the three worlds, and he is directly empowered by the Supreme Personality of Godhead. He is without change, and he is an incarnation of the Supreme known as a śaktyāveśa-avatāra. Being a liberated soul and completely learned, he understands that all material varieties are without meaning because their basic principle is nescience.

PURPORT

The reciters of these prayers are describing the transcendental qualities of Pṛthu Mahārāja. These qualities are summarized in the words *sākṣād bhagavān.* This indicates that Mahārāja Pṛthu is directly the Supreme Personality of Godhead and therefore possesses unlimited good qualities. Being an incarnation of the Supreme Personality of Godhead, Mahārāja Pṛthu could not be equaled in his excellent qualities. The Supreme Personality of Godhead is fully equipped with six kinds of opulences, and King Pṛthu was also empowered in such a way that he could display these six opulences of the Supreme Personality of Godhead in full.

The word *kūṭastha,* meaning "without change," is also very significant. There are two kinds of living entities—*nitya-mukta* and *nitya-baddha.* A *nitya-mukta* never forgets his position as the eternal servant of the Supreme Personality of Godhead. One who does not forget this position and knows that he is part and parcel of the Supreme Lord is *nitya-mukta.* Such a *nitya-mukta* living entity represents the Supersoul as His expansion. As stated in the *Vedas, nityo nityānām.* Thus the *nitya-mukta* living entity knows that he is an expansion of the supreme *nitya,* or the eternal Supreme Personality of Godhead. Being in such a position, he sees the material world with a different vision. The living entity who is *nitya-baddha,* or eternally conditioned, sees the material varieties as being actually different from one another. In this connection we should remember that the embodiment of the conditioned soul is considered to be like a dress. One may dress in different ways, but a really learned man does not take dresses into consideration. As stated in *Bhagavad-gītā:*

vidyā-vinaya-sampanne
brāhmaṇe gavi hastini

śuni caiva śvapāke ca
paṇḍitāḥ sama-darśinaḥ

"The humble sage, by virtue of true knowledge, sees with equal vision a learned and gentle *brāhmaṇa,* a cow, an elephant, a dog and a dog-eater [outcaste]." (Bg. 5.18)

Thus a learned man does not look upon the dresses that externally cover the living entity but sees the pure soul within the varieties of dress and knows very well that the varieties of dress are the creation of nescience (*avidyā-racitam*). Being a *śaktyāveśa-avatāra* empowered by the Supreme Personality of Godhead, Pṛthu Mahārāja did not change his spiritual position, and consequently there was no possibility of his viewing the material world as reality.

TEXT 20

अयं भुवो मण्डलमोदयाद्रे-
गोप्तैकवीरो नरदेवनाथः ।
आस्थाय जैत्रं रथमात्तचापः
पर्यस्यते दक्षिणतो यथार्कः ॥२०॥

ayaṁ bhuvo maṇḍalam odayādrer
goptaika-vīro naradeva-nāthaḥ
āsthāya jaitraṁ ratham ātta-cāpaḥ
paryasyate dakṣiṇato yathārkaḥ

ayam—this King; *bhuvaḥ*—of the world; *maṇḍalam*—the globe; *ā-udaya-adreḥ*—from the mountain where the first appearance of the sun is visible; *goptā*—will protect; *eka*—uniquely; *vīraḥ*—powerful, heroic; *nara-deva*—of all kings, gods in human society; *nāthaḥ*—the master; *āsthāya*—being situated on; *jaitram*—victorious; *ratham*—his chariot; *ātta-cāpaḥ*—holding the bow; *paryasyate*—he will circumambulate; *dakṣiṇataḥ*—from the southern side; *yathā*—like; *arkaḥ*—the sun.

TRANSLATION

This King, being uniquely powerful and heroic, will have no competitor. He will travel around the globe on his victorious chariot, holding his invincible bow in his hand and appearing exactly like the sun, which rotates in its own orbit from the south.

PURPORT

In this verse the word *yathārkaḥ* indicates that the sun is not fixed but is rotating in its orbit, which is set by the Supreme Personality of Godhead. This is confirmed in the *Brahma-saṁhitā* and also in other parts of *Śrīmad-Bhāgavatam.* In the Fifth Canto of *Śrīmad-Bhāgavatam* it is stated that the sun rotates in its own orbit at the rate of 16,000 miles per second. Similarly, *Brahma-saṁhitā* states: *yasyājñayā bhramati sambhṛta-kāla-cakraḥ.* The sun rotates in its own orbit according to the order of the Supreme Personality of Godhead. The conclusion is that the sun is not fixed in one place. As far as Pṛthu Mahārāja is concerned, it is indicated that his ruling power would extend all over the world. The Himalayan Mountains, from which the sunrise is first seen, are called *udayācala* or *udayādri.* It is herein indicated that Pṛthu Mahārāja's reign over the world would cover even the Himalayan Mountains and extend to the borders of all oceans and seas. In other words, his reign would cover the entire planet.

Another significant word in this verse is *naradeva.* As described in previous verses, the qualified king—be he King Pṛthu or any other king who rules over the state as an ideal king—should be understood to be God in human form. According to Vedic culture, the king is honored as the Supreme Personality of Godhead because he represents Nārāyaṇa, who also gives protection to the citizens. He is therefore *nātha*, or the proprietor. Even Sanātana Gosvāmī gave respect to the Nawab Hussain Shah as *naradeva,* although the Nawab was Mohammedan. A king or governmental head must therefore be so competent to rule over the state that the citizens will worship him as God in human form. That is the perfectional stage for the head of any government or state.

TEXT 21

अस्मै नृपालाः किल तत्र तत्र
बलिं हरिष्यन्ति सलोकपालाः ।
मंस्यन्त एषां स्त्रिय आदिराजं
चक्रायुधं तद्यश उद्धरन्त्यः ॥२१॥

asmai nṛpālāḥ kila tatra tatra
baliṁ hariṣyanti salokapālāḥ
maṁsyanta eṣāṁ striya ādi-rājaṁ
cakrāyudhaṁ tad-yaśa uddharantyaḥ

asmai—unto him; *nṛ-pālāḥ*—all the kings; *kila*—certainly; *tatra tatra*—here and there; *balim*—presentations; *hariṣyanti*—will offer; *sa*—with; *loka-pālāḥ*—the demigods; *maṁsyante*—will consider; *eṣām*—of these kings; *striyaḥ*—wives; *ādi-rājam*—the original king; *cakra-āyudham*—bearing the disc weapon; *tat*—his; *yaśaḥ*—reputation; *uddharantyaḥ*—carrying on.

TRANSLATION

When the King travels all over the world, other kings, as well as the demigods, will offer him all kinds of presentations. Their queens will also consider him the original king, who carries in his hands the emblems of club and disc, and will sing of his fame, for he will be as reputable as the Supreme Personality of Godhead.

PURPORT

As far as reputation is concerned, King Pṛthu is already known as the incarnation of the Supreme Personality of Godhead. The word *ādi-rājam* means "the original king." The original king is Nārāyaṇa, or Lord Viṣṇu. People do not know that the original king, or Nārāyaṇa, is actually the protector of all living entities. As confirmed in the *Vedas: eko bahūnāṁ yo vidadhāti kāmān* (*Kaṭha Up.* 2.2.13). Actually the Supreme Personality of Godhead is maintaining all living entities. The king, or *naradeva,* is His representative. As such, the king's duty is to personally supervise the distribution of wealth for the maintenance of all living entities. If he does so, he will be as reputable as Nārāyaṇa. As mentioned in this verse (*tad-yaśaḥ*), Pṛthu Mahārāja was actually carrying with him the reputation of the Supreme Personality of Godhead because he was actually reigning over the world in that capacity.

TEXT 22

अयं महीं गां दुदुहेऽधिराजः
प्रजापतिर्वृत्तिकरः प्रजानाम् ।
यो लीलयाद्रीन् स्वशरासकोट्या
भिन्दन् समां गामकरोद्यथेन्द्रः ॥२२॥

ayaṁ mahīṁ gāṁ duduhe 'dhirājaḥ
prajāpatir vṛtti-karaḥ prajānām
yo līlayādrīn sva-śarāsa-koṭyā
bhindan samāṁ gām akarod yathendraḥ

ayam—this King; *mahīm*—the earth; *gām*—in the form of a cow; *duduhe*—will milk; *adhirājaḥ*—extraordinary king; *prajā-patiḥ*—progenitor of mankind; *vṛtti-karaḥ*—providing living facility; *prajānām*—of the citizens; *yaḥ*—one who; *līlayā*—simply by pastimes; *adrīn*—mountains and hills; *sva-śarāsa*—of his bow; *koṭyā*—by the pointed end; *bhindan*—breaking; *samām*—level; *gām*—the earth; *akarot*—will make; *yathā*—as; *indraḥ*—the King of heaven, Indra.

TRANSLATION

This King, this protector of the citizens, is an extraordinary king and is equal to the prajāpati demigods. For the living facility of all citizens, he will milk the earth, which is like a cow. Not only that, but he will level the surface of the earth with the pointed ends of his bow, breaking all the hills exactly as King Indra, the heavenly King, breaks mountains with his powerful thunderbolt.

TEXT 23

विस्फूर्जयन्नाजगवं धनुः स्वयं
यदाचरत्क्ष्मामविषह्यमाजौ ।
तदा निलिल्युर्दिशि दिश्यसन्तो
लाङ्गूलमुद्यम्य यथा मृगेन्द्रः ॥२३॥

visphūrjayann ājagavaṁ dhanuḥ svayaṁ
yadācarat kṣmām aviṣahyam ājau
tadā nililyur diśi diśy asanto
lāṅgūlam udyamya yathā mṛgendraḥ

visphūrjayan—vibrating; *āja-gavam*—made of the horns of goats and bulls; *dhanuḥ*—his bow; *svayam*—personally; *yadā*—when; *acarat*—will travel; *kṣmām*—on the earth; *aviṣahyam*—irresistible; *ājau*—in battle; *tadā*—at that time; *nililyuḥ*—will hide themselves; *diśi diśi*—in all directions; *asantaḥ*—demoniac men; *lāṅgūlam*—tail; *udyamya*—keeping high; *yathā*—as; *mṛgendraḥ*—the lion.

TRANSLATION

When the lion travels in the forest with its tail turned upward, all menial animals hide themselves. Similarly, when King Pṛthu will travel over his kingdom and vibrate the string of his bow, which is made of the horns of goats and bulls and is irresistible in battle, all demoniac rogues and thieves will hide themselves in all directions.

PURPORT

It is very appropriate to compare a powerful king like Pṛthu to a lion. In India, *kṣatriya* kings are still called *simha,* which means "lion." Unless rogues, thieves and other demoniac people in a state are afraid of the executive head, who rules the kingdom with a strong hand, there cannot be peace or prosperity in the state. Thus it is most regrettable when a woman becomes the executive head instead of a lion-like king. In such a situation the people are considered very unfortunate.

TEXT 24

एषोऽश्वमेधाञ् शतमाजहार
सरस्वती प्रादुरभावि यत्र ।
अहार्षीद्यस्य हयं पुरन्दरः
शतक्रतुश्चरमे वर्तमाने ॥२४॥

eṣo 'śvamedhāñ śatam ājahāra
sarasvatī prādur abhāvi yatra
ahārṣīd yasya hayaṁ purandaraḥ
śata-kratuś carame vartamāne

eṣaḥ—this King; *aśvamedhān*—sacrifices known as *aśvamedha; śatam*—one hundred; *ājahāra*—will perform; *sarasvatī*—the river of the name Sarasvatī; *prāduḥ abhāvi*—became manifest; *yatra*—where; *ahārṣīt*—will steal; *yasya*—whose; *hayam*—horse; *purandaraḥ*—the Lord Indra; *śata-kratuḥ*—who performed one hundred sacrifices; *carame*—while the last sacrifice; *vartamāne*—is occurring.

TRANSLATION

At the source of the River Sarasvatī, this King will perform one hundred sacrifices known as aśvamedha. In the course of the last sacrifice, the heavenly King Indra will steal the sacrificial horse.

TEXT 25

एष स्वसद्मोपवने समेत्य
सनत्कुमारं भगवन्तमेकम् ।
आराध्य भक्त्यालभतामलं तज-
ज्ञानं यतो ब्रह्म परं विदन्ति ॥२५॥

eṣa sva-sadmopavane sametya
sanat-kumāraṁ bhagavantam ekam
ārādhya bhaktyālabhatāmalaṁ taj-
jñānaṁ yato brahma paraṁ vidanti

eṣaḥ—this King; *sva-sadma*—of his palace; *upavane*—in the garden; *sametya*—meeting; *sanat-kumāram*—Sanat-kumāra; *bhagavantam*—the worshipable; *ekam*—alone; *ārādhya*—worshiping; *bhaktyā*—with devotion; *alabhata*—he will achieve; *amalam*—without contamination; *tat*—that; *jñānam*—transcendental knowledge; *yataḥ*—by which; *brahma*—spirit; *param*—supreme, transcendental; *vidanti*—they enjoy, they know.

TRANSLATION

This King Pṛthu will meet Sanat-kumāra, one of the four Kumāras, in the garden of his palace compound. The King will worship him with devotion and will be fortunate to receive instructions by which one can enjoy transcendental bliss.

PURPORT

The word *vidanti* refers to one who knows something or enjoys something. When a person is properly instructed by a spiritual master and understands transcendental bliss, he enjoys life. As stated in *Bhagavad-gītā:*

brahma-bhūtaḥ prasannātmā
na śocati na kāṅkṣati
samaḥ sarveṣu bhūteṣu
mad-bhaktiṁ labhate parām

"One who is thus transcendentally situated at once realizes the Supreme Brahman. He never laments nor desires to have anything; he is equally disposed to every living entity. In that state he attains pure devotional service unto Me." (Bg. 18.54)

When one attains to the Brahman platform, he neither hankers nor laments. He actually partakes of transcendental blissful enjoyment. Although King Pṛthu was an incarnation of Viṣṇu, he nonetheless taught the people in his kingdom to take instructions from a spiritual master who represents the disciplic succession. Thus one can become fortunate and enjoy a blissful life even within this material world. In this verse the verb *vidanti* is sometimes taken to mean "understanding." Thus when a person understands Brahman, or the supreme source of everything, he enjoys a blissful life.

TEXT 26

तत्र तत्र गिरस्तास्ता इति विश्रुतविक्रमः ।
श्रोष्यत्यात्माश्रिता गाथाः पृथुः पृथुपराक्रमः ॥२६॥

tatra tatra giras tās tā
iti viśruta-vikramaḥ
śroṣyaty ātmāśritā gāthāḥ
pṛthuḥ pṛthu-parākramaḥ

tatra tatra—here and there; *giraḥ*—words; *tāḥ tāḥ*—many, various; *iti*—thus; *viśruta-vikramaḥ*—he whose chivalrous activities are widely reputed; *śroṣyati*—will hear; *ātma-āśritāḥ*—about himself; *gāthāḥ*—songs, narrations; *pṛthuḥ*—King Pṛthu; *pṛthu-parākramaḥ*—distinctly powerful.

TRANSLATION

In this way when the chivalrous activities of King Pṛthu come to be known to the people in general, King Pṛthu will always hear about himself and his activities.

PURPORT

To artificially advertise oneself and thus enjoy a so-called reputation is a kind of conceit. Pṛthu Mahārāja was famous amongst the people because of his chivalrous activities. He did not have to advertise himself artificially. One's factual reputation cannot be covered.

TEXT 27

दिशो विजित्याप्रतिरुद्धचक्रः
स्वतेजसोत्पाटितलोकशल्यः ।
सुरासुरेन्द्रैरुपगीयमान-
महानुभावो भविता पतिर्भुवः ॥२७॥

diśo vijityāpratiruddha-cakraḥ
sva-tejasotpāṭita-loka-śalyaḥ
surāsurendrair upagīyamāna-
mahānubhāvo bhavitā patir bhuvaḥ

diśaḥ—all directions; *vijitya*—conquering; *apratiruddha*—without check; *cakraḥ*—his influence or power; *sva-tejasā*—by his own prowess; *utpāṭita*—uprooted; *loka-śalyaḥ*—the miseries of the citizens; *sura*—of demigods; *asura*—of demons; *indraiḥ*—by the chiefs; *upagīyamāna*—being glorified; *mahā-anubhāvaḥ*—the great soul; *bhavitā*—he will become; *patiḥ*—the lord; *bhuvaḥ*—of the world.

TRANSLATION

No one will be able to disobey the orders of Pṛthu Mahārāja. After conquering the world, he will completely eradicate the threefold miseries of the citizens. Then he will be recognized all over the world. At that time both the suras and the asuras will undoubtedly glorify his magnanimous activities.

PURPORT

At the time of Mahārāja Pṛthu, the world was ruled by one emperor, although there were many subordinate states. Just as there are many united states in various parts of the world, in olden days the entire world was ruled through many states, but there was a supreme emperor who ruled over all subsidiary states. As soon as there were some discrepancies in the maintenance of the *varṇāśrama* system, the emperor would immediately take charge of the small states.

The word *utpāṭita-loka-śalyaḥ* indicates that Mahārāja Pṛthu completely uprooted all the miseries of his citizens. The word *śalya* means "piercing thorns." There are many kinds of miserable thorns that pierce the citizens of a state, but all competent rulers, even up to the reign of Mahārāja Yudhiṣṭhira, uprooted all the miserable conditions of the citizens. It is stated that during the reign of Mahārāja Yudhiṣṭhira there did not even exist severe cold or scorching heat, nor did the citizens suffer from any kind of mental anxiety. This is the standard of good government. Such a peaceful and prosperous government, devoid of anxiety, was established by Pṛthu Mahārāja. Thus the inhabitants of both saintly and demoniac planets were all engaged in glorifying the activities of Mahārāja Pṛthu. Persons or nations anxious to spread their influence all over the world should consider this point. If one is able to eradicate completely the threefold miseries of the citizens, he should aspire to rule the world. One should not aspire to rule for any political or diplomatic consideration.

Thus end the Bhaktivedanta purports of the Fourth Canto, Sixteenth Chapter, of the Śrīmad-Bhāgavatam, *entitled "Praise of King Pṛthu by the Professional Reciters."*

CHAPTER SEVENTEEN

Mahārāja Pṛthu Becomes Angry at the Earth

TEXT 1

मैत्रेय उवाच
एवं स भगवान् वैन्यः ख्यापितो गुणकर्मभिः ।
छन्दयामास तान् कामैः प्रतिपूज्याभिनन्द्य च ॥ १ ॥

maitreya uvāca
evaṁ sa bhagavān vainyaḥ
khyāpito guṇa-karmabhiḥ
chandayām āsa tān kāmaiḥ
pratipūjyābhinandya ca

maitreyaḥ uvāca—the great sage Maitreya continued to speak; *evam*—thus; *saḥ*—he; *bhagavān*—the Personality of Godhead; *vainyaḥ*—in the form of the son of King Vena; *khyāpitaḥ*—being glorified; *guṇa-karmabhiḥ*—by qualities and factual activities; *chandayām āsa*—pacified; *tān*—those reciters; *kāmaiḥ*—by various presentations; *pratipūjya*—offering all respects; *abhinandya*—offering prayers; *ca*—also.

TRANSLATION

The great sage Maitreya continued: In this way the reciters who were glorifying Mahārāja Pṛthu readily described his qualities and chivalrous activities. At the end, Mahārāja Pṛthu offered them various presentations with all due respect and worshiped them adequately.

TEXT 2

ब्राह्मणप्रमुखान् वर्णान् भृत्यामात्यपुरोधसः ।
पौराञ्जानपदान् श्रेणीः प्रकृतीः समपूजयत ॥ २ ॥

brāhmaṇa-pramukhān varṇān
bhṛtyāmātya-purodhasaḥ
paurāñ jāna-padān śreṇīḥ
prakṛtīḥ samapūjayat

brāhmaṇa-pramukhān—unto the leaders of the *brāhmaṇa* community; *varṇān*—to the other castes; *bhṛtya*—servants; *amātya*—ministers; *purodhasaḥ*—to the priests; *paurān*—to the citizens; *jāna-padān*—to his countrymen; *śreṇīḥ*—to different communities; *prakṛtīḥ*—to the admirers; *samapūjayat*—he gave proper respects.

TRANSLATION

King Pṛthu thus satisfied and offered all respect to all the leaders of the brāhmaṇas and other castes, to his servants, to his ministers, to the priests, citizens, general countrymen, people from other communities, admirers, as well as others, and thus they all became happy.

TEXT 3

विदुर उवाच
कस्माद्दधार गोरूपं धरित्री बहुरूपिणी ।
यां दुदोह पृथुस्तत्र को वत्सो दोहनं च किम् ॥ ३ ॥

vidura uvāca
kasmād dadhāra go-rūpaṁ
dharitrī bahu-rūpiṇī
yāṁ dudoha pṛthus tatra
ko vatso dohanaṁ ca kim

viduraḥ uvāca—Vidura inquired; *kasmāt*—why; *dadhāra*—took; *go-rūpam*—the shape of a cow; *dharitrī*—the earth; *bahu-rūpiṇī*—who has many other forms; *yām*—whom; *dudoha*—milked; *pṛthuḥ*—King Pṛthu; *tatra*—there; *kaḥ*—who; *vatsaḥ*—the calf; *dohanam*—the milking pot; *ca*—also; *kim*—what.

TRANSLATION

Vidura inquired from the great sage Maitreya: My dear brāhmaṇa, since mother earth can appear in different shapes, why did she take the shape of a cow? And when King Pṛthu milked her, who became the calf, and what was the milking pot?

TEXT 4

प्रकृत्या विषमा देवी कृता तेन समा कथम् ।
तस्य मेध्यं हयं देवः कस्य हेतोरपाहरत् ॥ ४ ॥

prakṛtyā viṣamā devī
kṛtā tena samā katham
tasya medhyaṁ hayaṁ devaḥ
kasya hetor apāharat

prakṛtyā—by nature; *viṣamā*—not level; *devī*—the earth; *kṛtā*—was made; *tena*—by him; *samā*—level; *katham*—how; *tasya*—his; *medhyam*—meant for offering in the sacrifice; *hayam*—horse; *devaḥ*—the demigod Indra; *kasya*—for what; *hetoḥ*—reason; *apāharat*—stole.

TRANSLATION

The surface of the earth is by nature low in some places and high in others. How did King Pṛthu level the surface of the earth, and why did the King of heaven, Indra, steal the horse meant for the sacrifice?

TEXT 5

सनत्कुमाराद्भगवतो ब्रह्मन् ब्रह्मविदुत्तमात् ।
लब्ध्वा ज्ञानं सविज्ञानं राजर्षिः कां गतिं गतः ॥ ५ ॥

sanat-kumārād bhagavato
brahman brahma-vid-uttamāt
labdhvā jñānaṁ sa-vijñānaṁ
rājarṣiḥ kāṁ gatiṁ gataḥ

sanat-kumārāt—from Sanat-kumāra; *bhagavataḥ*—the most powerful; *brahman*—my dear *brāhmaṇa; brahma-vit-uttamāt*—well versed in the Vedic knowledge; *labdhvā*—after achieving; *jñānam*—knowledge; *sa-vijñānam*—for practical application; *rāja-ṛṣiḥ*—the great saintly King; *kām*—which; *gatim*—destination; *gataḥ*—achieved.

TRANSLATION

The great saintly King, Mahārāja Pṛthu, received knowledge from Sanat-kumāra, who was the greatest Vedic scholar. After receiving knowl-

edge to be applied practically in his life, how did the saintly King attain his desired destination?

PURPORT

There are four Vaiṣṇava *sampradāyas* (systems) of disciplic succession. One *sampradāya* comes from Lord Brahmā, one from the goddess of fortune, one from the Kumāras headed by Sanat-kumāra, and one from Lord Śiva. These four systems of disciplic succession are still going on. As King Pṛthu has illustrated, one who is serious to receive transcendental Vedic knowledge must accept a *guru,* or spiritual master, in one of these four disciplic successions. It is said that unless one accepts a *mantra* from one of these *sampradāyas,* the so-called *mantra* will not act in Kali-yuga. Many *sampradāyas* have sprung up without authority, and they are misleading the people by giving unauthorized *mantras.* The rascals of these so-called *sampradāyas* do not observe the Vedic rules and regulations. Although they are addicted to all kinds of sinful activities, they still offer the people *mantras* and thus mislead them. Intelligent persons, however, know that such *mantras* will never be successful, and as such they never patronize such upstart spiritual groups. People should be very careful of these nonsensical *sampradāyas.* To get some facility for sense gratification, unfortunate people in this age receive *mantras* from these so-called *sampradāyas.* Pṛthu Mahārāja, however, showed by his example that one should receive knowledge from a bona fide *sampradāya.* Therefore Mahārāja Pṛthu accepted Sanat-kumāra as his spiritual master.

TEXTS 6-7

यच्चान्यदपि कृष्णस्य भवान् भगवतः प्रभोः ।
श्रवः सुश्रवसः पुण्यं पूर्वदेहकथाश्रयम् ॥ ६ ॥
भक्ताय मेऽनुरक्ताय तव चाधोक्षजस्य च ।
वक्तुमर्हसि योऽदुह्यद्वैन्यरूपेण गामिमाम् ॥ ७ ॥

yac cānyad api kṛṣṇasya
bhavān bhagavataḥ prabhoḥ
śravaḥ suśravasaḥ puṇyaṁ
pūrva-deha-kathāśrayam

bhaktāya me 'nuraktāya
tava cādhokṣajasya ca

vaktum arhasi yo 'duhyad
vainya-rūpeṇa gām imām

yat—which; *ca*—and; *anyat*—other; *api*—certainly; *kṛṣṇasya*—of Kṛṣṇa; *bhavān*—your good self; *bhagavataḥ*—of the Supreme Personality of Godhead; *prabhoḥ*—powerful; *śravaḥ*—glorious activities; *su-śravasaḥ*—who is very pleasing to hear about; *puṇyam*—pious; *pūrva-deha*—of His previous incarnation; *kathā-āśrayam*—connected with the narration; *bhaktāya*—unto the devotee; *me*—to me; *anuraktāya*—very much attentive; *tava*—of yourself; *ca*—and; *adhokṣajasya*—of the Lord, who is known as Adhokṣaja; *ca*—also; *vaktum arhasi*—please narrate; *yaḥ*—one who; *aduhyat*—milked; *vainya-rūpeṇa*—in the form of the son of King Vena; *gām*—cow, earth; *imām*—this.

TRANSLATION

Pṛthu Mahārāja was a powerful incarnation of Lord Kṛṣṇa's potencies; consequently any narration concerning his activities is surely very pleasing to hear, and it produces all good fortune. As far as I am concerned, I am always your devotee as well as a devotee of the Lord, who is known as Adhokṣaja. Please therefore narrate all the stories of King Pṛthu, who, in the form of the son of King Vena, milked the cow-shaped earth.

PURPORT

Lord Kṛṣṇa is also known as *avatārī*, which means, "one from whom all the incarnations emanate." In *Bhagavad-gītā* Lord Kṛṣṇa says, *ahaṁ sarvasya prabhavo mattaḥ sarvaṁ pravartate:* "I am the source of all spiritual and material worlds. Everything emanates from Me." (Bg. 10.8) Thus Lord Kṛṣṇa is the origin of everyone's appearance. As far as this material world is concerned, Lord Brahmā, Lord Viṣṇu and Lord Śiva are all emanations from Kṛṣṇa. These three incarnations of Kṛṣṇa are called *guṇa-avatāras*. The material world is governed by three material modes of nature, and Lord Viṣṇu, Lord Brahmā and Lord Śiva respectively take charge of the modes of goodness, passion and ignorance. Mahārāja Pṛthu is also an incarnation of those qualities of Lord Kṛṣṇa by which one rules over conditioned souls.

In this verse the word *adhokṣaja*, meaning "beyond the perception of the material senses," is very significant. No one can perceive the Supreme Personality of Godhead by mental speculation; therefore a person with a poor fund of knowledge cannot understand the Supreme Personality of

Godhead. Since one can only form an impersonal idea on the strength of one's material senses, the Lord is known as Adhokṣaja.

TEXT 8

सूत उवाच
चोदितो विदुरेणैवं वासुदेवकथां प्रति ।
प्रशस्य तं प्रीतमना मैत्रेयः प्रत्यभाषत ॥ ८ ॥

sūta uvāca
codito vidureṇaivaṁ
vāsudeva-kathāṁ prati
praśasya taṁ prīta-manā
maitreyaḥ pratyabhāṣata

sūtaḥ uvāca—Sūta Gosvāmī said; *coditaḥ*—inspired; *vidureṇa*—by Vidura; *evam*—thus; *vāsudeva*—of Lord Kṛṣṇa; *kathām*—narration; *prati*—about; *praśasya*—praising; *tam*—him; *prīta-manāḥ*—being very pleased; *maitreyaḥ*—the saint Maitreya; *pratyabhāṣata*—replied.

TRANSLATION

Sūta Gosvāmī continued: When Vidura became inspired to hear of the activities of Lord Kṛṣṇa in His various incarnations, Maitreya, also being inspired and being very pleased with Vidura, began to praise him. Then Maitreya spoke as follows.

PURPORT

Talk of *kṛṣṇa-kathā,* or topics about Lord Kṛṣṇa or His incarnations, is so spiritually inspiring that the reciter and hearer are never exhausted. That is the nature of spiritual talks. We have actually seen that one can never become satiated by hearing the conversations between Vidura and Maitreya. Both of them are devotees, and the more Vidura inquires, the more Maitreya is encouraged to speak. A symptom of spiritual talks is that no one feels tired. Thus upon hearing the questions of Vidura, the great sage Maitreya did not feel disgusted but rather felt encouraged to speak at greater length.

TEXT 9

मैत्रेय उवाच
यदाभिषिक्तः पृथुरङ्ग विप्रै-
रामन्त्रितो जनतायाश्च पालः ।

प्रजा निरन्ने क्षितिपृष्ठ एत्य
क्षुत्क्षामदेहाः पतिमभ्यवोचन् ॥ ९ ॥

maitreya uvāca
yadābhiṣiktaḥ pṛthur aṅga viprair
āmantrito janatāyāś ca pālaḥ
prajā niranne kṣiti-pṛṣṭha etya
kṣut-kṣāma-dehāḥ patim abhyavocan

maitreyaḥ uvāca—the great sage Maitreya said; *yadā*—when; *abhiṣiktaḥ*—was enthroned; *pṛthuḥ*—King Pṛthu; *aṅga*—my dear Vidura; *vipraiḥ*—by the *brāhmaṇas; āmantritaḥ*—was declared; *janatāyāḥ*—of the people; *ca*—also; *pālaḥ*—the protector; *prajāḥ*—the citizens; *niranne*—being without food grains; *kṣiti-pṛṣṭhe*—the surface of the globe; *etya*—coming near; *kṣudh*—by hunger; *kṣāma*—skinny; *dehāḥ*—their bodies; *patim*—to the protector; *abhyavocan*—they said.

TRANSLATION

The great sage Maitreya continued: My dear Vidura, at the time King Pṛthu was enthroned by the great sages and brāhmaṇas and declared to be the protector of the citizens, there was a scarcity of food grains. The citizens actually became skinny due to starvation. Therefore they came before the King and informed him of their real situation.

PURPORT

Information is given herein concerning the selection of the king by the *brāhmaṇas*. According to the *varṇāśrama* system, the *brāhmaṇas* are considered to be the heads of the society and therefore to be situated in the topmost social position. The *varṇāśrama-dharma,* the institution of four *varṇas* and four *āśramas,* is very scientifically designed. As stated in *Bhagavad-gītā, varṇāśrama-dharma* is not a man-made institution but is God-made. In this narration it is clearly indicated that the *brāhmaṇas* used to control the royal power. When an evil king like Vena ruled, the *brāhmaṇas* would kill him through their brahminical powers and would select a proper ruler by testing his qualifications. In other words, the *brāhmaṇas,* the intelligent men or great sages, would control the monarchical powers. Here we have an indication of how the *brāhmaṇas* elected King Pṛthu to the throne as the protector of the citizens. The citizens, being skinny due to hunger, approached the King and informed him that necessary action should be taken. The structure of the *varṇāśrama-dharma* was so nice that the *brāhmaṇas* would guide the head of state. The head of state would then give protection to the citizens. The *kṣatriyas* would take charge of protecting the people in general, and under the protection of the *kṣatriyas,* the *vaiśyas* would protect the cows, produce food grains and distribute them. *Śūdras,* the working class, would help the higher three classes by manual labor. This is the perfect social system.

TEXTS 10-11

वयं राजञ्जाठरेणाभितप्ता
यथाग्निना कोटरस्थेन वृक्षाः ।
त्वामद्य याताः शरणं शरण्यं
यः साधितो वृत्तिकरः पतिर्नः ॥१०॥
तन्नो भवानीहतु रातवेऽन्नं
क्षुधार्दितानां नरदेवदेव ।
यावन्न नङ्क्ष्यामह उज्झितोर्जा
वार्तापतिस्त्वं किल लोकपालः ॥११॥

vayaṁ rājañ jāṭhareṇābhitaptā
yathāgninā koṭara-sthena vṛkṣāḥ
tvām adya yātāḥ śaraṇaṁ śaraṇyaṁ
yaḥ sādhito vṛtti-karaḥ patir naḥ

tan no bhavān īhatu rātave 'nnaṁ
kṣudhārditānāṁ nara-deva-deva
yāvan na naṅkṣyāmaha ujjhitorjā
vārtā-patis tvaṁ kila loka-pālaḥ

vayam—we; *rājan*—O King; *jāṭhareṇa*—by the fire of hunger; *abhitaptāḥ*—very much aggrieved; *yathā*—just as; *agninā*—by the fire; *koṭara-sthena*—in the hollow of a tree; *vṛkṣāḥ*—trees; *tvām*—unto you; *adya*—today; *yātāḥ*—we have come; *śaraṇam*—shelter; *śaraṇyam*—worth taking shelter of; *yaḥ*—who; *sādhitaḥ*—appointed; *vṛtti-karaḥ*—one who gives employment; *patiḥ*—master; *naḥ*—our; *tat*—therefore; *naḥ*—to us; *bhavān*—Your Majesty; *īhatu*—please try; *rātave*—to give; *annam*—food grains; *kṣudhā*—with hunger; *arditānām*—suffering; *nara-deva-deva*—O supreme master of all kings; *yāvat na*—lest; *naṅkṣyāmahe*—we will perish; *ujjhita*—being bereft of; *ūrjāḥ*—food grains; *vārtā*—of occupational engagements; *patiḥ*—bestower; *tvam*—you; *kila*—indeed; *loka-pālaḥ*—the protector of the citizens.

TRANSLATION

Dear King, just as a tree with a fire burning in the hollow of the trunk gradually dries up, we are drying up due to the fire of hunger in our stomach. You are the protector of surrendered souls, and you have been appointed to give employment to us. Therefore we have all come to you for protection. You are not only a king, but the incarnation of God as well. Indeed, you are the King of all kings. You can give us all kinds of occupational engagements, for you are the master of our livelihood. Therefore, O King of all kings, please arrange to satisfy our hunger by the proper distribution of food grains. Please take care of us, lest we soon die for want of food.

PURPORT

It is the duty of the king to see that everyone in the social orders—*brāhmaṇas, kṣatriyas, vaiśyas* and *śūdras*—is fully employed in the state. Just as it is the duty of the *brāhmaṇas* to elect a proper king, it is the duty of the king to see that all the *varṇas*—the *brāhmaṇas, kṣatriyas, vaiśyas* and *śūdras*—are fully engaged in their respective occupational duties. It is here indicated that although the people were allowed to perform their duties, they were still unemployed. Although they were not lazy, they still could not produce sufficient food to satisfy their hunger. When the people are perplexed in this way, they should approach the head of government, and the president or king should take immediate action to mitigate the distress of the people.

TEXT 12

मैत्रेय उवाच

पृथुः प्रजानां करुणं निशम्य परिदेवितम् ।
दीर्घं दध्यौ कुरुश्रेष्ठ निमित्तं सोऽन्वपद्यत ॥१२॥

maitreya uvāca
pṛthuḥ prajānāṁ karuṇaṁ
niśamya paridevitam
dīrghaṁ dadhyau kuruśreṣṭha
nimittaṁ so 'nvapadyata

maitreyaḥ uvāca—the great saint Maitreya said; *pṛthuḥ*—King Pṛthu; *prajānām*—of the citizens; *karuṇam*—pitiable condition; *niśamya*—hearing;

paridevitam—lamentation; *dīrgham*—for a long time; *dadhyau*—contemplated; *kuru-śreṣṭha*—O Vidura; *nimittam*—the cause; *saḥ*—he; *anvapadyata*—found out.

TRANSLATION

After hearing this lamentation and seeing the pitiable condition of the citizens, King Pṛthu contemplated this matter for a long time to see if he could find out the underlying causes.

TEXT 13

इति व्यवसितो बुद्ध्या प्रगृहीतशरासनः ।
सन्दधे विशिखं भूमेः क्रुद्धस्त्रिपुरहा यथा ॥१३॥

iti vyavasito buddhyā
pragṛhīta-śarāsanaḥ
sandadhe viśikhaṁ bhūmeḥ
kruddhas tri-pura-hā yathā

iti—thus; *vyavasitaḥ*—having arrived at the conclusion; *buddhyā*—by intelligence; *pragṛhīta*—having taken up; *śarāsanaḥ*—the bow; *sandadhe*—fixed; *viśikham*—an arrow; *bhūmeḥ*—at the earth; *kruddhaḥ*—angry; *tri-pura-hā*—Lord Śiva; *yathā*—like.

TRANSLATION

Having arrived at a conclusion, the King took up his bow and arrow and aimed them at the earth, exactly as Lord Śiva destroyed the whole world out of anger.

PURPORT

King Pṛthu found out the cause for the scarcity of food grains. He could understand that it was not the people's fault, for they were not lazy in executing their duties. Rather, the earth was not producing sufficient food grains. This indicates that the earth can produce sufficiently if everything is properly arranged, but sometimes the earth can refuse to produce food grains for various reasons. The theory that there is a scarcity of food grains due to an increase of population is not a very sound theory. There are other causes that enable the earth to produce profusely or to stop producing. King Pṛthu found out the proper causes and took the necessary steps immediately.

TEXT 14

प्रवेपमाना धरणी निशाम्योदायुधं च तम् ।
गौः सत्यपाद्रवद्भीता मृगीव मृगयुद्रुता ॥१४॥

pravepamānā dharaṇī
niśāmyodāyudhaṁ ca tam
gauḥ saty apādravad bhītā
mṛgīva mṛgayu-drutā

pravepamānā—trembling; *dharaṇī*—the earth; *niśāmya*—seeing; *udāyudham*—having taken his bow and arrow; *ca*—also; *tam*—the King; *gauḥ*—a cow; *satī*—becoming; *apādravat*—began to flee; *bhītā*—very much afraid; *mṛgī iva*—like a deer; *mṛgayu*—by a hunter; *drutā*—being followed.

TRANSLATION

When the earth saw that King Pṛthu was taking his bow and arrow to kill her, she became very much afraid and began to tremble. She then began to flee, exactly as a deer, which runs very swiftly when followed by a hunter. Being afraid of King Pṛthu, she took the shape of a cow and began to run.

PURPORT

Just as a mother produces various children, both male and female, the womb of mother earth produces all kinds of living entities in various shapes. Thus it is possible for mother earth to take on innumerable shapes. At this time, in order to avoid the wrath of King Pṛthu, she took the shape of a cow. Since a cow is never to be killed, mother earth thought it wise to take the shape of a cow in order to avoid King Pṛthu's arrows. King Pṛthu, however, could understand this fact, and therefore he did not stop chasing the cow-shaped earth.

TEXT 15

तामन्वधावत्तद्वैन्यः कुपितोऽत्यरुणेक्षणः ।
शरं धनुषि सन्धाय यत्र यत्र पलायते ॥१५॥

tām anvadhāvat tad vainyaḥ
kupito 'tyaruṇekṣaṇaḥ

śaraṁ dhanuṣi sandhāya
yatra yatra palāyate

tām—the cow-shaped earth; *anvadhāvat*—he chased; *tat*—then; *vainyaḥ*—the son of King Vena; *kupitaḥ*—being very much angry; *ati-aruṇa*—very red; *īkṣaṇaḥ*—his eyes; *śaram*—an arrow; *dhanuṣi*—on the bow; *sandhāya*—placing; *yatra yatra*—wherever; *palāyate*—she flees.

TRANSLATION

Seeing this, Mahārāja Pṛthu became very angry, and his eyes became as red as the early morning sun. Placing an arrow on his bow, he chased the cow-shaped earth wherever she would run.

TEXT 16

सा दिशो विदिशो देवी रोदसी चान्तरं तयोः ।
धावन्ती तत्र तत्रैनं ददर्शानूद्यतायुधम् ॥१६॥

sā diśo vidiśo devī
rodasī cāntaraṁ tayoḥ
dhāvantī tatra tatrainaṁ
dadarśānūdyatāyudham

sā—the cow-shaped earth; *diśaḥ*—in the four directions; *vidiśaḥ*—randomly in other directions; *devī*—the goddess; *rodasī*—toward heaven and earth; *ca*—also; *antaram*—between; *tayoḥ*—them; *dhāvantī*—fleeing; *tatra tatra*—here and there; *enam*—the King; *dadarśa*—she saw; *anu*—behind; *udyata*—taken up; *āyudham*—his weapons.

TRANSLATION

The cow-shaped earth ran here and there in outer space between the heavenly planets and the earth, and wherever she ran, the King chased her with his bow and arrows.

TEXT 17

लोके नाविन्दत त्राणं वैन्यान्मृत्योरिव प्रजाः ।
त्रस्ता तदा निववृते हृदयेन विदूयता ॥१७॥

loke nāvindata trāṇaṁ
vainyān mṛtyor iva prajāḥ
trastā tadā nivavṛte
hṛdayena vidūyatā

loke—within the three worlds; *na*—not; *avindata*—could obtain; *trāṇam*—release; *vainyāt*—from the hand of the son of King Vena; *mṛtyoḥ*—from death; *iva*—like; *prajāḥ*—men; *trastā*—being very much afraid; *tadā*—at that time; *nivavṛte*—turned back; *hṛdayena*—within her heart; *vidūyatā*—very much aggrieved.

TRANSLATION

Just as a man cannot escape the cruel hands of death, the cow-shaped earth could not escape the hands of the son of Vena. At length the earth, fearful, her heart aggrieved, turned back in helplessness.

TEXT 18

उवाच च महाभागं धर्मज्ञापन्नवत्सल ।
त्राहि मामपि भूतानां पालनेऽवस्थितो भवान् ॥१८॥

uvāca ca mahā-bhāgaṁ
dharma-jñāpanna-vatsala
trāhi mām api bhūtānāṁ
pālane 'vasthito bhavān

uvāca—she said; *ca*—and; *mahā-bhāgam*—unto the great, fortunate King; *dharma-jña*—O knower of the principles of religion; *āpanna-vatsala*—O shelter of the surrendered; *trāhi*—save; *mām*—me; *api*—indeed; *bhūtānām*—of living entities; *pālane*—in protection; *avasthitaḥ*—situated; *bhavān*—Your Majesty.

TRANSLATION

Addressing the great opulent King Pṛthu as the knower of religious principles and shelter of the surrendered, she said: Please save me. You are the protector of all living entities. Now you are situated as the King of this planet.

PURPORT

The cow-shaped earth addressed King Pṛthu as *dharma-jña,* which refers to one who knows the principles of religion. The principles of religion dictate that a woman, a cow, a child, a *brāhmaṇa* and an old man must be given all protection by the king or anyone else. Consequently mother earth took the shape of a cow. She was also a woman. Thus she appealed to the King as one who knows the principles of religion. Religious principles also dictate that one is not to be killed if he surrenders. She reminded King Pṛthu that not only was he an incarnation of God, but he was situated as the King of the earth as well. Therefore his duty was to excuse her.

TEXT 19

स त्वं जिघांससे कस्माद्दीनामकृतकिल्बिषाम् ।
अहनिष्यत्कथं योषां धर्मज्ञ इति यो मतः ॥१९॥

sa tvaṁ jighāṁsase kasmād
dīnām akṛta-kilbiṣām
ahaniṣyat kathaṁ yoṣāṁ
dharma-jña iti yo mataḥ

saḥ—that very person; *tvam*—you; *jighāṁsase*—want to kill; *kasmāt*—why; *dīnām*—poor; *akṛta*—without having done; *kilbiṣām*—any sinful activities; *ahaniṣyat*—would kill; *katham*—how; *yoṣām*—a woman; *dharma-jñaḥ*—the knower of religious principles; *iti*—thus; *yaḥ*—one who; *mataḥ*—is considered.

TRANSLATION

The cow-shaped earth continued to appeal to the King: I am very poor and have not committed any sinful activities. I do not know why you want to kill me. Since you are supposed to be the knower of all religious principles, why are you so envious of me, and why are you so anxious to kill a woman?

PURPORT

The earth appealed to the King in two ways. A king who knows religious principles cannot kill anyone who has not committed sinful activities. Apart from this, a woman is not to be killed, even if she does commit some sinful activities. Since the earth was innocent and was also a woman, the King should not kill her.

TEXT 20

प्रहरन्ति न वै स्त्रीषु कृतागःस्वपि जन्तवः ।
किमुत त्वद्विधा राजन् करुणा दीनवत्सलाः ॥२०॥

praharanti na vai strīṣu
kṛtāgaḥsv api jantavaḥ
kim uta tvad-vidhā rājan
karuṇā dīna-vatsalāḥ

praharanti—strike; *na*—never; *vai*—certainly; *strīṣu*—women; *kṛta-āgaḥsu*—having committed sinful activities; *api*—although; *jantavaḥ*—human beings; *kim uta*—then what to speak of; *tvat-vidhāḥ*—personalities like you; *rājan*—O King; *karuṇāḥ*—merciful; *dīna-vatsalāḥ*—affectionate to the poor.

TRANSLATION

Even if a woman does commit some sinful activity, no one should place his hand upon her. And what to speak of you, dear King, who are so merciful. You are a protector, and you are affectionate to the poor.

TEXT 21

मां विपाट्याजरां नावं यत्र विश्वं प्रतिष्ठितम् ।
आत्मानं च प्रजाश्चेमाः कथमम्भसि धास्यसि ॥२१॥

māṁ vipāṭyājarāṁ nāvaṁ
yatra viśvaṁ pratiṣṭhitam
ātmānaṁ ca prajāś cemāḥ
katham ambhasi dhāsyasi

mām—me; *vipāṭya*—breaking to pieces; *ajarām*—very strong; *nāvam*—boat; *yatra*—where; *viśvam*—all worldly paraphernalia; *pratiṣṭhitam*—standing; *ātmānam*—yourself; *ca*—and; *prajāḥ*—your subjects; *ca*—also; *imāḥ*—all these; *katham*—how; *ambhasi*—in the water; *dhāsyasi*—you will hold.

TRANSLATION

The cow-shaped earth continued: My dear King, I am just like a strong boat, and all the paraphernalia of the world is standing upon me. If you break me to pieces, how can you protect yourself and your subjects from drowning?

PURPORT

Beneath the entire planetary system is the *garbha* water. Lord Viṣṇu lies on this *garbha* water, and from His abdomen a lotus stem grows, and all the planets within the universe are floating in the air being supported by this lotus stem. If a planet is destroyed, it must fall into the water of *garbha.* The earth therefore warned King Pṛthu that he could gain nothing by destroying her. Indeed, how would he protect himself and his citizens from drowning in the *garbha* water? In other words, outer space may be compared to an ocean of air, and each and every planet is floating on it just as a boat or island floats on the ocean. Sometimes planets are called *dvīpa,* or islands, and sometimes they are called boats. Thus the cosmic manifestation is partially explained in this reference by the cow-shaped earth.

TEXT 22

पृथुरुवाच
वसुधे त्वां वधिष्यामि मच्छासनपराङ्मुखीम् ।
भागं बर्हिषि या वृङ्क्ते न तनोति च नो वसु ॥२२॥

pṛthur uvāca
vasudhe tvāṁ vadhiṣyāmi
mac-chāsana-parāṅ-mukhīm
bhāgaṁ barhiṣi yā vṛṅkte
na tanoti ca no vasu

pṛthuḥ uvāca—King Pṛthu replied; *vasu-dhe*—my dear earthly planet; *tvām*—you; *vadhiṣyāmi*—I shall kill; *mat*—my; *śāsana*—rulings; *parāk-mukhīm*—disobedient to; *bhāgam*—your share; *barhiṣi*—in the *yajña; yā*—who; *vṛṅkte*—accepts; *na*—not; *tanoti*—does deliver; *ca*—and; *naḥ*—to us; *vasu*—produce.

TRANSLATION

King Pṛthu replied to the earthly planet: My dear earth, you have disobeyed my orders and rulings. In the form of a demigod you accepted your share of the yajñas we performed, but in return you have not produced sufficient food grains. For this reason I must kill you.

PURPORT

The cow-shaped earthly planet submitted that she was not only a woman, but was innocent and sinless as well. Thus she argued that she should not be killed. Besides, she pointed out that being perfectly religious-minded, the King could not violate the religious principles that forbade killing a woman. In reply, Mahārāja Pṛthu informed her that first of all she had disobeyed his orders. This was her first sinful activity. Secondly he accused her of taking her share in the *yajñas* (sacrifices) but not producing sufficient food grains in return.

TEXT 23

यवसं जग्ध्यनुदिनं नैव दोग्ध्यौधसं पयः ।
तस्यामेवं हि दुष्टायां दण्डो नात्र न शस्यते ॥२३॥

yavasaṁ jagdhy anudinaṁ
naiva dogdhy audhasaṁ payaḥ
tasyām evaṁ hi duṣṭāyāṁ
daṇḍo nātra na śasyate

yavasam—green grass; *jagdhi*—you eat; *anudinam*—daily; *na*—never; *eva*—certainly; *dogdhi*—you yield; *audhasam*—in the milk bag; *payaḥ*—milk; *tasyām*—when a cow; *evam*—thus; *hi*—certainly; *duṣṭāyām*—being offensive; *daṇḍaḥ*—punishment; *na*—not; *atra*—here; *na*—not; *śasyate*—is advisable.

TRANSLATION

Although you are eating green grass every day, you are not filling your milk bag so we can utilize your milk. Since you are willfully committing offenses, it cannot be said that you are not punishable due to your assuming the form of a cow.

PURPORT

A cow eats green grasses in the pasture and fills her milk bag with sufficient milk so that the cowherdsmen can milk her. *Yajñas* (sacrifices) are performed to produce sufficient clouds that will pour water over the earth. The word *payaḥ* can refer both to milk and to water. As one of the demigods, the earthly planet was taking her share in the *yajñas*—that is, she was eating green grass—but in return she was not producing sufficient food grains—that is, she was not filling her milk bag. Pṛthu Mahārāja was therefore justified in threatening to punish her for her offense.

TEXT 24

त्वं खल्वोषधिबीजानि प्राक् सृष्टानि स्वयम्भुवा ।
न मुञ्चस्यात्मरुद्धानि मामवज्ञाय मन्दधीः ॥२४॥

tvaṁ khalv oṣadhi-bījāni
prāk sṛṣṭāni svayambhuvā
na muñcasy ātma-ruddhāni
mām avajñāya manda-dhīḥ

tvam—you; *khalu*—certainly; *oṣadhi*—of herbs, plants and grains; *bījāni*—the seeds; *prāk*—formerly; *sṛṣṭāni*—created; *svayam-bhuvā*—by Lord Brahmā; *na*—do not; *muñcasi*—deliver; *ātma-ruddhāni*—hidden within yourself; *mām*—me; *avajñāya*—disobeying; *manda-dhīḥ*—less intelligent.

TRANSLATION

You have so lost your intelligence that, despite my orders, you do not deliver the seeds of herbs and grains—formerly created by Brahmā—now hidden within yourself.

PURPORT

While creating all the planets in the universe, Lord Brahmā also created the seeds of various grains, herbs, plants and trees. When sufficient water falls from the clouds, the seeds fructify and produce fruits, grains, vegetables, etc. By his example, Pṛthu Mahārāja indicates that whenever there is a scarcity in food production, the head of the government should take steps to see why production is being held up and what should be done to rectify the situation.

TEXT 25

अमूषां क्षुत्परीतानामार्तानां परिदेवितम् ।
शमयिष्यामि मद्बाणैर्भिन्नायास्तव मेदसा ॥२५॥

amūṣāṁ kṣut-parītānām
ārtānāṁ paridevitam
śamayiṣyāmi mad-bāṇair
bhinnāyās tava medasā

amūṣām—of all of them; *kṣudh-parītānām*—suffering from hunger; *ārtānām*—of the distressed; *paridevitam*—the lamentation; *śamayiṣyāmi*—I shall pacify; *mat-bāṇaiḥ*—by my arrows; *bhinnāyāḥ*—being cut into pieces; *tava*—of you; *medasā*—by the flesh.

TRANSLATION

Now, with the help of my arrows, I shall cut you to pieces and with your flesh satisfy the hunger-stricken citizens who are now crying for want of grains. Thus I shall satisfy the crying citizens of my kingdom.

PURPORT

Here we find some indication how the government can arrange for the eating of cow flesh. It is here indicated that in a rare circumstance when there is no supply of grains, the government may sanction the eating of meat. However, when there is sufficient food, the government should not allow the eating of cow's flesh just to satisfy the fastidious tongue. In other words, in rare circumstances, when people are suffering for want of grains, meat-eating or flesh-eating can be allowed, but not otherwise. The maintenance of slaughterhouses for the satisfaction of the tongue and the killing of animals unnecessarily should never be sanctioned by a government.

As described in the previous verse, animals or cows should be given sufficient grass to eat. If, despite a sufficient supply of grass, a cow does not supply milk, and there is an acute shortage of food, the dried-up cow may be utilized to feed the hungry masses of people. According to the law of necessity, first of all human society must try to produce food grains and vegetables, but if they fail in this, they can indulge in flesh-eating. Otherwise not. As human society is presently structured, there is sufficient production of grains all over the world. Therefore the opening of slaughterhouses cannot be supported. In some nations there is so much surplus grain that sometimes extra grain is thrown into the sea, and sometimes the government forbids further production of grain. The conclusion is that the earth produces sufficient grain to feed the entire population, but the distribution of this grain is restricted due to trade regulations and a desire for profit. Consequently in some places there is scarcity of grain and in others profuse production. If there were one government on the surface of the earth to handle the distribution of grain, there would be no question of scarcity, no necessity to open slaughterhouses, and no need to present false theories about overpopulation.

TEXT 26

पुमान् योषिदुत क्लीब आत्मसम्भावनोऽधमः ।
भूतेषु निरनुक्रोशो नृपाणां तद्वधोऽवधः ॥२६॥

pumān yoṣid uta klība
ātma-sambhāvano 'dhamaḥ
bhūteṣu niranukrośo
nṛpāṇāṁ tad-vadho 'vadhaḥ

pumān—a man; *yoṣit*—a woman; *uta*—also; *klībaḥ*—eunuch; *ātma-sambhāvanaḥ*—interested in self-maintenance; *adhamaḥ*—lowest of human-kind; *bhūteṣu*—to other living entities; *niranukrośaḥ*—without compassion; *nṛpāṇām*—for the kings; *tat*—of him; *vadhaḥ*—killing; *avadhaḥ*—not killing.

TRANSLATION

Any cruel person—be he a man, woman or impotent eunuch—who is only interested in his personal maintenance and has no compassion for other living entities, may be killed by the king. Such killing can never be considered actual killing.

PURPORT

The planet earth is actually a woman in her constitutional form, and as such she needs to be protected by the king. Pṛthu Mahārāja argues, however, that if a citizen within the state—be he man, woman or a eunuch—is not compassionate upon his fellow men, he or she may be killed by the king, and such killing is never to be considered actual killing. As far as the field of spiritual activities is concerned, when a devotee is self-satisfied and does not preach the glories of Kṛṣṇa, he is not considered a first-class devotee. A devotee who tries to preach, who has compassion upon innocent persons who have no knowledge of Kṛṣṇa, is a superior devotee. In his prayer to the Lord, Prahlāda Mahārāja said that he was not personally interested in liberation from this material world; rather, he did not wish to be liberated from this material condition until all fallen souls are delivered. Even in the material field, if a person is not interested in others' welfare, he should be considered to be condemned by the Personality of Godhead or His incarnation as Pṛthu Mahārāja.

TEXT 27

त्वां स्तब्धां दुर्मदां नीत्वा मायागां तिलशः शरैः ।
आत्मयोगबलेनेमा धारयिष्याम्यहं प्रजाः ॥२७॥

tvāṁ stabdhāṁ durmadāṁ
nītvā māyā-gāṁ tilaśaḥ śaraiḥ

ātma-yoga-balenemā
dhārayiṣyāmy ahaṁ prajāḥ

tvām—you; *stabdhām*—very much puffed up; *durmadām*—mad; *nītvā*—bringing into such a condition; *māyā-gām*—false cow; *tilaśaḥ*—into small particles like grains; *śaraiḥ*—by my arrows; *ātma*—personal; *yoga-balena*—by mystic power; *imāḥ*—all these; *dhārayiṣyāmi*—shall uphold; *aham*—I; *prajāḥ*—all the citizens, or all the living entities.

TRANSLATION

You are very much puffed up with pride and have become almost insane. Presently you have assumed the form of a cow by your mystic powers. Nonetheless I shall cut you into small pieces like grain, and I will uphold the entire population by my personal mystic powers.

PURPORT

The earth informed King Pṛthu that if he destroyed her, he and his subjects would all fall down into the waters of the *garbha* ocean. King Pṛthu now replies to that point. Although the earth assumed the shape of a cow by her mystic powers in order to be saved from being killed by the King, the King was nonetheless aware of this fact and would not hesitate to cut her to pieces, just like small bits of grain. As far as the destruction of the citizens is concerned, Mahārāja Pṛthu maintained that he could uphold everyone by his own mystic powers. He did not need the help of the earthly planet. Being the incarnation of Lord Viṣṇu, Pṛthu Mahārāja possessed the power of Saṅkarṣaṇa, which is explained by the scientists as the power of gravitation. The Supreme Personality of Godhead is holding millions of planets in space without any support; similarly, Pṛthu Mahārāja would not have had any difficulty supporting all his citizens and himself in space without the help of the planet earth. The Lord is known as Yogeśvara, master of all mystic powers. Consequently the planet earth was informed by the King that she need not worry about his standing without her help.

TEXT 28

एवं मन्युमयीं मूर्तिं कृतान्तमिव बिभ्रतम् ।
प्रणता प्राञ्जलिः प्राह मही सञ्जातवेपथुः ॥२८॥

evaṁ manyumayīṁ mūrtiṁ
kṛtāntam iva bibhratam

praṇatā prāñjaliḥ prāha
mahī sañjāta-vepathuḥ

evam—thus; *manyu-mayīm*—very much angry; *mūrtim*—form; *kṛta-antam*—death personified, Yamarāja; *iva*—like; *bibhratam*—possessing; *praṇatā*—surrendered; *prāñjaliḥ*—with folded hands; *prāha*—said; *mahī*—the earthly planet; *sañjāta*—arisen; *vepathuḥ*—trembling in her body.

TRANSLATION

At this time Pṛthu Mahārāja became exactly like Yamarāja, and his whole body appeared very angry. In other words, he was anger personified. After hearing him, the planet earth began to tremble. She surrendered, and with folded hands began to speak as follows.

PURPORT

The Supreme Personality of Godhead is death personified to miscreants and the supreme beloved Lord to the devotees. In *Bhagavad-gītā* the Lord says, *mṛtyuḥ sarva-haraś cāham*: "I am all-devouring death." (Bg. 10.34) Faithless unbelievers who challenge the appearance of God will be delivered by the Supreme Personality of Godhead when He appears before them as death. Hiraṇyakaśipu, for example, challenged the authority of the Supreme Personality of Godhead, and the Lord met him in the form of Nṛsiṁhadeva and killed him. Similarly, the planet earth saw Mahārāja Pṛthu as death personified, and she also saw him in the mood of anger personified. Therefore she began to tremble. One cannot challenge the authority of the Supreme Personality of Godhead in any circumstance. It is better to surrender unto Him and take His protection at all times.

TEXT 29

धरोवाच
नमः परस्मै पुरुषाय मायया
विन्यस्तनानातनवे गुणात्मने ।
नमः स्वरूपानुभवेन निर्धुत-
द्रव्यक्रियाकारकविभ्रमोर्मये ॥२९॥

dharovāca
namaḥ parasmai puruṣāya māyayā
vinyasta-nānā-tanave guṇātmane

namaḥ svarūpānubhavena nirdhuta-
dravya-kriyā-kāraka-vibhramormaye

dharā—the earthly planet; *uvāca*—said; *namaḥ*—I offer my obeisances; *parasmai*—unto the Transcendence; *puruṣāya*—unto the person; *māyayā*—by the material energy; *vinyasta*—expanded; *nānā*—various; *tanave*—whose forms; *guṇa-ātmane*—unto the source of the three modes of material nature; *namaḥ*—I offer my obeisances; *sva-rūpa*—of the real form; *anubhavena*—by understanding; *nirdhuta*—not affected by; *dravya*—matter; *kriyā*—action; *kāraka*—doer; *vibhrama*—bewilderment; *ūrmaye*—the waves of material existence.

TRANSLATION

The planet earth spoke: My dear Lord, O Supreme Personality of Godhead, You are transcendental in Your position, and by Your material energy You have expanded Yourself in various forms and species of life through the interaction of the three modes of material nature. Unlike some other masters, You always remain in Your transcendental position and are not affected by the material creation, which is subject to different material interactions. Consequently You are not bewildered by material activities.

PURPORT

After King Pṛthu gave his royal command, the planet earth in the shape of a cow could understand that the King was a directly empowered incarnation of the Supreme Personality of Godhead. Consequently the King knew everything past, present and future. Thus there was no possibility of the earth's cheating him. The earth was accused of hiding the seeds of all herbs and grains, and therefore she is preparing to explain how the seeds of these herbs and grains can be again exposed. The earth knew that the King was very angry with her, and she realized that unless she pacified his anger, there was no possibility of placing a positive program before him. Therefore in the beginning of her speech she very humbly presents herself as a part and parcel of the Supreme Personality of Godhead's body. She submits that the various bodily forms manifest in the physical world are but different parts and parcels of the supreme gigantic body. It is said that the lower planetary systems are parts and parcels of the legs of the Lord, whereas the upper planetary systems are parts and parcels of the Lord's head. The Lord creates this material world by His external energy, but this external energy is in one sense not different from Him. Yet at the same time the Lord is not directly manifest in the external energy but is always situated in the spiritual energy. As stated in *Bhagavad-gītā* (9.10), *mayādhyakṣeṇa prakṛtiḥ:* material nature is working under the direction of the Lord. Therefore the Lord is not unattached to the external energy, and He is addressed in this verse as *guṇa-ātmā,* the source of the three modes of material nature. As stated in *Bhagavad-gītā:*

sarvendriya-guṇābhāsaṁ
sarvendriya-vivarjitam
asaktaṁ sarva-bhṛc caiva
nirguṇam guṇa-bhoktṛ ca

"The Supersoul is the original source of all senses, yet He is without senses. He is unattached, although He is the maintainer of all living beings. He transcends the modes of nature, and at the same time He is the master of all modes of material nature." (Bg. 13.15)

Although the Lord is not attached to the external energy, He is nonetheless the master of it. The philosophy of Lord Caitanya, upholding that the Lord is simultaneously one with and different from His creation (*acintya-bhedābheda-tattva*), is very easily understandable in this connection. The planet earth explains that although the Lord is attached to the external energy, He is nonetheless *nirdhuta;* He is completely free from the activities of the external energy. The Lord is always situated in His internal energy. Therefore in this verse it is stated: *svarūpānubhavena.* The Lord remains completely in His internal potency and yet has full knowledge of the external energy as well as the internal energy, just as His devotee remains always in a transcendental position, keeping himself in the service of the Lord without becoming attached to the material body. Śrīla Rūpa Gosvāmī says that the devotee who is always engaged in the devotional service of the Lord is always liberated, regardless of his material situation. If it is possible for a devotee to remain transcendental, it is certainly possible for the Supreme Personality of Godhead to remain in His internal potency without being attached to the external potency. There should be no difficulty in understanding this situation. Just as a devotee is never bewildered by his material body, the Lord is never bewildered by the external energy of this material world. A devotee is not hampered by the material body, although he is situated in a physical body that runs according to so many material conditions, just as there are five kinds of air functioning within the body, and so many organs—the hands, legs, the tongue, genitals, rectum, etc.—all working differently. The spirit soul, the living entity who is in full knowledge of his position, is always engaged in chanting Hare Kṛṣṇa, Hare Kṛṣṇa, Kṛṣṇa Kṛṣṇa, Hare Hare/ Hare Rāma, Hare Rāma, Rāma Rāma, Hare Hare and is not concerned with the bodily functions. Although the Lord is connected with the material world, He is always situated in His spiritual energy and is always unattached to the functions of the material world. As far as the material body is concerned, there are six "waves" or symptomatic material conditions: hunger, thirst, lamentation, bewilderment, old age and death. The liberated soul is never concerned with these six physical interactions. The Supreme Personality of Godhead, being the all-powerful master of all energies, has some connection with the external energy, but He is always free from the interactions of the external energy in the material world.

TEXT 30

येनाहमात्मायतनं विनिर्मिता
धात्रा यतोऽयं गुणसर्गसङ्ग्रहः ।
स एव मां हन्तुमुदायुधः स्वरा-
डुपस्थितोऽन्यं शरणं कमाश्रये ॥३०॥

yenāhaṁ ātmāyatanaṁ vinirmitā
dhātrā yato 'yaṁ guṇa-sarga-saṅgrahaḥ
sa eva māṁ hantum udāyudhaḥ sva-rāḍ
upasthito 'nyaṁ śaraṇaṁ kam āśraye

yena—by whom; *aham*—I; *ātma-āyatanam*—resting place of all living entities; *vinirmitā*—was created; *dhātrā*—by the Supreme Lord; *yataḥ*—on account of whom; *ayam*—this; *guṇa-sarga-saṅgrahaḥ*—combination of different material elements; *saḥ*—He; *eva*—certainly; *mām*—me; *hantum*—to kill; *udāyudhaḥ*—prepared with weapons; *sva-rāṭ*—completely independent; *upasthitaḥ*—now present before me; *anyam*—other; *śaraṇam*—shelter; *kam*—unto whom; *āśraye*—I shall resort to.

TRANSLATION

The planet earth continued: My dear Lord, You are the complete conductor of the material creation. You have created this cosmic manifestation and the three material qualities, and therefore You have created me, the planet earth, the resting place of all living entities. Yet You are always fully independent, my Lord. Now that You are present before me and ready to kill me with Your weapons, let me know where I should go to take shelter, and tell me who can give me protection.

PURPORT

The planet earth herein exhibits the symptoms of full surrender before the Lord. As stated, no one can protect the person whom Kṛṣṇa is prepared to kill, and no one can kill the person whom Kṛṣṇa protects. Because the Lord was prepared to kill the planet earth, there was no one to give protection to her. We are all receiving protection from the Lord, and it is therefore proper that every one of us surrender unto Him. In *Bhagavad-gītā* the Lord instructs:

sarva-dharmān parityajya
mām ekaṁ śaraṇaṁ vraja
ahaṁ tvāṁ sarva-pāpebhyo
mokṣayiṣyāmi mā śucaḥ

"Abandon all varieties of religion and just surrender unto Me. I shall deliver you from all sinful reaction. Do not fear." (Bg. 18.66)

Śrīla Bhaktivinoda Ṭhākura sings: "My dear Lord, whatever I have—even my mind, the center of all material necessities, namely my home, my body and whatever I have in connection with this body—I now surrender unto You. You are now completely independent to act however You like. If You like, You can kill me, and if You like, You can save me. In any case, I am Your eternal servant, and You have every right to do whatever You like."

TEXT 31

य एतदादावसृजच्चराचरं
स्वमाययाऽऽत्माश्रययावितर्क्यया ।
तयैव सोऽयं किल गोप्तुमुद्यतः
कथं नु मां धर्मपरो जिघांसति ॥३१॥

ya etad ādāv asṛjac carācaraṁ
sva-māyayātmāśrayayāvitarkyayā
tayaiva so 'yaṁ kila goptum udyataḥ
kathaṁ nu māṁ dharma-paro jighāṁsati

yaḥ—one who; *etat*—these; *ādau*—in the beginning of creation; *asṛjat*—created; *cara-acaram*—moving and nonmoving living entities; *sva-māyayā*—by His own potency; *ātma-āśrayayā*—sheltered under His own protection; *avitarkyayā*—inconceivable; *tayā*—by that same *māyā; eva*—certainly; *saḥ*—

he; *ayam*—this King; *kila*—certainly; *goptum udyataḥ*—prepared to give protection; *katham*—how; *nu*—then; *mām*—me; *dharma-paraḥ*—one who is strictly following religious principles; *jighāṁsati*—desires to kill.

TRANSLATION

In the beginning of creation You created all these moving and non-moving living entities by Your inconceivable energy. Through this very same energy You are now prepared to protect the living entities. Indeed, You are the supreme protector of religious principles. Why are You so anxious to kill me, even though I am in the form of a cow?

PURPORT

The planet earth argues that there is no doubt that one who creates can also annihilate by His sweet will. The planet earth questions why she should be killed when the Lord is prepared to give protection to everyone. After all, it is the earth that is the resting place for all other living entities, and it is the earth that produces grains for them.

TEXT 32

नूनं बतेशस्य समीहितं जनै-
स्तन्मायया दुर्जययाकृतात्मभिः ।
न लक्ष्यते यस्त्वकरोदकारयद्-
योऽनेक एकः परतश्च ईश्वरः ॥३२॥

nūnaṁ bateśasya samīhitaṁ janais
tan-māyayā durjayayākṛtātmabhiḥ
na lakṣyate yas tv akarod akārayad
yo 'neka ekaḥ parataś ca īśvaraḥ

nūnam—surely; *bata*—certainly; *īśasya*—of the Supreme Personality of Godhead; *samīhitam*—activities, plan; *janaiḥ*—by people; *tat-māyayā*—by His potency; *durjayayā*—which is unconquerable; *akṛta-ātmabhiḥ*—who are not sufficiently experienced; *na*—never; *lakṣyate*—are seen; *yaḥ*—he who; *tu*—then; *akarot*—created; *akārayat*—caused to create; *yaḥ*—one who; *anekaḥ*—many; *ekaḥ*—one; *parataḥ*—by His inconceivable potencies; *ca*—and; *īśvaraḥ*—controller.

TRANSLATION

My dear Lord, although You are one, by Your inconceivable potencies You have expanded Yourself in many forms. Through the agency of Brahmā, You have created this universe. You are therefore directly the Supreme Personality of Godhead. Those who are not sufficiently experienced cannot understand Your transcendental activities because they are covered by Your illusory energy.

PURPORT

God is one, but He expands Himself in a variety of energies—the material energy, the spiritual energy, the marginal energy and so forth. Unless one is favored and especially endowed with grace, he cannot understand how the one Supreme Personality of Godhead acts through His different energies. The living entities are also the marginal energy of the Supreme Personality of Godhead. Brahmā is also one of these living entities, but he is especially empowered by the Supreme Personality of Godhead. Although Brahmā is supposed to be the creator of this universe, actually the Supreme Personality of Godhead is its ultimate creator. In this verse the word *māyayā* is significant. *Māyā* means "energy." Lord Brahmā is not the energetic but is one of the manifestations of the Lord's marginal energy. In other words, Lord Brahmā is only an instrument. Although sometimes plans appear contradictory, there is a definite plan behind all action. One who is experienced and is favored by the Lord can understand that everything is being done according to the Lord's supreme plan.

TEXT 33

सर्गादि योऽस्यानुरुणद्धि शक्तिभि-
र्द्रव्यक्रियाकारकचेतनात्मभिः ।
तस्मै समुन्नद्धनिरुद्धशक्तये
नमः परस्मै पुरुषाय वेधसे ॥३३॥

sargādi yo 'syānuruṇaddhi śaktibhir
dravya-kriyā-kāraka-cetanātmabhiḥ
tasmai samunnaddha-niruddha-śaktaye
namaḥ parasmai puruṣāya vedhase

sarga-ādi—creation, maintenance and dissolution; *yaḥ*—one who; *asya*—of this material world; *anuruṇaddhi*—causes; *śaktibhiḥ*—by His own potencies;

dravya—physical elements; *kriyā*—senses; *kāraka*—controlling demigods; *cetanā*—intelligence; *ātmabhiḥ*—consisting of false ego; *tasmai*—unto Him; *samunnaddha*—manifest; *niruddha*—potential; *śaktaye*—one who possesses these energies; *namaḥ*—obeisances; *parasmai*—unto the transcendental; *puruṣāya*—Supreme Personality of Godhead; *vedhase*—unto the cause of all causes.

TRANSLATION

My dear Lord, by Your own potencies You are the original cause of the material elements, as well as the performing instruments (the senses), the workers of the senses (the controlling demigods), the intelligence and the ego, as well as everything else. By Your energy You manifest this entire cosmic creation, maintain it and dissolve it. Through Your energy alone everything is sometimes manifest and sometimes not manifest. You are therefore the Supreme Personality of Godhead, the cause of all causes. I offer my respectful obeisances unto You.

PURPORT

All activities begin with the creation of the total energy, the *mahat-tattva.* Then, by the agitation of the three *guṇas,* the physical elements are created, as well as the mind, ego and the controllers of the senses. All of these are created one after another by the inconceivable energy of the Lord. In modern electronics, a mechanic may, by pushing only one button, set off an electronic chain reaction by which so many actions are carried out one after another. Similarly, the Supreme Personality of Godhead pushes the button of creation, and different energies create the material elements and various controllers of the physical elements, and their subsequent interactions follow the inconceivable plan of the Supreme Personality of Godhead.

TEXT 34

स वै भवानात्मविनिर्मितं जगद्
भूतेन्द्रियान्तःकरणात्मकं विभो ।
संस्थापयिष्यन्नज मां रसातला-
दभ्युज्जहाराम्भस आदिसूकरः ॥३४॥

sa vai bhavān ātma-vinirmitaṁ jagad
bhūtendriyāntaḥ-karaṇātmakaṁ vibho

saṁsthāpayiṣyann aja māṁ rasātalād
abhyujjahārāmbhasa ādi-sūkaraḥ

saḥ—He; *vai*—certainly; *bhavān*—Yourself; *ātma*—by Yourself; *vinirmitam*—manufactured; *jagat*—this world; *bhūta*—the physical elements; *indriya*—senses; *antaḥ-karaṇa*—mind, heart; *ātmakam*—consisting of; *vibho*—O Lord; *saṁsthāpayiṣyan*—maintaining; *aja*—O unborn; *mām*—me; *rasātalāt*—from the plutonic region; *abhyujjahāra*—took out; *ambhasaḥ*—from the water; *ādi*—original; *sūkaraḥ*—the boar.

TRANSLATION

My dear Lord, You are always unborn. Once in the form of the original boar, You rescued me from the waters in the bottom of the universe. Through Your own energy You created all the physical elements, the senses and the heart, for the maintenance of the world.

PURPORT

This refers to the time when Lord Kṛṣṇa appeared as the supreme boar, Varāha, and rescued the earth, which had been merged in water. The *asura* Hiraṇyākṣa had dislocated the earth from its orbit and thrown it beneath the waters of the Garbhodaka Ocean. Then the Lord, in the shape of the original boar, rescued the earth.

TEXT 35

अपामुपस्थे मयि नाव्यवस्थिताः
प्रजा भवानद्य रिरक्षिषुः किल ।
स वीरमूर्तिः समभूद्धराधरो
यो मां पयस्युग्रशरो जिघांससि ॥३५॥

apām upasthe mayi nāvy avasthitāḥ
prajā bhavān adya rirakṣiṣuḥ kila
sa vīra-mūrtiḥ samabhūd dharādharo
yo māṁ payasy ugra-śaro jighāṁsasi

apām—of the water; *upasthe*—situated on the surface; *mayi*—in me; *nāvi*—in a boat; *avasthitāḥ*—standing; *prajāḥ*—living entities; *bhavān*—Yourself; *adya*—now; *rirakṣiṣuḥ*—desiring to protect; *kila*—indeed; *saḥ*—He; *vīra*-

mūrtiḥ—in the form of a great hero; *samabhūt*—became; *dharā-dharaḥ*—the protector of the earthly planet; *yaḥ*—one who; *mām*—me; *payasi*—for the sake of milk; *ugra-śaraḥ*—with sharpened arrows; *jighāṁsasi*—you desire to kill.

TRANSLATION

My dear Lord, in this way You once protected me by rescuing me from the water, and consequently Your name has been famous as Dharādhara—He who holds the planet earth. Yet at the present moment, in the form of a great hero, You are about to kill me with sharpened arrows. I am, however, just like a boat on the water, keeping everything afloat.

PURPORT

The Lord is known as Dharādhara, meaning, "He who keeps the planet earth on His tusks as the boar incarnation." Thus the planet earth in the shape of a cow is accounting the contradictory acts of the Lord. Although He once saved the earth, He now wants to upset the earth, which is like a boat on water. No one can understand the activities of the Lord. Due to a poor fund of knowledge, human beings sometimes think the Lord's activities contradictory.

TEXT 36

नूनं जनैरीहितमीश्वराणा-
मस्मद्विधैस्तद्गुणसर्गमायया ।
न ज्ञायते मोहितचित्तवर्त्मभि-
स्तेभ्यो नमो वीरयशस्करेभ्यः ॥३६॥

nūnaṁ janair īhitam īśvarāṇām
asmad-vidhais tad-guṇa-sarga-māyayā
na jñāyate mohita-citta-vartmabhis
tebhyo namo vīra-yaśas-karebhyaḥ

nūnam—surely; *janaiḥ*—by the people in general; *īhitam*—activities; *īśvarāṇām*—of the controllers; *asmat-vidhaiḥ*—like me; *tat*—of the Personality of Godhead; *guṇa*—of the modes of material nature; *sarga*—which brings forth creation; *māyayā*—by Your energy; *na*—never; *jñāyate*—are understood; *mohita*—bewildered; *citta*—whose minds; *vartmabhiḥ*—way; *tebhyaḥ*—unto them; *namaḥ*—obeisances; *vīra-yaśaḥ-karebhyaḥ*—who bring renown to heroes themselves.

TRANSLATION

My dear Lord, I am also the creation of one of Your energies, composed of the three modes of material nature. Consequently I am bewildered by Your activities. Even the activities of Your devotees cannot be understood, and what to speak of Your pastimes. Thus everything appears to us to be contradictory and wonderful.

PURPORT

The activities of the Supreme Personality of Godhead in His various forms and incarnations are always uncommon and wonderful. It is not possible for a tiny human being to estimate the purpose and plans of such activities; therefore Śrīla Jīva Gosvāmī has said that unless the Lord's activities are accepted as inconceivable, they cannot be explained. The Lord is eternally existing as Kṛṣṇa, the Supreme Personality of Godhead, in Goloka Vṛndāvana. He has also simultaneously expanded Himself in innumerable forms, beginning with Lord Rāma, Lord Nṛsiṁha, Lord Varāha and all the incarnations coming directly from Saṅkarṣaṇa. Saṅkarṣaṇa is the expansion of Baladeva, and Baladeva is the first manifestation of Kṛṣṇa. Therefore all these incarnations are known as *kalā*.

The word *īśvarāṇām* refers to all the personalities of Godhead. As stated in *Brahma-saṁhitā:* (5.39) *rāmādi-mūrtiṣu kalā-niyamena tiṣṭhan.* In the *Śrīmad-Bhāgavatam* it is confirmed that all the incarnations are partial expansions or *kalā* of the Supreme Personality of Godhead. However, Kṛṣṇa is the original Supreme Personality of Godhead. One should not take the plural number of the word *īśvarāṇām* to mean that there are many Godheads. The fact is that God is one, but He exists eternally and expands Himself in innumerable forms and acts in various ways. Sometimes the common man is bewildered by all this and considers such activities contradictory, but they are not contradictory. There is a great plan behind all the Lord's activities.

For our understanding it is sometimes said that the Lord is situated in the heart of the thief as well as in the heart of the householder, but the Supersoul in the heart of the thief dictates, "Go and steal things from that particular house," and at the same time the Lord tells the householder, "Now be careful of thieves and burglars." These instructions to different persons appear contradictory, yet we should know that the Supersoul, the Supreme Personality of Godhead, has some plan, and we should not consider such activities contradictory. The best course is to surrender unto the Supreme

Personality of Godhead wholeheartedly, and, being protected by Him, remain peaceful.

Thus end the Bhaktivedanta purports of the Fourth Canto, Seventeenth Chapter, of the Śrīmad-Bhāgavatam, *entitled "Mahārāja Pṛthu Becomes Angry at the Earth."*

CHAPTER EIGHTEEN

Pṛthu Mahārāja Milks the Earth Planet

TEXT 1

मैत्रेय उवाच
इत्थं पृथुमभिष्टूय रुषा प्रस्फुरिताधरम् ।
पुनराहावनिर्भीता संस्तभ्यात्मानमात्मना ॥ १ ॥

maitreya uvāca
itthaṁ pṛthum abhiṣṭūya
ruṣā prasphuritādharam
punar āhāvanir bhītā
saṁstabhyātmānam ātmanā

maitreyaḥ uvāca—the great saint Maitreya continued to speak; *ittham*—thus; *pṛthum*—unto King Pṛthu; *abhiṣṭūya*—after offering prayers; *ruṣā*—in anger; *prasphurita*—trembling; *adharam*—his lips; *punaḥ*—again; *āha*—she said; *avaniḥ*—the earthly planet; *bhītā*—in fear; *saṁstabhya*—after settling; *ātmānam*—the mind; *ātmanā*—by the intelligence.

TRANSLATION

The great saint Maitreya continued to address Vidura: My dear Vidura, at that time, after the planet earth finished her prayers, King Pṛthu was still not pacified, and his lips trembled in great anger. Although the planet earth was frightened, she made up her mind and began to speak as follows in order to convince the King.

TEXT 2

संनियच्छाभिभो मन्युं निबोध श्रावितं च मे ।
सर्वतः सारमादत्ते यथा मधुकरो बुधः ॥ २ ॥

sanniyacchābhibho manyuṁ
nibodha śrāvitaṁ ca me
sarvataḥ sāram ādatte
yathā madhu-karo budhaḥ

sanniyaccha—please pacify; *abhibho*—O King; *manyum*—anger; *nibodha*—try to understand; *śrāvitam*—what is said; *ca*—also; *me*—by me; *sarvataḥ*—from everywhere; *sāram*—the essence; *ādatte*—takes; *yathā*—as; *madhu-karaḥ*—the bumblebee; *budhaḥ*—an intelligent person.

TRANSLATION

My dear Lord, please pacify your anger completely and patiently hear whatever I submit before you. Please turn your kind attention to this. I may be very poor, but a learned man takes the essence of knowledge from all places, just as a bumblebee collects honey from each and every flower.

TEXT 3

अस्मिँल्लोकेऽथवामुष्मिन्मुनिभिस्तत्त्वदर्शिभिः ।
दृष्टा योगाः प्रयुक्ताश्च पुंसां श्रेयःप्रसिद्धये ॥ ३ ॥

asmiĺ loke 'thavāmuṣmin
munibhis tattva-darśibhiḥ
dṛṣṭā yogāḥ prayuktāś ca
puṁsāṁ śreyaḥ-prasiddhaye

asmin—in this; *loke*—duration of life; *athavā*—or; *amuṣmin*—in the next life; *munibhiḥ*—by the great sages; *tattva*—the truth; *darśibhiḥ*—by those who have seen it; *dṛṣṭāḥ*—prescribed; *yogāḥ*—methods; *prayuktāḥ*—applied; *ca*—also; *puṁsām*—of the people in general; *śreyaḥ*—benefit; *prasiddhaye*—in the matter of obtaining.

TRANSLATION

To benefit all human society, not only in this life but in the next, the great seers and sages have prescribed various methods conducive to the prosperity of the people in general.

PURPORT

Vedic civilization takes advantage of the perfect knowledge presented in the *Vedas* and presented by the great sages and *brāhmaṇas* for the benefit of human society. Vedic injunctions are known as *śruti,* and the additional supplementary presentations of these principles, as given by the great sages, are known as *smṛti.* They follow the principles of Vedic instruction. Human society should take advantage of the instructions from both *śruti* and *smṛti.* If one wants to advance in spiritual life, he must take these instructions and follow the principles. In *Bhakti-rasāmṛta-sindhu,* Śrīla Rūpa Gosvāmī says that if one poses himself as advanced in spiritual life but does not refer to the *śrutis* and *smṛtis* he is simply a disturbance in society. One should follow the principles laid down in *śrutis* and *smṛtis* not only in one's spiritual life but in material life as well. As far as human society is concerned, it should follow the *Manu-smṛti* as well, for these laws are given by Manu, the father of mankind.

In the *Manu-smṛti* it is stated that a woman should not be given independence but should be given protection by her father, husband and elderly sons. In all circumstances a woman should remain dependent upon some guardian. Presently women are given full independence like men, but actually we can see that such independent women are no happier than those women who are placed under guardians. If people follow the injunctions given by the great sages, *śrutis* and *smṛtis,* they can actually be happy in both this life and the next. Unfortunately rascals are manufacturing so many ways and means to be happy. Everyone is inventing so many methods. Consequently human society has lost the standard ways of life, both materially and spiritually, and as a result people are bewildered, and there is no peace or happiness in the world. Although they are trying to solve the problems of human society in the United Nations, they are still baffled. Because they do not follow the liberated instructions of the *Vedas,* they are unhappy.

Two significant words used in this verse are *asmin* and *amuṣmin. Asmin* means "in this life," and *amuṣmin* means "in the next life." Unfortunately in this age, even exalted professors and learned men believe that there is no next life and that everything is finished in this life. Since they are rascals and fools, what advice can they give? Still they are passing as learned scholars and professors. In this verse the word *amuṣmin* is very explicit. It is the duty of everyone to mold his life in such a way that he will have a profitable next life. Just as a boy is educated in order to become happy later, one should be educated in this life in order attain an eternal and prosperous life after death. It is therefore essential that people follow what is given in the *śrutis* and *smṛtis* to make sure that the human mission is successful.

TEXT 4

तानातिष्ठति यः सम्यगुपायान् पूर्वदर्शितान् ।
अवरः श्रद्धयोपेत उपेयान् विन्दतेऽञ्जसा ॥ ४ ॥

tān ātiṣṭhati yaḥ samyag
upāyān pūrva-darśitān
avaraḥ śraddhayopeta
upeyān vindate 'ñjasā

tān—those; *ātiṣṭhati*—follows; *yaḥ*—anyone who; *samyak*—completely; *upāyān*—principles; *pūrva*—formerly; *darśitān*—instructed; *avaraḥ*—inexperienced; *śraddhayā*—with faith; *upetaḥ*—being situated; *upeyān*—the fruits of activities; *vindate*—enjoys; *añjasā*—very easily.

TRANSLATION

One who follows the principles and instructions enjoined by the great sages of the past can utilize these instructions for practical purposes. Such a person can very easily enjoy life and pleasures.

PURPORT

The Vedic principles (*mahājano yena gataḥ sa panthāḥ*) urge us to follow in the footsteps of great liberated souls. In this way we can receive benefit in both this life and the next, and we can also improve our material life. By following the principles laid down by great sages and saints of the past, we can very easily understand the aim of all life. The word *avaraḥ*, meaning "inexperienced," is very significant in this verse. Every conditioned soul is inexperienced. Everyone is *abodha-jāta*—born a fool and rascal. In democratic government at the present moment all kinds of fools and rascals are making decisions. But what can they do? What is the result of their legislation? They enact something today just to whimsically repeal it tomorrow. One political party utilizes a country for one purpose, and the next moment another political party forms a different type of government and nullifies all the laws and regulations. This process of chewing the chewed (*punaḥ punaś carvita-carvaṇānām*) will never make human society happy. In order to make all human society happy and prosperous, we should accept the standard methods given by liberated persons.

TEXT 5

ताननादृत्य योऽविद्वानर्थानारभते स्वयम् ।
तस्य व्यभिचरन्त्यर्था आरब्धाश्च पुनः पुनः ॥ ५ ॥

tān anādṛtya yo 'vidvān
arthān ārabhate svayam
tasya vyabhicaranty arthā
ārabdhāś ca punaḥ punaḥ

tān—those; *anādṛtya*—neglecting; *yaḥ*—anyone who; *avidvān*—rascal; *arthān*—schemes; *ārabhate*—begins; *svayam*—personally; *tasya*—his; *vyabhicaranty*—do not become successful; *arthāḥ*—purposes; *ārabdhāḥ*—attempted; *ca*—and; *punaḥ punaḥ*—again and again.

TRANSLATION

A foolish person who manufactures his own ways and means through mental speculation and does not recognize the authority of the sages who lay down unimpeachable directions is simply unsuccessful again and again in his attempts.

PURPORT

At the present moment it has become fashionable to disobey the unimpeachable directions given by the *ācāryas* and liberated souls of the past. Presently people are so fallen that they cannot distinguish between a liberated soul and a conditioned soul. A conditioned soul is hampered by four defects: he is sure to commit mistakes, he is sure to become illusioned, he has a tendency to cheat others, and his senses are imperfect. Consequently we have to take direction from liberated persons. This Kṛṣṇa consciousness movement directly receives instructions from the Supreme Personality of Godhead via persons who are strictly following His instructions. Although a follower may not be a liberated person, if he follows the supreme liberated Personality of Godhead, his actions are naturally liberated from the contamination of the material nature. Lord Caitanya therefore says: "By My order you may become a spiritual master." One can immediately become a spiritual master by having full faith in the transcendental words of the Supreme Personality of Godhead and by following His instructions. Materialistic men are not interested in taking directions from a liberated person, but they are very much interested in their concocted ideas, which make them repeatedly fail in their attempts. Because the entire world is now following the imperfect directions of conditioned souls, humanity is completely bewildered.

TEXT 6

पुरा सृष्टा ह्योषधयो ब्रह्मणा या विशाम्पते ।
भुज्यमाना मया दृष्टा असद्भिरधृतव्रतैः ॥ ६ ॥

purā sṛṣṭā hy oṣadhayo
brahmaṇā yā viśām pate
bhujyamānā mayā dṛṣṭā
asadbhir adhṛta-vrataiḥ

purā—in the past; *sṛṣṭāḥ*—created; *hi*—certainly; *oṣadhayaḥ*—herbs and food grains; *brahmaṇā*—by Lord Brahmā; *yāḥ*—all those which; *viśām pate*—O King; *bhujyamānāḥ*—being enjoyed; *mayā*—by me; *dṛṣṭāḥ*—seen; *asadbhiḥ*—by nondevotees; *adhṛta-vrataiḥ*—devoid of all spiritual activities.

TRANSLATION

My dear King, the seeds, roots, herbs and grains, which were created by Lord Brahmā in the past, are now being used by nondevotees, who are devoid of all spiritual understanding.

PURPORT

Lord Brahmā created this material world for the use of the living entities, but it was created according to a plan that all living entities who come into it to dominate it for sense gratification would be given directions by Lord Brahmā in the *Vedas* in order that they might ultimately leave it and return home, back to Godhead. All necessities grown on earth—namely fruits, flowers, trees, grains, animals and animal by-products—were created for use in sacrifice for the satisfaction of the Supreme Personality of Godhead, Viṣṇu. However, the planet earth in the shape of a cow herein submits that all these utilities are being used by nondevotees who have no plans for spiritual understanding. Although there are immense potencies within the earth for the production of grains, fruits and flowers, this production is checked by the earth itself when it is misused by nondevotees who have no spiritual goals. Everything belongs to the Supreme Personality of Godhead, and everything can be used for His satisfaction. Things should not be used for the sense gratification of the living entities. This is the whole plan of material nature according to the directions of this material nature.

In this verse the words *asadbhiḥ* and *adhṛta-vrataiḥ* are important. The word *asadbhiḥ* refers to the nondevotees. The nondevotees have been described in *Bhagavad-gītā* as *duṣkṛtinaḥ* (miscreants), *mūḍhāḥ* (asses or rascals), *narādhamāḥ* (lowest of mankind) and *māyayāpahṛta-jñānāḥ* (those who have lost their knowledge to the power of the illusory energy). All these persons are *asat*, nondevotees. Nondevotees are also called *gṛha-vrata*, whereas the devotee is called *dhṛta-vrata*. According to plans, the misguided conditioned souls who have come to lord it over material nature should be trained to become *dhṛta-vrata*. This means that they should take a vow to satisfy their senses or enjoy material life only by satisfying the senses of the Supreme Lord. Activities intended to satisfy the senses of the Surpeme Lord, Kṛṣṇa, are called *kṛṣṇārthe 'khila-ceṣṭāḥ*. This indicates that one can attempt all kinds of work, but one should do so to satisfy Kṛṣṇa. This is described in *Bhagavad-gītā* as *yajñārthāt karma*. The word *yajña* indicates Lord Viṣṇu. We should work only for His satisfaction. In modern times (Kali-yuga), however, people have forgotten Viṣṇu altogether, and they conduct their activities for sense gratification. Such people will gradually become poverty-stricken, for they cannot use things which are to be enjoyed by the Supreme Lord for their own sense gratification. If they continue like this, there will ultimately be a state of poverty, and no grains, fruits or flowers will be produced. Indeed, it is stated in the Twelfth Canto of *Bhāgavatam* that at the end of Kali-yuga people will be so polluted that there will no longer be any grains, wheat, sugar cane or milk.

TEXT 7

अपालितानादृता च भवद्भिर्लोकपालकैः ।
चोरीभूतेऽथ लोकेऽहं यज्ञार्थेऽग्रसमोषधीः ॥ ७ ॥

apālitānādṛtā ca
bhavadbhir loka-pālakaiḥ
corībhūte 'tha loke 'haṁ
yajñārthe 'grasam oṣadhīḥ

apālitā—without being taken care of; *anādṛtā*—being neglected; *ca*—also; *bhavadbhiḥ*—like your good self; *loka-pālakaiḥ*—by the governors or kings; *corībhūte*—being beset by thieves; *atha*—therefore; *loke*—this world; *aham*—

I; *yajña-arthe*—for the purpose of performing sacrifices; *agrasam*—have hidden; *oṣadhīḥ*—all the herbs and grains.

TRANSLATION

My dear King, not only are grains and herbs being used by nondevotees, but, as far as I'm concerned, I am not being properly maintained. Indeed, I am being neglected by kings who are not punishing these rascals who have turned into thieves by using grains for sense gratification. Consequently I have hidden all these seeds, which were meant for the performance of sacrifice.

PURPORT

That which happened during the time of Pṛthu Mahārāja and his father, King Vena, is also happening at this present moment. A huge arrangement exists for the production of large-scale industrial and agricultural products, but all these products are meant for sense gratification. Therefore despite such productive capacities there is scarcity because the world's population is full of thieves. The word *corībhūte* indicates that the population has turned to thievery. According to Vedic understanding, men are transformed into thieves when they plan economic development for sense gratification. It is also explained in *Bhagavad-gītā* that if one eats food grains without offering them to the Supreme Personality of Godhead, Yajña, he is a thief and liable to be punished. According to spiritual communism, all properties on the surface of the globe belong to the Supreme Personality of Godhead. The population has a right to use goods only after offering them to the Supreme Personality of Godhead. This is the process of accepting *prasāda.* Unless one eats *prasāda,* he is certainly a thief. It is the duty of governors and kings to punish such thieves and maintain the world nicely. If this is not done, grains will no longer be produced, and people will simply starve. Indeed, not only will people be obliged to eat less, but they will kill one another and eat their own flesh. They are already killing animals for flesh, so when there will no longer be grains, vegetables and fruits, they will kill their own sons and fathers and eat their flesh for sustenance.

TEXT 8

नूनं ता वीरुधः क्षीणा मयि कालेन भूयसा ।
तत्र योगेन दृष्टेन भवानादातुमर्हति ॥ ८ ॥

nūnaṁ tā vīrudhaḥ kṣīṇā
mayi kālena bhūyasā
tatra yogena dṛṣṭena
bhavān ādātum arhati

nūnam—therefore; *tāḥ*—those; *vīrudhaḥ*—herbs and grains; *kṣīṇāḥ*—deteriorated; *mayi*—within me; *kālena*—in course of time; *bhūyasā*—very much; *tatra*—therefore; *yogena*—by proper means; *dṛṣṭena*—acknowledged; *bhavān*—Your Majesty; *ādātum*—to take; *arhati*—ought.

TRANSLATION

Due to being stocked for a very long time, all the grain seeds within me have certainly deteriorated. Therefore you should immediately arrange to take these seeds out by the standard process, which is recommended by the ācāryas or śāstras.

PURPORT

When there is a scarcity of grain, the government should follow the methods prescribed in the *śāstra* and approved by the *ācāryas;* thus there will be a sufficient production of grains, and food scarcity and famine can be checked. *Bhagavad-gītā* recommends that we perform *yajña,* sacrifices. By the performance of *yajña,* sufficient clouds gather in the sky, and when there are sufficient clouds, there is also sufficient rainfall. In this way agricultural matters are taken care of. When there is sufficient grain production, the general populace eats the grains, and animals like cows, goats and other domestic animals eat the grasses and grains also. According to this arrangement, human beings should perform the sacrifices recommended in the *śāstras,* and if they do so there will no longer be food scarcity. In Kali-yuga, the only sacrifice recommended is *saṅkīrtana-yajña.*

In this verse there are two significant words: *yogena,* "by the approved method," and *dṛṣṭena,* "as exemplified by the former *ācāryas.*" One is mistaken if he thinks that by applying modern machines such as tractors, grains can be produced. If one goes to a desert and uses a tractor, there is still no possibility of producing grains. We may adopt various means, but it is essential to know that the planet earth will stop producing grains if sacrifices are not performed. The earth has already explained that because nondevotees are enjoying the production of food, she has reserved food seeds for the performance of sacrifice. Now, of course, atheists will not believe in this spiritual method of producing grains, but whether they believe or not, the fact remains that we are not independent to produce grain by mechanical means. As far as the approved method is concerned, it is enjoined in the *śāstras* that intelligent men in this age will take to the *saṅkīrtana* movement, and by so doing they shall worship the Supreme Personality of Godhead Lord Caitanya, whose bodily complexion is golden, and who is always accompanied by His confidential devotees to preach this Kṛṣṇa consciousness movement all over the world. In its present condition, the world can only be saved by introducing this *saṅkīrtana,* this Kṛṣṇa consciousness movement. As we have learned from the previous verse, one who is not in Kṛṣṇa consciousness is considered a thief. Even though he may be very materially advanced, a thief cannot be placed in a comfortable position. A thief is a thief, and he is punishable. Because people are without Kṛṣṇa consciousness, they have become thieves, and consequently they are being punished by the laws of material nature. No one can check this, not even by introducing so many relief funds and humanitarian institutions. Unless the people of the world take to Kṛṣṇa consciousness, there will be a scarcity of food and much suffering.

TEXTS 9-10

वत्सं कल्पय मे वीर येनाहं वत्सला तव ।
धोक्ष्ये क्षीरमयान् कामाननुरूपं च दोहनम् ॥ ९ ॥
दोग्धारं च महाबाहो भूतानां भूतभावन ।
अन्नमीप्सितमूर्जस्वद्भगवान् वाञ्छते यदि ॥१०॥

vatsaṁ kalpaya me vīra
yenāhaṁ vatsalā tava
dhokṣye kṣīramayān kāmān
anurūpaṁ ca dohanam

dogdhāraṁ ca mahā-bāho
bhūtānāṁ bhūta-bhāvana
annam īpsitam ūrjasvad
bhagavān vāñchate yadi

vatsam—a calf; *kalpaya*—arrange; *me*—for me; *vīra*—O hero; *yena*—by which; *aham*—I; *vatsalā*—affectionate; *tava*—your; *dhokṣye*—shall fulfill; *kṣīra-mayān*—in the form of milk; *kāmān*—desired necessities; *anurūpam*—according to different living entities; *ca*—also; *dohanam*—milking pot; *dog-

dhāram—milkman; *ca*—also; *mahā-bāho*—O mighty-armed one; *bhūtānām*—of all living entities; *bhūta-bhāvana*—O protector of the living entities; *annam*—food grains; *īpsitam*—desired; *ūrjaḥ-vat*—nourishing; *bhagavān*—your worshipable self; *vāñchate*—desires; *yadi*—if.

TRANSLATION

O great hero, protector of living entities, if you desire to relieve the living entities by supplying them sufficient grain, and if you desire to nourish them by taking milk from me, you should make arrangements to bring a calf suitable for this purpose and a pot in which the milk can be kept, as well as a milkman to do the work. Since I will be very much affectionate toward my calf, your desire to take milk from me will be fulfilled.

PURPORT

These are nice instructions for milking a cow. The cow must first have a calf so that out of affection for the calf she will voluntarily give sufficient milk. There must also be an expert milkman and a suitable pot in which to keep the milk. Just as a cow cannot deliver sufficient milk without being affectionate to her calf, the earth cannot produce sufficient necessities without feeling affection for those who are Kṛṣṇa conscious. Even though the earth's being in the shape of a cow may be taken figuratively, the meaning herein is very explicit. Just as a calf can derive milk from a cow, all living entities—including animals, birds, bees, reptiles, aquatics, etc.—can receive their respective foods from the planet earth provided that human beings are not *asat,* or *adhṛta-vrata,* as we have previously discussed. When human society becomes *asat,* or ungodly, or devoid of Kṛṣṇa consciousness, the entire world suffers. If human beings are well-behaved, animals will also receive sufficient food and be happy. The ungodly human being, ignorant of his duty to give protection and food to the animals, kills them to compensate for the insufficient production of grains. Thus no one is satisfied, and that is the cause for the present condition in today's world.

TEXT 11

समां च कुरु मां राजन्देववृष्टं यथा पयः ।
अपर्तावपि भद्रं ते उपावर्तेत मे विभो ॥११॥

samāṁ ca kuru māṁ rājan
deva-vṛṣṭaṁ yathā payaḥ

apartāv api bhadraṁ te
upāvarteta me vibho

samām—equally level; *ca*—also; *kuru*—make; *mām*—me; *rājan*—O King; *deva-vṛṣṭam*—fallen as rain by the mercy of King Indra; *yathā*—so that; *payaḥ*—water; *apartau*—when the rainy season has ceased; *api*—even; *bhadram*—auspiciousness; *te*—unto you; *upāvarteta*—it can remain; *me*—on me; *vibho*—O Lord.

TRANSLATION

My dear King, may I inform you that you have to make the entire surface of the globe level. This will help me, even when the rainy season has ceased. Rainfall comes by the mercy of King Indra. Rainfall will remain on the surface of the globe always keeping the earth moistened, and thus it will be auspicious for all kinds of production.

PURPORT

King Indra of the heavenly planets is in charge of throwing thunderbolts and giving rainfall. Generally thunderbolts are thrown on the tops of hills in order to break them to pieces. As these pieces are spread asunder in due course of time, the surface of the globe gradually becomes fit for agriculture. Level land is especially conducive to the production of grain. Thus the planet earth requested Mahārāja Pṛthu to level the surface of the earth, breaking up the high land and mountains.

TEXT 12

इति प्रियं हितं वाक्यं भुव आदाय भूपतिः ।
वत्सं कृत्वा मनुं पाणावदुहत्सकलौषधीः ॥१२॥

iti priyaṁ hitaṁ vākyaṁ
bhuva ādāya bhūpatiḥ
vatsaṁ kṛtvā manuṁ pāṇāv
aduhat sakalauṣadhīḥ

iti—thus; *priyam*—pleasing; *hitam*—beneficial; *vākyam*—words; *bhuvaḥ*—of the earth; *ādāya*—taking into consideration; *bhū-patiḥ*—the King; *vatsam*—calf; *kṛtvā*—making; *manum*—Svāyambhuva Manu; *pāṇau*—in his hands; *aduhat*—milked; *sakala*—all; *oṣadhīḥ*—herbs and grains.

TRANSLATION

After hearing the auspicious and pleasing words of the planet earth, the King accepted them. He then transformed Svāyambhuva Manu into a calf and milked all the herbs and grains from the earth in the form of a cow, keeping them in his cupped hands.

TEXT 13

तथापरे च सर्वत्र सारमाददते बुधाः ।
ततोऽन्ये च यथाकामं दुदुहुः पृथुभावितम् ॥१३॥

tathāpare ca sarvatra
sāram ādadate budhāḥ
tato 'nye ca yathā-kāmaṁ
duduhuḥ pṛthu-bhāvitām

tathā—so; *apare*—others; *ca*—also; *sarvatra*—everywhere; *sāram*—the essence; *ādadate*—took; *budhāḥ*—the intelligent class of men; *tataḥ*—thereafter; *anye*—others; *ca*—also; *yathā-kāmam*—as much as they desired; *duduhuḥ*—milked; *pṛthu-bhāvitām*—the earth planet controlled by Pṛthu Mahārāja.

TRANSLATION

Others, who were as intelligent as King Pṛthu, also took the essence out of the earthly planet. Indeed, everyone took this opportunity to follow in the footsteps of King Pṛthu and get whatever he desired from the planet earth.

PURPORT

The planet earth is also called *vasundharā.* The word *vasu* means "wealth," and *dharā* means "one who holds." All creatures within the earth fulfill the necessities required for human beings, and all living entities can be taken out of the earth by the proper means. As suggested by the planet earth, and accepted and initiated by King Pṛthu, whatever is taken from the earth—either from the mines, from the surface of the globe or from the atmosphere—should always be considered the property of the Supreme Personality of Godhead and should be used for Yajña, Lord Viṣṇu. As soon as the process of *yajña* is stopped, the earth will withold all productions—vegetables, trees, plants, fruits, flowers, other agricultural products, minerals, etc. As confirmed in *Bhagavad-gītā,* the process of *yajña* was instituted from the beginning of creation. By the regular performance of *yajña,* the equal distribution of wealth, and the restriction of sense gratification, the entire world will be made peaceful and prosperous. As already mentioned, in this age of Kali the simple performance of *saṅkīrtana-yajña*—the holding of festivals as initiated by the International Society for Krishna Consciousness—should be introduced in every town and village. Intelligent men should encourage the performance of *saṅkīrtana-yajña* by their personal behavior. This means that they should follow the process of austerity by restricting themselves from illicit sex life, meat-eating, gambling and intoxication. If the intelligent men, or the *brāhmaṇas* of society, would follow the rules and regulations, certainly the entire face of this present world, which is in such chaotic condition, would change, and people would be happy and prosperous.

TEXT 14

ऋषयो दुदुहुर्देवीमिन्द्रियेष्वथ सत्तम ।
वत्सं बृहस्पतिं कृत्वा पयश्छन्दोमयं शुचि ॥१४॥

ṛṣayo duduhur devīm
indriyeṣv atha sattama
vatsaṁ bṛhaspatiṁ kṛtvā
payaś chandomayaṁ śuci

ṛṣayaḥ—the great sages; *duduhuḥ*—milked; *devīm*—the earth; *indriyeṣu*—in the senses; *atha*—then; *sattama*—O Vidura; *vatsam*—the calf; *bṛhaspatim*—the sage Bṛhaspati; *kṛtvā*—making; *payaḥ*—milk; *chandaḥ-mayam*—in the form of the Vedic hymns; *śuci*—pure.

TRANSLATION

All the great sages transformed Bṛhaspati into a calf, and making the senses into a pot, they milked all kinds of Vedic knowledge to purify words, mind and hearing.

PURPORT

Bṛhaspati is the priest of the heavenly planets. Vedic knowledge was received in logical order by the great sages through Bṛhaspati for the benefit of human society, not only on this planet, but throughout the universes.

In other words, Vedic knowledge is considered one of the necessities for human society. If human society remains satisfied simply by taking grains from the planet earth as well as other necessities for maintaining the body, society will not be sufficiently prosperous. Humanity must have food for the mind and ear, as well as for the purpose of vibration. As far as transcendental vibrations are concerned, the essence of all Vedic knowledge is the *mahā-mantra*—Hare Kṛṣṇa, Hare Kṛṣṇa, Kṛṣṇa Kṛṣṇa, Hare Hare/ Hare Rāma, Hare Rāma, Rāma Rāma, Hare Hare. In Kali-yuga, if this Vedic *mahā-mantra* is chanted regularly and heard regularly by the devotional process of *śravaṇaṁ kīrtanam*, it will purify all societies, and thus humanity will be happy both materially and spiritually.

TEXT 15

कृत्वा वत्सं सुरगणा इन्द्रं सोममदूदुहन् ।
हिरण्मयेन पात्रेण वीर्यमोजो बलं पयः ॥१५॥

kṛtvā vatsaṁ sura-gaṇā
indraṁ somam adūduhan
hiraṇmayena pātreṇa
vīryam ojo balaṁ payaḥ

kṛtvā—making; *vatsam*—calf; *sura-gaṇāḥ*—the demigods; *indram*—Indra, King of heaven; *somam*—nectar; *adūduhan*—they milked out; *hiraṇmayena*—golden; *pātreṇa*—with a pot; *vīryam*—mental power; *ojaḥ*—strength of the senses; *balam*—strength of the body; *payaḥ*—milk.

TRANSLATION

All the demigods made Indra, the King of heaven, into a calf, and from the earth they milked the beverage soma, which is nectar. Thus they became very powerful in mental speculation and bodily and sensual strength.

PURPORT

In this verse the word *soma* means "nectar." *Soma* is a kind of beverage made in the heavenly planets from the moon to the kingdoms of the demigods in the various higher planetary systems. By drinking this *soma* beverage the demigods become more powerful mentally and increase their sensual power and bodily strength. The words *hiraṇmayena pātreṇa* indicate that this *soma* beverage is not an ordinary intoxicating liquor. The demigods would not touch any kind of liquor. Nor is *soma* a kind of drug. It is a different kind of beverage available in the heavenly planets. *Soma* is far different from the liquors made for demoniac people, as explained in the next verse.

TEXT 16

दैतेया दानवा वत्सं प्रह्लादमसुरर्षभम् ।
विधायादूदुहन् क्षीरमयःपात्रे सुरासवम् ॥१६॥

daiteyā dānavā vatsaṁ
prahlādam asura-ṛṣabham
vidhāyādūduhan kṣīram
ayaḥ-pātre surāsavam

daiteyāḥ—the sons of Diti; *dānavāḥ*—demons; *vatsam*—the calf; *prahlādam*—Prahlāda Mahārāja; *asura*—demon; *ṛṣabham*—the chief; *vidhāya*—making; *adūduhan*—they milked out; *kṣīram*—milk; *ayaḥ*—iron; *pātre*—in a pot; *surā*—liquor; *āsavam*—fermented liquids like beer.

TRANSLATION

The sons of Diti and the demons transformed Prahlāda Mahārāja, who was born in an asura family, into a calf, and they extracted various kinds of liquor and beer, which they put into a pot made of iron.

PURPORT

The demons also have their own types of beverage in the form of liquors and beers, just as the demigods use *soma-rasa* for their drinking purposes. The demons born of Diti take great pleasure in drinking wine and beer. Even today people of demoniac nature are very much addicted to liquor and beer. The name of Prahlāda Mahārāja is very significant in this connection. Because Prahlāda Mahārāja was born in a family of demons, as the son of Hiraṇyakaśipu, by his mercy the demons were and still are able to have their drinks in the forms of wine and beer. The word *ayaḥ* (iron) is very significant. Whereas the nectarean *soma* was put in a golden pot, the liquors and beers were put in an iron pot. Because the liquor and beer are inferior, they are placed in an iron pot, and because *soma-rasa* is superior, it is placed in a golden pot.

TEXT 17

गन्धर्वाप्सरसोऽधुक्षन् पात्रे पद्ममये पयः ।
वत्सं विश्वावसुं कृत्वा गान्धर्वं मधु सौभगम् ॥१७॥

gandharvāpsaraso 'dhukṣan
pātre padmamaye payaḥ
vatsaṁ viśvāvasuṁ kṛtvā
gāndharvaṁ madhu saubhagam

gandharva—inhabitants of the Gandharva planet; *apsarasaḥ*—the inhabitants of the Apsarā planet; *adhukṣan*—milked out; *pātre*—in a pot; *padmamaye*—made of a lotus; *payaḥ*—milk; *vatsam*—calf; *viśvāvasum*—of the name Viśvāvasu; *kṛtvā*—making; *gāndharvam*—songs; *madhu*—sweet; *saubhagam*—beauty.

TRANSLATION

The inhabitants of Gandharvaloka and Apsaroloka made Viśvāvasu into a calf, and they drew the milk into a lotus flower pot. The milk took the shape of sweet musical art and beauty.

TEXT 18

वत्सेन पितरोऽर्यम्णा कव्यं क्षीरमधुक्षत ।
आमपात्रे महाभागाः श्रद्धया श्राद्धदेवताः ॥१८॥

vatsena pitaro 'ryamṇā
kavyaṁ kṣīram adhukṣata
āma-pātre mahā-bhāgāḥ
śraddhayā śrāddha-devatāḥ

vatsena—by the calf; *pitaraḥ*—the inhabitants of Pitṛloka; *aryamṇā*—by the god of Pitṛloka, Aryamā; *kavyam*—offerings of food to ancestors; *kṣīram*—milk; *adhukṣata*—took out; *āma-pātre*—into an unbaked earthen pot; *mahā-bhāgāḥ*—the greatly fortunate; *śraddhayā*—with great faith; *śrāddha-devatāḥ*—the demigods presiding over *śrāddha* ceremonies in honor of deceased relatives.

TRANSLATION

The fortunate inhabitants of Pitṛloka, who preside over the funeral ceremonies, made Aryamā into a calf. With great faith they milked kavya, food offered to the ancestors, into an unbaked earthen pot.

PURPORT

In *Bhagavad-gītā* it is said, *pitṝn yānti pitṛ-vratāḥ.* Those who are interested in family welfare are called *pitṛ-vratāḥ.* There is a planet called Pitṛloka, and the predominating deity of that planet is called Aryamā. He is somewhat of a demigod, and by satisfying him one can help ghostly family members develop a gross body. Those who are very sinful and attached to their family, house, village or country do not receive a gross body made of material elements but remain in a subtle body composed of mind, ego and intelligence. Those who live in such subtle bodies are called ghosts. This ghostly position is very painful because a ghost has intelligence, mind and ego and wants to enjoy material life, but because he doesn't have a gross material body, he can only create disturbances for want of material satisfaction. It is the duty of family members, especially the son, to offer oblations to the demigod Aryamā, or Lord Viṣṇu. From time immemorial in India the son of a dead man goes to Gayā and, at a Viṣṇu temple there, offers oblations for the benefit of his ghostly father. It is not that everyone's father becomes a ghost, but the oblations of *piṇḍa* are offered to the lotus feet of Lord Viṣṇu so that if a family member happens to become a ghost, he will be favored with a gross body. However, if one is habituated to taking the *prasāda* of Lord Viṣṇu, there is no chance of his becoming a ghost or anything lower than a human being. In Vedic civilization there is a performance called *śrāddha* by which food is offered with faith and devotion. If one offers oblations with faith and devotion—either to the lotus feet of Lord Viṣṇu or to His representative in Pitṛloka, Aryamā—one's forefathers will attain material bodies to enjoy whatever material enjoyment is due them. In other words, they do not have to become ghosts.

TEXT 19

प्रकल्प्य वत्सं कपिलं सिद्धाः सङ्कल्पनामयीम् ।
सिद्धिं नभसि विद्यां च ये च विद्याधरादयः ॥१९॥

prakalpya vatsaṁ kapilaṁ
siddhāḥ saṅkalpanāmayīm

siddhiṁ nabhasi vidyāṁ ca
ye ca vidyādharādayaḥ

prakalpya—appointing; *vatsam*—calf; *kapilam*—the great sage Kapila; *siddhāḥ*—the inhabitants of Siddhaloka; *saṅkalpanā-mayīm*—proceeding from will; *siddhim*—yogic perfection; *nabhasi*—in the sky; *vidyām*—knowledge; *ca*—also; *ye*—those who; *ca*—also; *vidyādhara-ādayaḥ*—the inhabitants of Vidyādhara-loka, and so on.

TRANSLATION

After this, the inhabitants of Siddhaloka, as well as the inhabitants of Vidyādhara-loka, transformed the great sage Kapila into a calf, and making the whole sky into a pot, they milked out specific yogic mystic powers, beginning with aṇimā. Indeed, the inhabitants of Vidyādhara-loka acquired the art of flying in the sky.

PURPORT

The inhabitants of both Siddhaloka and Vidyādhara-loka are naturally endowed with mystic yogic powers by which they can not only fly in outer space without a vehicle but can also fly from one planet to another simply by exerting their will. Just as fish can swim within water, the residents of Vidyādhara-loka can swim in the ocean of air. As far as the inhabitants of Siddhaloka are concerned, they are endowed with all mystic powers. The *yogīs* in this planet practice the eightfold yogic mysticism—namely *yama, niyama, āsana, prāṇāyāma, pratyāhāra, dhāraṇā, dhyāna* and *samādhi.* By regularly practicing the yogic processes one after another, the *yogīs* attain various perfections; they can become smaller than the smallest, heavier than the heaviest, etc. They can even manufacture a planet, get whatever they like, and control whatever man they want. All the residents of Siddhaloka are naturally endowed with these mystic yogic powers. It is certainly a very wonderful thing if we see a person on this planet flying in the sky without a vehicle, but in Vidyādhara-loka such flying is as commonplace as a bird's flying in the sky. Similarly, in Siddhaloka all the inhabitants are great *yogīs,* perfect in mystic powers.

The name of Kapila Muni is significant in this verse because He was the expounder of the Sāṅkhya philosophical system, and His father, Kardama Muni, was a great *yogī* and mystic. Indeed, Kardama Muni prepared a great airplane, which was as large as a small town and had various gardens, palatial buildings, servants, maidservants, etc. With all this paraphernalia,

Kapiladeva's mother, Devahūti, and His father, Kardama Muni, traveled all over the universes and visited different planets.

TEXT 20

अन्ये च मायिनो मायामन्तर्धानाद्भुतात्मनाम् ।
मयं प्रकल्प्य वत्सं ते दुदुहुर्धारणामयीम् ॥२०॥

anye ca māyino māyām
antardhānādbhutātmanām
mayaṁ prakalpya vatsaṁ
te duduhur dhāraṇāmayīm

anye—others; *ca*—also; *māyinaḥ*—mystic magicians; *māyām*—mystic powers; *antardhāna*—disappearing; *adbhuta*—wonderful; *ātmanām*—of the body; *mayam*—the demon named Maya; *prakalpya*—making; *vatsam*—the calf; *te*—they; *duduhuḥ*—milked out; *dhāraṇā-mayīm*—proceeding from will.

TRANSLATION

Others also, the inhabitants of planets known as Kimpurusa-loka, made the demon Maya into a calf, and they milked out mystic powers by which one can disappear immediately from another's vision and appear again in a different form.

PURPORT

It is said that the inhabitants of Kimpuruṣa-loka can perform many wonderful mystic demonstrations. In other words, they can exhibit as many wonderful things as one can imagine. The inhabitants of this planet can do whatever they like, or whatever they imagine. Such powers are also mystic powers. The possession of such mystic power is called *īśitā.* The demons generally learn such mystic powers by the practice of *yoga.* In the *Daśama-skandha,* the Tenth Canto of *Śrīmad-Bhāgavatam,* there is a vivid description of how the demons appear before Kṛṣṇa in various wonderful forms. For instance, Bakāsura appeared before Kṛṣṇa and His cowherd boy friends as a gigantic crane. While present on this planet, Lord Kṛṣṇa had to fight with many demons who could exhibit the wonderful mystic powers of Kimpuruṣa-loka. Although the inhabitants of Kimpuruṣa-loka are naturally endowed with such powers, one can attain these powers on this planet by performing different yogic practices.

TEXT 21

यक्षरक्षांसि भूतानि पिशाचाः पिशिताशनाः ।
भूतेशवत्सा दुदुहुः कपाले क्षतजासवम् ॥२१॥

yakṣa-rakṣāṁsi bhūtāni
piśācāḥ piśitāśanāḥ
bhūteśa-vatsā duduhuḥ
kapāle kṣatajāsavam

yakṣa—the Yakṣas (the descendants of Kuvera); *rakṣāṁsi*—the Rākṣasas (meat-eaters); *bhūtāni*—ghosts; *piśācāḥ*—witches; *piśita-aśanāḥ*—who are all habituated to eating flesh; *bhūteśa*—Lord Śiva's incarnation Rudra; *vatsāḥ*—whose calf; *duduhuḥ*—milked out; *kapāle*—in the pot of skulls; *kṣata-ja*—blood; *āsavam*—a fermented beverage.

TRANSLATION

Then the Yakṣas, the Rākṣasas, ghosts and witches, who are habituated to eating flesh, transformed Lord Śiva's incarnation Rudra [Bhūtanātha] into a calf and milked out beverages made of blood and put them in a pot made of skulls.

PURPORT

There are some types of living entities in the form of human beings whose living conditions and eatables are most abominable. Generally they eat flesh and fermented blood, which is mentioned in this verse as *kṣata-jāsavam.* The leaders of such degraded men known as Yakṣas, Rākṣasas, *bhūtas, piśācas,* etc., are all in the mode of ignorance. They have been placed under the control of Rudra. Rudra is the incarnation of Lord Śiva and is in charge of the mode of ignorance in material nature. Another name of Lord Śiva is Bhūtanātha, meaning "master of ghosts." Rudra was born out of Brahmā's eyes when Brahmā was very angry at the four Kumāras.

TEXT 22

तथाहयो दन्दशूकाः सर्पा नागाश्च तक्षकम् ।
विधाय वत्सं दुदुहुर्बिलपात्रे विषं पयः ॥२२॥

tathāhayo dandaśūkāḥ
sarpā nāgāś ca takṣakam

vidhāya vatsaṁ duduhur
bila-pātre viṣaṁ payaḥ

tathā—similarly; *ahayaḥ*—snakes without hoods; *dandaśūkāḥ*—scorpions; *sarpāḥ*—cobras; *nāgāḥ*—big snakes; *ca*—and; *takṣakam*—Takṣaka, chief of the snakes; *vidhāya*—making; *vatsam*—calf; *duduhuḥ*—milked out; *bila-pātre*—in the pot of snake holes; *viṣam*—poison; *payaḥ*—as milk.

TRANSLATION

Thereafter cobras and snakes without hoods, large snakes, scorpions and many other poisonous animals took poison out of the planet earth as their milk and kept this poison in snake holes. They made a calf out of Takṣaka.

PURPORT

Within this material world there are various types of living entities, and the different types of reptiles and scorpions mentioned in this verse are also provided with their sustenance by the arrangement of the Supreme Personality of Godhead. The point is that everyone is taking his eatables from the planet earth. According to one's association with the material qualities, one develops a certain type of character. *Payaḥ-pānam bhujaṅgānām:* if one feeds a serpent milk, the snake will simply increase his venom. However, if one supplies milk to a talented sage or saint, the sage will develop finer brain tissues by which he can contemplate higher spiritual life. Thus the Lord is supplying everyone food, but according to the living entity's association with the modes of material nature, the living entity develops his specific character.

TEXTS 23-24

पशवो यवसं क्षीरं वत्सं कृत्वा च गोवृषम् ।
अरण्यपात्रे चाधुक्षन्मृगेन्द्रेण च दंष्ट्रिणः ॥२३॥
क्रव्यादाः प्राणिनः क्रव्यं दुदुहुः स्वे कलेवरे ।
सुपर्णवत्सा विहगाश्चरं चाचरमेव च ॥२४॥

paśavo yavasaṁ kṣīraṁ
vatsaṁ kṛtvā ca go-vṛṣam
araṇya-pātre cādhukṣan
mṛgendreṇa ca daṁṣṭriṇaḥ

kravyādāḥ prāṇinaḥ kravyaṁ
duduhuḥ sve kalevare
suparṇa-vatsā vihagāś
caraṁ cācaram eva ca

paśavaḥ—cattle; *yavasam*—green grasses; *kṣīram*—milk; *vatsam*—the calf; *kṛtvā*—making; *ca*—also; *go-vṛṣam*—the bull carrier of Lord Śiva; *araṇya-pātre*—in the pot of the forest; *ca*—also; *adhukṣan*—milked out; *mṛga-indreṇa*—by the lion; *ca*—and; *daṁṣṭriṇaḥ*—animals with sharp teeth; *kravya-adāḥ*—animals who eat raw flesh; *prāṇinaḥ*—living entities; *kravyam*—flesh; *duduhuḥ*—took out; *sve*—own; *kalevare*—in the pot of their body; *suparṇa*—Garuḍa; *vatsāḥ*—whose calf; *viha-gāḥ*—the birds; *caram*—moving living entities; *ca*—also; *acaram*—nonmoving living entities; *eva*—certainly; *ca*—also.

TRANSLATION

The four-legged animals like the cows made a calf out of the bull who carries Lord Śiva and made a milking pot out of the forest. Thus they got fresh green grasses to eat. Ferocious animals like tigers transformed a lion into a calf, and thus they were able to get flesh for milk. The birds made a calf out of Garuḍa and took milk from the planet earth in the form of moving insects and nonmoving plants and grasses.

PURPORT

There are many carnivorous birds descended from Garuḍa, the winged carrier of Lord Viṣṇu. Indeed, there is a particular type of bird that is very fond of eating monkeys. Eagles are fond of eating goats, and of course many birds eat only fruits and berries. Therefore the words *caram,* referring to moving animals, and *acaram,* referring to grasses, fruits and vegetables, are mentioned in this verse.

TEXT 25

वटवत्सा वनस्पतयः पृथग्रसमयं पयः ।
गिरयो हिमवद्वत्सा नानाधातून् स्वसानुषु ॥२५॥

vaṭa-vatsā vanas-patayaḥ
pṛthag rasamayaṁ payaḥ
girayo himavad-vatsā
nānā dhātūn sva-sānuṣu

vaṭa-vatsāḥ—making the banyan tree a calf; *vanaḥ-patayaḥ*—the trees; *pṛthak*—different; *rasa-mayam*—in the form of juices; *payaḥ*—milk; *girayaḥ*—the hills and mountains; *himavat-vatsāḥ*—making the Himalayas the calf; *nānā*—various; *dhātūn*—minerals; *sva*—own; *sānuṣu*—on their peaks.

TRANSLATION

The trees made a calf out of the banyan tree, and thus they derived milk in the form of many delicious juices. The mountains transformed the Himalayas into a calf, and they milked a variety of minerals into a pot made of the peaks of hills.

TEXT 26

सर्वे स्वमुख्यवत्सेन स्वे स्वे पात्रे पृथक् पयः ।
सर्वकामदुघां पृथ्वीं दुदुहुः पृथुभाविताम् ॥२६॥

sarve sva-mukhya-vatsena
sve sve pātre pṛthak payaḥ
sarva-kāma-dughāṁ pṛthvīṁ
duduhuḥ pṛthu-bhāvitām

sarve—all; *sva-mukhya*—by their own chiefs; *vatsena*—as the calf; *sve sve*—in their own; *pātre*—pots; *pṛthak*—different; *payaḥ*—milk; *sarva-kāma*—all desirables; *dughām*—supplying as milk; *pṛthvīm*—the earthly planet; *duduhuḥ*—milked out; *pṛthu-bhāvitām*—controlled by King Pṛthu.

TRANSLATION

The planet earth supplied everyone his respective food. During the time of King Pṛthu, the earth was fully under the control of the King. Thus all the inhabitants of the earth could get their food supply by creating various types of calves and putting their particular types of milk in various pots.

PURPORT

This is evidence that the Lord supplies food to everyone. As confirmed in the *Vedas: eko bahūnāṁ yo vidadhāti kāmān.* Although the Lord is one, He is supplying all necessities to everyone through the medium of the planet earth. There are different varieties of living entities on different planets, and they all derive their eatables from their planets in different forms. On the basis of these descriptions, how can one assume that there is no living entity on the moon? Every moon is earthly, being composed of the five elements. Every planet produces different types of food according to the needs of its residents. According to the Vedic *śāstras*, it is not true that the moon does not produce food nor that no living entity is living there.

TEXT 27

एवं पृथ्वादयः पृथ्वीमन्नादाः स्वन्नमात्मनः ।
दोहवत्सादिभेदेन क्षीरभेदं कुरूद्वह ॥२७॥

evaṁ pṛthv-ādayaḥ pṛthvīm
annādāḥ svannam ātmanaḥ
doha-vatsādi-bhedena
kṣīra-bhedaṁ kurūdvaha

evam—thus; *pṛthu-ādayaḥ*—King Pṛthu and others; *pṛthvīm*—the earth; *anna-adāḥ*—all living entities desiring food; *su-annam*—their desired foodstuff; *ātmanaḥ*—for self-preservation; *doha*—for milking; *vatsa-ādi*—by calves, pots and milkers; *bhedena*—different; *kṣīra*—milk; *bhedam*—different; *kuru-udvaha*—O chief of the Kurus.

TRANSLATION

My dear Vidura, chief of the Kurus, in this way King Pṛthu and all the others who subsist on food created different types of calves and milked out their respective eatables. Thus they received their various foodstuffs, which were symbolized as milk.

TEXT 28

ततो महीपतिः प्रीतः सर्वकामदुघां पृथुः ।
दुहितृत्वे चकारेमां प्रेम्णा दुहितृवत्सलः ॥२८॥

tato mahīpatiḥ prītaḥ
sarva-kāma-dughāṁ pṛthuḥ
duhitṛtve cakāremāṁ
premṇā duhitṛ-vatsalaḥ

tataḥ—thereafter; *mahī-patiḥ*—the King; *prītaḥ*—being pleased; *sarva-kāma*—all desirables; *dughām*—producing as milk; *pṛthuḥ*—King Pṛthu; *duhitṛtve*—treating as his daughter; *cakāra*—did; *imām*—unto the earthly planet; *premṇā*—out of affection; *duhitṛ-vatsalaḥ*—affectionate to his daughter.

TRANSLATION

Thereafter King Pṛthu was very satisfied with the planet earth, for she sufficiently supplied all food to various living entities. Thus he developed an affection for the planet earth, just as if she were his own daughter.

TEXT 29

चूर्णयन् स्वधनुष्कोट्या गिरिकूटानि राजराट् ।
भूमण्डलमिदं वैन्यः प्रायश्चक्रे समं विभुः ॥२९॥

cūrṇayan sva-dhanuṣ-koṭyā
giri-kūṭāni rāja-rāṭ
bhū-maṇḍalam idaṁ vainyaḥ
prāyaś cakre samaṁ vibhuḥ

cūrṇayan—making into pieces; *sva*—his own; *dhanuḥ-koṭyā*—by the power of his bow; *giri*—of the hills; *kūṭāni*—the tops; *rāja-rāṭ*—the Emperor; *bhū-maṇḍalam*—the whole earth; *idam*—this; *vainyaḥ*—the son of Vena; *prāyaḥ*—almost; *cakre*—made; *samam*—level; *vibhuḥ*—the powerful.

TRANSLATION

After this, the King of all kings, Mahārāja Pṛthu, leveled all rough places on the surface of the globe by breaking up the hills with the strength of his bow. By his grace the surface of the globe almost became flat.

PURPORT

Generally the mountainous and hilly portions of the earth are made flat by the striking of thunderbolts. Generally this is the business of King Indra of the heavenly planets, but King Pṛthu, an incarnation of the Supreme Personality of Godhead, did not wait for King Indra to break up the hills and mountains but did so himself by using his strong bow.

TEXT 30

अथास्मिन् भगवान् वैन्यः प्रजानां वृत्तिदः पिता ।
निवासान् कल्पयाश्चक्रे तत्र तत्र यथार्हतः ॥३०॥

athāsmin bhagavān vainyaḥ
prajānāṁ vṛtti-daḥ pitā
nivāsān kalpayāñ cakre
tatra tatra yathārhataḥ

atha—thus; *asmin*—on this earth planet; *bhagavān*—the Personality of Godhead; *vainyaḥ*—son of Vena; *prajānām*—of the citizens; *vṛtti-daḥ*—who supplies employment; *pitā*—a father; *nivāsān*—residences; *kalpayān*—suitable; *cakre*—make; *tatra tatra*—here and there; *yathā*—as; *arhataḥ*—desirable, suitable.

TRANSLATION

To all the citizens of the state, King Pṛthu was as good as a father. Thus he was visibly engaged in giving them proper subsistence and proper employment for subsistence. After leveling the surface of the globe, he earmarked different places for residential quarters, inasmuch as they were desirable.

TEXT 31

ग्रामान् पुरः पत्तनानि दुर्गाणि विविधानि च ।
घोषान् व्रजान् सशिबिरानाकरान् खेटखर्वटान् ॥३१॥

grāmān puraḥ pattanāni
durgāṇi vividhāni ca
ghoṣān vrajān sa-śibirān
ākarān kheṭa-kharvaṭān

grāmān—villages; *puraḥ*—cities; *pattanāni*—settlements; *durgāṇi*—forts; *vividhāni*—of different varieties; *ca*—also; *ghoṣān*—habitations for the milkmen; *vrajān*—pens for cattle; *sa-śibirān*—with camps; *ākarān*—mines; *kheṭa*—agricultural towns; *kharvaṭān*—mountain villages.

TRANSLATION

In this way the King founded many types of villages, settlements and towns and built forts, residences for cowherdsmen, stables for the animals, and places for the royal camps, mining places, agricultural towns and mountain villages.

TEXT 32

प्राक्पृथोरिह नैवैषा पुरग्रामादिकल्पना ।
यथासुखं वसन्ति स्म तत्र तत्राकुतोभयाः ॥३२॥

prāk pṛthor iha naivaiṣā
pura-grāmādi-kalpanā
yathā-sukhaṁ vasanti sma
tatra tatrākutobhayāḥ

prāk—before; *pṛthoḥ*—King Pṛthu; *iha*—on this planet; *na*—never; *eva*—certainly; *eṣā*—this; *pura*—of towns; *grāma-ādi*—of villages, etc.; *kalpanā*—planned arrangement; *yathā*—as; *sukham*—convenient; *vasanti sma*—lived; *tatra tatra*—here and there; *akutobhayāḥ*—without hesitation.

TRANSLATION

Before the reign of King Pṛthu there was no planned arrangement for different cities, villages, pasturing grounds, etc. Everything was scattered, and everyone constructed his residential quarters according to his own convenience. However, since King Pṛthu plans were made for towns and villages.

PURPORT

From this statement it appears that town and city planning is not new but has been coming down since the time of King Pṛthu. In India we can see regular planning methods evident in very old cities. In *Śrīmad-Bhāgavatam* there are many descriptions of such ancient cities. Even 5,000 years ago, Lord Kṛṣṇa's capital, Dvārakā, was well planned, and similar other cities—Mathurā, and Hastināpura (now New Delhi)—were also well planned. Thus the planning of cities and towns is not a modern innovation but was existing in bygone ages.

Thus end the Bhaktivedanta purports of the Fourth Canto, Eighteenth Chapter of the Śrīmad-Bhāgavatam, *entitled "Pṛthu Mahārāja Milks the Earth Planet."*

CHAPTER NINETEEN

King Pṛthu's One Hundred Horse Sacrifices

TEXT 1

मैत्रेय उवाच
अथादीक्षत राजा तु हयमेधशतेन सः ।
ब्रह्मावर्ते मनोः क्षेत्रे यत्र प्राची सरस्वती ॥ १ ॥

maitreya uvāca
athādīkṣata rājā tu
haya-medha-śatena saḥ
brahmāvarte manoḥ kṣetre
yatra prācī sarasvatī

maitreyaḥ uvāca—the sage Maitreya said; *atha*—thereafter; *adīkṣata*—took initiation; *rājā*—the King; *tu*—then; *haya*—horse; *medha*—sacrifices; *śatena*—to perform one hundred; *saḥ*—he; *brahmāvarte*—known as Brahmāvarta; *manoḥ*—of Svāyambhuva Manu; *kṣetre*—in the land; *yatra*—where; *prācī*—eastern; *sarasvatī*—the river named Sarasvatī.

TRANSLATION

The great sage Maitreya continued: My dear Vidura, King Pṛthu initiated the performance of one hundred horse sacrifices at the spot where the River Sarasvatī flows toward the East. This piece of land is known as Brahmāvarta, and it was controlled by Svāyambhuva Manu.

TEXT 2

तदभिप्रेत्य भगवान् कर्मातिशयमात्मनः ।
शतक्रतुर्न ममृषे पृथोर्यज्ञमहोत्सवम् ॥ २ ॥

tad abhipretya bhagavān
karmātiśayam ātmanaḥ
śata-kratur na mamṛṣe
pṛthor yajña-mahotsavam

tat abhipretya—considering this matter; *bhagavān*—the most powerful; *karma-atiśayam*—excelling in fruitive activities; *ātmanaḥ*—of himself; *śata-kratuḥ*—King Indra, who had performed a hundred sacrifices; *na*—not; *mamṛṣe*—did tolerate; *pṛthoḥ*—of King Pṛthu; *yajña*—sacrificial; *mahā-utsavam*—great ceremonies.

TRANSLATION

When the most powerful Indra, the King of heaven, saw this, he considered the fact that King Pṛthu was going to exceed him in fruitive activities. Thus Indra could not tolerate the great sacrificial ceremonies performed by King Pṛthu.

PURPORT

In the material world everyone who comes to enjoy himself or lord it over material nature is envious of others. This envy is also found in the personality of the King of heaven, Indra. As evident from revealed scriptures, Indra was several times envious of many persons. He was especially envious of great fruitive activities and the execution of *yoga* practices, or *siddhis*. Indeed, he could not tolerate them, and he desired to break them up. He was envious due to fear that those who performed great sacrifices for the execution of mystic *yoga* might occupy his seat. Since no one in this material world can tolerate another's advancement, everyone in the material world is called *matsara*, envious. In the beginning of *Śrīmad-Bhāgavatam* it is therefore said that *Śrīmad-Bhāgavatam* is meant for those who are completely *nirmatsara* (nonenvious). In other words, one who is not free from the contamination of envy cannot advance in Kṛṣṇa consciousness. In Kṛṣṇa consciousness, however, if someone excels another person, the devotee who is excelled thinks how fortunate the other person is to be advancing in devotional service. Such non-envy is typical of Vaikuṇṭha. However, when one is envious of his competitor, that is material. The demigods posted in the material world are not exempt from envy.

TEXT 3

यत्र यज्ञपतिः साक्षाद्भगवान् हरिरीश्वरः ।
अन्वभूयत सर्वात्मा सर्वलोकगुरुः प्रभुः ॥ ३ ॥

yatra yajña-patiḥ sākṣād
bhagavān harir īśvaraḥ
anvabhūyata sarvātmā
sarva-loka-guruḥ prabhuḥ

yatra—where; *yajña-patiḥ*—the enjoyer of all sacrifices; *sākṣāt*—directly; *bhagavān*—the Supreme Personality of Godhead; *hariḥ*—Lord Viṣṇu; *īśvaraḥ*—the supreme controller; *anvabhūyata*—became visible; *sarva-ātmā*—the Supersoul of everyone; *sarva-loka-guruḥ*—the master of all planets or the teacher of everyone; *prabhuḥ*—the proprietor.

TRANSLATION

The Supreme Personality of Godhead, Lord Viṣṇu, is present in everyone's heart as the Supersoul, and He is the proprietor of all planets and the enjoyer of the results of all sacrifices. He was personally present at the sacrifices made by King Pṛthu.

PURPORT

In this verse the word *sākṣāt* is significant. Pṛthu Mahārāja was a *śaktyāveśa-avatāra* incarnation of Lord Viṣṇu. Actually Pṛthu Mahārāja was a living entity, but he acquired specific powers from Lord Viṣṇu. Lord Viṣṇu, however, is directly the Supreme Personality of Godhead, and thus belongs to the category of *viṣṇu-tattva.* Mahārāja Pṛthu belonged to the *jīva-tattva.* The *viṣṇu-tattva* indicates God, whereas the *jīva-tattva* indicates the part and parcel of God. When God's part and parcel is especially empowered, he is called *śaktyāveśa-avatāra.* Lord Viṣṇu is herein described as *harir īśvaraḥ.* The Lord is so kind that He takes all miserable conditions away from His devotees. Consequently He is called *hari.* He is described as *īśvara* because He can do whatever He likes. He is the supreme controller. The supreme *īśvara puruṣottama* is Lord Kṛṣṇa. He exhibits His powers as *īśvara,* or the supreme controller, when He assures His devotee in *Bhagavad-gītā:* "Abandon all varieties of religion and just surrender unto Me. I shall deliver you from all sinful reaction. Do not fear." (Bg. 18.66) He can immediately make His devotee immune from all the reactions caused by sinful life if the devotee simply surrenders unto Him. He is described herein as *sarvātmā,* meaning that He is present in everyone's heart as the Supersoul, and as such He is the supreme teacher of everyone. If we are fortunate enough to take the lessons given by Lord Kṛṣṇa in *Bhagavad-gītā,* our lives immediately become successful. No one can give better instructions to human society than Lord Kṛṣṇa.

TEXT 4

अन्वितो ब्रह्मशर्वाभ्यां लोकपालैः सहानुगैः ।
उपगीयमानो गन्धर्वैर्मुनिभिश्चाप्सरोगणैः ॥ ४ ॥

anvito brahma-śarvābhyāṁ
loka-pālaiḥ sahānugaiḥ
upagīyamāno gandharvair
munibhiś cāpsaro-gaṇaiḥ

anvitaḥ—being accompanied; *brahma*—by Lord Brahmā; *śarvābhyām*—and by Lord Śiva; *loka-pālaiḥ*—by the predominating chiefs of all different planets; *saha anugaiḥ*—along with their followers; *upagīyamānaḥ*—being praised; *gandharvaiḥ*—by the residents of Gandharvaloka; *munibhiḥ*—by great sages; *ca*—also; *apsaraḥ-gaṇaiḥ*—by the residents of Apsaroloka.

TRANSLATION

When Lord Viṣṇu appeared in the sacrificial arena, Lord Brahmā, Lord Śiva and all the chief predominating personalities of every planet, as well as their followers, came with Him. When He appeared on the scene, the residents of Gandharvaloka, the great sages and the residents of Apsaroloka all praised Him.

TEXT 5

सिद्धा विद्याधरा दैत्या दानवा गुह्यकादयः ।
सुनन्दनन्दप्रमुखाः पार्षदप्रवरा हरेः ॥ ५ ॥

siddhā vidyādharā daityā
dānavā guhyakādayaḥ
sunanda-nanda-pramukhāḥ
pārṣada-pravarā hareḥ

siddhāḥ—the residents of Siddhaloka; *vidyādharāḥ*—the residents of Vidyādhara-loka; *daityāḥ*—the demoniac descendants of Diti; *dānavāḥ*—the *asuras; guhyaka-ādayaḥ*—the Yakṣas, etc.; *sunanda-nanda-pramukhāḥ*—headed by Sunanda and Nanda, the chief of Lord Viṣṇu's associates from Vaikuṇṭha; *pārṣada*—associates; *pravarāḥ*—most respectful; *hareḥ*—of the Supreme Personality of Godhead.

TRANSLATION

The Lord was accompanied by the residents of Siddhaloka, Vidyādharaloka, all the descendants of Diti, and the demons and the Yakṣas. He was also accompanied by His chief associates, headed by Sunanda and Nanda.

TEXT 6

कपिलो नारदो दत्तो योगेशाः सनकादयः ।
तमन्वीयुर्भागवता ये च तत्सेवनोत्सुकाः ॥ ६ ॥

kapilo nārado datto
yogeśāḥ sanakādayaḥ
tam anvīyur bhāgavatā
ye ca tat-sevanotsukāḥ

kapilaḥ—Kapila Muni; *nāradaḥ*—the great sage Nārada; *dattaḥ*—Dattātreya; *yoga-īśāḥ*—the masters of mystic power; *sanaka-ādayaḥ*—headed by Sanaka; *tam*—Lord Viṣṇu; *anvīyuḥ*—followed; *bhāgavatāḥ*—great devotees; *ye*—all those who; *ca*—also; *tat-sevana-utsukāḥ*—always eager to serve the Lord.

TRANSLATION

Great devotees who were always engaged in the service of the Supreme Personality of Godhead, as well as the great sages named Kapila, Nārada, and Dattātreya, and masters of mystic powers, headed by Sanaka Kumāra, all attended the great sacrifice with Lord Viṣṇu.

TEXT 7

यत्र धर्मदुघा भूमिः सर्वकामदुघा सती ।
दोग्धि स्माभीप्सितानर्थान् यजमानस्य भारत ॥ ७ ॥

yatra dharma-dughā bhūmiḥ
sarva-kāma-dughā satī
dogdhi smābhīpsitān arthān
yajamānasya bhārata

yatra—where; *dharma-dughā*—producing sufficient milk for religiosity; *bhūmiḥ*—the land; *sarva-kāma*—all desires; *dughā*—yielding as milk; *satī*—

the cow; *dogdhi sma*—fulfilled; *abhīpsitān*—desirable; *arthān*—objects; *yajamānasya*—of the sacrificer; *bhārata*—my dear Vidura.

TRANSLATION

My dear Vidura, in that great sacrifice the entire land came to be like the milk-producing kāma-dhenu, and thus, by the performance of yajña, all daily necessities for life were supplied.

PURPORT

In this verse the word *dharma-dughā* is significant, for it indicates *kāma-dhenu. Kāma-dhenu* is also known as *surabhi. Surabhi* cows inhabit the spiritual world, and, as stated in *Brahma-saṁhitā,* Lord Kṛṣṇa is engaged in tending these cows: *surabhīr abhipālayantam.* One can milk a *surabhi* cow as often as he likes, and the cow will deliver as much milk as one requires. Milk, of course, is necessary for the production of so many milk products, especially clarified butter, which is required for the performances of great sacrifices. Unless we are prepared to perform the prescribed sacrifices, our supply of the necessities of life will be checked. *Bhagavad-gītā* confirms that Lord Brahmā created human society along with *yajña,* the performance of sacrifice. *Yajña* means Lord Viṣṇu, the Supreme Personality of Godhead, and sacrifice means working for the satisfaction of the Supreme Personality of Godhead. In this age, however, it is very difficult to find qualified *brāhmaṇas* who can perform sacrifices as prescribed in the *Vedas.* Therefore it is recommended in *Śrīmad-Bhāgavatam* (*yajñaiḥ saṅkīrtana-prāyaiḥ*) that by performing *saṅkīrtana-yajña* and by satisfying the *yajña-puruṣa,* Lord Caitanya, one can derive all the results derived by great sacrifices in the past. King Pṛthu and others derived all the necessities of life from the earthly planet by performing great sacrifices. Now this *saṅkīrtana* movement has already been started by the International Society for Krishna Consciousness. People should take advantage of this great sacrifice and join in the Society's activities; then there will be no scarcity. If *saṅkīrtana-yajña* is performed, there will be no difficulty, not even in industrial enterprises. Therefore this system should be introduced in all spheres of life—social, political, industrial, commercial, etc. Then everything will run very peacefully and smoothly.

TEXT 8

ऊहुः सर्वरसान्नद्यः क्षीरदध्यन्नगोरसान् ।
तरवो भूरिवर्ष्माणः प्रासूयन्त मधुच्युतः ॥ ८ ॥

ūhuḥ sarva-rasān nadyaḥ
kṣīra-dadhy-anna-go-rasān
taravo bhūri-varṣmāṇaḥ
prāsūyanta madhu-cyutaḥ

ūhuḥ—bore; *sarva-rasān*—all kinds of tastes; *nadyaḥ*—the rivers; *kṣīra*—milk; *dadhi*—curd; *anna*—different kinds of food; *go-rasān*—other milk products; *taravaḥ*—trees; *bhūri*—great; *varṣmāṇaḥ*—having bodies; *prāsūyanta*—bore fruit; *madhu-cyutaḥ*—dropping honey.

TRANSLATION

The flowing rivers supplied all kinds of tastes—sweet, pungent, sour, etc.—and very big trees supplied fruit and honey in abundance. The cows, having eaten sufficient green grass, supplied profuse quantities of milk, curd, clarified butter and similar other necessities.

PURPORT

If rivers are not polluted and are allowed to flow in their own way, or sometimes allowed to flood the land, the land will become very fertile and able to produce all kinds of vegetables, trees and plants. The word *rasa* means "taste." Actually all *rasas* are tastes within the earth, and as soon as seeds are sown on the ground, various trees sprout up to satisfy our different tastes. For instance, sugar cane provides its juices to satisfy our taste for sweetness, and oranges provide their juices to satisfy our taste for a mixture of the sour and the sweet. Similarly, there are pineapples and other fruits. At the same time, there are chilis to satisfy our taste for pungency. Although the earth's ground is the same, different tastes arise due to different kinds of seeds. As Kṛṣṇa says in *Bhagavad-gītā, bījaṁ māṁ sarva-bhūtānām:* "I am the original seed of all existences." (Bg. 7.10) Therefore all arrangements are there. And as stated in *Īśopaniṣad: pūrṇam idam.* Complete arrangements for the production of all the necessities of life are made by the Supreme Personality of Godhead. People should therefore learn how to satisfy the *yajña-puruṣa,* Lord Viṣṇu. Indeed, the living entity's prime business is to satisfy the Lord because the living entity is part and parcel of the Lord. Thus the whole system is so arranged that the living entity must do his duty as he is constitutionally made. Without doing so, all living entities must suffer. That is the law of nature.

The words *taravo bhūri-varṣmāṇaḥ* indicate very luxuriantly grown, big-bodied trees. The purpose of these trees was to produce honey and varieties of fruit. In other words, the forest also has its purpose in supplying honey, fruits and flowers. Unfortunately in Kali-yuga, due to an absence of *yajña,* there are many big trees in the forests, but they do not supply sufficient fruits and honey. Thus everything is dependent on the performance of *yajña.* The best way to perform *yajña* in this age is to spread the *saṅkīrtana* movement all over the world.

TEXT 9

सिन्धवो रत्ननिकरान् गिरयोऽन्नं चतुर्विधम् ।
उपायनमुपाजह्रुः सर्वे लोकाः सपालकाः ॥ ९ ॥

sindhavo ratna-nikarān
girayo 'nnaṁ catur-vidham
upāyanam upājahruḥ
sarve lokāḥ sapālakāḥ

sindhavaḥ—the oceans; *ratna-nikarān*—heaps of jewels; *girayaḥ*—the hills; *annam*—eatables; *catuḥ-vidham*—four kinds of; *upāyanam*—presentations; *upājahruḥ*—brought forward; *sarve*—all; *lokāḥ*—the people in general of all planets; *sa-pālakāḥ*—along with the governors.

TRANSLATION

King Pṛthu was presented with various gifts from the general populace and predominating deities of all planets. The oceans and seas were full of valuable jewels and pearls, and the hills were full of chemicals and fertilizers. Four kinds of edibles were produced profusely.

PURPORT

As stated in *Īśopaniṣad,* this material creation is supplied with all the potencies for the production of all necessities required by the living entities—not only human beings, but animals, reptiles, aquatics, trees, etc. The oceans and seas produce pearls, coral and valuable jewels so that fortunate law-abiding people can utilize them. Similarly, the hills are full of chemicals so when rivers flow down from them the chemicals spread over the fields to fertilize the four kinds of foodstuffs. These are technically known as *carvya* (those edibles which are chewed), *lehya* (those which are licked up), *cūṣya* (those which are swallowed) and *peya* (those which are drunk).

Pṛthu Mahārāja was greeted by the residents of other planets and their presiding deities. They presented various gifts to the King and acknowledged him as the proper type of king by whose planning and activities everyone throughout the universe could be happy and prosperous. It is clearly indicated in this verse that the oceans and seas are meant for producing jewels, but in Kali-yuga the oceans are mainly being utilized for fishing. *Śūdras* and poor men were allowed to fish, but the higher classes like the *kṣatriyas* and *vaiśyas* would gather pearls, jewels and coral. Although poor men would catch tons of fish, they would not be equal in value to one piece of coral or pearl. In this age so many factories for the manufacture of fertilizers have been opened, but when the Personality of Godhead is pleased by the performance of *yajñas,* the hills automatically produce fertilizing chemicals, which help produce edibles in the fields. Everything is dependent on the people's acceptance of the Vedic principles of sacrifice.

TEXT 10

इति चाधोक्षजेशस्य पृथोस्तु परमोदयम् ।
असूयन् भगवानिन्द्रः प्रतिघातमचीकरत् ॥१०॥

iti cādhokṣajeśasya
pṛthos tu paramodayam
asūyan bhagavān indraḥ
pratighātam acīkarat

iti—thus; *ca*—also; *adhokṣaja-īśasya*—who accepted Adhokṣaja as his worshipable Lord; *pṛthoḥ*—of King Pṛthu; *tu*—then; *parama*—the topmost; *udayam*—opulence; *asūyan*—being envious of; *bhagavān*—the most powerful; *indraḥ*—the King of heaven; *pratighātam*—impediments; *acīkarat*—made.

TRANSLATION

King Pṛthu was dependent on the Supreme Personality of Godhead, who is known as Adhokṣaja. Because King Pṛthu performed so many sacrifices, he was superhumanly enhanced by the mercy of the Supreme Lord. King Pṛthu's opulence, however, could not be tolerated by the King of heaven, Indra, who tried to impede the progress of his opulence.

PURPORT

In this verse there are three significant purposes expressed in the words *adhokṣaja, bhagavān indraḥ* and *pṛthoḥ*. Mahārāja Pṛthu is an incarnation of Viṣṇu, yet he is a great devotee of Lord Viṣṇu. Although an empowered incarnation of Lord Viṣṇu, he is nonetheless a living entity. As such, he must be a devotee of the Supreme Personality of Godhead. Although one is empowered by the Supreme Personality of Godhead and is an incarnation, he should not forget his eternal relationship with the Supreme Personality of Godhead. In Kali-yuga there are many self-made incarnations, rascals, who declare themselves to be the Supreme Personality of Godhead. The words *bhagavān indraḥ* indicate that even a living entity can be as exalted and powerful as King Indra, for even King Indra is an ordinary living entity in the material world and possesses the four defects of the conditioned soul. King Indra is described herein as *bhagavān,* which is generally used in reference to the Supreme Personality of Godhead. In this case, however, King Indra is addressed as *bhagavān* because he has so much power in his hands. Despite his becoming *bhagavān,* he is envious of the incarnation of God, Pṛthu Mahārāja. The defects of material life are so strong that due to contamination King Indra becomes envious of an incarnation of God.

We should try to understand, therefore, how a conditioned soul becomes fallen. The opulence of King Pṛthu was not dependent on material conditions. As described in this verse, he was a great devotee of Adhokṣaja. The word *adhokṣaja* indicates the Personality of Godhead, who is beyond the expression of mind and words. However, the Supreme Personality of Godhead appears before the devotee in His original form of eternal bliss and knowledge. The devotee is allowed to see the Supreme Lord eye to eye, although the Lord is beyond the expression of our senses and beyond our direct perception.

TEXT 11

चरमेणाश्वमेधेन यजमाने यजुष्पतिम् ।
वैन्ये यज्ञपशुं स्पर्धन्नपोवाह तिरोहितः ॥११॥

carameṇāśvamedhena
yajamāne yajuṣ-patim
vainye yajña-paśuṁ spardhann
apovāha tirohitaḥ

carameṇa—by the last one; *aśvamedhena*—by the sacrifice of *aśvamedha-yajña; yajamāne*—when he was performing the sacrifice; *yajuḥ-patim*—for satisfaction of the Lord of *yajña,* Viṣṇu; *vainye*—the son of King Vena;

yajña-paśum—the animal meant to be sacrificed in the *yajña; spardhan*—being envious; *apovāha*—stole; *tirohitaḥ*—being invisible.

TRANSLATION

When Pṛthu Mahārāja was performing the last horse sacrifice [aśvamedha-yajña], King Indra, invisible to everyone, stole the horse intended for sacrifice. He did this because of his great envy of King Pṛthu.

PURPORT

King Indra is known as *śata-kratu,* which indicates that he has performed one hundred horse sacrifices (*aśvamedha-yajña*). We should know, however, that the animals sacrificed in the *yajña* were not killed. If the Vedic *mantras* were properly pronounced during the sacrifice, the animal sacrificed would come out again with a new life. That is the test for a successful *yajña.* When King Pṛthu performed one hundred *yajñas,* Indra became very envious because he did not want anyone to excel him. Being an ordinary living entity, he became envious of King Pṛthu, and, making himself invisible, he stole the horse and thus impeded the *yajña* performance.

TEXT 12

तमत्रिर्भगवानैक्षत्त्वरमाणं विहायसा ।
आमुक्तमिव पाखण्डं योऽधर्मे धर्मविभ्रमः ॥१२॥

tam atrir bhagavān aikṣat
tvaramāṇaṁ vihāyasā
āmuktam iva pākhaṇḍaṁ
yo 'dharme dharma-vibhramaḥ

tam—King Indra; *atriḥ*—the sage Atri; *bhagavān*—most powerful; *aikṣat*—could see; *tvaramāṇam*—moving very hastily; *vihāyasā*—in outer space; *āmuktam iva*—like a liberated person; *pākhaṇḍam*—imposter; *yaḥ*—one who; *adharme*—in irreligiosity; *dharma*—religiosity; *vibhramaḥ*—mistaking.

TRANSLATION

When King Indra was taking away the horse, he dressed himself to appear as a liberated person. Actually this dress is a form of cheating, for it falsely created an impression of religion. When Indra went into outer

space in this way, the great sage Atri saw him and understood the whole situation.

PURPORT

The word *pākhaṇḍa* used in this verse is sometimes pronounced *pāṣaṇḍa*. Both of these words indicate an imposter who presents himself as a very religious person but in actuality is sinful. Indra took up the saffron-colored dress as a way of cheating others. This saffron dress has been misused by many imposters who present themselves as liberated persons or incarnations of God. In this way people are cheated. As we have mentioned many times, the conditioned soul has a tendency to cheat; therefore this quality is also visible in a person like King Indra. It is understood that even King Indra is not liberated from the clutches of material contamination. Thus the word *āmuktam iva*, meaning "as if he were liberated," is used. The saffron dress worn by a *sannyāsī* announces to the world that he has renounced all worldly affairs and is simply engaged in the service of the Lord. Such a devotee is actually a *sannyāsī* or liberated person. In *Bhagavad-gītā* it is said:

anāśritaḥ karma-phalaṁ
kāryaṁ karma karoti yaḥ
sa sannyāsī ca yogī ca
na niragnir na cākriyaḥ

"One who is unattached to the fruits of his work and who works as he is obligated is in the renounced order of life, and he is the true mystic: not he who lights no fire and performs no work." (Bg. 6.1)

In other words, one who offers the results of his activities to the Supreme Personality of Godhead is actually a *sannyāsī* and *yogī*. Cheating *sannyāsīs* and *yogīs* have existed since the time of Pṛthu Mahārāja's sacrifice. This cheating was very foolishly introduced by King Indra. In some ages such cheating is very prominent, and in other ages not so prominent. It is the duty of a *sannyāsī* to be very cautious because, as stated by Lord Caitanya, *sannyāsīra alpa chidra sarva-loke gāya:* a little spot in a *sannyāsī's* character will be magnified by the public. Therefore, unless one is very sincere and serious, he should not take up the order of *sannyāsa*. One should not use this order as a means to cheat the public. It is better not to take up *sannyāsa* in this age of Kali because provocations are very strong in this age. Only a very exalted person advanced in spiritual understanding should attempt to take up *sannyāsa*. One should not adopt this order as a means of livelihood or for some material purpose.

TEXT 13

अत्रिणा चोदितो हन्तुं पृथुपुत्रो महारथः ।
अन्वधावत संक्रुद्धस्तिष्ठ तिष्ठेति चाब्रवीत् ॥१३॥

atriṇā codito hantuṁ
pṛthu-putro mahā-rathaḥ
anvadhāvata saṅkruddhas
tiṣṭha tiṣṭheti cābravīt

atriṇā—by the great sage Atri; *coditaḥ*—being encouraged; *hantum*—to kill; *pṛthu-putraḥ*—the son of King Pṛthu; *mahā-rathaḥ*—a great hero; *anvadhāvata*—followed; *saṅkruddhaḥ*—being very angry; *tiṣṭha tiṣṭha*—just wait, just wait; *iti*—thus; *ca*—also; *abravīt*—he said.

TRANSLATION

When the son of King Pṛthu was informed by Atri of King Indra's trick, he immediately became very angry and followed Indra to kill him, calling, "Wait! Wait!"

PURPORT

The words *tiṣṭha tiṣṭha* are used by a *kṣatriya* when he challenges his enemy. When fighting, a *kṣatriya* cannot flee from the battlefield. However, when a *kṣatriya* out of cowardice flees from the battlefield, showing his back to his enemy, he is challenged with the words *tiṣṭha tiṣṭha.* A real *kṣatriya* does not kill his enemy from behind, nor does a real *kṣatriya* turn his back on the battlefield. According to *kṣatriya* principle and spirit, one either attains victory or dies in the battlefield. Although King Indra was very exalted, being the King of heaven, he became degraded due to his stealing the horse intended for sacrifice. Therefore he fled without observing the *kṣatriya* principles, and the son of Pṛthu had to challenge him with the words *tiṣṭha tiṣṭha.*

TEXT 14

तं तादृशाकृतिं वीक्ष्य मेने धर्मं शरीरिणम् ।
जटिलं भस्मनाच्छन्नं तस्मै बाणं न मुञ्चति ॥१४॥

taṁ tādṛśākṛtiṁ vīkṣya
mene dharmaṁ śarīriṇam

jaṭilaṁ bhasmanācchannaṁ
tasmai bāṇaṁ na muñcati

tam—him; *tādṛśa-ākṛtim*—in such dress; *vīkṣya*—after seeing; *mene*—considered; *dharmam*—pious or religious; *śarīriṇam*—having a body; *jaṭilam*—having knotted hair; *bhasmanā*—by ashes; *ācchannam*—smeared all over the body; *tasmai*—unto him; *bāṇam*—arrow; *na*—not; *muñcati*—he did release.

TRANSLATION

King Indra was fraudulently dressed as a sannyāsī, having knotted his hair on his head and smeared ashes all over his body. Upon seeing such dress, the son of King Pṛthu considered Indra a religious man and pious sannyāsī. Therefore he did not release his arrows.

TEXT 15

वधान्निवृत्तं तं भूयो हन्तवेऽत्रिरचोदयत् ।
जहि यज्ञहनं तात महेन्द्रं विबुधाधमम् ॥१५॥

vadhān nivṛttaṁ taṁ bhūyo
hantave 'trir acodayat
jahi yajña-hanaṁ tāta
mahendraṁ vibudhādhamam

vadhāt—from killing; *nivṛttam*—stopped; *tam*—the son of Pṛthu; *bhūyaḥ*—again; *hantave*—for the purpose of killing; *atriḥ*—the great sage Atri; *acodayat*—encouraged; *jahi*—kill; *yajña-hanam*—one who impeded the performance of a *yajña; tāta*—my dear son; *mahā-indram*—the great heavenly King Indra; *vibudha-adhamam*—the lowest of all demigods.

TRANSLATION

When Atri Muni saw that the son of King Pṛthu did not kill Indra but returned deceived by him, Atri Muni again instructed him to kill the heavenly King because he thought that Indra had become the lowliest of all demigods due to his impeding the execution of King Pṛthu's sacrifice.

TEXT 16

एवं वैन्यसुतः प्रोक्तस्त्वरमाणं विहायसा ।
अन्वद्रवदभिक्रुद्धो रावणं गृध्रराडिव ॥१६॥

evaṁ vainya-sutaḥ proktas
tvaramāṇaṁ vihāyasā
anvadravad abhikruddho
rāvaṇaṁ gṛdhra-rāḍ iva

evam—thus; *vainya-sutaḥ*—the son of King Pṛthu; *proktaḥ*—being ordered; *tvaramāṇam*—Indra, who was moving hastily; *vihāyasā*—in the sky; *anvadravat*—began to chase; *abhikruddhaḥ*—being very angry; *rāvaṇam*—Rāvaṇa; *gṛdhra-rāṭ*—the king of vultures; *iva*—like.

TRANSLATION

Being thus informed, the grandson of King Vena immediately began to follow Indra, who was fleeing through the sky in great haste. He was very angry with him, and he chased him just as the king of the vultures chased Rāvaṇa.

TEXT 17

सोऽश्वं रूपं च तद्धित्वा तस्मा अन्तर्हितः स्वराट् ।
वीरः स्वपशुमादाय पितुर्यज्ञमुपेयिवान् ॥१७॥

so 'śvaṁ rūpaṁ ca tad dhitvā
tasmā antarhitaḥ sva-rāṭ
vīraḥ sva-paśum ādāya
pitur yajñam upeyivān

saḥ—King Indra; *aśvam*—the horse; *rūpam*—the false dress of a saintly person; *ca*—also; *tat*—that; *hitvā*—giving up; *tasmai*—for him; *antarhitaḥ*—disappeared; *sva-rāṭ*—Indra; *vīraḥ*—the great hero; *sva-paśum*—his animal; *ādāya*—having taken; *pituḥ*—of his father; *yajñam*—to the sacrifice; *upeyivān*—he came back.

TRANSLATION

When Indra saw that the son of Pṛthu was chasing him, he immediately abandoned his false dress and left the horse. Indeed, he disappeared from that very spot, and the great hero, the son of Mahārāja Pṛthu, returned the horse to his father's sacrificial arena.

TEXT 18

तत्तस्य चाद्भुतं कर्म विचक्ष्य परमर्षयः ।
नामधेयं ददुस्तस्मै विजिताश्व इति प्रभो ॥१८॥

tat tasya cādbhutaṁ karma
vicakṣya paramarṣayaḥ
nāmadheyaṁ dadus tasmai
vijitāśva iti prabho

tat—that; *tasya*—his; *ca*—also; *adbhutam*—wonderful; *karma*—activity; *vicakṣya*—after observing; *parama-ṛṣayaḥ*—the great sages; *nāmadheyam*—the name; *daduḥ*—they offered; *tasmai*—to him; *vijita-aśvaḥ*—Vijitāśva (he who has won the horse); *iti*—thus; *prabho*—my dear Lord Vidura.

TRANSLATION

My dear Lord Vidura, when the great sages observed the wonderful prowess of the son of King Pṛthu, they all agreed to give him the name Vijitāśva.

TEXT 19

उपसृज्य तमस्तीव्रं जहाराश्वं पुनर्हरिः ।
चषालयूपतश्छन्नो हिरण्यरशनं विभुः ॥१९॥

upasṛjya tamas tīvraṁ
jahārāśvaṁ punar hariḥ
caṣāla-yūpataś channo
hiraṇya-raśanaṁ vibhuḥ

upasṛjya—creating; *tamaḥ*—darkness; *tīvram*—dense; *jahāra*—took away; *aśvam*—the horse; *punaḥ*—again; *hariḥ*—King Indra; *caṣāla-yūpataḥ*—from the wooden instrument where the animals were sacrificed; *channaḥ*—being covered; *hiraṇya-raśanam*—tied with a gold chain; *vibhuḥ*—very powerful.

TRANSLATION

My dear Vidura, Indra, being the King of heaven and very powerful, immediately brought a dense darkness upon the sacrificial arena. Covering the whole scene in this way, he again took away the horse, which was chained with golden shackles near the wooden instrument where animals were sacrificed.

TEXT 20

अत्रिः सन्दर्शयामास त्वरमाणं विहायसा ।
कपालखट्वाङ्गधरं वीरो नैनमबाधत ॥२०॥

atriḥ sandarśayām āsa
tvaramāṇaṁ vihāyasā
kapāla-khaṭvāṅga-dharaṁ
vīro nainam abādhata

atriḥ—the great sage Atri; *sandarśayām āsa*—caused to see; *tvaramāṇam*—going very hastily; *vihāyasā*—in the sky; *kapāla-khaṭvāṅga*—a staff with a skull at the top; *dharam*—who carried; *vīraḥ*—the hero (King Pṛthu's son); *na*—not; *enam*—the King of heaven, Indra; *abādhata*—killed.

TRANSLATION

The great sage Atri again pointed out to the son of King Pṛthu that Indra was fleeing through the sky. The great hero, the son of Pṛthu, chased him again. But when he saw that Indra was carrying in his hand a staff with a skull at the top and was again wearing the dress of a sannyāsī, he still chose not to kill him.

TEXT 21

अत्रिणा चोदितस्तस्मै सन्दधे विशिखं रुषा ।
सोऽश्वं रूपं च तद्धित्वा तस्थावन्तर्हितः स्वराट् ॥२१॥

atriṇā coditas tasmai
sandadhe viśikhaṁ ruṣā
so 'śvaṁ rūpaṁ ca tad dhitvā
tasthāv antarhitaḥ sva-rāṭ

atriṇā—by the great sage Atri; *coditaḥ*—inspired; *tasmai*—for Lord Indra; *sandadhe*—fixed up; *viśikham*—his arrow; *ruṣā*—out of great anger; *saḥ*—King Indra; *aśvam*—horse; *rūpam*—the dress of a *sannyāsī; ca*—also; *tat*—that; *hitvā*—giving up; *tasthau*—he remained there; *antarhitaḥ*—invisible; *sva-rāṭ*—the independent Indra.

TRANSLATION

When the great sage Atri again gave directions, the son of King Pṛthu became very angry and placed an arrow on his bow. Upon seeing this, King Indra immediately abandoned the false dress of a sannyāsī and, giving up the horse, made himself invisible.

TEXT 22

वीरश्चाश्वमुपादाय पितृयज्ञमथाव्रजत् ।
तदवद्यं हरे रूपं जगृहुर्ज्ञानदुर्बलाः ॥२२॥

vīraś cāśvam upādāya
pitṛ-yajñam athāvrajat
tad avadyaṁ hare rūpaṁ
jagṛhur jñāna-durbalāḥ

vīraḥ—the son of King Pṛthu; *ca*—also; *aśvam*—the horse; *upādāya*—taking; *pitṛ-yajñam*—to the sacrificial arena of his father; *atha*—thereafter; *avrajat*—went; *tat*—that; *avadyam*—abominable; *hareḥ*—of Indra; *rūpam*—dress; *jagṛhuḥ*—adopted; *jñāna-durbalāḥ*—those with a poor fund of knowledge.

TRANSLATION

Then the great hero, Vijitāśva, the son of King Pṛthu, again took the horse and returned to his father's sacrificial arena. Since that time, certain men with a poor fund of knowledge have adopted the dress of a false sannyāsī. It was King Indra who introduced this.

PURPORT

Since time immemorial, the *sannyāsa* order has carried the *tridaṇḍa.* Later Śaṅkarācārya introduced the *ekadaṇḍi-sannyāsī.* A *tridaṇḍi-sannyāsī* is a Vaiṣṇava *sannyāsī,* and an *ekadaṇḍi-sannyāsī* is a Māyāvādī *sannyāsī.* There are many other types of *sannyāsīs* who are not approved by Vedic rituals. A type of pseudo-*sannyāsa* was introduced by Indra when he tried to hide himself from the attack of Vijitāśva, the great son of King Pṛthu. Now there are many different types of *sannyāsīs.* Some of them go naked, and some of them carry a skull and trident, generally known as *kāpālika.* All of them were introduced under some meaningless circumstances, and those who have a poor fund of knowledge accept these false *sannyāsīs* and their pretenses, although they are not bona fide guides to spiritual advancement. At the present moment some missionary institutions, without referring to the Vedic rituals, have introduced some *sannyāsīs* who engage in sinful activities. The sinful activities forbidden by the *śāstras* are illicit sex, intoxication, meat-eating and gambling. These so-called *sannyāsīs* indulge in all these activities. They eat meat and flesh, fish, eggs and just about everything. They sometimes drink with the excuse that without alcohol, fish and meat, it is impossible to remain in the cold countries near the arctic zone. These *sannyāsīs* introduce all these sinful activities in the name of serving the poor, and consequently poor animals are cut to pieces and go into the bellies of these *sannyāsīs.* As described in the following verses, such *sannyāsīs* are *pākhaṇḍīs.* Vedic literature states that a person who puts

Lord Nārāyaṇa on the level with Lord Śiva or Lord Brahmā immediately becomes a *pākhaṇḍī.* As stated in the *Purāṇas:*

yas tu nārāyaṇaṁ devaṁ
brahma-rudrādi-daivataiḥ
samatvenaiva vīkṣeta
sa pāṣaṇḍī bhaved dhruvam

In Kali-yuga the *pākhaṇḍīs* are very prominent. However, Lord Śrī Caitanya Mahāprabhu has tried to kill all these *pākhaṇḍīs* by introducing His *saṅkīrtana* movement. Those who take advantage of this *saṅkīrtana* movement of the International Society for Krishna Consciousness will be able to save themselves from the influence of these *pākhaṇḍīs.*

TEXT 23

यानि रूपाणि जगृहे इन्द्रो हयजिहीर्षया ।
तानि पापस्य खण्डानि लिङ्गं खण्डमिहोच्यते ॥२३॥

yāni rūpāṇi jagṛhe
indro haya-jihīrṣayā
tāni pāpasya khaṇḍāni
liṅgaṁ khaṇḍam ihocyate

yāni—all those which; *rūpāṇi*—forms; *jagṛhe*—accepted; *indraḥ*—the King of heaven; *haya*—the horse; *jihīrṣayā*—with a desire to steal; *tāni*—all those; *pāpasya*—of sinful activities; *khaṇḍāni*—signs; *liṅgam*—the symbol; *khaṇḍam*—the word *khaṇḍa; iha*—here; *ucyate*—is said.

TRANSLATION

Whatever different forms Indra assumed as a mendicant because of his desire to seize the horse were symbols of atheistic philosophy.

PURPORT

According to Vedic civilization, *sannyāsa* is one of the essential items in the program of the *varṇa-āśrama* institution. One should accept *sannyāsa* according to the *paramparā* system of the *ācāryas.* At the present moment, however, many so-called *sannyāsīs* or mendicants have no understanding of God consciousness. Such *sannyāsa* was introduced by Indra because of his jealousy of Mahārāja Pṛthu, and what he introduced is again appearing in the age of Kali. Practically none of the *sannyāsīs* in this age are bona fide. No one can introduce any new system into the Vedic way of life; if one does so out of malice, he is to be known as a *pāṣaṇḍī,* or atheist. In the Vaiṣṇava *tantra* it is said:

yas tu nārāyaṇaṁ devaṁ
brahma-rudrādi-daivataiḥ
samatvenaiva vīkṣeta
sa pāṣaṇḍī bhaved dhruvam

Although it is forbidden, there are many *pāṣaṇḍīs* who coin terms like *daridra-nārāyaṇa* and *svāmi-nārāyaṇa,* although not even such demigods as Brahmā and Śiva can be equal to Nārāyaṇa.

TEXTS 24-25

एवमिन्द्रे हरत्यश्वं वैन्ययज्ञजिघांसया ।
तद्गृहीतविसृष्टेषु पाखण्डेषु मतिर्नृणाम् ॥२४॥
धर्म इत्युपधर्मेषु नग्नरक्तपटादिषु ।
प्रायेण सज्जते भ्रान्त्या पेशलेषु च वाग्मिषु ॥२५॥

evam indre haraty aśvaṁ
vainya-yajña-jighāṁsayā
tad-gṛhīta-visṛṣṭeṣu
pākhaṇḍeṣu matir nṛṇām

dharma ity upadharmeṣu
nagna-rakta-paṭādiṣu
prāyeṇa sajjate bhrāntyā
peśaleṣu ca vāgmiṣu

evam—thus; *indre*—when the King of heaven; *harati*—stole; *aśvam*—the horse; *vainya*—of the son of King Vena; *yajña*—the sacrifice; *jighāṁsayā*—with a desire to stop; *tat*—by him; *gṛhīta*—accepted; *visṛṣṭeṣu*—abandoned; *pākhaṇḍeṣu*—toward the sinful dress; *matiḥ*—attraction; *nṛṇām*—of the people in general; *dharmaḥ*—system of religion; *iti*—thus; *upadharmeṣu*—toward false religious systems; *nagna*—naked; *rakta-paṭa*—red robed; *ādiṣu*—etc.; *prāyeṇa*—generally; *sajjate*—is attracted; *bhrāntyā*—foolishly; *peśaleṣu*—expert; *ca*—and; *vāgmiṣu*—eloquent.

TRANSLATION

In this way, King Indra, in order to steal the horse from King Pṛthu's sacrifice, adopted several orders of sannyāsa. Some of these sannyāsīs go naked, and sometimes they wear red garments and pass under the name of kāpālika. These are simply symbolic representations of their sinful activities. These so-called sannyāsīs are very much appreciated by sinful men because they are all godless atheists and very expert in putting forward arguments and reasons to support their case. We must know, however, that they are only passing as adherents of religion and are not so in fact. Unfortunately, bewildered persons accept them as religious, and being attracted to them, they spoil their life.

PURPORT

As stated in *Śrīmad-Bhāgavatam,* men in this age of Kali are short-lived, devoid of spiritual knowledge, and susceptible to accept false religious systems due to their unfortunate condition. Thus they always remain mentally disturbed. The Vedic *śāstras* practically prohibit the adoption of *sannyāsa* in the age of Kali because less intelligent men may accept the *sannyāsa* order for cheating purposes. Actually the only religion is the religion of surrender unto the Supreme Personality of Godhead. We must serve the Lord in Kṛṣṇa consciousness. All other systems of *sannyāsa* and religion are actually not bona fide. In this age they are simply passing for religious systems. This is most regrettable.

TEXT 26

तदभिज्ञाय भगवान् पृथुः पृथुपराक्रमः ।
इन्द्राय कुपितो बाणमादत्तोद्यतकार्मुकः ॥२६॥

tad abhijñāya bhagavān
pṛthuḥ pṛthu-parākramaḥ
indrāya kupito bāṇam
ādattodyata-kārmukaḥ

tat—that; *abhijñāya*—understanding; *bhagavān*—the incarnation of Godhead; *pṛthuḥ*—King Pṛthu; *pṛthu-parākramaḥ*—celebrated as very powerful; *indrāya*—upon Indra; *kupitaḥ*—being very angry; *bāṇam*—an arrow; *ādatta*—took up; *udyata*—having taken up; *kārmukaḥ*—the bow.

TRANSLATION

Mahārāja Pṛthu, who was celebrated as very powerful, immediately took up his bow and arrows and prepared to kill Indra himself, because Indra introduced such irregular sannyāsa orders.

PURPORT

It is the duty of the king not to tolerate any introduction of any irreligious systems. Since King Pṛthu was an incarnation of the Supreme Personality of Godhead, certainly his duty was to cut down all kinds of irreligious systems. Following in his footsteps, all heads of state should themselves be bona fide representatives of God and should cut down all irreligious systems. Unfortunately they are cowards who declare a secular state. Such a mentality is a way of compromising religious and irreligious systems, but because of this citizens are generally becoming uninterested in spiritual advancement. Thus the situation deteriorates to such an extent that human society becomes hellish.

TEXT 27

तमृत्विजः शक्रवधाभिसन्धितं
विचक्ष्य दुष्प्रेक्ष्यमसह्यरंहसम् ।
निवारयामासुरहो महामते
न युज्यतेऽत्रान्यवधः प्रचोदितात् ॥२७॥

tam ṛtvijaḥ śakra-vadhābhisandhitaṁ
vicakṣya duṣprekṣyam asahya-raṁhasam
nivārayām āsur aho mahā-mate
na yujyate 'trānya-vadhaḥ pracoditāt

tam—King Pṛthu; *ṛtvijaḥ*—the priests; *śakra-vadha*—killing the King of heaven; *abhisandhitam*—thus preparing himself; *vicakṣya*—having observed; *duṣprekṣyam*—terrible to look at; *asahya*—unbearable; *raṁhasam*—whose velocity; *nivārayām āsuḥ*—they forbade; *aho*—oh; *mahā-mate*—O great soul; *na*—not; *yujyate*—is worthy for you; *atra*—in this sacrificial arena; *anya*—others; *vadhaḥ*—killing; *pracoditāt*—from being so directed in the scriptures.

TRANSLATION

When the priests and all the others saw Mahārāja Pṛthu very angry and prepared to kill Indra, they requested him: O great soul, do not kill him,

for only sacrificial animals can be killed in a sacrifice. Such are the directions given by śāstra.

PURPORT

Animal killing is intended for different purposes. It tests the proper pronunciation of Vedic *mantras,* and an animal being put into the sacrificial fire should come out with a new life. No one should ever be killed in a sacrifice meant for the satisfaction of Lord Viṣṇu. How then could Indra be killed when he is actually worshiped in the *yajña* and accepted as part and parcel of the Supreme Personality of Godhead? Therefore the priests requested King Pṛthu not to kill him.

TEXT 28

वयं मरुत्वन्तमिहार्थनाशनं
ह्वयामहे त्वच्छ्रवसा हतत्विषम् ।
अयातयामोपहवैरनन्तरं
प्रसह्य राजन् जुहवाम तेऽहितम् ॥२८॥

vayaṁ marutvantam ihārtha-nāśanaṁ
hvayāmahe tvac-chravasā hata-tviṣam
ayātayāmopahavair anantaraṁ
prasahya rājan juhavāma te 'hitam

vayam—we; *marutvantam*—King Indra; *iha*—here; *artha*—of your interest; *nāśanam*—the destroyer; *hvayāmahe*—we shall call; *tvat-śravasā*—by your glory; *hata-tviṣam*—already bereft of his power; *ayātayāma*—never before used; *upahavaiḥ*—by *mantras* of invocation; *anantaram*—without delay; *prasahya*—by force; *rājan*—O King; *juhavāma*—we shall sacrifice in the fire; *te*—your; *ahitam*—enemy.

TRANSLATION

Dear King, Indra's powers are already reduced due to his attempt to impede the execution of your sacrifice. We shall call him by Vedic mantras, which were never before used, and certainly he will come. Thus by the power of our mantra, we shall cast him into the fire because he is your enemy.

PURPORT

By chanting the Vedic *mantras* properly in a sacrifice, one can perform many wonderful things. In Kali-yuga, however, there are no qualified *brāhmaṇas* who can chant the *mantras* properly. Consequently no attempt should be made to perform such big sacrifices. In this age the only sacrifice recommended is the *saṅkīrtana* movement.

TEXT 29

इत्यामन्त्र्य क्रतुपतिं विदुरास्यर्त्विजो रुषा ।
स्रुग्घस्ताञ्जुह्वतोऽभ्येत्य स्वयम्भूः प्रत्यषेधत ॥२९॥

ity āmantrya kratu-patiṁ
vidurāsyartvijo ruṣā
srug-ghastāñ juhvato 'bhyetya
svayambhūḥ pratyaṣedhata

iti—thus; *āmantrya*—after informing; *kratu-patim*—King Pṛthu, the master of the sacrifice; *vidura*—O Vidura; *asya*—of Pṛthu; *ṛtvijaḥ*—the priests; *ruṣā*—in great anger; *sruk-hastān*—with the sacrificial ladel in hand; *juhvataḥ*—performing the fire sacrifice; *abhyetya*—having begun; *svayam-bhūḥ*—Lord Brahmā; *pratyaṣedhata*—asked them to stop.

TRANSLATION

My dear Vidura, after giving the King this advice, the priests who had been engaged in performing the sacrifice called for Indra, the King of heaven, in a mood of great anger. When they were just ready to put the oblation on the fire, Lord Brahmā appeared on the scene and forbade them to start the sacrifice.

TEXT 30

न वध्यो भवतामिन्द्रो यद्यज्ञो भगवत्तनुः ।
यं जिघांसथ यज्ञेन यस्येष्टास्तनवः सुराः ॥३०॥

na vadhyo bhavatām indro
yad yajño bhagavat-tanuḥ
yaṁ jighāṁsatha yajñena
yasyeṣṭās tanavaḥ surāḥ

na—not; *vadhyaḥ*—ought to be killed; *bhavatām*—by all of you; *indraḥ*—the King of heaven; *yat*—because; *yajñaḥ*—a name of Indra; *bhagavat-tanuḥ*—part of the body of the Supreme Personality of Godhead; *yam*—whom;

jighāṁsatha—you wish to kill; *yajñena*—by performing sacrifice; *yasya*—of Indra; *iṣṭāḥ*—being worshiped; *tanavaḥ*—parts of the body; *surāḥ*—the demigods.

TRANSLATION

Lord Brahmā addressed them thus: My dear sacrificial performers, you cannot kill Indra, the King of heaven. It is not your duty. You should know that Indra is as good as the Supreme Personality of Godhead. Indeed, he is one of the most powerful assistants of the Personality of Godhead. You are trying to satisfy all the demigods by the performance of this yajña, but you should know that all these demigods are but parts and parcels of Indra, the King of heaven. How, then, can you kill him in this great sacrifice?

TEXT 31

तदिदं पश्यत महद्धर्मव्यतिकरं द्विजाः ।
इन्द्रेणानुष्ठितं राज्ञः कर्मैतद्विजिघांसता ॥३१॥

tad idaṁ paśyata mahad-
dharma-vyatikaraṁ dvijāḥ
indreṇānuṣṭhitaṁ rājñaḥ
karmaitad vijighāṁsatā

tat—then; *idam*—this; *paśyata*—just see; *mahat*—great; *dharma*—of religious life; *vyatikaram*—violation; *dvijāḥ*—O great *brāhmaṇas; indreṇa*—by Indra; *anuṣṭhitam*—performed; *rājñaḥ*—of the King; *karma*—activity; *etat*—this sacrifice; *vijighāṁsatā*—desiring to impede.

TRANSLATION

In order to make trouble and impede the performance of King Pṛthu's great sacrifice, King Indra has adopted some means that in the future will destroy the clear path of religious life. I draw your attention to this fact. If you oppose him any further, he will further misuse his power and introduce many other irreligious systems.

TEXT 32

पृथुकीर्तेः पृथोर्भूयात्तर्ह्येकोनशतक्रतुः ।
अलं ते क्रतुभिः स्विष्टैर्यद्भवान्मोक्षधर्मवित् ॥३२॥

pṛthu-kīrteḥ pṛthor bhūyāt
tarhy ekona-śata-kratuḥ
alaṁ te kratubhiḥ sviṣṭair
yad bhavān mokṣa-dharma-vit

pṛthu-kīrteḥ—of wide renown; *pṛthoḥ*—of King Pṛthu; *bhūyāt*—let it be; *tarhi*—therefore; *ekona-śata-kratuḥ*—he who performed ninety-nine *yajñas*; *alam*—there is nothing to be gained; *te*—of you; *kratubhiḥ*—by performing sacrifices; *su-iṣṭaiḥ*—well performed; *yat*—because; *bhavān*—yourself; *mokṣa-dharma-vit*—the knower of the path of liberation.

TRANSLATION

"Let there be only ninety-nine sacrificial performances for Mahārāja Pṛthu," Lord Brahmā concluded. Lord Brahmā then turned toward Mahārāja Pṛthu and informed him that since he was thoroughly aware of the path of liberation, what was the use in performing more sacrifices?

PURPORT

Lord Brahmā came down to pacify King Pṛthu regarding his continual performance of one hundred sacrifices. King Pṛthu was determined to perform one hundred sacrifices, and King Indra took this very seriously because Indra himself was known as the performer of one hundred sacrifices. Just as it is the nature of all living entities within this material world to become envious of their competitors, King Indra, although King of heaven, was also envious of King Pṛthu. Therefore, he wanted to stop him from performing one hundred sacrifices. Actually there was great competition, and King Indra, to satisfy his senses, began to invent so many irreligious systems to obstruct King Pṛthu. To stop these irreligious inventions, Lord Brahmā personally appeared in the sacrificial arena. As far as Mahārāja Pṛthu was concerned, he was a great devotee of the Supreme Personality of Godhead; therefore it was not necessary for him to perform the prescribed Vedic ritualistic ceremonies. Such ceremonies are known as *karma*, and there is no need for a devotee in the transcendental position to execute them. As the ideal king, however, it was King Pṛthu's duty to perform sacrifices. A compromise was therefore to be worked out. By the blessings of Lord Brahmā, King Pṛthu would become more famous than King Indra. Thus Pṛthu's determination to perform one hundred sacrifices was indirectly fulfilled by the blessings of Lord Brahmā.

TEXT 33

नैवात्मने महेन्द्राय रोषमाहर्तुमर्हसि ।
उभावपि हि भद्रं ते उत्तमश्लोकविग्रहौ ॥३३॥

naivātmane mahendrāya
roṣam āhartum arhasi
ubhāv api hi bhadraṁ te
uttamaśloka-vigrahau

na—not; *eva*—certainly; *ātmane*—nondifferent from you; *mahā-indrāya*—pon the King of heaven, Indra; *roṣam*—anger; *āhartum*—to apply; *arhasi*—ou ought; *ubhau*—both of you; *api*—certainly; *hi*—also; *bhadram*—good ortune; *te*—unto you; *uttama-śloka-vigrahau*—incarnations of the Supreme ersonality of Godhead.

TRANSLATION

Lord Brahmā continued: Let there be good fortune to both of you, for ou and King Indra are both part and parcel of the Supreme Personality of Godhead. Therefore you should not be angry with King Indra, who is nondifferent from you.

TEXT 34

मास्मिन्महाराज कृथाः स्म चिन्तां
निशामयास्मद्वच आदृतात्मा ।
यद्ध्यायतो दैवहतं नु कर्तुं
मनोऽतिरुष्टं विशते तमोऽन्धम् ॥३४॥

māsmin mahārāja kṛthāḥ sma cintāṁ
niśāmayāsmad-vaca ādṛtātmā
yad dhyāyato daiva-hataṁ nu kartuṁ
mano 'tiruṣṭaṁ viśate tamo 'ndham

mā—do not; *asmin*—in this; *mahā-rāja*—O King; *kṛthāḥ*—do; *sma*—as done in the past; *cintām*—agitation of the mind; *niśāmaya*—please consider; *asmat*—my; *vacaḥ*—words; *ādṛta-ātmā*—being very respectful; *yat*—because; *dhyāyataḥ*—of he who is contemplating; *daiva-hatam*—that which is thwarted by providence; *nu*—certainly; *kartum*—to do; *manaḥ*—the mind; *atiruṣṭam*—very angry; *viśate*—enters; *tamaḥ*—darkness; *andham*—dense.

TRANSLATION

My dear King, don't be agitated and anxious because your sacrifices have not been properly executed due to providential impediments. Kindly take my words with great respect. We should always remember that if something happens by providential arrangement, we should not be very sorry. The more we try to rectify such reversals, the more we enter into the darkest region of materialistic thought.

PURPORT

Sometimes the saintly or very religious person also has to meet with reversals in life. Such incidents should be taken as providential. Although there may be sufficient cause for being unhappy, one should avoid counteracting such reversals because the more we become implicated in rectifying such reversals, the more we enter into the darkest regions of material anxiety. Lord Kṛṣṇa has also advised us in this connection. We should tolerate things instead of becoming agitated.

TEXT 35

क्रतुर्विरमतामेष देवेषु दुरवग्रहः ।
धर्मव्यतिकरो यत्र पाखण्डैरिन्द्रनिर्मितैः ॥३५॥

kratur viramatām eṣa
deveṣu duravagrahaḥ
dharma-vyatikaro yatra
pākhaṇḍair indra-nirmitaiḥ

kratuḥ—the sacrifice; *viramatām*—let it stop; *eṣaḥ*—this; *deveṣu*—amongst the demigods; *duravagrahaḥ*—addiction to unwanted things; *dharma-vyatikaraḥ*—violation of religious principles; *yatra*—where; *pākhaṇḍaiḥ*—by sinful activities; *indra*—by the King of heaven; *nirmitaiḥ*—manufactured.

TRANSLATION

Lord Brahmā continued: Stop the performance of these sacrifices, for they have induced Indra to introduce so many irreligious aspects. You

should know very well that even amongst the demigods there are many unwanted desires.

PURPORT

There are many competitors in ordinary business affairs, and the *karma-kāṇḍa* chapters of the *Vedas* sometimes cause competition and envy amongst *karmīs.* A *karmī* must be envious because he wishes to enjoy material pleasures to their fullest extent. That is the material disease. Consequently there is always competition amongst *karmīs,* either in ordinary business affairs or in the performance of *yajña.* Lord Brahmā's purpose was to end the competition between Lord Indra and Mahārāja Pṛthu. Because Mahārāja Pṛthu was a great devotee and incarnation of God, he was requested to stop the sacrifices so that Indra might not further introduce irreligious systems, which are always followed by criminal-minded people.

TEXT 36

एभिरिन्द्रोपसंसृष्टैः पाखण्डैर्हारिभिर्जनम् ।
ह्रियमाणं विचक्ष्वैनं यस्ते यज्ञध्रुगश्वमुट् ॥३६॥

ebhir indropasaṁsṛṣṭaiḥ
pākhaṇḍair hāribhir janam
hriyamāṇaṁ vicakṣvainaṁ
yas te yajña-dhrug aśva-muṭ

ebhiḥ—by these; *indra-upasaṁsṛṣṭaiḥ*—created by the King of heaven, Indra; *pākhaṇḍaiḥ*—sinful activities; *hāribhiḥ*—very attractive to the heart; *janam*—the people in general; *hriyamāṇam*—being carried away; *vicakṣva*—just see; *enam*—these; *yaḥ*—one who; *te*—your; *yajña-dhruk*—creating a disturbance in the performance of the sacrifice; *aśva-muṭ*—who stole the horse.

TRANSLATION

Just see how Indra, the King of heaven, was creating a disturbance in the midst of the sacrifice by stealing the sacrificial horse. These attractive sinful activities, which he has introduced, will be carried out by the people in general.

PURPORT

As stated in *Bhagavad-gītā:*

yad yad ācarati śreṣṭhas
tat tad evetaro janaḥ

sa yat pramāṇaṁ kurute
lokas tad anuvartate

"Whatever action is performed by a great man, common men follow in his footsteps. And whatever standards he sets by exemplary acts, all the world pursues." (Bg 3.21)

For his own sense gratification, King Indra thought to defeat Mahārāja Pṛthu in the performance of one hundred horse sacrifices. Consequently he stole the horse and hid himself amid so many irreligious personalities, taking on the guise of a false *sannyāsī.* Such activities are attractive to the people in general; therefore they are dangerous. Lord Brahmā thought that instead of allowing Indra to further introduce such irreligious systems, it would be better to stop the sacrifice. A similar stance was taken by Lord Buddha when people were overly engrossed in the animal sacrifices recommended by Vedic instructions. Lord Buddha had to introduce the religion of nonviolence by contradicting the Vedic sacrificial instructions. Actually in the sacrifices the slaughtered animals were given a new life, but people without such powers were taking advantage of such Vedic rituals and unnecessarily killing poor animals. Therefore Lord Buddha had to deny the authority of the *Vedas* for the time being. One should not perform sacrifices that will induce reversed orders. It is better to stop such sacrifices.

As we have repeatedly explained, due to a lack of qualified brahminical priests in Kali-yuga, it is not possible to perform the ritualistic ceremonies recommended in the *Vedas.* Consequently the *śāstras* instruct us to perform the *saṅkīrtana-yajña.* By the *saṅkīrtana* sacrifice, the Supreme Personality of Godhead, in His form of Lord Caitanya, will be satisfied and worshiped. The entire purpose of performing sacrifices is to worship the Supreme Personality of Godhead, Viṣṇu. Lord Viṣṇu or Lord Kṛṣṇa is present in His form of Lord Caitanya; therefore people who are intelligent should try to satisfy Him by performing *saṅkīrtana-yajña.* This is the easiest way to satisfy Lord Viṣṇu in this age. People should take advantage of the injunctions in different *śāstras* concerning sacrifices in this age and not create unnecessary disturbances during the sinful age of Kali. In Kali-yuga men all over the world are very expert in opening slaughterhouses for killing animals, which they eat. If the old ritualistic ceremonies were observed, people would be encouraged to kill more and more animals. In Calcutta there are many butcher shops which keep a deity of the goddess Kālī, and animal eaters think it proper to purchase animal flesh from such shops in hope that they are eating the remnants of food offered to goddess Kālī. They do not know that goddess Kālī never accepts nonvegetarian food because she is the chaste wife of Lord Śiva. Lord Śiva is also a great Vaiṣṇava and never eats nonvegetarian food, and the goddess Kālī accepts the remnants of food left by Lord Śiva. Therefore there is no possibility of her eating flesh or fish. Such offerings are accepted by the associates of goddess Kālī known as *bhūtas*, *piśācas* and Rākṣasas, and those who take the *prasāda* of goddess Kālī in the shape of flesh or fish are not actually taking the *prasāda* left by goddess Kālī, but the food left by the *bhūtas* and *piśācas*.

TEXT 37

भवान् परित्रातुमिहावतीर्णो
धर्मं जनानां समयानुरूपम् ।
वेनापचारादवलुप्तमद्य
तद्देहतो विष्णुकलासि वैन्य ॥३७॥

bhavān paritrātum ihāvatīrṇo
dharmaṁ janānāṁ samayānurūpam
venāpacārād avaluptam adya
tad-dehato viṣṇu-kalāsi vainya

bhavān—Your Majesty; *paritrātum*—just to deliver; *iha*—in this world; *avatīrṇaḥ*—incarnated; *dharmam*—religious system; *janānām*—of the people in general; *samaya-anurūpam*—according to the time and circumstances; *vena-apacārāt*—by the misdeeds of King Vena; *avaluptam*—almost vanished; *adya*—at the present moment; *tat*—his; *dehataḥ*—from the body; *viṣṇu*—of Lord Viṣṇu; *kalā*—part of a plenary portion; *asi*—you are; *vainya*—O son of King Vena.

TRANSLATION

O King Pṛthu, son of Vena, you are the part and parcel expansion of Lord Viṣṇu. Due to the mischievous activities of King Vena, religious principles were almost lost. At that opportune moment you descended as the incarnation of Lord Viṣṇu. Indeed, for the protection of religious principles you have appeared from the body of King Vena.

PURPORT

The way in which Lord Viṣṇu kills the demons and protects the faithful is mentioned in *Bhagavad-gītā:*

paritrāṇāya sādhūnāṁ
vināśāya ca duṣkṛtām
dharma-saṁsthāpanārthāya
sambhavāmi yuge yuge

"In order to deliver the pious and to annihilate the miscreants, as well as to reestablish the principles of religion, I advent Myself millennium after millennium." (Bg. 4.8)

In two hands Lord Viṣṇu always carries a club and a *cakra* to kill demons, and in His other two hands He holds a conchshell and a lotus to give protection to His devotees. When His incarnation is present on this planet or in this universe, the Lord kills the demons and protects His devotees simultaneously. Sometimes Lord Viṣṇu appears in His person as Lord Kṛṣṇa or Lord Rāma. All of these appearances are mentioned in the *śāstras.* Sometimes He appears as a *śaktyāveśa-avatāra* like Lord Buddha. As explained before, these *śaktyāveśa-avatāras* are incarnations of Viṣṇu's power invested in a living entity. Living entities are also part and parcel of Lord Viṣṇu, but they are not as powerful; therefore when a living entity descends as an incarnation of Viṣṇu, he is especially empowered by the Lord.

When King Pṛthu is described as an incarnation of Lord Viṣṇu, it should be understood that he is a *śaktyāveśa-avatāra,* part and parcel of Lord Viṣṇu, and is specifically empowered by Him. Any living being acting as the incarnation of Lord Viṣṇu is thus empowered by Lord Viṣṇu to preach the *bhakti* cult. Such a person can act like Lord Viṣṇu and defeat demons by arguments and preach the *bhakti* cult exactly according to the principles of *śāstra.* As indicated in *Bhagavad-gītā,* whenever we find someone extraordinary preaching the *bhakti* cult, we should know that he is especially empowered by Lord Viṣṇu or Lord Kṛṣṇa. As confirmed in *Caitanya-caritāmṛta, kṛṣṇa-śakti vinā nahe tāra pravartana:* one cannot explain the glories of the holy name of the Lord without being specifically empowered by Him. If one criticizes or finds fault with such an empowered personality, one is to be considered an offender against Lord Viṣṇu and is punishable. Even though such offenders may dress as Vaiṣṇavas with false *tilaka* and *mālā,* they are never forgiven by the Lord if they offend a pure Vaiṣṇava. There are many instances of this in the *śāstras.*

TEXT 38

स त्वं विमृश्यास्य भवं प्रजापते
सङ्कल्पनं विश्वसृजां पिपीपृहि ।

ऐन्द्रीं च मायामुपधर्ममातरं
प्रचण्डपाखण्डपथं प्रभो जहि ॥३८॥

sa tvaṁ vimṛśyāsya bhavaṁ prajāpate
saṅkalpanaṁ viśva-sṛjāṁ pipīpṛhi
aindrīṁ ca māyām upadharma-mātaraṁ
pracaṇḍa-pākhaṇḍa-pathaṁ prabho jahi

saḥ—the aforesaid; *tvam*—you; *vimṛśya*—considering; *asya*—of the world; *bhavam*—existence; *prajā-pate*—O protector of the people; *saṅkalpanam*—the determination; *viśva-sṛjām*—of the progenitors of the world; *pipīpṛhi*—just fulfill; *aindrīm*—created by the King of heaven; *ca*—also; *māyām*—illusion; *upadharma*—of the irreligious system of so-called *sannyāsa; mātaram*—the mother; *pracaṇḍa*—furious, dangerous; *pākhaṇḍa-patham*—the path of sinful activities; *prabho*—O Lord; *jahi*—please conquer.

TRANSLATION

O protector of the people in general, please consider the purpose of your being incarnated by Lord Viṣṇu. The irreligious principles created by Indra are but mothers of so many unwanted religions. Please therefore stop these imitations immediately.

PURPORT

Lord Brahmā addresses King Pṛthu as *prajāpate* just to remind him of his great responsibility in maintaining the peace and prosperity of the citizens. Mahārāja Pṛthu was empowered by the Supreme Personality of Godhead for this purpose only. It is the duty of the ideal king to see that people are properly executing religious principles. Lord Brahmā especially requested King Pṛthu to conquer the pseudo-religious principles produced by King Indra. In other words, it is the duty of the state or king to put a stop to pseudo-religious systems produced by unscrupulous persons. Originally a religious principle is one, given by the Supreme Personality of Godhead, and it comes through the channel of disciplic succession in two forms. Lord Brahmā requested Pṛthu Mahārāja to desist in his unnecessary competition with Indra, who was determined to stop Pṛthu Mahārāja from completing one hundred *yajñas*. Instead of creating adverse reactions, it was better for Mahārāja Pṛthu to stop the *yajñas* in the interest of his original purpose as an incarnation. This purpose was to establish good government and set things in the right order.

TEXT 39

मैत्रेय उवाच

इत्थं स लोकगुरुणा समादिष्टो विशाम्पतिः ।
तथा च कृत्वा वात्सल्यं मघोनापि च सन्दधे ॥३९॥

maitreya uvāca
itthaṁ sa loka-guruṇā
samādiṣṭo viśām patiḥ
tathā ca kṛtvā vātsalyaṁ
maghonāpi ca sandadhe

maitreyaḥ uvāca—the great sage Maitreya continued to speak; *ittham*—thus; *saḥ*—King Pṛthu; *loka-guruṇā*—by the original teacher of all people, Lord Brahmā; *samādiṣṭaḥ*—being advised; *viśām patiḥ*—king, master of the people; *tathā*—in that way; *ca*—also; *kṛtvā*—having done; *vātsalyam*—affection; *maghonā*—with Indra; *api*—even; *ca*—also; *sandadhe*—concluded peace.

TRANSLATION

The great sage Maitreya continued: When King Pṛthu was thus advised by the supreme teacher, Lord Brahmā, he abandoned his eagerness to perform yajñas and with great affection concluded a peace with King Indra.

TEXT 40

कृतावभृथस्नानाय पृथवे भूरिकर्मणे ।
वरान्ददुस्ते वरदा ये तद्बर्हिषि तर्पिताः ॥४०॥

kṛtāvabhṛtha-snānāya
pṛthave bhūri-karmaṇe
varān dadus te varadā
ye tad-barhiṣi tarpitāḥ

kṛta—having performed; *avabhṛtha-snānāya*—taking bath after the sacrifice; *pṛthave*—unto King Pṛthu; *bhūri-karmaṇe*—famous for performing many virtuous acts; *varān*—benedictions; *daduḥ*—gave; *te*—all of them; *vara-dāḥ*—the demigods, bestowers of benedictions; *ye*—who; *tat-barhiṣi*—in the performance of such a *yajña; tarpitāḥ*—became pleased.

TRANSLATION

After this, Pṛthu Mahārāja took his bath, which is customarily taken after the performance of a yajña, and received the benedictions and due blessings of the demigods, who were very pleased by his glorious activities.

PURPORT

Yajña means Lord Viṣṇu, for all *yajña* is meant to please the Supreme Personality of Godhead, Lord Viṣṇu. Since the demigods automatically become very pleased with the performance of sacrifice, they bestow benediction upon the executors of *yajñas.* When one pours water on the root of a tree, the branches, trunks, twigs, flowers and leaves are all satisfied. Similarly, when one gives food to the stomach, all parts of the body are rejuvenated. In the same way, if one simply satisfies Lord Viṣṇu by the performance of *yajña,* one satisfies all the demigods automatically. In turn, the demigods offer their benedictions to such a devotee. A pure devotee therefore does not ask benedictions directly from the demigods. His only business is to serve the Supreme Personality of Godhead. Thus he is never in need of those things supplied by the demigods.

TEXT 41

विप्राः सत्याशिषस्तुष्टाः श्रद्धया लब्धदक्षिणाः ।
आशिषो युयुजुः क्षत्तरादिराजाय सत्कृताः ॥४१॥

viprāḥ satyāśiṣas tuṣṭāḥ
śraddhayā labdha-dakṣiṇāḥ
āśiṣo yuyujuḥ kṣattar
ādi-rājāya sat-kṛtāḥ

viprāḥ—all the *brāhmaṇas; satya*—true; *āśiṣaḥ*—whose benedictions; *tuṣṭāḥ*—being very satisfied; *śraddhayā*—with great respect; *labdha-dakṣiṇāḥ*—who obtained rewards; *āśiṣaḥ*—benedictions; *yuyujuḥ*—offered; *kṣattaḥ*—O Vidura; *ādi-rājāya*—upon the original King; *sat-kṛtāḥ*—being honored.

TRANSLATION

With great respect, the original King, Pṛthu, offered all kinds of rewards to the brāhmaṇas present at the sacrifice. Since all these brāhmaṇas were very much satisfied, they gave their heartfelt blessings to the King.

TEXT 42

त्वयाऽऽहूता महाबाहो सर्व एव समागताः ।
पूजिता दानमानाभ्यां पितृदेवर्षिमानवाः ॥४२॥

tvayāhūtā mahā-bāho
sarva eva samāgatāḥ
pūjitā dāna-mānābhyāṁ
pitṛ-devarṣi-mānavāḥ

tvayā—by you; *āhūtāḥ*—were invited; *mahā-bāho*—O great mighty-armed one; *sarve*—all; *eva*—certainly; *samāgatāḥ*—assembled; *pūjitāḥ*—were honored; *dāna*—by charity; *mānābhyām*—and by respect; *pitṛ*—the inhabitants of Pitṛloka; *deva*—demigods; *ṛṣi*—great sages; *mānavāḥ*—as well as common men.

TRANSLATION

All the great sages and brāhmaṇas said: O mighty King, by your invitation all classes of living entities have attended this assembly. They have come from Pitṛloka and the heavenly planets, and great sages as well as common men have attended this meeting. Now all of them are very much satisfied by your dealing and charity toward them.

Thus end the Bhaktivedanta purports of the Fourth Canto, Nineteenth Chapter, of the Śrīmad-Bhāgavatam, *entitled "King Pṛthu's One Hundred Horse Sacrifices."*